Rhetoric and Literature

P9-AGH-961

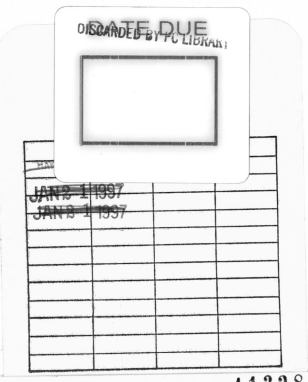

DATE DUE

DISCARDED BY PC LIBRARY

JAN 2 1 1997			
JAN 2 1 1997			

PE 1408
.C289

41328

PENINSULA COLLEGE LIBRARY
PORT ANGELES WASHINGTON

Rhetoric and Literature

P. JOSEPH CANAVAN
Head of English and Humanities
Mount San Antonio College

McGRAW-HILL BOOK COMPANY
New York St. Louis San Francisco Düsseldorf Johannesburg
Kuala Lumpur London Mexico Montreal New Delhi
Panama Paris São Paulo Singapore Sydney Tokyo Toronto

41328

Library of Congress Cataloging in Publication Data

Canavan, P   Joseph.
   Rhetoric and literature.

   Includes bibliographies.
      1. English language—Rhetoric.   2.   College readers.
I.   Title.
PE1408.C289   808'.04275   74-1232
ISBN 0-07-009705-4

RHETORIC AND LITERATURE

Copyright © 1974   by McGraw-Hill, Inc. All rights reserved.
Printed in the United States of America. No part of this publication
may be reproduced, stored in a retrieval system, or transmitted, in any
form or by any means, electronic, mechanical, photocopying, recording, or
otherwise, without the prior written permission of the publisher.

1234567890DODO7987654

This book was set in Vega by Rocappi, Inc.
The editors were David Edwards and David Dunham;
the production supervisor was Bill Greenwood.
R. R. Donnelly & Sons Company was printer and binder.

PE 1408
. C289

ACKNOWLEDGMENTS

Edwin Barton, "The Day Sing Sing Licked Us." *Coronet,* December 1960. Copyright © 1960 by Esquire, Inc. Reprinted by permission of Esquire, Inc.

"A Basic Method to Teach Swimming," *Good Housekeeping Magazine,* August 1969. Copyright © 1969 by the Hearst Corporation. Reprinted by permission.

Lerone Bennett, "The Convert," *Negro Digest,* January 1963. Copyright © 1963 by Negro Digest. Reprinted by permission of *Black World* and Lerone Bennett.

John Berryman, "The Ball Poem," from *Short Poems* by John Berryman. Copyright 1948 by John Berryman. Reprinted by permission of Farrar, Straus & Giroux, Inc.

Peter Blake, "Today's Suburbia," from *God's Own Junkyard* by Peter Blake. Copyright © 1964 by Peter Blake. Reprinted by permission of Holt, Rinehart & Winston, Inc.

Joseph P. Blank, "Face to Face with Hurricane Camille," *Reader's Digest,* March 1970. Copyright © 1970 by The Reader's Digest Association, Inc. Reprinted by permission.

Ray Bradbury, "The Wonderful Ice Cream Suit." Copyright © 1958 by Ray Bradbury. Reprinted by permission of Harold Matson Company, Inc.

Gwendolyn Brooks, "When you have forgotten Sunday: the love story," from *The World of Gwendolyn Brooks* by Gwendolyn Brooks. Copyright 1945 by Gwendolyn Brooks Blakely. Reprinted by permission of Harper & Row, Publishers, Inc.

Glenn R. Capp, *How to Communicate Orally,* 2d ed. Copyright © 1966 by Prentice-Hall, Inc. Reprinted by permission.

Frank G. Carpenter, *Cairo to Kisumu.* Copyright 1923 by Frank G. Carpenter. Reprinted by permission of the Estate of Frances Carpenter Huntington.

Bruce Catton, "Grant and Lee: A Study in Contrast," from *The American Story,* edited by E. S. Miers. Copyright © 1956 by Broadcast Music. Reprinted by permission of Hawthorn Book, Inc.

Anton Chekhov, "Ward No. 6," from *The Portable Russian Reader,* edited and translated by Bernard Guilbert Guerney. Copyright 1947 by the Viking Press, Inc. Reprinted by permission.

John Collier, "The Chaser." Copyright 1941 and 1968 by John Collier. Reprinted by permission of Harold Matson Company, Inc. Originally appeared in *The New Yorker.*

Don Cook, "Britian's 'Thin Blue Line'—Police Prefer Tolerance to Carrying Guns," *Los Angeles Times,* April 6, 1972. Copyright © 1972 by Los Angeles Times. Reprinted by permission.

e. e. cummings, "since feeling is first," from *Complete Poems 1913–1962* by e. e. cummings. Copyright 1926 by Horace Liveright, copyright 1954 by e. e. cummings. Reprinted by permission of Harcourt Brace Jovanovich, Inc.

Eliot Daley, "What Produced Those Pot-Smoking, Rebellious, Demonstrating Kids?—Television," *TV Guide,* November 7, 1970. Copyright © 1970 by Triangle Publications, Inc. Reprinted by permission of *TV Guide Magazine.*

C. A. D'Alonzo, "The Loneliness of the Alcoholic," *The Drinking Problem and Its Control.* Copyright © 1959 by Gulf Publishing Co. Reprinted by permission of Gulf Publishing Company.

Robert Gorham Davis, *Handbook for English.* Reprinted by permission of Robert Gorham Davis, Theodore Morrison, the President and Fellows of Harvard University, and Harvard University Press.

Garrett DeBell, editor, *The Environmental Handbook.* Copyright © 1970 by Garrett De-Bell. Reprinted by permission of Ballantine Books, Inc., a Division of Random House, Inc.

Alexis de Tocqueville, "Causes of the Restless Spirit of Americans," *Democracy in America, Vol. II.* Copyright © 1963 by Alfred A. Knopf, Inc. Reprinted by permission.

Peter F. Drucker, "How to Take the Profit Out of Hard Drugs," *Saturday Review,* May 13, 1972. Copyright © 1972 by Saturday Review Company. Reprinted by permission.

Louise Dudley and Austin Faricy, *The Humanities, 4th ed.* Copyright © 1967 by McGraw-Hill, Inc. Reprinted by permission of McGraw-Hill Book Company.

John P. East, "Why So Few Conservatives on Campus?" The New Guard, May 1970. Copyright © 1970 by Young Americans for Freedom, Inc. Reprinted by permission.

T. S. Eliot, "The Love Song of J. Alfred Prufrock," from *Collected Poems 1901–1962* by T. S. Eliot. Copyright 1936 by Harcourt Brace Jovanovich, Inc., copyright © 1963 by T. S. Eliot. Reprinted by permission of Harcourt Brace Jovanovich and Faber and Faber Ltd.

Kenneth Fearing, "Portrait," from *New and Selected Poems* by Kenneth Fearing. Reprinted by permission of Indiana University Press.

Robert Frost, "Stopping by Woods on a Snowy Evening," from *The Poetry of Robert Frost,* edited by Edward Connery Lathem. Copyright © 1923 and 1969 by Holt, Rinehart & Winston, Inc., copyright © 1951 by Robert Frost. Reprinted by permission of Holt, Rinehart & Winston, Inc.

Jose Ortega y Gasset, *The Revolt of the Masses.* Copyright 1932 by W. W. Norton & Company, Inc., copyright © 1960 by Teresa Carey. Reprinted by permission of W. W. Norton & Company, Inc., and George Allen & Unwin Ltd.

Richard Gordon, "The Common Cold." Copyright © 1954 by The Atlantic Monthly Company, Boston, Mass. Reprinted by permission.

Robert B. Greenough and George L. Kittredge, *Words and Their Ways in English Speech.* Copyright © 1900, 1901 by Macmillan Company. Reprinted by permission of The Macmillan Company.

Thomas Hardy, "The Man He Killed," from *Collected Poems* by Thomas Hardy. Copyright 1925 by Macmillan Publishing Company, Inc. Reprinted by permission of The Macmillan Publishing Company, the Trustees of the Hardy Estate, Macmillan London & Basingstoke, and the Macmillan Company of Canada, Ltd.

Theodore W. Hatlen, *Drama: Principles and Plays.* Copyright © 1967 by Meredith Publishing Company. Reprinted by permission of Appleton-Century-Crofts, Inc.

"Have You Ever Been Convicted of a Felony," *Clinton Herald,* 1945. Copyright 1945 by The Clinton Herald Company.

Ernest Hemingway, "A Clean, Well-lighted Place," from *Winner Take Nothing* by Ernest Hemingway. Copyright 1933 by Charles Scribner's Sons. Reprinted by permission.

James Hodgson, "Think again before Sending Your Child to College," *Family Weekly,* September 17, 1972. Copyright © 1972 by Family Weekly, Inc. Reprinted by permission.

Rod W. Horton and Herbert W. Edwards, *Backgrounds of American Literary Thought, 2d ed.* Copyright 1952 by Appleton-Century-Crofts. Copyright © 1967 by Meredith Publishing Company. Reprinted by permission of Appleton-Century-Crofts, Educational Division, Meredith Publishing Co.

Rod W. Horton and Vincent F. Hopper, *Backgrounds of European Literature.* Copyright 1954 by Meredith Publishing Co. Reprinted by permission of Appleton-Century-Crofts, Educational Division, Meredith Publishing Co.

Langston Hughes, "I, Too," from *Selected Poems* by Langston Hughes. Copyright 1929 by Alfred A. Knopf, Inc., and renewed 1954 by Langston Hughes. Reprinted by permission of Alfred A. Knopf, Inc.

Thomas Henry Huxley, *Autobiography and Selected Essays,* by Thomas Henry Huxley. Reprinted by permission of Houghton Mifflin Company.

Washington Irving, "The Legend of Sleepy Hollow," from *Selected Writings of Washington Irving,* edited by Saxe Commins. Copyright 1945 by Random House, Inc. Reprinted by permission.

T. K. Irwin, "Noise Pollution: Despite the Furor, the Problem Still Grows," *Family Weekly,* November 21, 1971. Copyright © 1971 by Family Weekly, Inc. Reprinted by permission.

Randall Jarrell, "Eighth Air Force," from *The Complete Poems of Randal Jarrell.* Copyright © 1947, 1969 by Mrs. Randall Jarrell. Reprinted by permission of Farrar, Straus & Giroux, Inc.

Leroi Jones, "for hettie," from *Preface to a Twenty Volume Suicide Note* by Leroi Jones. Copyright © 1961 by Leroi Jones. Reprinted by permission of Corinth Books.

X. J. Kennedy, "Who Killed King Kong?" *Dissent,* volume vii, number 2, Spring 1960. Reprinted by permission.

Russell Kirk, "Conservative Tide Grows in an Effort to Stem the Drift," and "Conservatives Take Practical Tack Seeking Order, Change," *San Gabriel Valley Tribune,* September 23, 1969. Copyright © 1969 by *San Gabriel Valley Tribune.*

Joseph Wood Krutch, "On Law and Order," *This Week Magazine,* October 19, 1973. Copyright © 1969 by United Newspapers Magazine Corporation. Reprinted by permission of Mrs. Joseph Wood Krutch.

Paul Lehr, Herbert Zim, and R. Will Burnett, *Weather—A Golden Guide.* Copyright 1965 and 1967 by Western Publishing Company, Inc. Reprinted by permission.

Max Lerner, "The Games Nations Play," *Los Angeles Times,* December 5, 1971. Copyright © 1971 by *Los Angeles Times.* Reprinted by permission.

Carson McCullers, "The Jockey," from *The Ballad of the Sad Cafe.* Copyright © 1955 by Carson McCullers. Reprinted by permission of Houghton Mifflin Company.

Judith McPherson, "Killers in the Air," *Health,* May-June 1970. Copyright © 1970 by American Osteopathic Association. Reprinted by permission of the American Osteopathic Association and Judith McPherson.

Millie McWhirter, "The Short-Short Story," *Writer's Digest,* January 1969. Copyright © 1969 by *Writer's Digest.* Reprinted by permission of F. & M. Publishing Corporation and Curtis Brown, Ltd.

Oscar Mandel, "Mobility and the United States," *The American Scholar,* volume 27, number 2, Spring 1958. Copyright © 1958 by the United Chapters of Phi Beta Kappa. Reprinted by permission.

David L. Martin, "Schoolboy Sports a Bone-crushing Financial Problem," *Los Angeles Times,* July 9, 1972. Condensed from an article in *The American School Board Journal,* August 1972. Copyright © 1972 by the National School Boards Association. All rights reserved. Reprinted by permission.

Marianne Moore, "Poetry," from *Collected Poems* by Marianne Moore. Copyright 1935 by Marianne Moore, renewed 1963 by Marianne Moore and T. S. Eliot. Reprinted by permission of The Macmillan Company.

Alan Morehead, *The Blue Nile,* revised edition. Copyright © 1962 and 1972 by Alan Moorehead. Reprinted by permission of Harper & Row, Publishers, Inc., Laurence Pollinger Ltd., and Hamish Hamilton Ltd.

Thomas B. Morgan, "The American War Game," *Esquire,* October 1965. Copyright © 1965 by Esquire, Inc.; copyright © 1974 by Thomas B. Morgan. Reprinted by permission.

Allan Nevins and Henry Steel Commager, *A Pocket History of the U.S.* Copyright © 1956 by Allan Nevins and Henry Steele Commager. Reprinted by permission of Washington Square Press, a division of Simon & Schuster, Inc.

Ruth Pintar, "Football Banquet Affair," *Teen,* October 1967. Reprinted by permission.

Edith Raskin, "The Hidden Landscape," "Types of Volcanoes," and "The Earth Ball," from *Many Worlds: Seen and Unseen* by Edith Raskin. Copyright 1954 by Edith Raskin. Reprinted by permission.

David Riesman, Nathan Glazer and Reuel Denney, *The Lonely Crowd.* Twelfth printing, August 1965. Copyright 1950 by Yale University Press. Reprinted by permission of Yale University Press.

Edwin Arlington Robinson, "Richard Cory," from *Children of the Night* by Edwin Arlington Robinson. Reprinted by permission of Charles Scribner's Sons.

Theodore Roethke, "Elegy for Jane," from *Collected Poems of Theodore Roethke.* Copyright 1950 by Theodore Roethke. Reprinted by permission of Doubleday & Company, Inc.

Lenore Romeny, "Men, Women—and Politics," *Look Magazine,* April 16, 1971. Copyright © 1971 by Cowles Communications, Inc. Reprinted by permission.

luis omar salinos, "Aztec Angel," from *Crazy Gypsy.* Reprinted by permission.

Anne Sexton, "Her Kind," from *Bedlam and Part Way Back* by Anne Sexton. Copyright © 1960 by Anne Sexton. Reprinted by permission of Houghton Mifflin Company.

Dorothy Z. Seymour, "Black Children, Black Speech," *Commonweal,* November 19, 1967. Copyright © 1967 by Commonweal Publishing Company, Inc. Reprinted by permission of Commonweal Publishing Company, Inc.

Irwin Shaw, "The Girls in Their Summer Dresses," from *Selected Short Stories of Irwin Shaw.* Copyright 1939, renewed 1967 by Irwin Shaw. Reprinted by permission of Random House, Inc.

"Song of Dawn Boy" from *American Indian Poetry* by George Cronyn. Copyright 1934 by Liveright Publishing Corporation. Copyright © renewed 1962 by George Cronyn. Reprinted by permission of Liveright Publishing Corporation.

Theodore Sorenson, "Dangers Facing the University," *Columbia Journal of World Business,* November-December 1969. Copyright © 1969 by the Trustees of Columbia University in the City of New York. Reprinted by permission.

Athelstan Spilhaus, "The Next Industrial Revolution," *Science,* volume 167, March 27, 1970, p. 1673. Copyright © 1970 by the American Association for the Advancement of Science. Reprinted by permission.

John Steinbeck, "The Chrysanthemums," from *The Long Valley* by John Steinbeck. Copyright © 1968 by John Steinbeck. Reprinted by permission of The Viking Press.

Gloria Steinem, "Why We Need a Woman President in 1976." Copyright © 1970 by Gloria Steinem. Reprinted by permission of the Sterling Lord Agency, Inc.

J. C. Stobart, "Athens and Rome," from *The Grandeur That Was Rome.* Copyright © 1962 by Sidgwick & Jackson, Ltd. All rights reserved. Reprinted by permission of Hawthorn Books, Inc.

May Swenson, "Woman," from *Iconographs* by May Swenson. Copyright © 1968 by May Swenson. Reprinted by permission of Charles Scribner's Sons. First appeared in *New American Review #3.*

Dylan Thomas, "Fern Hill," from *The Poems of Dylan Thomas.* Copyright 1946 by New Directions Publishing Corporation. Reprinted by permission of New Directions Publishing Corporation, J. M. Dent & Sons, Ltd., and the Trustees for the Copyrights of the late Dylan Thomas.

John Updike, "Ex-Basketball Player," from *The Carpentered Hen and Other Tame Creatures* by John Updike. Copyright © 1957 by John Updike. Reprinted by permission of Harper & Row, Publishers, Inc. Originally appeared in *The New Yorker.*

T. Walter Wallbank and Alastair M. Taylor, *Civilization: Past and Present.* Copyright 1954 by Scott, Foresman and Company. Reprinted by permission.

Webster's New World Dictionary of the American Language, second college edition. Copyright © 1970 by The World Publishing Company. Reprinted by permission.

James Wellard, "Tin Hinan," from *The Great Saraha.* Copyright © 1964 and 1965 by James Wellard. Reprinted by permission of E. P. Dutton & Company, Inc., and Curtis Brown Ltd.

Jessamyn West, "Sixteen," from *Cress Delahanty* by Jessamyn West. Copyright © 1946 by Jessamyn West. Reprinted by permission of Harcourt Brace Jovanovich, Inc.

Donald E. Westlake, "Love Stuff, Cops-and-Robbers Style." Copyright © 1972 by the Times-Mirror Company. Reprinted by permission of the author and Henry Morrison, Inc., his agent.

T. Harry Williams, *Lincoln and His Generals.* Copyright 1952 by Alfred A. Knopf, Inc. Reprinted by permission.

Edmund Wilson, *Europe Without Boedeker,* 2d ed. Copyright © 1947 and 1966 by Edmund Wilson. Reprinted by permission of Farrar, Straus & Giroux, Inc.

Elizabeth C. Winship, "Ireland, Israel—Alike Yet Different," *Boston Globe,* August 25, 1970. Copyright © 1970 by the Boston Globe. Reprinted by permission.

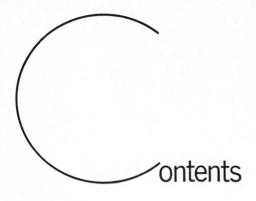

Contents

Preface — xxi

1 INTRODUCTION TO WRITING — 1
"The Sad Young Men" by Rod W. Horton and Herbert W. Edwards — 4
"What Produced Those Pot-smoking, Rebellious, Demonstrating Kids?—Television!" by Eliot Daley — 9
Discussion One/Television and Youth — 14
Topics for Written Assignments or Discussion — 15

2 WRITING THE PARAGRAPH — 17
Introductory Paragraphs — 18
Assignment/Introduction — 20
Middle Paragraphs — 20
Assignment/Basic Frames or Orders of Paragraph Organization — 27
Assignment/Topic Sentence — 30
Assignment/Writing the Paragraph — 31
Assignment/Writing the Paragraph — 34
Guide to the Paragraph — 41
Assignment/Comparison and Contrast — 42
Assignment/Writing the Paragraph — 45
Transitional Paragraphs — 48
Assignment/Transitional Paragraphs — 48
Transitions within the Paragraph (Coherence) — 49
Assignment/Paragraph Coherence — 54
Concluding Paragraphs — 54
"Who Killed King Kong?" by X. J. Kennedy — 56
Structure Review One/Paragraph Organization — 60
Answer Section — 61

3 PLANNING THE PAPER — 63
Select a Subject — 64
Preliminary Search for Material — 64
Assignment/Preliminary Search for Material — 67
Limit the Subject — 68
Assignment/Limiting the Subject — 69

Gather Material 70
Assignment/Gathering Material 70
Organize the Material 70
Assignment/Informal Outline 73
Assignment/Outlining 79
Assignment/Outlining 79
Assignment/Outlining 81
Write the First Draft 81
Revise the First Draft 81
Prepare the Final Paper 82
"Britain's 'Thin Blue Line'—Police Prefer Tolerance to Carrying
  Guns" by Don Cook 83
Structure Review Two/Analyzing the Plan 86
Answer Section 88

4 NARRATION AND DESCRIPTION 91
Narration 92
"Face to Face with Hurricane Camille" by Joseph P. Blank ... 94
Structure Review Three/Narration 100
Guide to Narration 102
"The Day Sing Sing Licked Us" by Edwin D. Barton 102
Structure Review Four/Narration 107
Assignment/Structuring Narration 109
Assignment/Writing Narration 109
Description 109
Assignment/Identifying Figures of Speech 111
Guide to Description 116
"Tin Hinan" by James Wellard 117
Structure Review Five/Description 120
Assignment/Effective Choice of Words 121
Assignment/Point of View 122
"The Blue Nile" by Alan Moorhead 123
Structure Review Six/Description 128
Assignment/Writing Description 130
Answer Section 130

5 COMPARISON, CONTRAST, AND ANALOGY 133
Comparison 136
"The American War Game" by Thomas B. Morgan 138
Structure Review Seven/Comparison 147
Assignment/Writing Comparison 149
Contrast 149
"Athens and Rome" by J. C. Stobart 152
"Grant and Lee: A Study in Contrasts" by Bruce Catton 154
Structure Review Eight/Contrast 158
"Ireland, Israel—Alike yet Different" by Elizabeth C. Winship ... 159
Structure Review Nine/Comparison and Contrast 162
"Love Stuff, Cops-and-Robbers Style" by Donald E. Westlake ... 163
Assignment/Contrast 165
Discussion Two/Films 165
Assignment/Writing Contrast and Comparison 165

Analogy 165
"The Games Nations Play" by Max Lerner 166
Answer Section 168

6 PROCESS AND CLASSIFICATION 169
Instructional Process 169
"A Basic Method to Teach Swimming" 170
Structure Review Ten/Instructional Process 172
"The Short-Short Story" by Millie McWhirter 174
Structure Review Eleven/Instructional Process 178
Informational Process 179
"The Hidden Landscape" by Edith Raskin 180
Structure Review Twelve/Informational Process 182
Assignment/Writing the Instructional Process 182
Assignment/Writing the Informational Process 183
Classification 183
Assignment/Basic for Classification 184
"The Common Cold" by Richard Gordon 186
"Types of Volcanoes" by Edith Raskin 187
Structure Review Thirteen/Classification 189
Assignment/Writing Classification 190
Answer Section 190

7 PARTITION AND CAUSAL ANALYSIS 193
Physical Partition 194
"The Earth Ball" by Edith Raskin 194
Structure Review Fourteen/Physical Partition 196
"Today's Suburbia" by Peter Blake 197
Assignment/Physical Partition 199
Conceptual Partition 199
"Think Again before Sending Your Child to College"
  by James D. Hodgson 200
"The Next Industrial Revolution" by Athelstan Spilhaus 202
Structural Review Fifteen/Conceptual Partition 204
Assignment/Analyzing the Conceptual Partition 205
"Dangers Facing the University" by Theodore Sorenson 205
"The Loneliness of the Alcoholic" by C. A. D'Alonzo 206
Structural Review Sixteen/Conceptual Partition 209
"How to Take the Profits out of Hard Drugs" by Peter F. Drucker 210
Discussion Three/Drugs 214
Assignment/Writing the Conceptual Partition 214
"Noise Pollution: Despite Furor, the Problem Still Grows"
  by T. K. Irwin 216
Structure Review Seventeen/Causal Analysis 219
"Have You Ever Been Convicted of a Felony?" 220
Discussion Four/Youth and Crime 221
"Why So Few Conservatives on Campus?" by John P. East 221
Structure Review Eighteen/Causal Analysis 225
Assignment/Writing Causal Analysis 227
Answer Section 227

8 DEFINING AND COMBINING   231
Dictionary Definition   232
Assignment/Dictionary Definition   234
Assignment/Simple Definitions and Errors in Defining   234
Formal Definition   235
Extended Definition   237
"What Was the Renaissance?" by T. Walter Wallbank and
    Alastair M. Taylor   237
"Conservatives Take Practical Tack Seeking Order, Change"
    by Russell Kirk   241
Structure Review Nineteen/Definition   244
Assignment/Writing Definition   245
Combination of Methods   245
"On Law and Order" by Joseph Wood Krutch   247
Discussion Five/Law and Order   249
Answer Section   249

9 PERSUASION   251
Strategies of Dishonest Persuasion   253
Assignment/Analogy   258
Honest Persuasion   259
"Churchill's Speech to the House of Commons"   260
Assignment/Persuasion   265
Structuring the Persuasion Paper   265
Assignment/The Issues   267
"Schoolboy Sports a Bone-crushing Financial Problem"
    by David L. Martin   270
Structure Review Twenty/Persuasion   275
"Men, Women—and Politics" by Lenore Romney   276
Discussion Six/Women's Liberation   279
"Why We Need a Woman President in 1976" by Gloria Steinem   279
Structure Review Twenty-One/Persuasion   283
Assignment/Writing Persuasion   285
Answer Section   286

CONTEMPORARY LITERATURE   287

POETRY   287
"Songs of Dawn Boy"   287
"Poetry" by Marianne Moore   289
"The Love Song of J. Alfred Prufrock" by T. S. Eliot   290
"When You Have Forgotten Sunday: The Love Story"
    by Gwendolyn Brooks   295
"for hettie" by LeRoi Jones   296
"since feeling is first" by e. e. cummings   297
"Aztec Angel" by luis omar salinas   297
"I, Too, Sing America" by Langston Hughes   299
"Stopping by Woods on a Snowy Evening" by Robert Frost   300
"The Man He Killed" by Thomas Hardy   301
"Eighth Air Force" by Randall Jarrell   302
"Portrait" by Kenneth Fearing   303

"ex-basketball player" by John Updike   304
"Richard Cory" by Edwin Arlington Robinson   306
"Women" by May Swenson   306
"her kind" by Anne Sexton   307
"Elegy for Jane" by Theodore Roethke   308
"The Ball Poem" by John Berryman   309
"Fern Hill" by Dylan Thomas   310

SHORT STORIES   312
"The Girls in Their Summer Dresses" by Irwin Shaw   312
"Sixteen" by Jessamyn West   319
"The Chaser" by John Collier   325
"A Clean, Well-lighted Place" by Ernest Hemingway   327
"The Jockey" by Carson McCullers   331
"Football Banquet Affair" by Ruth Pintar   336
"The Wonderful Ice Cream Suit" by Ray Bradbury   345
"The Convert" by Lerone Bennett, Jr.   363
"The Chrysanthemums" by John Steinbeck   376

Correction Key for Written Assignments   385
Checklist for Correctness   387

Index   389

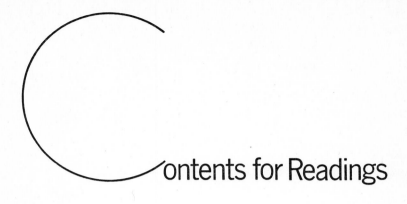

ontents for Readings

YOUTH
"The Sad Young Men" by Rod W. Horton and Herbert W. Edwards   4
"What Produced Those Pot-smoking, Rebellious, Demonstrating
  Kids—Television!" by Eliot Daley   9
"Elegy for Jane" by Theodore Roethke   308
"The Ball Poem" by John Berryman   309
"Fern Hill" by Dylan Thomas   310
"Sixteen" by Jassamyn West   319
"Football Banquet Affair" by Ruth Pintar   336

MOVIES
"Who Killed King Kong?" by X. J. Kennedy   56
"Love Stuff, Cops-and-Robbers Style" by Donald E. Westlake   163

WAR AND VIOLENCE
"Britain's 'Thin Blue Line'—Police Prefer Tolerance to Carrying
  Guns" by Don Cook   83
"The American War Game" by Thomas B. Morgan   138
"Dangers Facing the University" by Theodore Sorenson   205
"Churchill's Speech to the House of Commons"   260
"The Man He Killed" by Thomas Hardy   301
"Eighth Air Force" by Randall Jarrell   302

MINORITIES
"The Wonderful Ice Cream Suit" by Ray Bradbury   345
"The Convert" by Lerone Bennett, Jr.   363
"Aztec Angel" by luis omar salinas   297
"I, Too, Sing America" by Langston Hughes   299

PEOPLE
"Face to Face with Hurricane Camille" by Joseph P. Blank   94
"The Day Sing Sing Licked Us" by Edwin D. Barton   102
"Grant and Lee: A Study in Contrasts" by Bruce Catton   154

PLACES
"Tin Hinan" by James Wellard   117

"The Blue Nile" by Alan Moorhead   123
"Athens and Rome" by J. C. Stobart   152
"Ireland, Israel—Alike yet Different" by Elizabeth C. Winship   159
"The Hidden Landscape" by Edith Raskin   180
"The Earth Ball" by Edith Raskin   194

POLITICS
"The Games Nations Play" by Max Lerner   166
"Why So Few Conservatives on Campus?" by John P. East   221
"Conservatives Take Practical Tack Seeking Order, Change"
   by Russell Kirk   241

POLLUTION
"Noise Pollution: Despite Furor, the Problem Still Grows"
   by T. K. Irwin   216

SOCIETY
"Today's Suburbia" by Peter Blake   197
"The Next Industrial Revolution" by Athelstan Spilhaus   202
"Have You Ever Been Convicted of a Felony? in *The Clinton Herald*   220
"On Law and Order" by Joseph Wood Krutch   247

EDUCATION
"Think Again before Sending Your Child to College"
   by James Hodgson   200
"Schoolboy Sports a Bone-crushing Financial Problem"
   by David L. Martin   270

ALCOHOL AND DRUGS
"The Loneliness of the Alcoholic" by C. A. D'Alonzo   206
"How to Take the Profit out of Hard Drugs" by Peter F. Drucker   210

WOMEN
"Men, Women—and Politics" by Lenore Romney   276
"Why We Need a Woman President in 1976" by Gloria Steinem   279
"Women" by May Swenson   306
"her kind" by Anne Sexton   307

LOVE AND MARRIAGE
"When You Have Forgotten Sunday: The Love Story"
   by Gwendolyn Brooks   295
"for hettie" by LeRoi Jones   296
"since feeling is first" by e. e. cummings   297
"The Girls in Their Summer Dresses" by Irwin Shaw   312
"The Chaser" by John Collier   325

ALIENATION AND REFLECTION
"The Love Song of J. Alfred Prufrock" by T. S. Eliot   290
"Stopping by Woods on a Snowy Evening" by Robert Frost   300
"Portrait" by Kenneth Fearing   303
"ex-basketball player" by John Updike   304
"Richard Cory" by Edwin Arlington Robinson   306
"A Clean, Well-lighted Place" by Ernest Hemingway   327
"The Jockey" by Carson McCullers   331
"The Chrysanthemums" by John Steinbeck   376

GENERAL INTEREST
"A Basic Method to Teach Swimming"   170
"The Short-Short Story" by Millie McWhirter   174
"The Common Cold" by Richard Gordon   186
"What Was the Renaissance?" by T. Walter Wallbank and
    Alastair M. Taylor   237
"Types of Volcanoes" by Edith Raskin   187
"Songs of Dawn Boy"   287
"Poetry" by Marianne Moore   289

reface

This book was written to help the student who wishes and needs to organize his thought effectively for written communication in college. Most of the writing he will do, such as reports, compositions, essay examinations, assigned papers, and various other written assignments, are relatively short pieces of writing demanding of him a proficiency in the techniques and skills of organizing and developing narration, description, exposition, and persuasion. In this book, the student will find considerable detailed information about organizing and developing thought for written communication. He will also have the opportunity to read many excellent essays by experienced writers which will serve as models for structuring his own writing and as sources for class discussion of ideas that may suggest topics for compositions and other required written assignments. Finally, he will be required to do writing of his own so that he can put into practice what he is learning.

The organization of the material is simple; it consists of four logical divisions. The first three chapters prepare the student for the writing process. This division explains the kind of writing the student will do for successful completion of most programs of study, introduces him to the structure of the essay, discusses the organization and development of the different kinds of paragraphs in juxtaposition with the requirements of a good paragraph—unity, order, coherence, and completeness—and gives him such information that will help him plan the paper before he begins writing.

Chapter 4 considers development of thought by narration and description—a logical unit since these types are organized by the natural orders of time (narration) and space (description) that are inherent within them.

Chapters 5 through 8, the largest division of the book, concentrate on the methods of organizing and developing thought in a form known as exposition. The treatment of this material—the purpose of which is to inform and explain—is more detailed and complete than in the other divisions since proficiency in expository skills and techniques is most essential for success in college writing. Comparison, contrast, analogy, process, classification, partition, causal analysis, and definition—the basic methods of exposition—are treated separately so that the student will understand better the skills and techniques especially suited to each method. Nevertheless, a concluding part of this division stresses developing thought by a combination of methods, which is more characteristic of the writing process.

Chapter 9 presents strategies of persuasion and methods of writing a successful argumentative paper.

The supporting text—Structure Reviews, Questions for Discussion, and various assignments—is designed to supplement the explanation of the various methods of developing thought so that the student will have an opportunity to practice what he is learning.

Each of the twenty-one Structure Reviews consists of questions for rhetorical analysis of essays by experienced writers. Thus, the student will be able to reinforce and review the rhetorical information presented in the text with practical applications closely related to that material. Written assignments will further implement this design.

Six of the essays by experienced writers are followed by Questions for Discussion. These questions will serve to stimulate class discussion and are sources of ideas for the student's own writing and discussion. They may be used by the student and instructor for rhetorical analysis as well. Most of the essays selected for models of good writing were chosen also because they treat contemporary topics of interest to the student. They may also provide ideas for the student's own writing and for discussion.

The book includes a section of poems and short stories by contemporary writers. Each poem and short story is followed by questions for discussion and analysis. Thus, the book provides a variety of reading experiences for the student. The book, therefore, is designed as a rhetoric reader with a separate Table of Contents for each purpose. In the Contents for the readings, the selections are arranged thematically.

The approach to teaching writing in this book stresses four tried and proven methods: (1) explaining simply and completely enough the skills and techniques of effective writing so that the student may learn how to write well; (2) presenting selections that illustrate interesting and successful writing so that by an analysis of these models the student may see for himself the ways experienced writers organize and develop their thought; (3) giving the student ample opportunity to practice and apply the knowledge he is gaining; and (4) providing the student with essays, poems, and short stories so that he may enjoy the enriching experience that good literature offers.

P. Joseph Canavan

Introduction to Writing

The beginning writer does not usually associate written communication with the thinking process. If he thinks about writing, he relates it to spelling, grammar, and punctuation errors and remembers those arduous hours he spent in the writing class trying to think of something to write about. In his mind also remains the vivid image of a returned paper marked in red with a variety of symbols, each indicating some kind of failure. Because he has been concentrating so much on the mechanical processes of structuring written assignments, he has become less concerned with the possibilities of written communication. He does not realize that it offers him an opportunity to present effectively his thoughts concerning an almost unlimited variety of subjects that grow out of knowledge assimilated in different courses and his own life's experiences.

In college, you and other beginning writers will be asked to demonstrate your skills in organizing and developing your thought by written assignments, among which are reports, compositions, research papers, and supplementary papers.

Suppose, for example, your instructor in a history, sociology, or literature class gave you an essay examination with a question or questions about the younger generation of the 1920s like the following.

1 What were the causes and effects of the revolt of the younger generation of the 1920s?
2 Compare and/or contrast the revolt of the younger generation of the 1920s with the revolt of the younger generation today.
3 How did the younger generation of the 1920s face the challenge of a rapidly changing world?
4 Define the expression "generation gap."
5 In what ways did Greenwich Village set the pattern for the revolt of the younger generation of the 1920s?
6 Place the young people involved in the revolt of the 1920s into three classes or categories on the basis of similar characteristics.

How would you limit, organize, and develop your answer to question 2 if the time limit were fifteen minutes? Forty-five minutes? 2½ hours? How would you limit, organize, and develop your thought if the instructor asked you to write on five of these questions in fifty minutes? Two hours? Three hours?

Suppose the same instructor asked you to write a paper of your choice on "The Revolt of the Younger Generation in the 1920s." Your sources for the paper might be class lectures, your textbooks, supplementary readings, interviews, or films. How would you limit, organize, and develop your thought for an out-of-class paper of approximately 500 words? For an in-class written assignment (approximately fifty minutes)? For a research paper of approximately 2,000 words?

Written assignments and essay questions like those mentioned above are not designed simply to test your knowledge about a particular subject and give you a grade in the course. If this were their only purpose, such assignments would scarcely justify the time and energy that you would expend to satisfactorily complete them. They are also devices that show how well you have assimilated knowledge about a subject and how well you have organized and developed your thought within the limitations of the assignment.

Frequently, in college written assignments, you are given a topic by the instructor to develop or asked questions by him. With this kind of assignment, your problem is to understand the directions and give the instructor exactly what the question or the assignment demands. With this kind of written assignment, you must, therefore, realize that the nature of the question or assignment has already limited your treatment of the subject to a particular aspect of the topic that the instructor wants developed. You must also limit your development of the topic to satisfy the time requirements. Your problem, then, is to select from a variety of information that you have accumulated about the subject those specifics that will best answer the question or develop the limited topic most effectively in a certain time.

As you read the model paragraphs that follow, answering the question, In what ways did Greenwich Village set the pattern for the revolt of the younger generation of the 1920s? notice how the writers limit their knowledge about the much broader subject to this one aspect of it. They begin with a clearly stated main idea—Greenwich Village set the pattern—and use paragraph 1 to explain Greenwich Village to the reader, following in paragraph 2 with supporting material showing how the rest of the country imitated life in the "Village."

Greenwich Village set the pattern. Since the Seventies a dwelling place for artists and writers who settled there because living was cheap, the Village had long enjoyed a dubious reputation for Bohemianism and eccentricity. It had also harbored enough major writers, especially in the decade before World War I, to support its claim to being the intellectual center of the nation. After the war, it was only natural that hopeful young writers, their minds and pens inflamed against war, Babbittry, and "Puritanical" gentility, should flock to the traditional artistic center (where living was still cheap in 1919) to pour out their new-found creative strength, to tear down the old world, to flout the morality of their grandfathers, and to give all to art, love, and sensation.

Soon they found their imitators among the non-intellectuals. As it became more and more fashionable throughout the country for young persons to defy the law and the conventions and to add their own little matchsticks to the conflagration of "flaming youth," it was Greenwich Village that fanned the flames. "Bohemian" living became a fad. Each town had its "fast" set which prided itself on its unconventionality, although in reality this self-conscious unconventionality was rapidly becoming a standard feature of the country club class—and its less affluent imitators—throughout the nation. Before long the movement had become officially recognized by the pulpit (which denounced it), by the movies and magazines (which made it attractively naughty while pretending to denounce it), and by advertising (which obliquely encouraged it by selling everything from cigarettes to automobiles with the implied promise that their owners would be rendered sexually irresistible). Younger brothers and sisters of the war generation, who had been playing with marbles and dolls during the battles of Belleau Wood and Chateau-Thierry, and who had suffered no real disillusionment or sense of loss, now began to imitate the manners of their elders and play with the toys of vulgar rebellion. Their parents were shocked, but before long they found themselves and their

SOURCE NOTE: Rod W. Horton and Herbert W. Edwards, "The Sad Young Men," in Horton and Edwards, *Backgrounds of American Literary Thought,* pp. 319–320. Copyright © 1967 by Meredith Publishing Company. Permission of Appleton-Century-Crofts, Inc., division of Meredith Corporation.

friends adopting the new gaiety. By the middle of the decade, the "wild party" had become as commonplace a factor in American life as the flapper, the Model T, or the Dutch Colonial home in Floral Heights.

In another kind of written assignment, the instructor allows you to select a subject and develop it with a method or variety of methods that will best fulfill your purpose and give order to the kind of material that you have gathered from your research or your knowledge of the subject or both. Listed below are some topics that illustrate this kind of assignment.

The Tragedy at Pearl Harbor

Living in a New Mexico Commune

The Various Ways to Reach Our Campus

What Is a Campus Activist?

Amazing Similarities between the Deaths of Abraham Lincoln and John F. Kennedy

A Profile of a Gentleman—Robert E. Lee

Jefferson Davis—A Hero of a Lost Cause

Why Young People Aren't Going to College

The Busiest Place on Campus

How to Take Class Notes Efficiently

Why We Lost the Big Game

As you read the model essay below that treats in more detail a subject we have been using for illustrative purposes, observe the structural organization of the *whole* piece of writing. Focus your attention, therefore, on the *whole* and notice how the individual parts—the introductory paragraph, the middle paragraphs, and the final paragraph—relate to the writers' purpose and smoothly and logically fulfill that purpose. Study the individual paragraphs or paragraph units (a series of paragraphs developing one single main idea) to see how they are organized, relate to the central thought of the whole, and develop new but related stages of the developing thought.

THE SAD YOUNG MEN*
Rod W. Horton and Herbert W. Edwards

1 No aspect of life in the Twenties has been more commented upon and sensationally romanticized than the so-called Revolt of the Younger Generation. The slightest mention of the decade brings nostalgic recollections to the

*Source note: Rod W. Horton and Herbert W. Edwards, "The Sad Young Men," in Horton and Edwards, *Backgrounds of American Literary Thought*," pp. 315–322. Copyright © 1967 by Meredith Publishing Company. Permission of Appleton-Century-Crofts, Inc., division of Meredith Corporation.

middle-aged and curious questionings by the young: memories of the deliciously illicit thrill of the first visit to a speakeasy, of the brave denunciation of Puritan morality, and of the fashionable experimentations in amour in the parked sedan on a country road; questions about the naughty, jazzy parties, the flask-toting "sheik," and the moral and stylistic vagaries of the "flapper" and the "drugstore cowboy." "Were young people really so wild?" present-day students ask their parents and teachers. "Was there really a Younger Generation problem?" The answers to such inquiries must of necessity be "yes" and "no"—"yes" because the business of growing up is always accompanied by a Younger Generation Problem; "no" because what seemed so wild, irresponsible, and immoral in social behavior at the time can now be seen in perspective as being something considerably less sensational than the degeneration of our jazz-mad youth.

2   Actually, the revolt of the young people was a logical outcome of conditions in the age. First of all, it must be remembered that the rebellion was not confined to the United States, but affected the entire Western world as a result of the aftermath of the first serious war in a century. Second, in the United States it was reluctantly realized by some—subconsciously if not openly—that our country was no longer isolated in either politics or tradition and that we had reached an international stature that would forever prevent us from retreating behind the artificial walls of a provincial morality or the geographical protection of our two bordering oceans.

3   The rejection of Victorian gentility was, in any case, inevitable. The booming of American industry, with its gigantic, roaring factories, its corporate impersonality, and its large-scale aggressiveness, no longer left any room for the code of polite behavior and well-bred morality fashioned in a quieter and less competitive age. War or no war, as the generations passed, it became increasingly difficult for our young people to accept standards of behavior that bore no relationship to the bustling business medium in which they were expected to battle for success. The war acted merely as a catalytic agent in this breakdown of the Victorian social structure, and by precipitating our young people into a pattern of mass murder it released their inhibited violent energies which, after the shooting was over, were turned in both Europe and America to the destruction of an obsolescent nineteenth-century society.

4   Thus in a changing world youth was faced with the challenge of bringing our mores up to date. But at the same time it was tempted, in America at least, to escape its responsibilities and retreat behind an air of naughty alcoholic sophistication and a pose of Bohemian immorality. The faddishness, the wild spending of money on transitory pleasures and momentary novelties, the hectic air of gaiety, the experimentation in sensation—sex, drugs, alcohol, perversions—were all part of the pattern of escape, an escape made possible by a general prosperity and a post-war fatigue with politics, economic restrictions, and international responsibilities. Prohibition afforded the young the additional opportunity of making their pleasures illicit, and the much-publi-

cized orgies and defiant manifestoes of the intellectuals crowding into Greenwich Village gave them a pattern and a philosophic defense for their escapism. And like most escapist sprees, this one lasted until the money ran out, until the crash of the world economic structure at the end of the decade called the party to a halt and forced the revellers to sober up and face the problems of the new age.

5 The rebellion started with World War I. The prolonged stalemate of 1915–1916, the increasing insolence of Germany toward the United States, and our official reluctance to declare our status as a belligerent were intolerable to many of our idealistic citizens, and with typical American adventurousness enhanced somewhat by the strenuous jingoism of Theodore Roosevelt, our young men began to enlist under foreign flags. In the words of Joe Williams, in John Dos Passos' *U.S.A.,* they "wanted to get into the fun before the whole thing turned belly up." For military service, in 1916–1917, was still a romantic occupation. The young men of college age in 1917 knew nothing of modern warfare. The strife of 1861–1865 had popularly become, in motion picture and story, a magnolia-scented soap opera, while the one hundred-days' fracas with Spain in 1898 had dissolved into a one-sided victory at Manila and a cinematic charge up San Juan Hill. Furthermore, there were enough high school assembly orators proclaiming the character-forming force of the strenuous life to convince more than enough otherwise sensible boys that service in the European conflict would be of great personal value, in addition to being idealistic and exciting. Accordingly, they began to join the various armies in increasing numbers, the "intellectuals" in the ambulance corps, others in the infantry, merchant marine, or wherever else they could find a place. Those who were reluctant to serve in a foreign army talked excitedly about Preparedness, occasionally considered joining the National Guard, and rushed to enlist when we finally did enter the conflict. So tremendous was the storming of recruitment centers that harassed sergeants actually pleaded with volunteers to "go home and wait for the draft," but since no self-respecting person wanted to suffer the disgrace of being drafted, the enlistment craze continued unabated.

6 Naturally, the spirit of carnival and the enthusiasm for high military adventure were soon dissipated once the eager young men had received a good taste of twentieth-century warfare. To their lasting glory, they fought with distinction, but it was a much altered group of soldiers who returned from the battlefields in 1919. Especially was this true of the college contingent, whose idealism had led them to enlist early and who had generally seen a considerable amount of action. To them, it was bitter to return to a home town virtually untouched by the conflict, where citizens still talked with the naive Fourth-of-July bombast they themselves had been guilty of two or three years earlier. It was even more bitter to find that their old jobs had been taken by the stay-at-homes, that business was suffering a recession that prevented the opening up of new jobs, and that veterans were considered problem children and less desirable than non-veterans for whatever business opportunities did exist. Their very homes were often uncomfortable to them; they had outgrown town and families and had developed a sudden bewildering world-weariness which neither they nor their relatives could understand. Their energies had been whipped up and their naivete destroyed by the war and now, in sleepy Gopher Prairies all over the country, they were being asked to curb those energies and resume the pose of self-deceiving Victorian innocence that they now felt to be as outmoded as the notion that their fighting had "made the world safe for democracy." And, as if home town conditions were not enough, the returning veteran also had to face the sodden, Napoleonic cynicism of Versailles, the hypocritical do-goodism of Prohibition, and the smug patriotism of the war profiteers. Something in the tension-ridden youth of America had to "give" and, after a short period of bitter resentment, it "gave" in the form of a complete overthrow of genteel standards of behavior.

7   Greenwich Village set the pattern. Since the Seventies a dwelling place for artists and writers who settled there because living was cheap, the Village had long enjoyed a dubious reputation for Bohemianism and eccentricity. It had also harbored enough major writers, especially in the decade before World War I, to support its claim to being the intellectual center of the nation. After the war, it was only natural that hopeful young writers, their minds and pens inflamed against war, Babbittry, and "Puritanical" gentility, should flock to the traditional artistic center (where living was still cheap in 1919) to pour out their new-found creative strength, to tear down the old world, to flout the morality of their grandfathers, and to give all to art, love, and sensation.

8   Soon they found their imitators among the non-intellectuals. As it became more and more fashionable throughout the country for young persons to defy the law and the conventions and to add their own little matchsticks to the conflagration of "flaming youth," it was Greenwich Village that fanned the flames. "Bohemian" living became a fad. Each town had its "fast" set which prided itself on its unconventionality, although in reality this self-conscious unconventionality was rapidly becoming a standard feature of the country club class—and its less affluent imitators—throughout the nation. Before long the movement had become officially recognized by the pulpit (which denounced it), by the movies and magazines (which made it attractively naughty while pretending to denounce it), and by advertising (which obliquely encouraged it by selling everything from cigarettes to automobiles with the implied promise that their owners would be rendered sexually irresistible). Younger brothers and sisters of the war generation, who had been playing with marbles and dolls during the battles of Belleau Wood and Chateau-Thierry, and who had suffered no real disillusionment or sense of loss, now began to imitate the manners of their elders and play with the toys of vulgar rebellion. Their parents were shocked, but before long they found themselves and their

friends adopting the new gaiety. By the middle of the decade, the "wild party" had become as commonplace a factor in American life as the flapper, the Model T, or the Dutch Colonial home in Floral Heights.

9   Meanwhile, the true intellectuals were far from flattered. What they had wanted was an America more sensitive to art and culture, less avid for material gain, and less susceptible to standardization. Instead, their ideas had been generally ignored, while their behavior had contributed to that standardization by furnishing a pattern of Bohemianism that had become as conventionalized as a Rotary luncheon. As a result, their dissatisfaction with their native country, already acute upon their return from the war, now became even more intolerable. Flaming diatribes poured from their pens denouncing the materialism and what they considered to be the cultural boobery of our society. An important book rather grandiosely entitled *Civilization in the United States,* written by "thirty intellectuals" under the editorship of J. Harold Stearns, was the rallying point of sensitive persons disgusted with America. The burden of the volume was that the best minds in the country were being ignored, that art was unappreciated, and that big business had corrupted everything. Journalism was a mere adjunct to money-making, politics were corrupt and filled with incompetents and crooks, and American family life so devoted to making money and keeping up with the Joneses that it had become joyless, patterned, hypocritical, and sexually inadequate. These defects would disappear if only creative art were allowed to show the way to better things, but since the country was blind and deaf to everything save the glint and ring of the dollar, there was little remedy for the sensitive mind but to emigrate to Europe where "they do things better." By the time *Civilization in the United States* was published (1921), most of its contributors had taken their own advice and were living abroad, and many more of the artistic and would-be artistic had followed suit.

10   It was in their defiant, but generally short-lived, European expatriation that our leading writers of the Twenties learned to think of themselves, in the words of Gertrude Stein, as the "lost generation." In no sense a movement in itself, the "lost generation" attitude nevertheless acted as a common denominator of the writing of the times. The war and the cynical power politics of Versailles had convinced these young men and women that spirituality was dead; they felt as stunned as John Andrews, the defeated aesthete in Dos Passos' *Three Soldiers,* as rootless as Hemingway's wandering alcoholics in *The Sun Also Rises.* Besides Stein, Dos Passos, and Hemingway, there were Lewis Mumford, Ezra Pound, Sherwood Anderson, Matthew Josephson, J. Harold Stearns, T. S. Eliot, E. E. Cummings, Malcolm Cowley, and many other novelists, dramatists, poets, and critics who tried to find their souls in the Antibes and on the Left Bank, who directed sad and bitter blasts at their native land, and who, almost to a man, drifted back within a few years out of sheer homesickness, to take up residence on coastal islands and in New

England farmhouses and to produce works ripened by the tempering of an older, more sophisticated society.

11 For actually the "lost generation" was never lost. It was shocked, uprooted for a time, bitter, critical, rebellious, iconoclastic, experimental, often absurd, more often misdirected—but never "lost." A decade that produced, in addition to the writers listed above, such figures as Eugene O'Neill, Edna St. Vincent Millay, F. Scott Fitzgerald, William Faulkner, Sinclair Lewis, Stephen Vincent Benét, Hart Crane, Thomas Wolfe, and innumerable others could never be written off as sterile, even by itself in a moment of self-pity. The intellectuals of the Twenties, the "sad young men," as F. Scott Fitzgerald called them, cursed their luck but didn't die; escaped but voluntarily returned; flayed the Babbitts but loved their country, and in so doing gave the nation the liveliest, freshest, most stimulating writing in its literary experience.

In the closing pages of this chapter is an essay on today's youth. It is the first in a series of selections in the book designed to develop your skill in evaluating the thinking of others concerning the problems and issues of your time and to provide you with a stimulus for topics for your written assignments.

Read the questions for discussion that follow each essay first; then read the essay. Become a critical reader by asking the following questions.

1 What is the writer's purpose?
2 What is the central thought or thesis that he develops?
3 Does he support his opinions with facts and details that make the meaning of the generalization acceptable to you?
4 What are the weak points in his presentation?
5 Do you agree with his conclusion or conclusions?

WHAT PRODUCED THOSE POT-SMOKING, REBELLIOUS,
DEMONSTRATING KIDS?—TELEVISION!*
Eliot Daley

1 Whatever happened to some of these kids today? How come they smoke pot, sleep around, demonstrate, and drop out? And why won't they study in our schools, work at our jobs, and kill in our wars? What got into them?
2 Television did.
3 Those born within a few years of 1950 never experienced a reality that didn't include massive doses of television. They spent more time with TV than with their parents or teachers. For the first time, an unsanctioned source

*SOURCE NOTE: Eliot Daley, "What Produced Those Pot-smoking, Rebellious, Demonstrating Kids?—Television!" *TV Guide.* Copyright © 1971 by Triangle Publications, Inc.

taught our children most of what they learned about our culture. And they have been profoundly shaped by what they learned—and mislearned. Their slogans reveal how staggeringly different these TV kids really are.

4   They don't just think we're square or corny. That's not what many of them are saying. They are suspicious of our intentions. They do not *trust us.*

5   What an assertion! How can we have a society—or any relationship— without trust? What made them feel we didn't have their best interests at heart?

6   Well, for one thing, we let TV rob them of their childhood. Back in what should have been the simple intimacy and security of preschool days, we let the world bust in on them. Adult banality, precocious commercialism, visions of evil all flooded their waking hours.

7   Most of the children's programming in the early '50s was originally produced for older audiences in theaters. Very young children must have been confused by the unmitigated mayhem of the "cartoons." How was a 4-year-old sitting alone before the TV set supposed to know why big cats chased small birds and ate them? From Tweetie and Sylvester to Popeye or The Road Runner, virtually every cartoon swamped them with the same theme: for some totally obscure reason, the big people are just bent on beating hell out of the little people. With a little luck, a weapon and a trick, the small may survive *this* time. But there's always next time . . .

8   For thousands of hours these pre-Oedipal[1] kids watched the (wicked) Powerful incessantly harass the (innocent) Weak. Is it any wonder they don't trust the Establishment?

9   But that's only part of it. Commercials really took their toll, too. Never before have advertisers so systematically assaulted the judgment and will power of preschoolers!

10   It worked, of course. Seventy per cent of children ask for stuff they see on TV—and 89 per cent of their parents buy it for them.

Do your own thing

11   Who can blame them for wanting to escape "our thing"? Hard on the heels of the evening news, with its roster of victims of our civilization, came the prime-time hours of affluent indolence. From Lucy and Desi onward, TV has held up both the exaggerated and the genuine banalities of middle-class existence. The result is many of the young are embarrassed to be what, in very fact, they are.

12   The specter of a middle-class life sent them scurrying for alternatives. Through the glass eye of TV, our children saw "our thing" as the child saw the Emperor without any clothes: bombastic, mindless, naked and vain. In all

[1] Refers to the early years of childhood before a strong attachment to the parent of the opposite sex shows itself. Roughly, prepuberty.

these years, can you name more than a couple of adults on TV whose adulthood was depicted as significant and fulfilling? Men tended to rely on money or weapons for their strength; women were shrewish or conveniently missing altogether.

13 Unfortunately, parents' own habits compounded the distorted vision of adulthood. They spent less time sharing with their children whatever satisfactions they enjoyed as adults—because they were too busy watching that new TV machine. In 1949, only about a third of U.S. homes even had a radio playing after supper on Sunday nights. But by 1958, almost two-thirds of American families were glued to the tube by 8 P.M. Something new had been added. And something else was lost.

Now!

14 That's when the kids want things. Now. Yesterday would have been better. (Tomorrow? Out of the question!) What makes them so darned impatient? Don't they know that things take time?

15 No, they don't. In fact, TV taught them that things *don't* take time. They happened on cue. Every problem had a solution. Every program had a conclusion. There were no alternatives to explore (no time for that). There were no human idiosyncrasies to consider (power or deceit will prevail). Opinions, rights, feelings of others? Irrelevant. Due process of law? What a laugh! The Eisenhower Commission on television violence reported that 80 per cent of all violent conflicts on TV are resolved without ever bothering with due process of law. Should we really wonder that some radicals ignore law—and then expect amnesty?

16 It is a particular shame that this generation witnessed so much cut-rate "justice" and superficial "problem-solving." Because they also became more aware than anyone of the enormity of intolerable social problems. So they have more sense of outrage—and less sense of change-process—than preceding generations. TV never demonstrated the distinction between awareness and understanding, imperative and strategy, product and process.

17 And because they spent tens of thousands of hours squatting before the set, they didn't find it out on their own. All the hours that previous generations spent fort-building, club-forming and friend-making, this bunch spent in relatively passive spectatorship. And so their passion for healing is frustrated by their procedural incompetence, and "patience" becomes an intolerable luxury synonymous with the indifference overindulged by their elders.

Hell, no! We won't go!

18 Lots of these kids have no stomach for killing. Not for national honor or any other reason. They're holed up in colleges, graduate schools and foreign countries hoping to avoid the draft.

19 TV has been a major factor again. War used to be remote. It was easy to glorify. Combatants never saw the "enemy" until a split-second of kill-or-be-killed.

20 But the pathetic peasants of Vietnam have been in our homes every day for five or six years now. Holding mangled children. Scurrying for shelter. Being shot and chased and badgered by grotesque armies indistinguishable in their effect. All these kids have seen are the ravages of war. Every single day. After day after day.

21 On top of that, they don't share many of our prejudices and stereotypes about "foreigners." That's another legacy of TV. Before these kids ever entered kindergarten, they had spent more time seeing people of other lands than we had in our first 20 years. And they came to know them as people, with faces and names and personalities and families—not as anonymous masses of "Japs" or "Russkies." Consequently, when they see people who live in other lands being killed, they react differently; sociologist Herbert Gans found that, on viewing TV films of the war in Vietnam, 75 per cent of teen-agers surveyed said they felt "sick, horrible, badly"; but 75 per cent of adults felt "more hawkish"!

Tomorrow has been canceled

22 The younger generation expects to die soon. The *majority* of collegians fear they'll be dead within the next two decades! (Surveys consistently reveal this.) How come? Is it The Bomb? Or is it The War?

23 Partly. But it's also television. Through TV they have been swept into a crescendo of violence that castrates confidence in a future. So much fictional and authentic violence has bombarded them that it becomes hard to distinguish between fiction and fact.

24 When this generation was preschool age, only one show *(Dragnet)* involving guns was among the Top 10 broadcast. Just five years later, seven of the Top 10 programs were saturated with killing. Listen to the titles: *Gunsmoke, Have Gun—Will Travel, The Rifleman, Maverick, Tales of Wells Fargo, Wagon Train, The Texan.*

25 Then a real live Texan devastated them once and for all. As the bullets crashed into John F. Kennedy, the hero-worshipping dreams and vicarious aspirations of a whole generation were shattered. If this princely creature could be reduced to nothing by madness, on what could a future be built? *These youngsters plunged with their families into an average of 34 hours of immersion in television coverage of the John F. Kennedy assassination and funeral.*

26 TV chronicled in minute detail the wreckage of their aspirations. It portrayed in anguished incredulity the utter insecurity and ultimate futility of what has been The American Dream, Camelot-come-true.

27 No TV event, no public event, before or since, equaled that experience.

Not in hours broadcast, personnel involved, expense incurred, viewers watch-ing—or impact felt.

28 Things just never got any better. The next November they watched an earthy Lyndon B. Johnson ground the hawkish Barry Goldwater—and then fly off himself, escalating the horror of Vietnam and further foreclosing their fu-ture.

29 They came to know other public men, too. And just when TV had made them personally known, it showed them shot to death. These kids were there when towering men of the '60's fell. Fiction became fact. Those more willing to kill than die survived and the kids had already had enough of killing.

Let it all hang out

30 Teen-agers avoid TV like the plague. No segment of our population watches less. The kids are out making music.

31 *Making* music, not just listening to it. They're playing guitars, kazoos, washtubs—anything they can get their hands on. They want to get into the act. They sat impassively during their most formative years, mesmerized by TV. Now they've traded the meaningless picture of TV for the pictureless meaning of music.

32 No one should doubt the importance of their music. Sometimes merely raucous and rapacious, more often their music is profoundly searching, poi-gnantly vulnerable. It dignifies their humanity in a way television never did.

33 Then the films pick up the beat and visualize their new-found rhythm of life. "Blow-Up" and "Easy Rider" illustrated their perceptions and perplexi-ties. "Elvira Madigan" and "Romeo and Juliet" celebrated their futility.

34 Both music and films have become occasions for communion among the young. Now hundreds of thousands of young pilgrims surge to a Woodstock music festival to be pressed together in the flesh. No more electronic images! They want to be where there's *life*.

Turn on!

35 Teen-agers are the shock troops of a culture hooked on drugs. At a $100,000,000 annual clip, many TV commercials encourage us to expect mir-acles from drugs. The young apparently have been convinced. Soaring after Utopia or Nirvana or Ultimate Reality, their crash landings have made lurid news.

36 Ironically, the last 20 years have been the age of genuine miracle drugs—including many of the Brand Name products. But some were deceptively ad-vertised. Moreover, we deceived ourselves. We thought we could buy tempo-rary relief indefinitely and would never have to grapple with the roots of our dissatisfaction. Now we're all reaping the whirlwind. (Same thing with sex. Teen-agers don't hold a sacrosanct view of human sexuality. It's just sort of there. No particular value or virtue involved. And that's the way they saw it on TV. Sex is just another marketing tool. Use it to tease a would-be buyer of cat food or razor blades or something. Sex: use as needed to grease the Gross National Product. Of *course* the kids don't value it. We didn't.)

There's a new world coming

37 TV turned them on to more than drugs and sex, though. This younger generation is excitingly and energetically rejuvenating our whole visual environment. They are flocking into art and filmmaking courses in record numbers. They are splashing psychedelic art everywhere, designing and wearing unique clothes, exercising our eyes with their graffiti and optical poetry. Everywhere we turn, they stimulate our sight.

38 Eventually, they may even stimulate our vision, as well as our sight. For this generation was sent, when very young, on a prolonged pilgrimage in the twilight zone where reality and fantasy merge. TV obliterated boundaries of mind and material for them.

39 Consequently, they don't settle for the mundane definition of reality we swallowed unquestioningly. They're hungry to probe deeper. Hallucinogenic drugs, mysticism, hypnosis, astrology, religious agony and ecstasy. They are sometimes fearless and frequently foolish in their quest. But they are questing, like never before.

40 This pioneer TV generation has blazed new trails. True, television has taken its toll—trivializing adulthood, exploiting childhood, ignoring needs while fabricating wants. But we also know that television is capable of decreasing prejudice, increasing wonder and anathematizing war. And we've scarcely begun to take it seriously.

DISCUSSION ONE/TELEVISION AND YOUTH

1 Compare the organization and development of the paragraphs in this essay with the paragraphs in "The Sad Young Men." What similarities and differences do you notice between the two?

2 If you knew that this essay was written for *TV Guide* and that "The Sad Young Men" was written for a textbook entitled *Backgrounds of American Literary Thought,* would this fact explain in part the difference in the style of the two selections?

3 What is Daley's purpose in writing this essay?

4 What reasons does Daley offer to explain the statement that young people do not trust their parents?

5 Why, according to Daley, do teen-agers avoid TV?

6 Do you think that young people of your generation watch TV very much? Why? Why not?

7 In your opinion, do TV commercials encourage young people to expect miracles from drugs?

8 What weak points do you see in Daley's presentation?

9 Do you agree with Daley's conclusions?

10 Would you have explained the rebellion of youth in another way?

TOPICS FOR WRITTEN ASSIGNMENTS OR DISCUSSION

1 Problems of Youth
2 Choosing a Career
3 Why I Won't (Will) Get Married
4 Why Go to College
5 My Parents and I
6 Choosing Friends
7 Working and Getting an Education
8 Spending Leisure Time
9 I Thought I Had All the Answers
10 Young People in Politics
11 Youth and Religion
12 Tomorrow's Dreams
13 Values to Live By
14 Youth Is Too Short a Time
15 What I Want out of Life

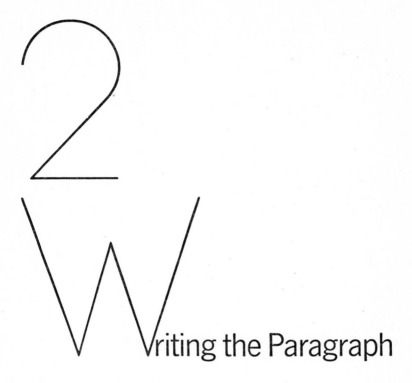

Writing the Paragraph

A piece of writing like "The Sad Young Men" is simply organized. It consists of words joined together to form certain kinds of sentences: commands, questions, statements, exclamations. Each sentence expresses a complete thought. Sentences are organized around a stated or implied main idea into a paragraph or a paragraph unit (two or more paragraphs organized around and developing a main idea). Paragraphs are organized around a central thought *(thesis)* or a *statement of purpose* to form a *whole* piece of writing.

In breaking down the structural organization of "The Sad Young Men," you will find that the essay, like so many other pieces of writing, divides logically into paragraphs with particular functions: to introduce the subject *(introduction)* in paragraph 1, to support and develop the thesis (the *body* or *middle*) in paragraphs 2 through 9, to bring the discussion to an end *(conclusion)* in paragraphs 10 and 11, and to carry the reader smoothly from one phase of the developing thought to another phase *(transitional paragraphs)*.

What is a paragraph? A paragraph is a series of sentences related to one another that revolve around and develop an expressed (some-

times implied) main idea. There are four kinds of paragraphs: introductory paragraphs, body or middle paragraphs, concluding paragraphs, and transitional paragraphs.

INTRODUCTORY PARAGRAPHS

Introductory paragraphs serve to gain reader interest and present
background material or other kinds of explanatory information necessary for a better understanding of what will follow. Some introductory
paragraphs include the *thesis statement*—a single sentence expressing the central thought of the piece of writing. Others include, along
with the thesis statement, a clear indication of the direction of the
writer's flowing thought.

In "The Sad Young Men," the function of the first paragraph is introductory. Horton and Edwards begin by mentioning the interest in the
Twenties by young people today. In addition, they discuss the questions that present-day students are asking their parents and teachers:
Was there really a Younger Generation problem? Were young people
really so wild? Their answers are yes and no.[1]

No aspect of life in the Twenties has been more commented upon and sensationally romanticized than the so-called Revolt of the Younger Generation.
The slightest mention of the decade brings nostalgic recollections to the middle-aged and curious questioning by the young: memories of the deliciously
illicit thrill of the first visit to a speakeasy, of the brave denunciation of Puritan
morality, and of the fashionable experimentations in amour in the parked sedan on a country road; questions about the naughty, jazzy parties, the flask-
toting "sheik," and the moral and stylistic vagaries of the "flapper" and the
"drugstore cowboy." "Were young people really so wild?" present-day students ask their parents and teachers. "Was there really a Younger Generation
problem?" The answers to such questions must of necessity be "yes" and
"no"—"yes" because the business of growing up is always accompanied by
a Younger Generation Problem; "no" because what seemed so wild, irresponsible, and immoral in social behavior at the time can now be seen in
perspective as being something considerably less sensational than the degeneration of our jazz-mad youth.

In the next model introductory paragraph, the writer states clearly
his thesis:

> The greatest threat to our cities is not air pollution, the poor,
> the blacks, the white racists, the automobile, or "the system."

[1] Rod W. Horton and Herbert W. Edwards, "The Sad Young Men" in Horton and Edwards, *Back-grounds of American Literary Thought*, p. 315. Copyright © 1967 by Meredith Publishing Company. Permission of Appleton-Century-Crofts, Inc., division of Meredith Corporation.

Thesis   *The greatest threat is our present narcotics laws.* They make the 99 per cent of us who are free from addiction the main victims of this monstrous plague.[2]

In the following introduction, consisting of four paragraphs, the writer states clearly in paragraph 4 his thesis and indicates that he will give reasons why the American public refuses to let King Kong "rest in peace."[3]

Introductory material

The ordeal and spectacular death of King Kong, the giant ape, undoubtedly have been witnessed by more Americans than have ever seen a performance of *Hamlet, Iphigenia at Aulis,* or even *Tobacco Road.* Since RKO-Radio Pictures first released *King Kong,* a quarter-century has gone by; yet year after year, from prints that grow more rain-beaten, from sound tracks that grow more tinny, ticket-buyers by thousands still pursue Kong's luckless fight against the forces of technology, tabloid journalism, and the DAR. They see him chloroformed to sleep, see him whisked from his jungle isle to New York and placed on show, see him burst his chains to roam the city (lugging a frightened blonde), at last to plunge from the spire of the Empire State Building, machine-gunned by model airplanes.

Introduction

Through Kong may die, one begins to think his legend unkillable. No clearer proof of his hold upon the popular imagination may be seen than what emerged one catastrophic week in March 1955, when New York WOR-TV programmed *Kong* for seven evenings in a row (a total of sixteen showings). Many a rival network vice-president must have scowled when surveys showed that *Kong*—the 1933 B-picture—had lured away fat segments of the viewing populace from such powerful competitors as Ed Sullivan, Groucho Marx and Bishop Sheen.

Introduction

But even television has failed to run *King Kong* into oblivion. Coffee-in-the-lobby cinemas still show the old hunk of hokum, with the apology that in its use of composite shots and animated models the film remains technically interesting. And no other monster in movie history has won so devoted a popular audience. None of the plodding mummies, the stultified draculas, the whitecoated Lugosis with their shiny pinball-machine laboratories, none of the invisible stranglers, berserk robots, or menaces from Mars has ever enjoyed so many resurrections.

[2] Peter F. Drucker, "How to Take the Profit out of Hard Drugs," *Saturday Review,* May 13, 1972, pp. 26–27.
[3] X. J. Kennedy, "Who Killed King Kong?" *Dissent* (Spring 1960), p. 213.

Question   Why does the American public refuse to let King Kong rest in
Answers   peace? It is true, I'll admit, that *Kong* outdid every monster movie before or since in sheer carnage. Producers Cooper and
Schoedsack crammed into it dinosaurs, headhunters, riots,
aerial battles, bullets, bombs, bloodletting. Heroine Fay Wray,
whose function is mainly to scream, shuts her mouth for hardly
one uninterrupted minute from first reel to last. It is also true
that *Kong* is larded with good healthy sadism, for those whose
joy it is to see the frantic girl dangled from cliffs and harried by
Thesis   pterodactyls. *But it seems to me that the abiding appeal of the
giant ape rests on other foundations.* (Italics added)

ASSIGNMENT/INTRODUCTION

Write a paragraph that will serve to introduce a subject. Include a
clear statement of the thesis and gain reader interest.

MIDDLE PARAGRAPHS

The middle paragraphs—those in the body or middle of the piece of
writing between the introduction and the conclusion—are of two
kinds: *supporting and transitional.*

Supporting paragraphs

In "The Sad Young Men," Horton and Edwards state their thesis in the
last paragraph of the essay: "The intellectuals of the Twenties, the
'sad young men,' as F. Scott Fitzgerald called them, cursed their luck
but didn't die; escaped but voluntarily returned; flayed the Babbitts but
loved their country, and in so doing gave the nation the liveliest, freshest, most stimulating writing in its literary experience."

    They support their thesis by providing historical material concern-
ing the revolt of the younger generation of the Twenties in a series of
paragraphs and paragraph units between the introduction and conclusion. Each paragraph or paragraph unit develops a new but related
aspect of the thought stated in the thesis. Read again the middle paragraphs of that essay and observe how frequently the first sentence
states clearly the main idea of the material that follows and indicates a
new but related stage of the developing thought. Be alert to these
sentences:

Actually the revolt of the young people was a logical outcome of conditions in
the age. (paragraph 2)

The rejection of Victorian gentility was, in any case, inevitable. (paragraph 3)

The rebellion started with World War I. (paragraph 5)

Greenwich Village set the pattern. (paragraph 7)

Meanwhile the true intellectuals were far from flattered. (paragraph 9)

The supporting paragraph or paragraph unit is organized and developed in much the same way as an essay or composition. As a matter of fact, it is customary for writers explaining paragraph structure to think of the usual paragraph in the middle of a piece of writing as a "composition in miniature." The main idea of the paragraph, although sometimes implied by the writer, is usually stated in the first sentence, called a *topic sentence*. This sentence corresponds to the *thesis sentence* or *statement of purpose sentence* in the essay or composition. The main idea of the model paragraph that follows is stated in the first sentence; it reads: "Meanwhile, the true intellectuals were far from flattered."[4]

Meanwhile, the true intellectuals were far from flattered. What they had wanted was an America more sensitive to art and culture, less avid for material gain, and less susceptible to standardization. Instead, their ideas had been generally ignored, while their behavior had contributed to that standardization by furnishing a pattern of Bohemianism that had become as conventionalized as a Rotary luncheon. As a result, their dissatisfaction with their native country, already acute upon their return from the war, now became even more intolerable. Flaming diatribes poured from their pens denouncing the materialism and what they considered to be the cultural boobery of our society. An important book rather grandiosely entitled *Civilization in the United States,* written by "thirty intellectuals" under the editorship of J. Harold Stearns, was the rallying point of sensitive persons disgusted with America. The burden of the volume was that the best minds in the country were being ignored, that art was unappreciated, and that big business had corrupted everything. Journalism was a mere adjunct to money-making, politics were corrupt and filled with incompetents and crooks, and American family life so devoted to making money and keeping up with the Joneses that it had become joyless, patterned, hypocritical, and sexually inadequate. These defects would disappear if only creative art were allowed to show the way to better things, but since the country was blind and deaf to everything save the glint and ring of the dollar, there was little remedy for the sensitive mind but to emigrate to Europe where "they do things better." By the time *Civilization in the United States* was published (1921), most of its contributors had taken their own advice and were living abroad, and many more of the artistic and would-be artistic had followed suit.

[4] Horton and Edwards, op. cit., pp. 320–321.

The main idea is developed by examples, explanations, repetitions, reasons, facts, similarities, differences, causes, effects, classes, parts—various kinds of details and specifics that support the writer's point of view stated in the topic sentence or make the meaning of the topic sentence clear. This supporting material may be compared to the *middle paragraphs* of an essay or composition. In the model paragraph, the writers give reasons why the "intellectuals were far from flattered." They also give examples of works by these men which voiced their dissatisfaction. They state that the best minds in the country were being ignored, "that art was unappreciated, that big business had corrupted everything." They attack journalism, politics, and family life and point out that "these defects would disappear if only creative art were allowed to show the way to better things. . . ."

Often a writer will restate the main idea of the topic sentence in different words in the final sentence of the paragraph, a device similar to closing the longer piece of writing with a *conclusion.* In the model paragraph, the writers emphasize the meaning of the main idea by closing the paragraph with a result arising from the defects in American culture; they write: "By the time *Civilization in the United States* was published (1921), most of its contributors had taken their own advice and were living abroad, and many more of the artistic and would-be artistic had followed suit."

Middle paragraphs like the model paragraph we are discussing are expository or developmental in function; that is, they serve to support, amplify, and explain the thesis of the larger piece of writing. If they do their job effectively, they should have four characteristics: *unity, completeness, order,* and *coherence.* In other words, a good paragraph must develop a single topic only. Any time a writer strays away from the main idea with material that does not relate to that major point and support or explain it, he destroys paragraph unity. You have seen how the writers of the model paragraph gained unity by presenting supporting material for the opening generalization that read: "the true intellectuals were far from flattered." Each reason and example in that paragraph belonged there because it explained or supported the topic sentence.

A good paragraph must be complete. Regardless of its length, a good paragraph develops the main idea so that the reader will understand it if it requires explanation and will accept the point of view if the main idea is in the form of a generalization. In the model paragraph, the writers felt that their topic sentence needed additional clarification; therefore, they followed it with an explanatory sentence; it read: "What they had wanted was an America more sensitive to art and culture, less avid for material gain, and less susceptible to standardization." To support the point of view expressed in the topic sentence, the writers of the model paragraph present much factual material, hence the length of the paragraph.

A good paragraph must have some kind of order of development so that the reader can move smoothly and logically through the flowing thought. The writers of the model paragraph organized their thought by moving the reader from an opening generalization in the topic sentence through material that supported it. Later, you will learn that this pattern of organizing expository thought is the most popular.

Finally, a good paragraph must have coherence, possessing qualities of continuity and "togetherness" so that the reader can readily sense the relationship of the parts to the main idea and to one another and move onward without pauses or gaps in the developing thought. In subsequent pages of this book, you will learn much about achieving coherence in your writing. You will learn that the unity and order of the model paragraph contribute much to its coherence. You will learn also that certain transitional words like "meanwhile," "instead," "as a result," and "but" play a significant role in carrying the reader smoothly onward and making clear the relationship of ideas. In addition, you will learn of the importance of pronoun reference in achieving coherence.

There are four basic patterns, frames, or orders of paragraph organization and development:

1 General to particular
2 Particular to general
3 General to particular to general
4 Question to answer.

Patterns or frames

GENERAL TO PARTICULAR
In developing and organizing thought in the paragraph by moving the reader from the general (topic sentence) through the particular (the supporting or explanatory material), a writer begins with a clear and usually concise statement of the main idea in the first sentence and follows with sentences that explain, support, and illustrate that central thought, making its meaning more understandable for the reader as the thought moves onward.

The model that follows is a middle paragraph unit in "The Sad Young Men."[5]

[5] Ibid., pp. 319–320.

Topic sentence

Explanation

Explanation

Support

Support

Greenwich Village set the pattern. Since the Seventies a dwelling place for artists and writers who settled there because living was cheap, the Village had long enjoyed a dubious reputation for Bohemianism and eccentricity. It had also harbored enough major writers, especially in the decade before World War I, to support its claim to being the intellectual center of the nation. After the war, it was only natural that hopeful young writers, their minds and pens inflamed against war, Babbittry, and "Puritanical" gentility, should flock to the traditional artistic center (where living was still cheap in 1919) to pour our their new-found creative strength, to tear down the old world, to flout the morality of their grandfathers, and to give all to art, love, and sensation.

New but related phase

Repeat of main idea stated in paragraph 1

Support

Support

Support

Support

Repeat of main idea

Soon they found their imitators among the non-intellectuals. As it became more and more fashionable throughout the country for young persons to defy the law and the conventions and to add their own little matchsticks to the conflagration of "flaming youth," *it was Greenwich Village that fanned the flames.* "Bohemian" living became a fad. Each town had its "fast" set which prided itself on its unconventionality, although in reality this self-conscious unconventionality was rapidly becoming a standard feature of the country club class—and its less affluent imitators—throughout the nation. Before long the movement had become officially recognized by the pulpit (which denounced it), by the movies and magazines (which made it attractively naughty while pretending to denounce it), and by advertising (which obliquely encouraged it by selling everything from cigarettes to automobiles with the implied promise that their owners would be rendered sexually irresistible). Younger brothers and sisters of the war generation, who had been playing with marbles and dolls during the battles of Belleau Wood and Chateau-Thierry, and who had suffered no real disillusionment or sense of loss, now began to imitate the manners of their elders and play with the toys of vulgar rebellion. Their parents were shocked, but before long they found themselves and their friends adopting the new gaiety. By the middle of the decade, the "wild party" had become as commonplace a factor in American life as the flapper, the Model T, or the Dutch Colonial home in Floral Heights. (Italics added.)

Sometimes the main idea is stated in a sentence other than the first sentence or last sentence. A very common position other than these positions is the middle sentence of the paragraph. In this structure, the writer will begin moving in one direction and reverse the flow of thought by placing the main idea in the middle of the paragraph. In the model paragraph below, the writer uses the first sentence to carry the reader back to the thought expressed in the previous paragraph or paragraphs. Then, he moves the reader onward to another but related aspect of the thesis by placing the main idea of the paragraph in sentence 2.

Topic sentence	Thus in a changing world youth was faced with the challenge of bringing our mores up to date. *But at the same time it was tempted, in America at least, to escape its responsibilities and retreat behind an air of naughty alcoholic sophistication and a pose of Bohemian immorality.* The faddishness, the wild spend-
Support	ing of money on transitory pleasures and momentary novelties, the hectic air of gaiety, the experimentation in sensation—sex, drugs, alcohol, perversions—were all part of the pattern of escape, an escape made possible by a general prosperity and a post-war fatigue with politics, economic restrictions, and inter-
Support	national responsibilities. Prohibition afforded the young the additional opportunity of making pleasures illicit, and the much-publicized orgies and defiant manifestoes of the intellectuals crowding into Greenwich Village gave them a pattern and a
Conclusion	philosophic defense for their escapism. And like most escapist sprees, this one lasted until the money ran out, until the crash of the world economic structure at the end of the decade called the party to a halt and forced the revellers to sober up and face the problems of the new age.[6] (Italics added.)

PARTICULAR TO GENERAL

In the following model, the writer reverses the order by beginning with the supporting material and moving on to a statement of the main idea in the final sentence (topic sentence).

First paragraph of support	. . . Americans are reacting against the unpleasant prospect of the mass society, in which—as Emerson wrote—"Things are in the saddle, and ride mankind." They mean to stave off either Huxley's "Brave New World" or Orwell's "1984." During the liberal era now passing away, and more conspicuously in the totalist states of our century, the person seems reduced to less and less, while centralized arbitrary power bulks greater and greater.

As Big Government, big labor, and big business reduce old

[6] Ibid., pp. 316–317.

Support		independence and opportunity for the average citizen, as increasingly American life is directed from Washington, the public looks for some alternative to this drift toward a standardized,
Topic sentence		monotonous, perhaps servile existence. *Conservatism may be that alternative.*[7] (Italics added.)

GENERAL TO PARTICULAR TO GENERAL

In the next model paragraph, the writer starts with a topic sentence, moves into the support with a discussion of "our little houses" to explain his main idea and concludes with a restatement of the main idea in slightly different words. By repeating the main idea in slightly different words in the final sentence, a writer gives it additional emphasis.

General	Topic sentence	(2) *In today's Suburbia, it is virtually impossible to create outdoor spaces of any character.* Individual little houses plonked down on individual little lots do not form continuous "walls" of the sort we still find along the cobblestone streets of Beacon Hill.
	Support	Our little houses form, at best, a ragged fence, full of gaps; they face each other across wide streets
to	Support	and deep front yards, so that the distances between them are likely to measure at least 100 feet; and because our little houses are generally low-slung,
Particular	Support	the "ragged fences" created by them, together with the wide distances between parallel "fences," add up to absolutely nothing in terms of definable, outdoor space. For any "outdoor room," just like any
to	Support	indoor room, depends for its success upon the proportions of height to width to length. Suburbia's streets are "outdoor rooms" 100 feet wide, lined (if you look closely) with ragged walls that may be 12 feet high, and completed at each end by an inter-
General	Restatement of main idea	section or, possibly, a fire hydrant. *No city builder of the Middle Ages or the Renaissance would have dared to propose anything so ridiculously amorphous; if he had, his fellow citizens would have run him out of town.*[8] (Italics added.)

---

[7] Russell Kirk, "Conservative Tide Grows in an Effort to Stem the Drift," *San Gabriel Valley Tribune,* Covina, Calif.
[8] Peter Blake, "Today's Suburbia," *God's Own Junkyard,* p. 20. Copyright © 1964 by Peter Blake. Permission of Holt, Rinehart and Winston.

QUESTION TO ANSWER

In organizing with this method of development, a writer asks a question and answers it with enough material to satisfy the reader's understanding. In the model paragraph that follows, the writer asks the question, answers it, and follows with the supporting material.

Question	Is it really possible for old differences in sound, structure, and vocabulary to persist from the West African languages of slave
Answer	days into present-day inner city Black English? Easily. Nothing else really explains such regularity of language habits, most of which persist among black people in various parts of the West-
Support	ern Hemisphere. For a long time scholars believed that certain speech forms used by Negroes were merely leftovers from ar-
Support	chaic English preserved in the speech of early English settlers in America and copied by their slaves. But this theory has been
Support	greatly weakened, largely as the result of the work of a black linguist, Dr. Lorenzo Dow Turner of the University of Chicago.
Conclusion	Dr. Turner studied the speech off the Carolina coast and found so many traces of West African languages that he thoroughly discredited the archaic-English theory.[9]

ASSIGNMENT/BASIC FRAMES OR ORDERS OF PARAGRAPH ORGANIZATION

1 Write a topic sentence for a paragraph or paragraph unit that would be part of the supporting material for a thesis derived from the following broad subjects:

    a Authority and Me
    b Small Town Amusements
    c College Is Obsolete
    d The Price of Textbooks
    e Movies Are Worse Than Ever (Movies Are Better Than Ever)

2 Select one topic sentence from the first assignment and list in sentence form under it as many ideas as you can that will serve as supporting material.

3 Write a paragraph or paragraph unit using the material in assignment 2. Organize and develop the thought by moving from general to particular to general.

Organizing the support

Within these orders or frames of organization, especially the general to particular, a writer may arrange or organize his supporting or ex-

---

[9] Dorothy Z. Zeymour, "Black Children, Black Speech," *Commonweal,* Nov. 19, 1971, pp. 175–178.

planatory sentences (ideas) in a variety of ways depending upon the kind of material and his purpose. If his purpose was to explain the Depression of 1929 or violence in the streets, he would most logically arrange his ideas by cause and effect or effect and cause. If he was interested in showing the likenesses between the Romans and the Greeks or the differences between these two peoples and cultures, he would organize by comparison (likenesses) or contrast (differences). If he was telling a story, he would use the natural order of time. If he was describing a person, place, or thing, he would move his reader with him through space as his eyes moved from bottom to top, top to bottom, front to back, back to front, etc. Some of the most common methods of organizing the sentences of the support are the following:

BY EXAMPLE OR ILLUSTRATION

Using examples and illustrative material to support or explain a main idea is a very common and very effective method of organizing the ideas of support. This kind of supporting material makes clear the vague and abstract image the generalization leaves in the reader's mind. Good examples and illustrative material make the vague and abstract more concrete and the general more specific. In the model paragraph that follows, the writer states in the topic sentences that the crooks in the films of the 1930s and 1940s were better than life. Left on his own the reader could explain this generalization in a variety of ways. The crooks of those days were more efficient in their robberies than modern crooks, more humane, more honest with each other, or more considerate of the poor. Thus, the reader might receive an entirely different meaning from the one intended by the writer. To avoid this kind of thinking on the part of the reader and to make perfectly clear what he meant by the generalization, the writer cites specific examples.

Topic sentence	*But not only the crooks were better than life in those movies; the whole world was.* The DA really didn't take bribes. Reporters loved their jobs so much they constantly risked death to
Example	bring in a story. Justices of the peace would put on a ratty bathrobe and marry a sweet young couple on the lam at any
Example	hour of the night. And when bank robbers got to the bank there was a parking space out front.[10] (Italics added.)

BY TIME

In organizing material by time, a writer simply moves onward in the natural order in which the events or happenings occurred. In the mod-

[10] Donald E. Westlake, "Love Stuff, Cops-and-Robbers Style," *Los Angeles Times Calendar,* May 7, 1972, p. 14. Copyright © 1972 by the Los Angeles Times Company.

el paragraph that follows, the writer organizes his ideas in order of time sequence. He carries his reader through a series of incidents beginning with the seizing of the king in August 1792 and ending with his execution by guillotine on January 21, 1793.

August 1792	But the initiative proved to be of little advantage to the French armies, and as defeat followed defeat and Paris itself was threatened, the people took action. In August, 1792, the Parisian radicals, led by Danton, invaded the royal palace, seized the king after he had appealed to the assembly for protection, and forced the terrified legislature to dissolve itself in favor of a National Convention which was to prepare a new republican
September 22	constitution. On September 22, following a long awaited French victory against the invading forces of the Duke of Brunswick, the National Convention enthusiastically resolved that from this date on royalty was abolished in France, the emigrés were forever banished, and Year I of the Republic had begun. With the establishment of the Republic, Louis XVI had but few weeks to
December 1792	live. In December, 1792, he was brought to trial and condemned to death by a close vote. On the following January 21
January 21, 1793	he was executed, and within a few months Marie-Antoinette and other members of his family followed him to the guillotine.[11]

BY SPACE

In organizing by the natural order of space, a writer moves through space from top to bottom, from bottom to top, from a distance to up close, from up close to a distance, from ceiling to floor, from floor to ceiling, from left to right, from right to left. As his eyes move through space, he describes what he sees and carries the reader along with him. In the next model paragraph, the writer takes the reader into a "spacious room which takes up the whole wing." His eyes move to the wall, the ceiling, the windows, and the floor. Finally he notes the smell that "gives you the impression that you are entering a menagerie."

Walls Ceiling	Next you enter a large, spacious room which takes up the whole wing—that is, if the entry is not taken into consideration. The *walls* here are daubed over with a dirty light-blue paint; the *ceiling* is covered with soot, as in a smoke-house: it is evident that the furnaces here smoke in winter and give off asphyxiat-
Windows Floor	ing fumes. The *windows* are made hideous by iron bars on the inside. The *floor* is gray and splintery. There is a *stench* of sau-

[11] Rod W. Horton and Vincent F. Hopper, *Backgrounds of European Literature*, p. 372. Copyright © 1954 by Meredith Corporation. Permission of Appleton-Century-Crofts, Inc., division of Meredith Corporation.

erkraut, of charred lamp-wicks, of bedbugs and ammonia, and from the very first this stench gives you the impression that you are entering a menagerie.[12] (Italics added.)

BY ORDER OF CLIMAX

In the next order of development, a writer moves from the least important to the most important supporting or explanatory points. Thus, he moves in order of ascending importance of the supporting material. In the model paragraph below, the writer begins by discussing the Tsar who submits a document to his fellow-rulers, discusses the feeble nature of the document, explains that all but two of the rulers signed it, and closes with the name of the document—the most important point in the discussion.

Among the mystic group was no less a personage than Tsar Alexander. Throughout his life he proved himself remarkably sensitive to all the changing winds of opinion. On the fall of Napoleon he submitted a document to his fellow-rulers which he requested them to sign and by the terms of which they pledged themselves to govern their states in accordance with precepts abstracted by him from the New Testament. As the document, a mass of well-meaning platitudes, failed to commit the rulers of Europe to anything politically tangible or practical, all but two signed it. One of the two was George III of Great Britain, who, owing to insanity, had been replaced by a regent; the other was the sultan of Turkey, who, as a Mohammedan, was spared the humiliation of attaching his name to a docu-
Most important point ment reeking with Christian sentiments. This harmless communication, not unfairly characterized by the cynical Metternich as verbiage, has received the name of the Holy Alliance.[13]

ASSIGNMENT/TOPIC SENTENCE

Following is a list of possible topic sentences. Read each topic sentence. If you feel that it is weak, rewrite the sentence.

1 Parents weaken their authority in the home.
2 Skiing is a dangerous sport.
3 Some television commercials are (sickening) (very interesting), etc.
4 That discovery meant new hope for my friend.

---

[12] Anton Chekhov, "Ward No. 6" in Bernard Guilbert Guerney (trans.), *Portable Russian Reader.* Copyright © 1947 by The Viking Press.
[13] Ferdinand Schevill, *A History of Europe,* new and rev. ed., p. 451. Copyright © 1951 by Harcourt, Brace & World, Inc.

5 Big Sur is my kind of country.
6 The game was won in the final minute.
7 Sherlock Holmes was a master at drawing inferences.
8 The student leaders set the pattern.
9 Carbon dioxide is a dangerous air pollutant.
10 The team prepared for the big game.

ASSIGNMENT/WRITING THE PARAGRAPH

1 Using any topic sentence that you rewrote or accepted in the previous assignment, write a general-to-particular paragraph organized and developed by examples, by order of climax, or by both methods.
2 Write a paragraph or paragraph unit organized and developed by space order or time order.

BY WHOLE TO PARTS

In organizing thought by breaking down a subject into parts, a writer will usually announce the analysis in the first sentence, often indicating the parts into which he will break down his subject. He will then treat each part separately, presenting sufficient information concerning the division in order to make clear its nature for the reader. Often a writer will help the reader to distinguish the parts by using figures (1), (2), (3), etc., or the guide words "first," "second," "third," etc. In the model paragraph that follows, the writer breaks down the whole (the future of our cities) into parts: inhabitants, function, and organization. He indicates the divisions with the guide words "first," "second," "third."

Main idea	*With a very, very few exceptions, our cities seem to be headed for a grim future indeed—unless we determine to make some radical changes.* That future looks something like this: first, our cities will be inhabited solely by the very poor (generally colored) and the very rich (generally white)—plus a few divisions
Parts indicated by guide words	of police to protect the latter from the former. Second, they will become *primarily* places to work in—places for office buildings and for light industry. Third, they will become totally ghettofied—not merely in terms of racial segregation, but also in terms of usage: there will be office ghettos, industrial ghettos, apartment ghettos, amusement or culture ghettos (like Manhattan's gold-plated Rockefeller ghetto, *Lincoln Center*), bureaucratic ghettos, shopping ghettos, medical-center ghettos. In
Conclusion	other words, there will be virtually no mixed uses of streets or of

neighborhoods, so that most areas of the city will be alive for mere fractions of each day or weeks, and as deserted as Wall Street on a weekend for the rest of the time.[14] (Italics added.)

BY REASONS

In organizing thought by reasons, a writer explains a happening, a situation, a problem, or an event by simply presenting the reasons for its origin. In the model paragraph that follows, the writers explain the reasons for the increase in organized violence, using various guide words to identify the separate reasons, such as "more pertinent reasons," "first," "second," "third," "along with these technological reasons," "furthermore."

Reason 1	More pertinent reasons for the increase in organized violence are found first in the rise of the automobile, which made it easier for crooks to escape the scene of the crime and to spread
Reason 2	their operations over a much wider area; second, improvements in firearms during World War I which made them more
Reason 3	deadly effective; third, in the lack of laws controlling the sale of these weapons or the lack of enforcement of such laws as did
Other reasons	exist. Along with these technological reasons went even more important psychological and economic ones. American veneration for the successful operator, enhanced by the actions of the "robber barons" of the post-Civil War era, often blinded one to immoral means when those means were employed in the sacred practice of amassing a fortune. Furthermore, the growth of American business through combination and monopolistic practices demonstrated the power of large enterprise and taught the crooked elements to turn from petty individual thievery to big-time "rackets," large-scale operations organized with big-business efficiency and cold-steel impersonality, and controlled by one or two ruthlessly powerful "big shots."[15]

BY CAUSE TO EFFECT

In developing by cause to effect, a writer begins with a cause or causes and follows with its effect or effects. In the model paragraph that follows, the writers begin with a cause—the Civil War—and show its effects on both sections; then they follow with separate effects on a defeated South and a victorious North.

Cause	The Civil War worked a revolution in American society and economy, North as well as South. Although the roots of modern

[14] Blake, op. cit., p. 23.
[15] Horton and Edwards, op. cit., pp. 308–309.

America go deep into the prewar years, we can date its actual emergence from the war itself. That conflict gave an immense stimulus to industry, speeded up the exploitation of natural resources, the development of large-scale manufacturing, the rise of investment banking, the extension of foreign commerce, and brought to the fore a new generation of "captains of industry" and "masters of capital." It enormously accelerated the
Effects   construction of the railway and telegraph network and ushered in the railroad age. It put a premium upon inventions and labor-saving devices and witnessed the large-scale application of these to agriculture as well as to industry. It threw open vast new areas for farming and grazing, developed fresh markets for farm produce, and inaugurated both the agricultural revolution and the farm problem. It created conditions favorable to the growth of cities and offered work to the hundreds of thousands of immigrants who soon crowded into the New World. In the
South   South, defeat largely destroyed the planter class, freed the Negro, revolutionized farm economy, brought a new middle class to the fore, and laid the foundations for that New South which
North   was to emerge during the next generation. In the North it opened up new fields to investment and to speculation, created a host of war millionaires, and hastened the process of the concentration of control of resources, industry, and finance in the great urban centers, the subordination of the South and West to the Northeast, and the creation of new class divisions to take the place of the old.[16]

BY EFFECT TO CAUSE

In organizing thought by effect to cause, the writer reverses the order by first presenting an effect or effects and then showing their cause or causes.

In the following paragraph, the writer begins by stating an effect: ". . . there is something surprising in this strange unrest of so many happy [American] men, restless in the midst of abundance." He follows this statement with the causes of the unrest.[17]

At first sight there is something surprising in this strange unrest
Effect   of so many happy men, restless in the midst of abundance. The spectacle itself is, however, as old as the world; the novelty is to

[16] Allan Nevins and Henry Steele Commager, *A Pocket History of the United States*, pp. 240–241. Copyright © 1942, 1951, 1956 by Allan Nevins and Henry Steele Commager. Permission of Washington Square Press.
[17] Alexis de Tocqueville, "Causes of the Restless Spirit of Americans," *Democracy in America*, vol. 11, p. 137. Copyright © 1963 by Alfred A. Knopf.

Cause

Explana-
tion

Cause

see a whole people furnish an exemplification of it. Their taste for physical gratifications must be regarded as the original source of that secret inquietude that the actions of the Americans betray, and of that inconstancy of which they afford fresh examples every day. He who has set his heart exclusively upon the pursuit of worldly welfare is always in a hurry, for he has but a limited time at his disposal to reach it, to grasp it, and to enjoy it. The recollection of the brevity of life is a constant spur to him. Besides the good things which he possesses, he every instant fancies a thousand others which death will prevent him from trying if he does not try them soon. This thought fills him with anxiety, fear, and regret, and keeps his mind in ceaseless trepidation, which leads him perpetually to change his plans and his abode. If in addition to the taste for physical well-being a social condition be superadded, in which the laws and customs make no condition permanent, here is a great additional stimulant to this restlessness of temper. Men will then be seen continually to change their track, for fear of missing the shortest cut to happiness. It may readily be conceived that if men, passionately bent upon physical gratifications, desire eagerly, they are also easily discouraged: as their ultimate object is to enjoy, the means to reach that object must be prompt and easy, or the trouble of acquiring the gratification would be greater than the gratification itself. Their prevailing frame of mind, then, is at once ardent and relaxed, violent and enervated. Death is often less dreaded than perseverance in continuous efforts to one end.

ASSIGNMENT/WRITING THE PARAGRAPH

1 Write a paragraph or paragraph unit organized and developed by moving from the whole through the parts.
2 Write a paragraph or paragraph unit organized and developed (*a*) by reasons, (*b*) by causes, (*c*) by effects, (*d*) by any combination of the first three.

BY CLASSES
In classifying, a writer breaks down a subject into classes. In developing thought by classification, a writer gives order and meaning to a seemingly unrelated number of persons, places, things, ideas, and experiences by sorting them out and placing them in a group with other members that share similar characteristics. In classifying, a writer asks and answers two questions: What is this a kind of? What are kinds of this? Volcanoes, for example, may be broken down into

four types on the basis of the manner they erupt. An active volcano that erupts in a mildly explosive manner every half hour or so is called a Strombolian volcano because it is like the active volcano on the island of Stromboli, north of Sicily. Thus, we have answered the question, What is this a kind of? If a new volcano were discovered, we would place it in one of the four classes on the basis of its characteristics. If it erupted in a passive manner very often, we would categorize it as the Hawaiian type. If it erupted in a manner so violent that it split its cone, we would classify this new volcano as the Vulcanian type, etc. Thus, we have answered the question, What are kinds of this?

This kind of classification is called a *simple system of classification* because the writer breaks down the subject into major divisions only. In the model classification that follows, the writer breaks down listeners into four groups: (1) nonlisteners, (2) half-listeners, (3) passive acceptance listeners, and (4) discriminating listeners.

Listeners can be classified into four groups: (1) Some do not listen; they "tune the speaker out" and think of matters foreign to the speaker's subject. They get little from a speech. (2) Some only half-listen; their spasmodic listening fluctuates all the way from careful attention to no attention. They understand fragments of the speech but they do not see the idea as a whole. (3) Some listen with passive acceptance; they accept all the speaker says without question. Because of their lack of discrimination, they add little to what the speaker says from their own experiences. (4) Some listen with discrimination; this critical type of listener gets the most from a speech. If you adopt the following measures you will soon find yourself a member of this group.[18]

Suppose, for example, you want to develop by classification a fairly exhaustive treatment of a subject such as clouds. You might break down clouds on the basis of altitude into four families and eight subfamilies. This system of classification is called a *complex system of classification* because the writer breaks down his subject into divisions, subdivisions, and—if necessary—into further subdivisions. A plan of this complex system of classification of clouds might look something like the following:

Clouds

Purpose of the classification: to explain the different kinds of clouds

Basis for the classification: altitude of the cloud

High Clouds	Middle Clouds	Stratus
Cirrus	Altostratus	Nimbostratus
Cirrocumulus	Altocumulus	Stratocumulus
Cirro stratus	Low Clouds	Towering Clouds

[18] Glenn R. Capp, *How to Communicate Orally,* 2d ed., p. 53. Copyright © 1966 by Prentice-Hall, Inc.

In the model classification paragraph that follows, observe the complex system of classification to make clear the major class called low clouds. The writer breaks down low clouds into three subfamilies: stratus, nimbostratus, and stratocumulus. He presents characteristics that identify each class.

Low clouds have bases that range in height from near the earth's surface to 6,500 feet. There are three main kinds: Stratus is a low, quite uniform sheet, like fog, with the base above the ground. Dull-gray stratus clouds often make a heavy, leaden sky. Only fine drizzle can fall from true stratus clouds, because there is little or no vertical movement in them. Nimbostratus are the true rain clouds. Darker than ordinary stratus, they have a wet look, and streaks of rain often extend to the ground. They often are accompanied by low scud clouds (fractostratus) when the wind is strong. Stratocumulus are irregular masses of clouds spread out in a rolling or puffy layer. Gray with darker shading, stratocumulus do not produce rain but sometimes change into nimbostratus, which do. The rolls or masses then fuse together and the lower surface becomes indistinct with rain.[19]

The extent to which a writer divides and subdivides and subdivides depends upon his purpose. In other words, seldom will you find it necessary to discuss every possible subdivision of a class that can be subdivided and then subdivided further. In addition, you may find items that do not fit neatly into any grouping. You would be wise, however, to explain to the reader why your classification is not exhaustive and why some items do not fit in a particular division.

By classifying, the writers explaining clouds are saying that any cloud composed almost entirely of ice crystals with a base averaging 20,000 feet above the earth may be placed in the family of high clouds. If this cloud was formed at 25,000 feet and above, looked "thin, wispy, and feathery," and was frequently blown into "feathery strands called 'mares tails,' " it would be placed in the subfamily under high clouds as a cirrus cloud. If the cloud had a base ranging in height from near the earth's surface to 6,500 feet, it would be classified as a low cloud. If it was a "low, quite uniform sheet, like fog," had a base above the ground, possessed little vertical movement, and contained only a fine drizzle, it would be classified as a low stratus cloud.

How does a writer classify? A writer first classifies according to his purpose or interest. You might, for example, break down the students on your campus into different groups depending upon your purpose. If you wish to tell the reader something about their politics, you might

[19] Paul E. Lehr, R. Will Burnett, and Herbert S. Zim, *Weather*. Copyright © 1957 by The Golden Press, Inc. and reprinted with permission of the publisher.

break them down into four political groups resulting from a survey that you conducted.

Republicans	Democrats	Independents	Others
25%	45%	20%	10%

If you wanted to tell something about the socioeconomic backgrounds of the students on your campus, your survey might result in the following grouping. The basis for the classes would be the income of the parents.

Below $10,000	$10,000 to $20,000	Above $20,000
30%	60%	10%

If your purpose was to tell something about the proportion of students on campus who were working, your survey might result in the following grouping.

Full-Time Employment (30 hours or more)	Part-Time Employment (approximately 15 hours)	No Employment
30%	50%	20%

In classifying, a writer breaks down his subject on some basis that will suit his purpose. He will frequently state the basis in the classification. Below are listed some opening sentences of classifications illustrating *statement of basis for the classification.*

In the subsurface component of any terrestrial habitat the organisms are divisible into three groups on the basis of their size.

On the basis of the manner in which they erupt volcanoes may be classified into four types.

Clouds are classified according to how they are formed. There are two basic types.

Dunes may take several forms, depending on the supply of sand, the lay of the land, the restricting vegetation, and the steadiness of the direction of the winds.

After determining his purpose and the basis for classifying that will fulfill his purpose, a writer must firmly establish his classes by presenting a sufficient number of characteristics to identify a member of a class and make it possible to place other entities in that class if the occasion arises. Read again the model classification of the low cloud and its subfamilies, observing the characteristics of the three subdivisions: stratus, nimbostratus, and stratocumulus.

As you read the model classification paragraph that follows, review what you have learned about classifying by answering the following questions.

1 What is the writer's purpose?
2 What is he sorting out?
3 Into how many classes does the writer divide pollution?
4 How does he establish the basis for the classification?
5 Is it a complex or simple system of classification?
6 Why does the writer place DDT in the second class?

Pollution is of two types. One sort results from an excess of some fairly ordinary substance—smoke, or solid waste—which cannot be absorbed or transmuted rapidly enough to offset its introduction into the environment, thus causing changes the great cycle is not prepared for. (All organisms have wastes and by-products, and these are indeed part of the total biosphere: energy is passed along the line and refracted in various ways, "the rainbow body." This is cycling, not pollution.) The other sort is powerful modern chemicals and poisons, products of recent technology, which the biosphere is totally unprepared for. Such is DDT and similar chlorinated hydrocarbons—nuclear testing fallout and nuclear waste—poison gas, germ and virus storage and leakage by the military; and chemicals which are put into food, whose long-range effects on human beings have not been properly tested.[20]

Finally, in establishing your classes, make sure that the classes are mutually exclusive. In other words, do not make the error of overlapping, or cross-ranking. Such a mistake makes it impossible to develop the classification. In some cases, overlapping results in absurdity. If you were to break down the student body into the following groups, you would be making a mistake that borders on the absurd.

High School Graduates   Athletes   Scholars   Republicans

It is obvious that many students could be placed in each of these classes. John could be a high school graduate, be on the football team, be an honor student with a grade point average of 3.5, and be a Republican. If you were to break down teachers on campus into the three following groups, you would be cross-ranking.

Good Teachers   Bad Teachers   Experienced Teachers

An experienced teacher might be a bad teacher in spite of her years in the field; thus, you have overlapping of classes.

BY COMPARISON

A writer may organize and develop his thought in the paragraph or paragraph unit by showing similarities between two or among three or more persons, places, or things. This method of development is called

---

[20] Garrett DeBell (ed.), *Environmental Handbook.* Copyright © 1970 by Garrett DeBell. A Ballantine/ Friends of the Earth Book.

comparison. In structuring thought by comparison, a writer shows the likenesses between his subjects to fulfill a specific purpose. In the model paragraph below, the writer announces the comparison in the first sentence and follows with a number of similarities between Rome and Greece.

Statement	The resemblances between Rome and Greece are very clearly
Compari-son	marked. In many respects they are visibly of the same family, and though we no longer speak as loosely of "Aryan" and "In-
	do-European" as did the ethnologists and philologists of the nineteenth century, yet there remains an obvious kinship of lan-
Points of	guage, customs, and even dress. Many of the most obvious
compari-son	similarities, such as those of religion and literature, are now seen to be the result of later borrowing, but there remains a distinct cousinship; both peninsulas may be regarded as exhib-
	iting phases of a common Mediterranean culture, reposing pos-sibly on a common aboriginal stock which has been variously influenced by intruding tribes and by geographical condi-tions.[21]

BY CONTRAST

In the next model paragraph, the writer develops his thought by contrast (differences). He uses a pattern of organization of his contrasting points known as *subject at a time,* presenting points in the first paragraph that characterize the Pueblo Indians and following with points of difference in the second paragraph that characterize the Dobu.[22]

	The Pueblo Indians are pictured as a peaceable, cooperative society, in which no one wishes to be thought a great man and everyone wishes to be thought a good fellow. Sexual relations are taken with little jealousy or other violent response; infidelity
Pueblo In-dians	is not severely punished. Death, too, is taken in stride, with little violent emotion; indeed, emotion is, in general, subdued. While there are considerable variations in economic status, there is little display of economic power and even less of political power; there is a spirit of cooperation with family and commu-nity.
Dobu	The Dobu, by contrast, are portrayed as virtually a society of paranoids in which each man's hand is against his neighbor's

[21] J. C. Stobart, "Athens and Rome," *The Grandeur That Was Rome,* 4th ed., p. 2. Copyright © 1962 by Sedwick & Jackson Ltd. Permission of Hawthorn Books, Inc., 70 Fifth Avenue, New York, New York.
[22] David Riesman, *The Lonely Crowd,* p. 272. Copyright © 1950 by the Yale University Press. Permis-sion of the Yale University Press.

Points of
contrast

in sorcery, theft, and abuse; in which husband and wife alternate as captives of the spouse's kin, and in which infidelity is deeply resented. Dobuan economic life is built on sharp practice in interisland trading, on an intense feeling for property rights, and on a hope of getting something for nothing through theft, magic, and fraud. . . .

The writer of the next model contrast organizes his difference by a method called *alternating pattern.* He first presents one point concerning popular words and follows with a contrasting point related to learned words. He will follow with this kind of alternation until he has exhausted all the points of contrast, using more than one paragraph if necessary.

Statement
of contrast

Point by
point

The difference between popular and learned words may be easily seen in a few examples. We may describe a girl as "lively" or as "vivacious." In the first case, we are using a native English formation from the familiar noun *life.* In the latter, we are using a Latin derivative which has precisely the same meaning. Yet the atmosphere of the two words is quite different. No one ever got the adjective *lively* out of a book. It is part of everybody's vocabulary. We cannot remember a time when we did not know it, and we feel sure that we learned it long before we were able to read. On the other hand, we must have passed several years of our lives before learning the word *vivacious.* We may even remember the first time that we saw it in print or heard it from some grown-up friend who was talking over our childish heads. Both *lively* and *vivacious* are good English words, but *lively* is "popular" and *vivacious* is "learned". . . .[23]

BY KNOWN TO UNKNOWN

A special form of comparison is called *analogy.* In developing thought by analogy, a writer makes the unknown and unfamiliar clear and understandable to the reader by comparing it to a subject that is known and familiar to the reader. Thomas Henry Huxley defines education as he sees it. He reveals his idea of education by comparing the game of life (education) to a game of chess—a subject much simpler and better known to the reader.[24]

[23] Robert B. Greenough and George L. Kittredge, *Words and Their Ways in English Speech,* p. 20. Copyright © 1929 by Greenough and Kittredge. Permission of The Macmillan Company.
[24] Thomas Henry Huxley, *Autobiography and Selected Essays,* p. 39. Copyright © 1909 by Houghton Mifflin Company.

Stating the
analogy

Suppose it were perfectly certain that the life and fortune of every one of us would, one day or other, depend upon his winning or losing a game at chess. Don't you think that we should all consider it to be a primary duty to learn at least the names and the moves of the pieces; to have a notion of a gambit, and a keen eye for all the means of giving and getting out of check? Do you not think that we should look with a disapprobation amounting to scorn upon the father who allowed his son, or the state which allowed its members, to grow up without knowing a pawn from a knight?

Game of
chess and
game of
life

Yet it is a very plain and elementary truth that the life, the fortune and the happiness of every one of us, and, more or less, of those who are connected with us, do depend upon our knowing something of the rules of a game infinitely more difficult and complicated than chess. It is a game which has been played for untold ages, every man and woman of us being one of the two players in a game of his or her own. The chess-board is the world, the pieces are the phenomena of the universe, the rules of the game are what we call the laws of Nature. The player on the other side is hidden from us. We know that his play is always fair, just and patient. But also we know, to our cost, that he never overlooks a mistake, or makes the smallest allowance for ignorance. To the man who plays well, the highest stakes are paid, with that sort of overflowing generosity with which the strong shows delight in strength. And one who plays ill is checkmated—without haste, but without remorse. . . .

Definition
of educa-
tion

Well, what I mean by Education is learning the rules of this mighty game. In other words, education is the instruction of the intellect in the laws of Nature, under which name I include not merely things and their forces, but men and their ways; and the fashioning of the affections and of the will into an earnest and loving desire to move in harmony with those laws. For me, education means neither more nor less than this.

GUIDE TO THE PARAGRAPH

1 *Completeness* has been achieved when the reader is willing to accept the generalization of the topic sentence or its meaning because the writer has offered sufficient support or explanatory material to establish his point of view.
2 *Coherence* is the quality of continuity and "togetherness" in a paragraph that enables the reader to sense the relationship of the parts to the main idea and to one another so that he follows the flow of thought without pauses and gaps.

3 A *main idea* is an expression of the writer's purpose. It gives the paragraph unity of thought.

4 *Major support* consists of statements that develop and make acceptable the generalization or meaning of the topic sentence.

5 *Minor support* consists of statements that make acceptable the generalizations expressed in the major supporting statements.

6 A *paragraph* is a series of sentences that relate to and develop the main idea.

7 A *paragraph unit* is a series of paragraphs that relate to and develop a single main idea.

8 A *topic sentence* is a concise statement of a main idea. It is usually expressed in the first or second sentence of the paragraph.

9 *Paragraph unity* has been achieved when each sentence contributes something to developing the main idea.

ASSIGNMENT/COMPARISON AND CONTRAST

1 Write a paragraph or paragraph unit organized and developed by comparison. Below are some suggested topics.

  a Two or more friends
  b Two or more schools
  c Two or more activities, such as sports, dancing, hobbies
  d Two or more places
  e Two or more works of art
  f Two or more famous individuals
  g Two or more teachers, employers, kings, etc.
  h Two or more beliefs
  i Two or more organizations, clubs, political parties, etc.
  j Two or more movies, television programs, etc.

2 Write a paragraph or paragraph unit organized and developed by contrast. You may use the suggested topics in the previous assignment to aid you in selecting a contrast. Develop by subject-at-a-time organization; then develop the same contrast by alternating pattern.

BY DEFINITION

Frequently, in defining a word or term, a writer discovers the dictionary meaning is not sufficient to make meaning clear. With words or terms like "democracy," "literary criticism," "personality," "pollution," and "naturalism," he extends the simple definition to a paragraph, a paragraph unit—even a whole essay. In defining, a writer will usually combine one or more methods, such as those we have been discussing in this chapter. In most defining, the writer implies, rather than states, the topic sentence because the nature of defining indicates clearly to the reader the main idea and reveals his purpose: to limit the meaning of a word or term and make its meaning clear.

Some methods of defining, not previously discussed, are by giving (1) the historical meaning, (2) the etymology, (3) a negative definition, (4) a formal definition, or (5) multiple definitions with the writer's choice. A writer may define by presenting the historical meanings of the word. The word "nice," for example, over several centuries has meant at one time or another "foolish," "wanton," "strange," "lazy," "coy," "modest," "fastidious," "refined," "precise," "subtle," "slender," "critical," "attentive," "minute," "accurate," "dainty," "appetizing," "agreeable." Words like "derrick," "bobby," "malapropism," and "sandwich" have very interesting histories. (See *A Dictionary Study Guide* for use with *Webster's New World Dictionary of the American Language,* Prentice-Hall, Inc., Englewood Cliffs, N.J.)

Second, a writer may present the etymology of the word, that is, the origin and development of the word. Words like "bonfire," "Niagra," and "dada" have interesting etymologies. An etymological search will reveal that way back in language history the words "rat," "raze," "razor," and "rasher" (of bacon) are related.

Third, to make the meaning of his word clear, a writer will present a negative meaning and then follow with the meaning that he wants the reader to accept. A writer, for example, might define "naturalism" as it is used in literature in the following way: "By naturalism, I do not mean a faithful adherence to nature and realism. I use the term to mean a positive philosophy based on man's acceptance of defeat and despair so that he can face the certain adversities of life courageously."

Fourth, a writer may use a *formal definition;* that is, he may place the word or term in a general class (genus) and by presenting details show how it differs from all the other members of that class. Actually, the writer establishes subclasses to a major class on the basis of differences in this method of defining. Let us define four words with this method of defining.

Major Class: Discourse
Term to be defined
Defining terms (genus or class and differences)

Exposition	is a form of discourse (genus) that informs or explains (difference).
Narration	is a form of discourse that tells a story.
Description	is a form of discourse that creates a word picture of a person, place, thing, or experience.
Argumentation	is a form of discourse that seeks to convince the reader of the truth of a given proposition or thesis.

Let us illustrate the formal definition further by using this method to define the following words and terms: "science" (at the top of the ladder of abstraction), "natural science," "social science," "physics," and "sociology."

A science is a systematized knowledge derived from observation, study, and experimentation carried on in order to determine the nature or principles of what is being studied.

A natural science is a systematized knowledge (genus) of nature and the physical world, including zoology, botany, chemistry, physics, geology, etc. (difference).

A social science is a branch of science (genus) that deals with the institutions and functioning of human society and with the interpersonal relationships of individuals as members of society.

Physics is a natural science (genus) dealing with the properties, changes, interactions, etc., of matter and energy in which energy is considered to be continuous (difference).

Sociology is the science of human society and of social relations, organization, and change (genus); it is the study of the beliefs, values, interrelationships, etc., of societal groups and of the principles or processes governing social phenomena (difference).

Fifth, a writer will present various definitions of a word and then follow with his choice and reasons for it, for example, the word "personality."

In the model definition paragraph that follows, the writer defines the word "symbol" in this manner."[25]

Main idea	A second term that calls for explanation is the symbol. A symbol
Definition	is a sign that by common agreement stands for something else.
	It is a kind of shorthand whereby long or complicated facts may
Examples	be expressed in a short time or space. The bands on the sleeve
	of a railway conductor indicate how long he has been in the
	service of the company. Stars, bars, eagles, and maple leaves
	indicate rank in the army. Certain tunes on the radio tell what
	programs are to follow.
Related	*The world is full of symbols:* a pin tells what fraternal organi-
main idea	zation one belongs to. One type of ring tells that a woman is
	married and another that she is engaged. One could make an
	interesting story from the symbolism of hats, the sailor's cap,
	the opera hat, the cowboy's wide-brimmed hat, etc. Often a

[25] Louise Dudley and Austin Faricy, *The Humanities,* 4th ed., pp. 32–34. Copyright © 1960 by McGraw-Hill Book Company.

Further discussion with examples	person is recognized by his symbol. Mercury, the messenger of the gods, may usually be identified by his winged sandals, his staff entwined with snakes (caduceus) and his flat hat (petasos). The caduceus had magical powers over sleeping, waking, and dreaming, and as such become identified with healing. It is now the symbol of the medical profession and of the Army Medical Corps. Bacchus, the god of wine, is usually portrayed with grapes or grape leaves. In the painting by Execias, *Dionysus Sailing the Sea,* we recognize Bacchus (Dionysus) by the grapes and grape leaves which fill the upper part of the picture. The story is that one day while he was asleep, Bacchus was taken aboard a ship by some sailors who wished to sell him into slavery. When the god awoke he asked them to take him to Naxos. When they refused, vines laden with grapes grew up around the mast, and the mariners were changed into dolphins.
Related main idea	*There are many symbols of the Christian Church:* Peter is represented with a key because of Christ's saying that he gave Peter the keys of the kingdom of heaven (Matt. 16: 19). Paul is represented as a bald old man carrying a sword. In Dürer's paintings of the four saints both Peter and Paul may be recognized by their symbols. The symbols of the four evangelists, Matthew, Mark, Luke, and John, were well known in the Middle Ages and are frequently found today. Matthew is symbolized as
Examples	a winged man, Mark a winged lion, Luke a winged ox, and John an eagle. We see these in a characteristic setting in the tympanum, or curved space above the door, of the church of St. Trophime at Arles, France. Christ is in the center with his hands raised in blessing and around him are the symbols of the four evangelists. (Italics added.)

ASSIGNMENT/WRITING THE PARAGRAPH

Write an extended definition organized and developed by any method of defining or any combination of methods. Select some term or expression that you believe needs defining before you can discuss with your friends some particular issue, problem, activity, or happening. Below are some suggested topics.

1 Violence
2 Generation gap
3 Authority
4 Teenage music
5 Good literature
6 Frustration

 7 A good guy
 8 A bad guy
 9 Excitement
10 Waste
11 Five-man defense
12 Feedback
13 Intelligence
14 Courage
15 Slang

BY A COMBINATION OF METHODS

Frequently, a writer will organize and develop his paragraph with more than one method. In the model paragraph unit below, the writers begin with a clearly stated topic sentence. They support this main idea by describing for the reader what a person would see as he approaches a medieval town and walks through it. This description emphasizes the influence of religion on the life of the people—the great cathedral, the vast numbers of ecclesiastics, the local shrine, an arrival of a papal delegate, and many other buildings owned by the Church.

With the transitional sentence in the middle of the paragraph which reads: "For the Church performed many tasks other than that of religion," the writers lead the reader into another related but different aspect of the developing thought expressed in the opening topic sentence. They state this new idea in the next sentence; it reads: "It was the one great social organization of the Middle Ages." They support this main idea with examples in the remainder of the paragraph and continue with the support in the following paragraph.[26]

Main idea

By moving
outside the
town into
the city

The universality of the Church brought its influence into every home. *Approaching a medieval town,* one would see above the thick city walls the tapering spires of the cathedral, the largest and most centrally located structure in the community. *Entering the city,* the modern visitor would be amazed to see the narrow streets filled with ecclesiastics—black- and yellow-cowled monks rubbing shoulders with steel-helmeted soldiers of a lord bishop's retinue, nuns and their charges hurrying past tavern doors to escape coarse comments, pilgrims staring at unfamiliar objects while searching out the local shrine, and perhaps a cavalcade clattering over the uneven road and announcing the arrival of a great papal legate from overseas. Many buildings

[26] T. Walter Wallbank and Alastair M. Taylor, *Civilization: Past and Present,* 3rd ed., pp. 407–408. Copyright © 1954 by Scott, Foresman and Company.

New phase

Support

Leaving
the city

would be church property. Churches, monasteries, colleges, hospitals, or almshouses would meet the eye, as well as the elegant palace of the bishop. For the Church performed many tasks other than that of religion. *It was the one great social organization of the Middle Ages.* Monks built bridges and repaired roads; the Church's hospitals and almshouses took care of the lepers and the poor; the schools and colleges of the Church were the sole places of education; its courts had jurisdiction over every Christian's moral and religious acts.

The Church supervised the amusements of the populace, and the church porch was the setting of popular religious dramas, or mystery plays. When one left the city behind, he would see wayside shrines along the highway, parish church steeples everywhere, and the massive buildings of a monastery, whose inmates were engaged (at least during the earlier Middle Ages) in transcribing manuscripts, writing chronicles or local histories, teaching the peasants new methods of farming, tending vineyards, fishing in nearby waters, and making new discoveries in animal husbandry. (Italics added.)

In the last sentence of paragraph 2, the writers return again to the description, moving the reader onward to sights he sees as he leaves the city behind.

In summary, the middle paragraphs may be organized and developed in a variety of ways. There are four basic patterns of movement:

General to particular

Particular to general

General to particular to general

Question to answer

Within these frames, a writer may organize his supporting material depending upon his purpose and the kind of material by:

Examples and illustrations

Time

Space

Order of climax

Whole to parts

Reasons

Cause to effect, effect to cause

Classes

Comparison

Contrast

Known to unknown (analogy)

Definition

A combination of methods

TRANSITIONAL PARAGRAPHS

The transitional paragraph is usually a very short paragraph, some-times only a single sentence. It serves to carry the reader smoothly onward from one stage of the thought to a related but different stage. In the transitional paragraph, a writer may sum up the main ideas of the previous discussion; he may tell his reader what he intends to do in the next division of the developing thought, or he may repeat a certain point or points for emphasis. In the model transitional para-graph that follows, the writer tells his reader that in the future discus-sion he will examine the points by which a republic differs from a pure democracy so that we "shall comprehend both the nature of the cure and the efficacy which it must derive from the Union."

A republic, by which I mean a government in which the scheme of represen-tation takes place, opens a different prospect, and promises the cure for which we are seeking. Let us examine the points in which it varies from pure democracy, and we shall comprehend both the nature of the cure and the efficacy which it must derive from the Union.[27]

In the next model paragraph, the writer summarizes and emphasizes a point in the previous discussion.

In short, the outlook of the feudal baron was too limited. He often lost sight of the welfare of the whole people in his preoccupation with the problems and needs of his petty feudal domain. People can best live in harmony and ad-vance materially when they subscribe to one central government which takes the larger view of their affairs. Under feudalism there were too many conflict-ing loyalties.[28]

ASSIGNMENT/TRANSITIONAL PARAGRAPHS
Study the two model paragraphs that follow. Write a paragraph explaining their function.

[27] James Madison, "The Federalist," no. X.
[28] Wallbank and Taylor, op. cit., p. 358.

Paragraph 1

The criticism directed at the government on the ground of political ineptitude and failure served to swell the stream of social-economic criticism which had set in with the very beginning of the eighteenth century and which concerned itself with every institution and every intellectual position inherited from the past. The whole European intelligentsia participated in this movement, usually called the Enlightenment. Having treated the Enlightenment with a certain fullness in the previous chapter, we may content ourselves at this point with repeating that, although the movement began in England, not only did Frenchmen become its greatest propagandists, but the French champions sprang preponderantly from the bourgeoisie. They sprang, therefore, from the very class with which we have just become acquainted as the most vital element of the third estate.[29]

Paragraph 2

From the two dozen or more feudal units that filled the map of Europe in the eleventh century, England, France, and Spain arose as pioneers in national unification. Our main case study in the rise of the national state will be England. Although outdistanced in international affairs by France and Spain until the eighteenth century, England was the first country to achieve a completely organized nationhood. The story of England also merits highlighting because it involves such important developments as the growth of the common law and the genesis of a system of representative government—the Parliament.[30]

TRANSITIONS WITHIN THE PARAGRAPH (COHERENCE)

Coherence within a paragraph means that its thought flows smoothly and logically onward without gaps and pauses in its progression. Coherence is achieved by unity, order, and transitional devices that tie one sentence to another or to another paragraph. Thus, a paragraph with unity—that is, a group of sentences revolving around and developing a main idea—is also a paragraph with coherence. Furthermore, a paragraph with order—that is, a paragraph organized and developed effectively by any one method or a combination of methods of development—is also a paragraph with coherence. Gaining coherence, however, means more than achieving unity and order; it means connecting the separate but related ideas or links in the chain of thought with certain transitional devices that act like signposts and guide the reader through that thought. The most common transitional devices are the following:

[29] Schevill, op. cit., pp. 389–390.
[30] Wallbank and Taylor, op. cit., p. 452.

1 Transitional words and expressions
2 Pronouns
3 Repeated words or groups of words
4 Synonyms
5 Transitional sentences

The paragraph below possesses unity and order and appears at first glance to be an effective paragraph. However, when you compare it with the original paragraph that follows it, you will observe how various transitional devices lead the reader more smoothly and logically onward.

Paragraph without Transitions:

Main idea	This is only one aspect of the problem. *There is the wider gap between generations since the rate of social development has*
Support	*speeded up.* The tastes and habits of young people today differ markedly from those of the thirties, let alone the twenties. Influ-
Support	ences by the tastes and habits of their early years, the "fathers" are inclined to think these things are absolutes and to deny their children the right to independent creativity which they de-
Repeat of the main idea	manded from their own parents. The artificial conflicts, in which a dance or the width of trousers is elevated to the dignity of crucial issues.[31] (Italics added.)

Paragraph with Transitions.

But this is *only one* aspect of the problem. Another no less essential, is the wider gap between generations since the rate of social development has speeded up. *The tastes and habits* of *young people* today differ markedly from those of the *young people* of the thirties, let alone of the twenties. Still influenced by the *tastes and habits* of their own youth, the "fathers" are inclined to think these habits and tastes are absolutes and to deny their children the right to independent creativity which they demanded from their own parents. Hence the artificial conflicts, in which a dance or the width of trousers is elevated to the dignity of crucial issues.[32] (Italics added.)

In additional to unity and order, the writer of the paragraph above uses the following transitional devices:

1 Transitional words and expressions
but   another   still   hence
2 Pronouns
those   their   these   they   their

---

[31] Igor Kon, "Young People and Society," *Soviet Life,* May 1966, pp. 11–12.
[32] Ibid.

3 Repeated words or groups of words
tasks and habits   young people
4 Synonyms (word substitutes)
of the young people   young people of the thirties
their own parents   their own youth
the fathers

Let us consider each of the transitional devices more fully.

Transitional words and expressions

The following transitional words and expressions are grouped under their function in the paragraph.

To explain or give example

for example	as an example
for instance	in particular
for one thing	that is
in this way	in this manner
namely	frequently
such as	especially
specifically	occasionally
to illustrate	

To indicate time sequence of ideas

first	
second	another
third	still another
in the next place	the following
in the beginning	next
in addition	besides
in the first place	the former
and	the latter
and then	again
also	moreover
	indeed

To indicate comparison

likewise	at the same time
similarly	in like manner
in the same way	

To indicate contrast

on the one hand	
on the other hand	conversely
on the contrary	but
however	yet
in contrast	whereas

To indicate reason, cause, effect

because	hence
since	consequently
for	finally
all in all	accordingly
as a result	and so
therefore	as a consequence

To indicate summary or conclusion

in brief	at last
in short	finally
thus	to summarize
to conclude	in summary
in conclusion	to sum up

To indicate repetition

and so again	indeed
to repeat	in other words
I repeat	to recapitulate
as has been said	in fact

Pronouns

Pronouns carry the reader backward to an antecedent—the word, usually a single noun, for which the pronoun stands. Thus, using pronouns as noun substitutes aids coherence by tying one sentence or part of a sentence to a previous sentence or part of a sentence.

John dribbled the ball slowly and carefully down the floor. As *he* crossed the center line, *he* glanced quickly above *him* to the scoreboard hanging down from the roof of the arena. *It* read: Valley 60, Readville 60 with 10 seconds left in the game. *He* put on a burst of speed and looked anxiously for a *teammate who* might be breaking for the basket. *All* were guarded closely. When *he* reached the top of the foul circle, *he* stopped, faked to his left, leaving his man a step behind *him,* and threw the ball into the air toward the basket. *It* sailed through the hoop without hitting the rim. *John* had won the big game. (Italics added.)

Repeated words or groups of words

In the model paragraph that follows, the writer keeps the loneliness of the alcoholic in the reader's mind by repetition of that feeling.

The alcoholic is a *lonely* man. He is *lonely* when he is *alone,* and being an alcoholic he must be *alone* a great deal of the time. He has difficulty tolerating himself. He thinks he has to drink, so he does—then he hates himself for his drinking. He is, in other words, *lonely* in his Jekyll and Hyde role: one is the guy who drinks and tries to rationalize to himself a reason or need for doing so. The other is the fellow who realizes he shouldn't drink, and is aware that alcohol is ruining him.[33] (Italics added.)

Synonyms

Synonyms are words with a meaning similar to the original word, for example, "house," "home," and "dwelling"; "fear," "trepidation," "panic," "apprehension," "fright," and "terror." The use of synonyms is illustrated in the two contrived paragraphs that follow.

Paragraph without Synonyms:

Bad luck is the word that best sums up my football career in high school. In my first year, I had the *bad luck* to break my leg in a practice game before the freshman season began. The next year I was a victim of *bad luck* again when I tripped in the shower and broke my shoulder the day before my first varsity game. In my junior year my *bad luck* took a different path. I fumbled the ball on our own 2-yard line with one minute left to play. Our opponents scored on the next play and beat us 7 to 6. My senior year was no different. I had the *bad luck* to tear a cartilage in my right knee and watched the remaining seven games from the bench. *Bad luck* and football are synonymous in my vocabulary. (Italics added.)

Paragraph with Synonyms:

Bad luck is the word that best sums up my football career in high school. In my first year, I had the *misfortune* to break my leg in a practice game before the freshman season began. The next year I was the victim of *adversity* again when I tripped in the shower and broke my shoulder the day before my first varsity game. In my junior year, my *ill fortune* took a different path. I fumbled the ball on our own 2-yard line with one minute left to play. Our opponents scored on the next play and beat us 7 to 6. My senior year was no different. I had the *misfortune* to tear a cartilage in my right knee and watched the remaining seven games from the bench. *Bad luck* and football are synonymous in my vocabulary. (Italics added.)

Transitional sentence

Frequently a writer will lead his reader smoothly through his developing thought by using the final sentence in a paragraph to indicate the main idea that he will develop in the following paragraph. In the model

[33] C. A. D'Alonzo, "The Loneliness of the Alcoholic," *The Drinking Problem—and Its Control*, pp. 13–16. Copyright © 1959 by Gulf Publishing Company of Houston, Texas.

paragraph unit that follows, the writer uses the final sentence of the first paragraph to introduce the reader to the main thought of the next paragraph.

The problem of the generations does not reduce itself simply to the fact that the status of fathers and sons are more equal today while the differences between them are greater. *Another, and a very important factor, is the longer life span.*

The term *"aging population"* sounds dismal. Actually it is not. What it denotes is a greater proportion of aged people because of a longer average life expectancy. In many developed countries the proportion of people who are 60 and older exceeds 15 per cent. In our country average life expectancy has increased from 32 years in 1913 to the present 70 years. The process is progressive, of course, and it poses problems—for example, the problem of prolonging not only one's life, but one's capacity for work as well, or the problem of combining harmoniously the activity of old and young people.[34] (Italics added.)

ASSIGNMENT/PARAGRAPH COHERENCE
Write a paragraph or paragraph unit making use of various transitional devices to carry the reader smoothly through your flowing thought.

CONCLUDING PARAGRAPHS

Although some papers, especially short papers, do not require a formal conclusion, a concluding sentence in some cases or a concluding paragraph or paragraphs in other situations can be a very important part of the writing process. The conclusion functions to give the reader the feeling that the writer has completed his discussion. It serves also to emphasize the thesis, the writer's purpose, or certain points the writer wishes the reader to remember. There are a variety of ways to conclude a paper.

Some of the less effective ways for concluding your papers are with an appropriate quotation or an anecdote or by leaving the development open for further discussion.

Some suggestions for effective conclusions are the following:

1 A summary of the main points of the discussion
2 A statement of the thesis
3 A restatement of the thesis (first stated in the first paragraph)
4 A consideration of the broader implications of the topic

[34] Kon, op. cit., pp. 11–12.

5 A recommendation for future action
6 A means of emphasizing a key point or points (not a summary)
7 Any combination of these objectives

Study the model concluding paragraphs that follow. Some of them are the concluding paragraphs for essays from which the model introductions that you studied earlier were excerpted. Others are conclusions from essays in the book. If you choose, you may study the introductions and conclusion to these essays at this time.

Model 1: From "Britain's 'Thin Blue Line'—Police Prefer Tolerance to Carrying Guns," reprinted in full in Chapter 3.

Thus, on balance, the general attitude and policy of tolerance and the "thin blue line" still seems to work in containing violence.

The police in Britain are always ready to cooperate with peaceful demonstrators, providing them with an escort of bored bobbies along a specified line of march. And even when such restrictions do not appeal to the demonstrators the British remain determined to try to avoid violence.[35]

Model 2: From "Love Stuff, Cops-and-Robbers Style," reprinted in full in Chapter 5.

So even in a deromanticized world, even as a businessman among businessmen, the crook still has one advantage over most heroes of fiction. Stepping outside society, operating without regard for those proliferating rules that hem in the rest of us, he is the one of the few businesses where romance can still happen. Not as frequently as when gang members were putting their kid brothers through medical school, but sometimes; they do get that occasional helicopter ride. And we get to ride along with them.[36]

Model 3: From "The Next Industrial Revolution," reprinted in full in Chapter 7.

The next industrial revolution is on our doorstep. Let us be the revolutionaries who shape it, rather than have it happen—and shape us.[37]

Model 4: From "On Law and Order," reprinted in full in Chapter 7.

There will never be a reign of law and order until those engaged in the various protests now epidemic everywhere know with certainty when they have gone

[35] Don Cook, "Britain's 'Thin Blue Line'—Police Prefer Tolerance to Carrying Guns," *Los Angeles Times,* Apr. 16, 1972, sec. G, p. 4. Copyright © 1972 by the Los Angeles Times Company.
[36] Westlake, op. cit., p. 14.
[37] Athelstan Spilhaus, "The Next Industrial Revolution," *Science,* Mar. 27, 1970, p. 1273. Copyright © 1970 by the American Association for the Advancement of Science, 1515 Massachusetts Ave., N.W., Washington, D.C.

beyond the legal limit and, if they have, what penalties will be imposed upon them.[38]

Model 5: From "How to Take the Profit out of Hard Drugs," reprinted in full in Chapter 7.

But all this, bluntly, is completely secondary. The first and overriding concern now must be the nonaddicts. The first task is to make the city livable again.

The first prescription for the survival of our cities is not "Law and Order"; it must be "Freedom from Fear."[39]

Model 6: From "Who Killed King Kong?" reprinted in full in Chapter 2.

Every day in the week on a screen somewhere in the world, King Kong relives his agony. Again and again he expires on the Empire State Building, as audiences of the devout assist his sacrifice. We watch him die, and by extension kill the ape within our bones, but these little deaths of ours occur in prosaic surroundings. We do not die on a tower, New York before our feet, nor do we give our lives to smash a few flying machines. It is not for us to bring to a momentary standstill the civilization in which we move. King Kong does this for us. And so we kill him again and again, in much-spliced celluloid, while the ape in us expires from day to day, obscure, in desperation.[40]

Read the model essay that follows. This selection is the first in a series of structure reviews. Be prepared to answer questions on the structure of the essay. Most of these structure reviews have answers at the end of the chapter in which they appear. Others, like the model essays you will read in Chapter 4, are without answers. Your instructor may use this kind of structure review for oral discussion, for testing you on what you have learned about organizing and developing thought, or for both purposes.

WHO KILLED KING KONG?
X. J. Kennedy

1 The ordeal and spectacular death of King Kong, the giant ape, undoubtedly have been witnessed by more Americans than have ever seen a performance of *Hamlet, Iphigenia at Aulis,* or even *Tobacco Road.* Since RKO-Radio Pictures first released *King Kong,* a quarter-century has gone by; yet year after year, from prints that grow more rain-beaten, from sound tracks that

SOURCE NOTE: X. J. Kennedy, "Who Killed King Kong?" *Dissent,* Spring 1960, pp. 213–215.

[38] Joseph Wood Krutch, "On Law and Order," *This Week Magazine,* Oct. 19, 1969, p. 2. Copyright © 1969 by United Newspapers Magazine Corporation, 485 Lexington Avenue, New York, N.Y. 10017.
[39] Drucker, op. cit., p. 26.
[40] Kennedy, op. cit., p. 215.

grow more tinny, ticket-buyers by thousands still pursue Kong's luckless fight against the forces of technology, tabloid journalism, and the DAR. They see him chloroformed to sleep, see him whisked from his jungle isle to New York and placed on show, see him burst his chains to roam the city (lugging a frightened blonde), at last to plunge from the spire of the Empire State Building, machine-gunned by model airplanes.

2   Though Kong may die, one begins to think his legend unkillable. No clearer proof of his hold upon the popular imagination may be seen than what emerged one catastrophic week in March 1955, when New York WOR-TV programmed *Kong* for seven evenings in a row (a total of sixteen showings). Many a rival network vice-president must have scowled when surveys showed that *Kong*—the 1933 B-picture—had lured away fat segments of the viewing populace from such powerful competitors as Ed Sullivan, Groucho Marx and Bishop Sheen.

3   But even television has failed to run *King Kong* into oblivion. Coffee-in-the-lobby cinemas still show the old hunk of hokum, with the apology that in its use of composite shots and animated models the film remains technically interesting. And no other monster in movie history has won so devoted a popular audience. None of the plodding mummies, the stultified draculas, the whitecoated Lugosis with their shiny pinball-machine laboratories, none of the invisible stranglers, berserk robots, or menaces from Mars has ever enjoyed so many resurrections.

4   Why does the American public refuse to let King Kong rest in peace? It is true, I'll admit, that *Kong* outdid every monster movie before or since in sheer carnage. Producers Cooper and Schoedsack crammed into it dinosaurs, headhunters, riots, aerial battles, bullets, bombs, bloodletting. Heroine Fay Wray, whose function is mainly to scream, shuts her mouth for hardly one uninterrupted minute from first reel to last. It is also true that *Kong* is larded with good healthy sadism, for those whose joy it is to see the frantic girl dangled from cliffs and harried by pterodactyls. But it seems to me that the abiding appeal of the giant ape rests on other foundations.

5   Kong has, first of all, the attraction of being manlike. His simian nature gives him one huge advantage over giant ants and walking vegetables in that an audience may conceivably identify with him. Kong's appeal has the quality that established the Tarzan series as American myth—for what man doesn't secretly image himself a huge hairy howler against whom no other monster has a chance? If Tarzan recalls the ape in us, then Kong may well appeal to that great-granddaddy primordial brute from whose tribe we have all deteriorated.

6   Intentionally or not, the producers of *King Kong* encourage this identification by etching the character of Kong with keen sympathy. For the ape is a figure in a tradition familiar to moviegoers: the tradition of the pitiable monster. We think of Lon Chaney in the role of Quasimodo, of Karloff in the origi-

nal *Frankenstein.* As we watch the Frankenstein monster's fumbling and disastrous attempts to befriend a flower-picking child, our sympathies are enlisted with the monster in his impenetrable loneliness. And so with Kong. As he roars in his chains, while barkers sell tickets to boobs who gape at him, we perhaps feel something more deep than pathos. We begin to sense something of the problem that engaged Eugene O'Neill in *The Hairy Ape:* the dilemma of a displaced animal spirit forced to live in a jungle built by machines.

7 *King Kong,* it is true, had special relevance in 1933. Landscapes of the depression are glimpsed early in the film when an impresario, seeking some desperate pretty girl to play the lead in a jungle movie, visits souplines and a Woman's Home Mission. In Fay Wray—who's been caught snitching an apple from a fruitstand—his search is ended. When he gives her a big feed and a movie contract, the girl is magic-carpeted out of the world of the National Recovery Act. And when, in the film's climax, Kong smashes that very Third Avenue landscape in which Fay had wandered hungry, audiences of 1933 may well have felt a personal satisfaction.

8 What is curious is that audiences of 1960 remain hooked. For in the heart of urban man, one suspects, lurks the impulse to fling a bomb. Though machines speed him to the scene of his daily grind, though IBM comptometers ("freeing the human mind from drudgery") enable him to drudge more efficiently once he arrives, there comes a moment when he wishes to turn upon his machines and kick hell out of them. He wants to hurl his combination radio-alarmclock out the bedroom window and listen to its smash. What subway commuter wouldn't love—just for once—to see the downtown express smack head-on into the uptown local? Such a wish is gratified in that memorable scene in *Kong* that opens with a wide-angle shot: interior of a railway car on the Third Avenue El. Straphangers are nodding, the literate refold their newspapers. Unknown to them, Kong has torn away a section of trestle toward which the train now speeds. The motorman spies Kong up ahead, jams on the brakes. Passengers hurtle together like so many peas in a pail. In a window of the car appear Kong's bloodshot eyes. Women shriek. Kong picks up the railway car as if it were a rat, flips it to the street and ties knots in it, or something. To any commuter the scene must appear one of the most satisfactory pieces of celluloid ever exposed.

9 Yet however violent his acts, Kong remains a gentleman. Remarkable is his sense of chivalry. Whenever a fresh boa constrictor threatens Fay, Kong first sees that the lady is safely parked, then manfully thrashes her attacker. (And she, the ingrate, runs away every time his back is turned.) Atop the Empire State Building, ignoring his pursuers, Kong places Fay on a ledge as tenderly as if she were a dozen eggs. He fondles her, then turns to face the Army Air Force. And Kong is perhaps the most disinterested lover since Cyrano: his attentions to the lady are utterly without hope of reward. After all,

between a five-foot blonde and a fifty-foot ape, love can hardly be more than an intellectual flirtation. In his simian way King Kong is the hopelessly yearning lover of Petrarchan convention. His forced exit from his jungle, in chains, results directly from his single-minded pursuit of Fay. He smashes a Broadway theater when the notion enters his dull brain that the flashbulbs of photographers somehow endanger the lady. His perilous shinnying up a skyscraper to pluck Fay from her boudoir is an act of the kindliest of hearts. He's impossible to discourage even though the love of his life can't lay eyes on him without shrieking murder.

10 The tragedy of King Kong, then, is to be the beast who at the end of the fable fails to turn into the handsome prince. This is the conviction that the scriptwriters would leave with us in the film's closing line. As Kong's corpse lies blocking traffic in the street, the entrepreneur who brought Kong to New York turns to the assembled reporters and proclaims: "That's your story, boys —it was Beauty killed the Beast!" But greater forces than those of the screaming Lady have combined to lay Kong low, if you ask me. Kong lives for a time as one of those persecuted near-animal souls bewildered in the middle of an industrial order, whose simple desires are thwarted at every turn. He climbs the Empire State Building because in all New York it's the closest thing he can find to the clifftop of his jungle isle. He dies, a pitiful dolt, and the army brass and publicity-men cackle over him. His death is the only possible outcome to as neat a tragic dilemma as you can ask for. The machine-guns do him in, while the manicured human hero (a nice clean Dartmouth boy) carries away Kong's sweetheart to the altar. O, the misery of it all. There's far more truth about upper-middle-class American life in *King Kong* than in the last seven dozen novels of John P. Marquand.

11 A Negro friend from Atlanta tells me that in movie houses in colored neighborhoods throughout the South, *Kong* does a constant business. They show the thing in Atlanta at least every year, presumably to the same audiences. Perhaps this popularity may simply be due to the fact that *Kong* is one of the most watchable movies ever constructed, but I wonder whether Negro audiences may not find some archetypical appeal in this serio-comic tale of a huge black powerful free spirit whom all the hardworking white policemen are out to kill.

12 Every day in the week on a screen somewhere in the world, King Kong relives his agony. Again and again he expires on the Empire State Building, as audiences of the devout assist his sacrifice. We watch him die, and by extension kill the ape within our bones, but these little deaths of ours occur in prosaic surroundings. We do not die on a tower, New York before our feet, nor do we give our lives to smash a few flying machines. It is not for us to bring to a momentary standstill the civilization in which we move. King Kong does this for us. And so we kill him again and again, in much-spliced celluloid, while the ape in us expires from day to day, obscure, in desperation.

STRUCTURE REVIEW ONE/PARAGRAPH ORGANIZATION

Name _____ Class _____

Answer each question in the space provided below it.

1 What is the central thought of the essay? In what paragraph is it stated or implied?

2 What is the function of the first four paragraphs? How does the writer attempt to gain reader interest?

3 What is the main idea that gives unity to the paragraph unit consisting of paragraphs 1 through 3? In what paragraph is it expressed?

4 What is the organizational pattern of paragraph 1? paragraph 2? Discuss the movement of thought and the kind of support in your answer.

5 What is the main idea that gives unity to paragraphs 5 and 6?

6 How does the writer tie the thought of paragraph 7 which has a special relevance for audiences of 1933 with the thought of paragraph 8 which has relevance for audiences of the 1960s?

7 How is the King Kong of paragraph 9 different from the earlier Kong? What word in the first sentence of paragraph 9 indicates a change in the direction of thought? Does the topic sentence of the paragraph clearly indicate the change of thought?

8 What word in the first sentence of paragraph 10 indicates another change in the direction of the writer's thought?

9 What is the special function of paragraph 12?

10 What is the writer's conclusion concerning the film *King Kong*?

ANSWER SECTION

STRUCTURE REVIEW ONE

1 Mr. X. J. Kennedy presents reasons why the film *King Kong* has remained popular throughout the years. Two sentences in paragraph 4 reveal the thesis: (1) "Why does the American public refuse to let King Kong rest in peace," and (2) "But it seems to me that the abiding appeal of the giant ape rests on other foundations."

2 The first four paragraphs serve to introduce the subject and gain reader interest. The writer shows how popular the film has been; thus, he anticipates that his readers will begin to wonder why it has been so popular.

3 The main idea is the popularity of the film. In the next to the last sentence of paragraph 3, Kennedy writes, "And no other monster in movie history has won so devoted a popular audience." He elaborates on this idea in the sentence that follows.

4 The movement is from general to particular. The supporting material consists mainly of examples and factual material concerning the film's popularity.

5 Kong has, first of all, the attraction of being manlike.

6 The feeling of frustration within man toward society and his desire to strike out against it are developed in both paragraphs. The members of the audience would like to destroy something, just as Kong destroyed Third Avenue.

7 Kong remains a gentleman. This is stated in the topic sentence of paragraph 9. It is preceded by the guide words "Yet however violent his acts," indicating a change in direction to contrast.

8 The guide word "then" indicates a summary or conclusion reached from the previous discussion.

9 It is the concluding paragraph. The writer gives the reason why we kill the ape again and again.

10 He concludes that we watch *King Kong* because in killing Kong we are able to give vent to our anger; thus, we kill a little of ourselves each time we see the film, leaving us more desperate than ever.

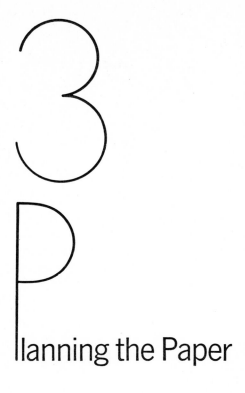

lanning the Paper

In the two previous chapters, you were given much information about how to structure, organize, and develop the paragraph, the paragraph unit, and the longer piece of writing. You should be ready now to organize your own thoughts into sentences, paragraphs, and compositions. How would you, then, go about selecting a topic, researching it, and organizing and developing the material for a composition of approximately 500 words for a writing class or as a paper of the same length for a history, sociology, or literature assignment?

To develop your thought for this kind of written assignment, follow these suggested steps.

1 Select a subject.
2 Make a preliminary search for material.
3 Limit the subject.
4 Gather material.
5 Organize the material.
6 Write the first draft.
7 Revise the first draft.
8 Prepare the final paper.

SELECT A SUBJECT

If possible select a subject from your own experience that you know something about and that you believe will interest others besides your instructor. Begin your search for a subject by listing broad areas of interest; for example, in the manner that follows:

amusements	cars	music	sports
animals	communism	painting	travel
antiques	education	politics	youth
art	the ghetto	pollution	violence
camping	hobbies	religion	war

If you are aware of people, places, things, happenings in the world, whether it be on campus, such as the athletic field, the cafeteria, the club meeting, the drama department, the classroom, or in the town, the home, the city, you will find ample subjects for written communication. You must observe life and question yourself and others about it.

PRELIMINARY SEARCH FOR MATERIAL

Whether or not you have decided upon exactly what you want to say about your selected subject, begin now to gather information on it from your own experiences, class lectures, research in books and periodicals in the library, and discussion with other individuals. In addition to accumulating information about the subject, this preliminary investigation will help you think about it and may lead to a selection of a topic that will lend itself to the kind of development required by the time and space requirements of the assignment. It may also tell you that you do not have enough knowledge and information to treat the subject or that the subject is too limited for treatment.

Your college library is an excellent place to begin your search for material. Although there is not space here to discuss in detail the abundance of sources in the library, the following is a list of general reference works that will be useful in your preliminary search. (This material was excerpted from *The Library Research Paper,* 4th ed., by P. Joseph Canavan and Lawrence D. Parker, published by Kendall/ Hunt Publishing Company, Dubuque, Iowa. Copyright © 1971 by Canavan and Parker.)

General reference sources

1 Bibliographies to bibliographies
   Besterman, Theodore, *World Bibliography of Bibliographies,* 4th ed., Geneva: Societas Bibliographia, 1965–1966, 5 vols., including index.

(Useful in locating older bibliographies. Arranged by subject and indexed by author.)

Bibliographic Index: A Cumulative Bibliography of Bibliographies, 1937 to date, New York: H. W. Wilson Co., 1938 to date. (Lists current bibliographies contained in books, periodicals, and pamphlets. A subject index only.)

2 Catalogs

The Booklist and *Subscription Books Bulletin,* 1905 to date, Chicago: American Library Association, 1905 to date. (A subject-author-title guide to current books.)

Books in Print. 1948 to date, New York: R. R. Bowker Co., 1948 to date, 2 vols. (An author-title index to the *Publisher's Trade List Annual.*)

British Books in Print; the Reference Catalogue of Current Literature, 1965 to date, 2 vols. (An author-title list of all books in print and on sale in the British Empire. Formerly the Reference Catalogue of Current Literature, last published 1961.)

Publisher's Trade List Annual, 1873 to date, New York: R. R. Bowker Co., 1873 to date. (A compilation of publishers' catalogs arranged under the names of publishers. *Books in Print,* 1948, is the author-title index. *Subject Guide to Books in Print* was added in 1957.)

The Reader's Adviser, 11th ed., ed. by Winifred F. Courtney, New York: R. R. Bowker Co., 1968–1969, 2 vols. (A fully annotated guide to subjects in the humanities and the social sciences.)

Standard Catalog for Public Libraries, 4th ed., 1958, New York: H. W. Wilson Co., 1959. Annual supplements. (An annotated list of titles. It has a particularly useful author-title-subject index.)

Subject Guide to Books in Print, 1957 to date, New York: R. R. Bowker Co., 1957 to date, 2 vols. (A companion volume to *Books in Print,* listing under subject the books to be found.)

The United States Catalog; Books in Print January 1, 1928, 4th ed., New York: H. W. Wilson Co., 1928. (An author-subject-title index to all books published in the United States from 1898 to January 1, 1928. Information includes publisher, price, and date of publication.)

The Cumulative Book Index: A World List of Books in the English Language, 1928 to date, New York: H. W. Wilson Co., 1933 to date. (A continuation and expansion of *The United States Catalog.* It lists books published in the English language anywhere in the world.)

United States Library of Congress, *A Catalog of Books Represented by Library of Congress Printed Cards Issued to July 31, 1942,* Ann Arbor, Mich.: Edwards Brothers, 1942–1946, 167 vols., plus supplements 1942–1947. (A photographic reproduction of the Library of Congress card catalog in Washington. It lists eighteen cards on each page.)

When using these indexes, the student should usually start with the most recent volume and work back in time. He should look at the prefatory and introductory pages for explanations of symbols and abbreviations used, guides to using the index, and lists of periodicals included.

3 Indexes to magazines, newspapers, and essays

Ayer Directory of Newspapers and Periodicals, Philadelphia: N. W. Ayer and Sons, 1880 to date. (Gives information on the history, circulation, politics, and editors of newspapers and magazines in the United States and Canada. Originally entitled *American Newspaper Annual and Directory.*)

Essay and General Literature Index, 1900–1933, ed. by Minnie E. Sears and Miriam Shaw, New York: H. W. Wilson Co., 1934. (Kept up to date by half-year, annual, three-year, and seven-year supplements. Arranged in two parts—an author-subject-distinctive title index to essays and articles, and a list of books indexed. Sometimes referred to as the *Essay Index.*)

Guide to U.S. Government Serials and Periodicals, 1964 ed., McLean, Va.: Documents Index, 1966, 4 vols. (Includes serials, periodicals, releases, field agency publications, and other ephemeral publications of the U.S. government.)

International Index to Periodical Literature, 1907–1965, New York: H. W. Wilson Co., 1916–1965. (Title changed to *Social Sciences and Humanities Index* in 1965.)

Social Sciences and Humanities Index: formerly *International Index,* , 1965 to date, New York: H. W. Wilson Co., 1965 to date. (These are author-subject indexes to scholarly, highly specialized, and international periodicals not included in *Readers' Guide.* Chiefly concerned with subjects in the humanities and social sciences.)

New York Times Index, 1913 to date, New York, New York Times, 1913 to date. (A specific subject index to news articles in the *New York Times,* giving date, page, and column of each article. It also may be used as a guide to similar articles in other newspapers of the same date.)

Nineteenth Century Readers' Guide to Periodical Literature, 1890–1899, with *Supplementary Indexing,* 1900–1922, New York: H. W. Wilson Co., 1944, 2 vols. (An author-title-subject index that extends the *Readers' Guide* backward into the last decade of the nineteenth century.)

Palmer's Index to "The [London] Times" Newspaper, 1790–1941, Corsham, Wilts, Palmer, London, England, 1868–1943. (Valuable as an index to old copies of the *London Times.*)

Poole's Index to Periodical Literature, 1802–1907, rev. ed. with suppls., Boston: Houghton, Mifflin Co., c. 1877–1908, 7 vols. (A subject index to articles in nineteenth-century English and American magazines.)

Readers' Guide to Periodical Literature, 1900 to date, New York: H. W. Wilson Co., 1905 to date. (An author-subject-title index to popular magazines.)

"The [London] Times" or *Index to "The Times,"* 1906 to date. (An index to recent copies of the *London Times.*)

Ulrich's International Periodicals Directory, 11th ed., ed. by E. C. Graves, New York: R. R. Bowker Co., 1965–1966, 2 vols. (A guide to current foreign and domestic periodicals.)

Union List of Serials in Libraries of the United States and Canada, 3d ed., ed. by Edna Brown Titus, New York: H. W. Wilson Co., 1965, 5 vols. (A list of the periodicals contained in United States and Canadian libraries.)

4 Encyclopedias

Chambers' Encyclopaedia, new rev. ed., London: Pergamon, 1966, 15 vols. (Contains brief articles written by outstanding scholars. It is often more current than the *Encyclopaedia Britannica.*)

Collier's Encyclopedia, New York: Collier, 24 vols. (Aimed at the college level, but coverage is usually not so detailed as in the *Britannica* or the *Americana.* It has continuous revision and is supplemented by annual *Collier Yearbook.*)

Encyclopedia Americana, New York: Encyclopedia Americana Corp., 30 vols. (Contains excellent short articles, alphabetized word by word, and bibliographies on history, places, institutions, and industries, as well as summaries of famous books. It is especially valuable in the fields of science, business, and government. It now has continuous revision with each new printing. Older sets are kept up to date by the *Americana Annual.*)

Encyclopaedia Britannica, Chicago: Encyclopaedia Britannica, 24 vols. (A famous English encyclopedia containing articles, alphabetized letter by letter, written by recognized specialists in each field. It has excellent bibliographies at the end of articles. Since 1936 it also has had continuous revision with each new printing. Older sets are kept up to date by the *Britannica Book of the Year.*)

New International Encyclopedia, 2d ed., New York: Dodd, Mead, and Co., 1914–1916, 23 vols. Reissued, slightly revised, 1922 and 1927. Suppls. 1925 (2 vols.) and 1930 (2 vols.). (Contains good bibliographies and biographical articles on older Americans. Annual volumes are *The New International Year Book,* 1932 to date.)

ASSIGNMENT/PRELIMINARY SEARCH FOR MATERIAL

Underneath each subject, list three possible sources of information. Use the various sources in the previous list to aid you in your investigation.

1 Pollution

   a

   b

   c

2 The Aztecs

   a

   b

   c

3 Professional Basketball

   a

   b

   c

4 Saint Peter's Cathedral in Rome

   a

   b

   c

LIMIT THE SUBJECT

Perhaps as you were doing the preliminary investigation into the subject, you may have decided on a purpose for writing and what specific phase of the subject you intend to develop. If you have not reached that stage at this time, you will certainly have come to the conclusion that to attempt to treat a topic like Communism, Sports, Religion, or Youth in the time and space requirements of most college written assignments would be a fruitless endeavor. Any effort to develop broad and general subjects like those in your original listing would undoubtedly lead to a presentation of a series of loosely related generalizations of little interest to your reader.

Begin limiting your subject by writing down under the broad subject a title that indicates one aspect of the subject. Observe how titles like those below limit the earlier broad subjects of Politics, Painting, Religion, The Ghetto, Camping, Pollution, Education, and Violence.

You must limit your subject if you are going to treat it effectively in a 300- to 500-word paper. You must begin to focus on one aspect of the topic and state a point of view or reveal an attitude about it. In other words, you arrive at a purpose or a central thought about the subject around which the subsequent discussion revolves. You may state this unifying thought in a *thesis statement* or *statement of purpose.* Observe how much more clearly defined is the writer's purpose in the sentences stating the purpose or the thesis (central thought) that follow as compared with the titles for the same subjects given above them. These selections are in this book.

1 "The Common Cold" (written by Richard Gordon, p. 186)

Statement of purpose: These home cures generally follow one of three distinct courses, and each reflects the psychology of the sufferer; let us examine them in detail. They are (1) the Fresh-Air Treatment, (2) the Scientific Attack, (3) the Coddle.

2 "The American War Game" (written by Thomas B. Morgan, p. 138)
Statement of purpose: It is therefore in the interest of peace that one should inquire into the nature of the "war" game.

3 "Dangers Facing the University" (written by Theodore Sorenson, p. 205)
Statement of thesis: The university is in danger.

4 "The Loneliness of the Alcoholic" (written by C. A. D'Alonzo, p. 206)
Statement of thesis: The alcoholic is a lonely man.

5 "The Next Industrial Revolution" (written by Athelstan Spilhaus, p. 202)
Statement of thesis: I believe we must base the next industrial revolution—a planned one—on the thesis that there is no such a thing as waste, that waste is simply some useful substance that we do not yet have the wit to use.

ASSIGNMENT/LIMITING THE SUBJECT

Using the technique below, limit five broad or general subjects of your own choosing that you might wish later to develop into an essay.

Alcoholism
  the Alcoholic
    Characteristics of the Alcoholic
    Thesis: The alcoholic is a lonely man.
    Thesis: The alcoholic has abnormal fear.
    Thesis: The alcoholic is a liar, a cheat, and a deceitful person.

Sports
  College Sports
    Football
    Thesis: College football takes too much time.
    Thesis: Games films are invaluable aids for the coach and players.
    Thesis: Offensive blocking is the art of taking punishment.

Let us review the process of limiting the subject with a final example. In seeking a topic for a written assignment of approximately 500 words, you began with the broad area of interest "Youth." Aware that this subject was too vague and general for the time and space demands of the paper, you decided on one phase of the subject by considering the "Revolt of the Younger Generation in the 1920s." Finally you focused your thought on a point of view concerning the more limited subject by phrasing a central thought in a thesis sentence:

THESIS: The revolt of the younger generation of the 1920s was a logical outcome of the conditions of the age in which they lived.

GATHER MATERIAL

Your preliminary gathering of material and limiting of the topic should have indicated whether you need to research the subject further. In searching for additional material, make use of the various sources of your library. But, remember that this search is not concerned with the broad subject of the previous investigation; it must focus on the limited topic expressed by the thesis. Your investigation into "Revolt of the Younger Generation in the 1920s" will center chiefly on gathering information supporting the view that the revolt was the logical outcome of the conditions of that time. Your thesis statement, therefore, narrows your field of research.

ASSIGNMENT/GATHERING MATERIAL

Underneath the topics listed below, express a thesis sentence. Research this more limited topic than the previous assignment. Fill in the blanks with three sources.

1 Pollution
Thesis:
a
b
c

2 The Aztecs
Thesis:
a
b
c

3 Professional Basketball
Thesis:
a
b
c

4 Saint Peter's Cathedral in Rome
Thesis:
a
b
c

ORGANIZE THE MATERIAL

Organizing thought for a written assignment begins as soon as you select a subject. These early steps, you now know, are directed toward focusing your thinking about a subject so that it may be communicated effectively in the time and space demands of the assignment. You have reached the stage now where you must organize a mass of material around a central thought and move logically and effectively from a beginning through a middle or support to a conclusion.

You know, however, at this stage of developing your thought about a subject that the organizational plan and method or methods of developing should begin to take shape in your mind if the material has not already indicated them. Perhaps you are confused by the seemingly illogical process of arriving at a point where your thought begins to take shape for further development into a unified whole as you saw in the model essay on the younger generation in the 1920s.

In reaching the stage in your writing where you phrase a thesis statement, you may have discarded or modified many approaches along the way. You might have begun with only the subject in mind and without a purpose or a clearly defined central thought. You may have started with a general idea of what you wanted to say and reached the point where you stated that central thought clearly in a thesis. Or you may have been one of the lucky ones who knew exactly what you wanted to do and had a clearly defined thesis in mind at the beginning. Still again, you may have changed your subject one or more times before deciding on a suitable topic for further development. All this effort is part of the writing process.

Though these early stages may have been time-consuming and illogical, the processes of limiting the subject, gathering information to develop it completely, and stating the central thought or thesis are the most important ones in writing the long paper or composition. Without this kind of prewriting and thinking through the subject before actually writing, your chances of effective communication would be very small. Too often the beginning writer will put his thoughts on paper without knowing exactly what he wishes to say, whether he has enough knowledge to say it, or without knowing where he is going once he has begun to write. As a result, he rambles on and on, letting one idea lead him on to another without establishing the relationships of the parts to each other and to the central thought of the whole piece of writing. Thus, he loses his reader in a mass of disorganized and confusing thought about a subject whose central idea never becomes clear.

Informal outline

To help you structure your thoughts about a subject during the early stages in the writing process, this book, like many other books on writing, recommends that you begin organizing the piece of writing with an *informal* or *scratch outline.*

In preparing this kind of outline, begin by writing down the thesis and beneath it jot down as many ideas about it as you can. Plan the writing of the paper so that you do not have to do this step all at one time. Write down some ideas; go away from the paper for awhile; do something else. Then, come back and think about the subject again. Write down any additional ideas. Research it some more if it is necessary to acquire sufficient material for development. Continue this process until you have exhausted your thought about the subject. As an example of an informal listing of ideas, the following thought groups were jotted down under a thesis for a composition on air pollution.

THESIS: Pollutants in the air are endangering the health of the people of the world.

1 Smog in the world
2 Smog in Los Angeles
3 Inversion layer
4 Industrial smog
5 Automobile pollutants
6 Danger of air pollution
7 Number of air pollutants
8 Eleven identifiable air pollutants
9 Many unidentified air pollutants
10 Sulfur dioxide most well-known
11 Production of sulfur dioxide
12 Danger level for humans
13 Effect on plants
14 Sulfuric acid
15 Dangers of sulfuric acid
16 Carbon monoxide—a known killer
17 Why dangerous
18 Automobile exhaust
19 Number of automobiles in California
20 Excess of freeways
21 Smog devices
22 Supervision of automobiles

As you were listing ideas, some form of organization may have come into your mind. At least, logical groupings into main headings with supporting material under them should begin to emerge as you are working with and thinking about the material. Your next step is to group the material into major headings and place under these future main ideas the items that in your opinion belong with them as supporting material. In this operation, you may eliminate any weak or irrelevant points, that is, those items which, in your opinion, will not develop the thesis. Your groupings might look like the following informal outline. Note the number of items eliminated from the earlier listing.

THESIS: Two air pollutants are a danger to our health.

Dangerous air pollutants
    Threat to the world health
    Smog in the major cities
    70 percent of air pollutants still unidentified
    List of known air pollutants
    Thesis statement
Sulfur dioxide
    Most widely publicized
    How formed
    Danger level for humans
    Lethal effects on plants in various places
Carbon monoxide
    Why dangerous
    Automobile exhaust
    Increasing number of automobiles

The scratch or informal outline is satisfactory for organizing most short papers and brief written assignments and answers to examination questions that do not require long and complicated development.

ASSIGNMENT/INFORMAL OUTLINE
Prepare an informal outline for development of any one of the subjects that you investigated for the assignment on gathering material: Pollution, The Aztecs, Professional Basketball, or Saint Peter's Cathedral in Rome.

THESIS:

Formal outline

In structuring the formal outline, write the title of the paper in the center of the page. Underneath the title and to the far left margin, write *thesis statement* and follow it with a concise statement of your thesis. Indicate your major divisions of thought (main ideas of paragraphs or paragraph units) with Roman numerals I, II, III, etc. Underneath these

major headings place the subheadings (indicating support or explanatory material) indicated by the capital letters A, B, C, etc. If additional
subdividing is necessary use the numbers 1, 2, 3, etc., and for further
subdividing under this division, the small letters of the alphabet a, b, c,
etc. Most papers do not require that the introduction and conclusion
be included in the formal outline. However, sometimes, because the
introduction is fully developed with considerable important information for the reader, it is best to include it in the outline as shown below.

TITLE

THESIS STATEMENT:
Introduction: _____
                A. _____
                B. _____
                C. _____
                    1. _____
                    2. _____

Study the model outline form that follows.

TITLE

THESIS STATEMENT:
   I. _____
     A. _____
         1. _____
         2. _____
             a. _____
             b. _____
             c. _____
     B. _____
         1. _____
         2. _____
         3. _____
         4. _____
     C. _____
     D. _____
         1. _____
         2. _____
  II. _____
     A. _____
     B. _____
     C. _____
     D. _____

III. _____

  A. _____

    1. _____

    2. _____

    3. _____

    4. _____

  B. _____

    1. _____

      a. _____

      b. _____

    2. _____

      a. _____

      b. _____

      c. _____

  C. _____

    1. _____

    2. _____

    3. _____

  D. _____

If we are subdividing our thought into logical divisions or stages, we cannot have a I without a II, an A without a B, a 1 without a 2, or an a without a b.

There are three kinds of formal outlines: the *sentence outline,* the *topic outline,* and the *paragraph outline.* The sentence outline is best for structuring thought in long and complicated papers because each of the major headings and the minor headings is expressed in a complete sentence. Thus, the sentence outline forces you to think through each stage of your developing thought before writing. In addition, it will give your instructor or reader a better picture of exactly what you intend to do and enable him to more accurately follow each stage of

KILLERS IN THE AIR

THESIS STATEMENT: Air pollutants are threatening our world with devastation and death.

  I. Air pollutants are a hazard to health, even the cause of many deaths.

    A. People, plants, and animals sicken and die.

    B. Masonry crumbles, metal corrodes, and rubber and leather become hard and brittle.

SOURCE NOTE: The material for the outline examples was taken from an article in the May–June issue of *Health* entitled "Killers in the Air" and written by Judith McPherson, R.N.

    C. The air carries a startling mixture of harmful substances.
        1. Seventy percent of pollutants are still unidentified.
        2. A list of the identified air pollutants includes sulfur dioxide, carbon (soot), carbon monoxide, and asbestos.

II. Sulfur dioxide is the most widely publicized of the dangerous air pollutants.
    A. It is produced mainly by burning coal and certain fuel oils.
    B. Sulfur dioxide attacks plant life.
        1. Both flowers and trees can be damaged, even killed by it.
           a. Thousands of acres of deciduous forest in Montana, Tennessee, Ontario, and British Columbia have been destroyed by it.
           b. Lettuce and spinach have been practically eliminated as healthy crops in the Los Angeles Basin.
        2. Citrus yields in the Los Angeles Basin have been cut in half.
    C. Sulfur dioxide can be lethal to humans.
        1. When the level of sulfur dioxide in the air is at 0.11 part per million for three days, it will have an adverse effect on the health of the contaminated community.
        2. When it is at a level of 0.52 part per million for three days, authorities have come to expect an increased death rate.

III. Carbon or soot is another dangerous pollutant.
    A. It is a product of fuel combustion.
    B. In New York, Chicago, and Detroit more than 730 tons of suspended particles, including carbon, are deposited in each square mile every year.
    C. Soot soils clothes, penetrates closed windows, defaces fresh-fallen snow, and gets in our eyes.
    D. Soot carries cancer-causing hydrocarbons beyond the protective mucociliary lining of the lungs.
        1. Hydrocarbons are found specifically in petroleum, natural gas, and coal.
        2. Jets spew out large quantities of hydrocarbons.
           a. It is estimated that one four-engine jet at full takeoff throttle produces the per-minute equivalent in pollution of 6,000 automobiles.
           b. Exhaust from the first plane in a takeoff lineup is sucked into the ventilation system of the plane following—and so on through the line.

IV. Carbon monoxide, odorless and colorless, is a known killer.
    A. It is dangerous because of the body's normal arrangement for oxygen transport.

1. The red blood cells contain hemoglobin, with which oxygen combines freely for transport to the target tissues and which then freely releases the oxygen for local use.
2. Like oxygen, carbon monoxide has a great affinity for hemoglobin; but unlike oxygen, carbon monoxide forms a tight bond with hemoglobin and is not freely released again.
3. Even when air contains only small quantities of carbon monoxide, the situation is dangerous, because molecule after molecule of hemoglobin is rendered unavailable for carrying oxygen.
4. Thus the body receives insufficient oxygen, and asphyxiation results.

B. Carbon monoxide is among the pollutants released in automobile exhaust.
1. Oxygen deprivation can affect persons who drive for prolonged periods on heavily trafficked roads.
2. Studies are presently under way to demonstrate the connection between highway accidents and blood levels of carbon monoxide in drivers.

V. The auto braking system is also a pollution culprit since it discharges particles of asbestos into the atmosphere.
A. Such particles are found in significant amounts in the lungs of urban dwellers.
B. Dr. Dubos has said, "there is no doubt that asbestos is a great health hazard."

You begin the topic outline in the same way as the sentence outline by writing the title and beneath it a complete statement of the thesis. Then, instead of expressing the major headings and minor headings in complete statement sentences, you suggest that thought with a word or group of words (a topic). It is an easy-to-construct outline and is very helpful in organizing thought for short papers, class lectures, and other assignments where the expression of the complete idea at each stage of the developing thought is not essential. A topic outline for "Killers in the Air" would look like the following:

KILLERS IN THE AIR

THESIS STATEMENT: Air pollutants are threatening our world with devastation and death.

I. Pollutants—a health hazard
  A. Effect on people, plants, and animals
  B. Effect on masonry, metal, rubber, and leather

PENINSULA COLLEGE LIBRARY
PORT ANGELES WASHINGTON

    C. Harmful substances in the air
       1. 70 percent unidentified pollutants
       2. List of identified pollutants
II. Sulfur dioxide most widely publicized
    A. Production
    B. Effect on plant life
       1. Damages or kills flowers and trees
          a. Destroyed deciduous forests in various places
          b. Effect on lettuce and spinach
       2. Attacks citrus in Los Angeles Basin
    C. Effect on humans
       1. Level of 0.11 part per million
       2. Level of 0.52 part per million
III. Carbon (soot)
    A. Production
    B. Quantities in various cities
    C. Effects
    D. Cancer-causing hydrocarbons
       1. Where found
       2. Jets
          a. Amount jets produce
          b. Jet exhaust
IV. Carbon monoxide
    A. Reason for danger
       1. Hemoglobin and oxygen
       2. Reaction of carbon monoxide with hemoglobin
       3. Effect of small quantities of carbon monoxide
       4. Asphyxiation
    B. Automobile exhaust
       1. Effect on humans
       2. Present studies
  V. Automobile braking system and asbestos
    A. Amounts in the lungs of urban dwellers
    B. Report of Dr. Dubos

The *paragraph outline* is of very little use to the beginning student except in preparing for the written examination. It presents only a rough guide to the organization of the material since the writer will give only the title, the thesis statement, and the main headings (topic sentences) of the separate divisions of the paper.

ASSIGNMENT/OUTLINING

Below are a number of items in a listing on the subject of drama. The title of the paper is "The Appeals of Drama" and the thesis statement reads: "The dramatic experience is very often a blend of several satisfactions." Select from the list four items that you consider major headings.

1 Drama tells an interesting story.

2 Men love to hear someone tell of excitement and adventure.

3 One should compare Ibsen with Arthur Miller.

4 Sir Laurence Olivier is an exciting Hamlet.

5 A drama is a means of extending ourselves beyond the narrow circle of everyday existence.

6 A theatergoer identifies with the characters and action on the stage.

7 He sees in the play universal patterns of behavior.

8 An audience finds pleasure in witnessing an achievement.

9 He appreciates the skill of the director, actor, and stage designer.

10 He enjoys comparing certain productions with other productions and acting with other acting.

11 Tragedy is serious.

12 Tragedy evokes a catharsis—a purging away, a cleansing of the ignoble, the mean, the base.

13 The dramatic experience is also a spiritual one.

14 The great works of drama depict great characters exploring the spiritual issues of life.

15 "Wonders are many, and none is more wonderful than man," said Sophocles.

ASSIGNMENT/OUTLINING

Study the sentence outline below. Rewrite the outline as a topic outline. The major headings are the correct headings for the previous assignment.

THE APPEALS OF DRAMA

THESIS: The dramatic experience is very often a blend of several satisfactions.

    I. Drama tells an interesting story.

        A. Man has always found delight in sharing tales of adventure and excitement, struggle and conflict.

            1. In primitive days, man, sitting by a fire, enjoyed hearing what happened next.

SOURCE NOTE: The material for this and the following assignment was taken with certain modifications from the following source: Theodore W. Hatlen, *Drama: Principles & Plays*, New York: Appleton-Century-Crofts, pp. 6–7. Copyright © 1967 by Meredith Publishing Company. Permission by Meredith Publishing Company.

      2. He has always listened with rapt attention to eyewitness accounts of happenings.

      3. He loves to listen to those who have a gift for re-creating an experience.

  B. More compelling is man's desire to see the events for himself.

      1. Narration, therefore, has become dramatization.

      2. The spectator shares the story vicariously when he sees it reenacted.

II. The audience finds pleasure in witnessing an achievement, in considering the manner in which a thing is done.

  A. The theatergoer may take naïve pleasure in the illusions created by the designer and the technical crew through their skillful use of canvas, lumber, paint, and light.

  B. As a connoisseur of performances, the spectator will find pleasure in comparing the acting of certain great performers in the same role.

      1. He may compare Sir Laurence Olivier's Hamlet with that of Sir Maurice Evans or Sir John Gielgud.

      2. He may compare Thomas Mitchell's Willie Loman with that of Lee Cobb.

  C. He notes the effectiveness of the ensemble acting.

  D. He observes the director's adroit use of pace and rhythm.

  E. He notes the actor's ability to react as well as to speak.

  F. He is aware of the appropriateness of the scenery in reinforcing the mood of the play.

III. A third satisfaction provided by the theater is its function as a means of extending ourselves beyond the narrow circle of everyday existence.

  A. The spectator's sympathies are aroused as he identifies himself with the characters and action before him.

  B. He becomes emotionally involved in the outcome.

  C. He often sees in the play universal patterns of behavior that parallel his own.

IV. The dramatic experience can also be a spiritual one.

  A. Aristotle suggested that tragedy is serious.

      1. It is elevated in scale.

      2. It evokes a catharsis—a purging away, a cleansing of the ignoble, the mean, the base.

  B. The great works of drama depict great characters exploring the great issues of life.

      1. "Wonders are many, and none is more wonderful than man," said Sophocles.

    2. The sufferings of Greek characters like Antigone and Oedipus were positive statements about the Greek view of life.

    3. The medieval dramatist in composing Everyman had the high purpose of presenting the process of salvation to mankind.

  C. In the masterpieces of drama, good and evil are ruthlessly examined, choices are made and judgments rendered which indicate the distilled wisdom of the race.

  D. Man's loftiest ideas and aspirations have been the significant content of drama.

ASSIGNMENT/OUTLINING

Construct a topic outline for a composition titled "Why I Came to College."

WRITE THE FIRST DRAFT

When you have completed the outline, you are ready to begin writing the first draft of the paper. Most of your thinking about the subject and organization of thought will have been done by this time, especially if you have constructed a sentence outline. The object of the first draft is to get your ideas on paper as quickly as possible. Use your outline as a guide, but modify it if necessary. If you cannot get started by developing an introduction, begin at the part that comes most easily and write the rest around it. Do not worry about punctuation, grammar, usage, and spelling at this time as you can work on correctness in the revision. Leave space in the margins and between the lines for revisions. When you have finished the first draft, set it aside, preferably overnight.

REVISE THE FIRST DRAFT

When you return to the paper, read it aloud. Make corrections in the margins and between lines. When you have finished, rewrite the paper with the improvements. Use the following questions for your revision.

Title

1 Is it interesting?

2 Does it indicate what the paper is about?

Thesis

1 Does it adequately limit the subject for the space and time requirements of the written assignment?

2 Does it express clearly the central thought that will lead to unity in development?

3 Is the thesis sentence expressed in specific terms so that it emphasizes the main idea?

Introduction

1 Does the paper require a formal introduction?
2 Will the introduction catch the reader's attention and make him want to read the material that follows?
3 Does the introduction tell the reader what the paper is about?
4 Does the introduction contain definitions and background material if those kinds of information are necessary for the reader's understanding?

Middle Paragraphs

1 Do the middle paragraphs relate to and develop the thesis?
2 Does each paragraph or paragraph unit have unity, order, coherence, and completeness?

Conclusion

1 Is the reader left hanging in the air?
2 Are there any unnecessary or irrelevant details in this paragraph?
3 Are there any new or undeveloped ideas in the final paragraph?
4 Does the paragraph bring the discussion to an end?

In checking your paper for correctness, make use of the information at the end of the book.

PREPARE THE FINAL PAPER

After you have finished your revision, write or type the final draft following the directions of your instructor. Most requirements are similar to the following:

1 Write legibly in blue or black ink or type double space on one side of the paper only (usually the paper is 8½ by 11 inches). Use lined paper for handwritten papers, unlined for typewritten papers.
2 In handwritten papers, center the title on the top line of the first page and leave a space between it and the first line of the composition. Do not enclose the title in quotation marks unless it is itself quoted material. With typewritten papers, center the title about 2½ inches from the top of the first page and leave about 1½ inches between it and the first line of the composition.
3 Leave margins—2 inches at the left and 1½ inches at top, right, and bottom. Indicate paragraph indentions by leaving ½ inch. With typewritten papers new paragraphs are indicated by leaving five spaces.
4 Number the pages after the first page in the upper right-hand corner in arabic numerals: 2, 3, 4, etc.

5 Hand in the paper flat with a title page on which you put whatever information the instructor wishes. The title page usually includes your name, the title of the composition, and the date.

Read the following model essay. Be prepared to answer questions on its structural organization.

BRITAIN'S "THIN BLUE LINE"—POLICE PREFER TOLERANCE TO
CARRYING GUNS
Don Cook

1 When the unarmed police of Britain have to face a mob of potentially violent demonstrators—as occasionally they must even in this law-abiding society—they use a technique unlike that of any other police force in the world.

2 They link arms and close up against the demonstrators face-to-face. There are no plastic shields or protective gear or truncheons, no weapons and no tear gas. The police are trained and instructed to act, in the words of a senior police commissioner, "as a defensive absorbent sponge." They also are expected to show tolerance and even humor, if possible, and above all to avoid behavior which would be provocative or incite the militants in any mob to real violence.

3 Of course the "thin blue line" is broken on occasion, and truncheons are brought into play by police reserves. The British press has printed its share of photos of demonstrators being hustled into police wagons with their arms twisted behind them and their faces streaming with blood. But it is still difficult to get anybody in Britain to call a policeman a pig.

4 Without any doubt, there is a violent streak in British character. From Shakespeare to Ian Fleming there is violence in British literature, and British history for all its romance and pageantry is not much less bloody than the history of France or Spain. Cromwell in Ireland, the Sepoy rebellion in India, the Boer War, the subjugation and rule of the British Empire, the very style and panache with which the British army still whets its appetite on a whiff of grapeshot—all attest to a ruthless, icy quality with which the British can act when they feel it necessary.

5 Nevertheless, among themselves and undisturbed, there is nothing the British treasure more than the national image of a peace-loving, law-abiding, nonviolent society. The very closeness of living on a crowded industrialized island has bred a long tradition and habit of respect for the law as the arbiter of society. No people in the world form queues as automatically and patiently as the British—whether they are boarding a bus or buying a cup of tea.

SOURCE NOTE: Don Cook, "Britain's 'Thin Blue Line'—Police Prefer Tolerance to Carrying Guns," *Los Angeles Times,* Apr. 16, 1972, sec. G, p. 4. Copyright © 1972 by the Los Angeles Times Company.

6 Not one British policeman in a hundred would declare that he thinks he ought to be carrying a gun to do his job. The policeman who shepherds school children across a traffic intersection is the same policeman who is called upon for crowd control.

7 To a remarkable degree in a period in which violence is on the rise, tolerance remains the key to the British attitude. It is, however, a tolerance possible only because it is based on the strong public support for law and order which is part of British national character and which is backed up by a judiciary which can be swift and even ruthless when prosecutions for violence reach the courts.

8 The very speed with which the law can act in Britain—as compared with the United States—is vital to the British way of coping with violence.

9 Perhaps for the very reason of the traditions and self-image of a nonviolent society, the British are currently involved in an almost continuous public and political discussion of "what to do about violence."

10 By U.S. standards, their problem is miniscule.

11 "Teacher Said To Have Broken a Pupil's Jaw" ran a headline in the Times of London a few weeks ago. The incident became something of a national test case on the legal rights of a teacher who is attacked by a student to strike back. It was a case of "the law" intervening to set a limit on tolerance of violence.

12 A 15-year-old student, husky and well-developed, became rude, abusive and obstreperous in a classroom in Birmingham. The teacher tried to restrain the boy, and finally clipped him on the chin and laid him out cold—breaking the boy's jaw in the process. The parents sued the teacher for damages. It then developed that the boy by his own admission had taken LSD. Said the British judge in charging the jury:

13 "Have we really reached a stage in schools in this country where an insolent pupil has to be treated with all the courtesies of visiting royalty? Whatever may be the views of some of our most advanced theoreticians, the law does not require a teacher to have the patience of a saint."

14 The teacher was acquitted.

15 In a tight and homogeneous society such as Britain's, a single case of this kind can set the tone for the courts, the teachers and the pupils throughout the country.

16 Nevertheless, violence poses an increasing problem in Britain, with the police more often encountering situations in which a retreat in the face of threatened violence is the better way of preserving public order.

17 William F. Deedes, a Conservative member of Parliament and the chairman of the House of Commons Home Affairs Committee, cites a recent case during the long coal miners strike in February, in which 1,500 miners converged on Westminster. The miners demanded entry into the Parliament building to protest the slowness with which their pay claim was being dealt. Tempers were high—particularly among Tory members of the House of Commons who judged that the miners had already overdone things by picketing the electric power plants and carrying their strike to a secondary boycott.

18 "I rounded up some of the members of my committee and took them outside to witness the scene," Deedes said. "There were perhaps 150 policemen trying to control 10 times their number, and I said to my colleagues—all right, you are the police commissioner. What orders are you now going to give the policemen? Are you going to tell them to pull out their batons and break up the demonstrators, or are you going to let them into the building?"

19 Against instructions to keep the miners out, the police gave way and allowed about 500 of the demonstrators to enter St. Stephens Hall to make their protest. Right of assembly, right of protest, right of demonstration had been preserved—and the public peace had been preserved as well, even though a literal local order had been breached.

20 "A dual policy suggests itself," said Deedes, in discussing the problem of containing violence. "First it is to contain the challenge peaceably if possible in the interests of public safety. Then, when the law is defied, to identify the organizers and later summons them under the appropriate law. If they fail to appear, they can be arrested, but there is no occasion to raise the temperature of a demonstration by arresting them on the spot."

21 In a very British way, this combines tolerance and firmness—demonstrate now but pay later.

22 To keep the problem within bounds, the government has the past two weeks taken several steps which Deedes describes as "warning shots across the bows." On the order of Home Secretary Reginald Maudling there is to be a review of violence in films, triggered in particular by the films "A Clockwork Orange" and "Klute."

23 Meanwhile, the British Broadcasting Corp., taking the hint of the government's mood, has also instigated an examination of the degree and necessity of violence in its television programs. British commercial television is quietly following suit.

24 And the minister of education has ordered a study of violence among school children with the aim of establishing causes of classroom disturbances and the best methods of dealing with it.

25 Thus, on balance, the general attitude and policy of tolerance and the "thin blue line" still seems to work in containing violence.

26 The police in Britain are always ready to cooperate with peaceful demonstrators, providing them with an escort of bored bobbies along a specified line of march. And even when such restrictions do not appeal to the demonstrators the British remain determined to try to avoid violence.

STRUCTURE REVIEW TWO/ANALYZING THE PLAN

Name _____ Class _____

Answer each question in the space provided below it.

1 Does the writer state clearly his thesis at the beginning? at the end of the essay?

2 How does the writer indicate his purpose in the introductory paragraphs?

3 Which paragraph do you consider to be the first of the middle paragraphs or body of the essay?

4 In the middle paragraphs, how many major points in support of his view does the writer consider? In other words, what are the topic sentences of the paragraphs or paragraph units that constitute the middle or body of the essay?

5 What is the main idea of paragraph 4? With what kind of support does the writer develop his main idea?

6 How does the guide word "nevertheless" in paragraph 5 and paragraph 16 help the reader follow the change in the direction of the writer's thought?

7 What is the function of paragraph 15? paragraph 21?

8 What main idea unifies the paragraph unit consisting of paragraphs 11 through 15?

9 What paragraphs develop the main idea stated in paragraph 16?

10   What is the function of the final paragraph?

ANSWER SECTION

STRUCTURE REVIEW TWO

1   He states his thesis in the final paragraph.

2   He gives an example of a technique "unlike that of any other police force in the world." Then, in paragraph 2, he explains the method of tolerance that the police force uses; he writes, "The police are trained and instructed to act, in the words of a senior police commissioner, 'as a defensive absorbent sponge.'" "They also are expected to show tolerance and even humor, if possible, and above all to avoid behavior which would be provocative or incite the militants in any mob to real violence."

3   Paragraph 5. "Nevertheless, among themselves and undisturbed, there is nothing the British treasure more than the national image of a peace-loving, law-abiding, nonviolent society."
This is the first point that supports the reasons for the "Thin Blue Line."

4   The middle paragraphs may be broken down into five major points signaled by the following topic sentences.

   a   Paragraphs 5 and 6 develop the first main point. The topic sentence is stated above—"Nevertheless, among themselves. . . ."

   b   Paragraphs 7 and 8 develop the second major point:
"It is, however, a tolerance possible only because it is based on the strong public support for law and order which is part of British national character and which is backed up by a judiciary which can be swift and even ruthless when prosecutions for violence reach the courts."

   c   The paragraph unit consisting of paragraphs 9 through 15 develops the writer's third point.
"The British are currently involved in an almost continuous public and political discussion of 'what to do about violence.'"

   d   Point four is developed in paragraphs 16 through 21. This paragraph unit is introduced by the main idea that reads:
"A retreat in the face of violence is the better way of preserving public order."

   e   The final point (number 5) is developed in the paragraph unit made up of paragraphs 22 to 24.
"To keep the problem within bounds, the government has the past two weeks taken several steps which Deedes describes as 'warning shots across the bows.'"

5   The main idea of paragraph 4, stated in the first line, reads, "Without any doubt, there is a violent streak in British character." It is supported with examples from English history.

6 The guide word "nevertheless," in paragraphs 5 and 16, means "in spite of that" or "however." It leads the reader smoothly into a change in the direction of the writer's thought to contrasting statements to what he has just been discussing.

7 They serve to conclude the previous discussion by stating a result of those circumstances. Thus, they serve to emphasize the main point he uses to support his thesis. In addition, they mark clearly the end of a particular part of the discussion.

8 See answer to question 4, part *c* above.

9 See answer to question 4, part *d* above.

10 To conclude the paper by stating the thesis.

4 Narration and Description

The traditional methods of developing thought for written communication are *narration, description, exposition,* and *persuasion (argumentation).* In the remaining pages of this book, each order of organizing and developing thought will be treated in some detail. At this time, however, let us briefly introduce you to the orders of development so that you can see the variety of choices that have proved successful in organizing thought.

Often in working with a subject, you will find that the order of development is inherent in the material itself; thus, narration and description may be grouped in a class of *natural order of development. Narration* tells a story. You will find that the events that make up the action of the story move along in the *natural order of time (chronological order),* beginning usually with the earliest incidents and progressing through a related chain of occurrences to the high point of the action. In *description* (painting a verbal picture of some person, place, or thing), you move through the *natural order of space (spatial order)* from left to right, right to left, top to bottom, bottom to top, etc.

In developing thought for *exposition,* where your purpose is to inform or explain, you will find it necessary to impose some kind of order on the material depending upon your purpose and the nature of the supporting material. Thus, the kinds of development best suited for exposition may be grouped into the class of *imposed order of development.* The same is true of *persuasion,* where your purpose is to convince a reader to accept your point of view.

Exposition may be organized and developed by a variety of effective orders or methods. You may develop by *comparison* in order to show likenesses between two or among three or more persons, places, things, or ideas. You may *contrast* to show differences. You may develop by *analogy* to make clear and meaningful the unfamiliar by comparing it to the familiar (a subject known by the reader). You may wish to give directions or show how something is done or how something happened so you organize and develop a *process.* For convenience in explaining a subject or proving a point of view about it, you may break a subject down into its component parts *(partition),* into classes *(classification),* or into *causes* and *effects* or *effects* and *causes* *(causal analysis).* You may find it necessary to define terms or expressions beyond the simple dictionary meaning; therefore you write an *extended definition.* Finally, even though one method will be dominant in the organization because of your purpose or intent, you will organize and develop your thought, more often than not, by a *combination of methods.*

When you have learned to organize with these methods, you will also be able to make good use of them in writing the persuasion paper.

NARRATION

Narration tells a story. It has a beginning, a middle, and an end, even though it may start in the middle or at some other point in the action and move backward to the earlier happenings. Narration moves through *time,* usually starting with the earliest happenings and moving through incidents and events in order of their occurrence. Narration revolves around people in some kind of *struggle (conflict)* against other people, nature, society, or themselves. In the conflict, the leading character *(protagonist)* battles against some force or forces *(antagonist)* with the outcome of the struggle usually in doubt. As the action progresses, intensity increases and tension builds until the highest point in the struggle *(climax)* is reached. The story then moves rapidly to a conclusion *(denouement).* Action *(plot)* usually dominates narration; however, some narratives focus on *character, theme* (the idea behind the story), *atmosphere* (the mood or tone).

NOTE: At this time, the student may wish to read the short stories in the last section.

In telling a story, a writer cannot possibly recount everything that takes place; therefore, he selects those incidents and happenings that will best fulfill his purpose. In the model narration that follows, "Face to Face with Hurricane Camille," the writer Joseph P. Blank does not attempt to tell us everything that happened from the time the Koshaks decided to "batten down and ride it out." Instead, he presents a series of events that focus on the struggle between the Koshaks and hurricane Camille that "brought a night of terror such as few people have ever experienced."

The organizational pattern is simple—an introduction, a middle, and a conclusion. In the early paragraphs (1–6), Blank gives the time and place of the action *(setting)*. In addition, he introduces the characters and emphasizes the might of hurricane Camille. He moves through time, beginning with preparations during the day and moving onward to 7:00 P.M. when the hurricane really begins.

He organizes the middle by statements concerning the hurricane and follows with incidents showing how the Koshaks and their friends struggled against each onslaught. "As the wind mounted to a roar, the house began leaking. . . . At 8:30, the power failed, and Pop Koshak turned on the generator" (paragraph 7). "The roar of the hurricane now was overwhelming" (paragraph 8). "The wind sounded like the roar of a train passing a few yards away" (paragraph 13). "A moment later, the hurricane, in one mighty swipe, lifted the entire roof off the house and skimmed it 40 feet through the air" (paragraph 18). Each new attack by Camille brings heroic action by the Koshaks. As the intensity of the storm increases, so does the tension since it appears that the Koshaks cannot possibly survive. They retreat up the stairs because the living room and the fireplace and its chimney collapse; as two walls begin to disintegrate, they race from the sanctuary of the bedroom into the television room, the one farthest from the direction of the storm. They pray for their lives. "Pop Koshak raged silently, frustrated at not being able to do anything to fight Camille." Finally, they face the entire might of Camille—"the world seemed to be breaking apart." "The floor tilted"; "a third wall gave way"; "water lapped across the slanting floor." They decide to place the kids on a door if the floor goes. Tension is at its highest; all seems lost. "In that moment [the climax], the wind slightly diminished, and the water stopped rising. Then the water began receding. The main thrust of Camille had passed. The Koshaks and their friends had survived."

In the final paragraphs, the writer tells of efforts of the Koshaks and other Gulfport families to reorganize their lives. In the final paragraph, Joseph P. Blank restates the purpose in the reflection of Grandmother Koshak: "We lost practically all our possessions, but the family came through it. When I think of that, I realize we lost nothing important."

In addition to selectivity, character, plot, atmosphere, setting, and conflict, *point of view* is also important in organizing and developing narration. Point of view is the manner in which a writer tells his story; it indicates through whose eyes the reader will view the action. Point of view, like time movement, gives order to the events or happenings. Moreover, it shows the relationship of the narrator (the teller of the story) to the action. A very commonly used point of view is *third person omniscient* (an all-knowing view) because it permits the writer to tell everything he chooses and to express the feelings and thoughts of the characters involved in the action. In "Face to Face with Hurricane Camille," we see the action, for the most part, through the eyes of John Koshak, Jr., the protagonist. But, we see many more incidents than those John Koshak, Jr., himself experiences, and we know the thoughts and feelings of the various characters in the struggle. Thus, the point of view is third person omniscient. If Joseph P. Blank had limited the action to simply what John Koshak, Jr., saw and felt, he would have written the story in the *third person objective.* Another common point of view, especially for personal experience stories, is the *first person,* using the pronoun "I." The writer himself may be the protagonist (see "Football Banquet Affair" and "The Convert" in the final section), or the writer may tell the story by a minor character in the first person. Other points of view are the third person plural ("they") and the second person ("you"), in which the reader becomes part of the action.

FACE TO FACE WITH HURRICANE CAMILLE

Joseph P. Blank

Introduction
Time
Place

1   John Koshak, Jr., knew that Hurricane Camile would be bad. Radio and television warnings had sounded throughout that Sunday, last August 17, as Camille lashed northwestward across the Gulf of Mexico. It was certain to pummel Gulfport, Miss., where the Koshaks lived. Along the coasts of Louisiana, Mississippi and Alabama, nearly 150,000 people fled inland to

Introduces
characters
in the story

safer ground. But, like thousands of others in the coastal communities, John was reluctant to abandon his home unless the family—his wife, Janis, and their seven children, aged 3 to 11—was clearly endangered.

2   Trying to reason out the best course of action, he talked with his father and mother, who had moved into the ten-room

Source note: Joseph P. Blank, "Face to Face with Hurricane Camille," *Reader's Digest,* March 1970, pp. 62–67. Copyright © 1970 by the Reader's Digest Association, Inc.

house with the Koshaks a month earlier from California. He also consulted Charles Hill, a longtime friend, who had driven from Las Vegas for a visit.

Background

3 John, 37—whose business was right there in his home (he designed and developed educational toys and supplies, and all of Magna Products' correspondence, engineering drawings and art work were there on the first floor)—was familiar with the power of a hurricane. Four years earlier, Hurricane Betsy had demolished his former home a few miles west of Gulfport (Koshak had moved his family to a motel for the night). But that house had stood only a few feet above sea level. "We're elevated 23 feet," he told his father, "and we're a good 250 yards from the sea. The place has been here since 1915, and no hurricane has ever bothered it. We'll probably be as safe here as anyplace else."

Mention of conflict—man versus hurricanes

4 The elder Koshak, a gruff, warmhearted expert machinist of 67, agreed. "We can batten down and ride it out," he said. "If we see signs of danger, we can get out before dark."

Preparations for struggle begins movement through time

5 The men methodically prepared for the hurricane. Since water mains might be damaged, they filled bathtubs and pails. A power failure was likely, so they checked out batteries for the portable radio and flashlights, and fuel for the lantern. John's father moved a small generator into the downstairs hallway, wired several light bulbs to it and prepared a connection to the refrigerator.

Time element Beginning of hurricane Middle section

6 Rain fell steadily that afternoon; gray clouds scudded in from the Gulf on the rising wind. The family had an early supper. A neighbor, whose husband was in Vietnam, asked if she and her two children could sit out the storm with the Koshaks. Another neighbor came by on his way inland—would the Koshaks mind taking care of his dog?

Time sequence

7 It grew dark before seven o'clock. Wind and rain now whipped the house. John sent his oldest son and daughter upstairs to bring down mattresses and pillows for the younger children. He wanted to keep the group together on one floor. "Stay away from the windows," he warned, concerned about glass flying from storm-shattered panes. As the wind mounted to a roar, the house began leaking—the rain seemingly driven right through the walls. With mops, towels, pots and buckets the Koshaks began a struggle against the rapidly spreading water. At 8:30, power failed, and Pop Koshak turned on the generator.

Increase of tension as storm increases in violence Time sequence

8 The roar of the hurricane now was overwhelming. The house shook, and the ceiling in the living room was falling

piece by piece. The French doors in an upstairs room blew in with an explosive sound, and the group heard gun-like reports as other upstairs windows disintegrated. Water rose above their ankles.

Details of the strug-gle as con-flict devel-ops

9 Then the front door started to break away from its frame. John and Charlie put their shoulders against it, but a blast of water hit the house, flinging open the door and shoving them down the hall. The generator was doused, and the lights went out. Charlie licked his lips and shouted to John, "I think we're in real trouble. That water tasted salty." The sea had reached the house, and the water was rising by the minute!

10 "Everybody out the back door to the cars!" John yelled. "We'll pass the children along between us. Count them! Nine!"

11 The children went from adult to adult like buckets in a fire brigade. But the cars wouldn't start; the electrical systems had been killed by water. The wind was too strong and the water too deep to flee on foot. "Back to the house!" John yelled. "Count the children! Count nine!"

12 As they scrambled back, John ordered, "Everybody on the stairs!" Frightened, breathless and wet, the group settled on the stairs, which were protected by two interior walls. The children put the cat, Spooky, and a box with her four kittens on the landing. She peered nervously at her litter. The neighbor's dog curled up and went to sleep.

13 The wind sounded like the roar of a train passing a few yards away. The house shuddered and shifted on its founda-tions. Water inched its way up the steps as first-floor outside

Conflict heightens

walls collapsed. No one spoke. Everyone knew there was no escape; they would live or die in the house.

14 Charlie Hill had more or less taken responsibility for the neighbor and her two children. The mother was on the verge of panic. She clutched his arm and kept repeating, "I can't swim, I can't swim."

15 "You won't have to," he told her, with outward calm. "It's bound to end soon."

16 Grandmother Koshak reached an arm around her hus-band's shoulder and put her mouth close to his ear. "Pop," she said, "I love you." He turned his head and answered, "I love you"—and his voice lacked its usual gruffness.

17 John watched the water lap at the steps, and felt a crush-ing guilt. He had underestimated the ferocity of Camille. He had assumed that what had never happened could not happen. He held his head between his hands, and silently prayed: "Get us through this mess, will You?"

18 A moment later, the hurricane, in one mighty swipe, lifted the entire roof off the house and skimmed it 40 feet through the air. The bottom steps of the staircase broke apart. One wall began crumbling on the marooned group.

Information to tell reader about the power of the hurricane

Dr. Robert H. Simpson, director of the National Hurricane Center in Miami, Fla., graded Hurricane Camille as "the greatest recorded storm ever to hit a populated area in the Western Hemisphere." In its concentrated breadth of some 70 miles it shot out winds of nearly 200 m.p.h. and raised tides as much as 30 feet. Along the Gulf Coast it devastated everything in its swath: 19,467 homes and 709 small businesses were demolished or severely damaged. It seized a 600,000-gallon Gulfport oil tank and dumped it 3½ miles away. It tore three large cargo ships from their moorings and beached them. Telephone poles and 20-inch-thick pines cracked like guns as the winds snapped them.

To the west of Gulfport, the town of Pass Christian was virtually wiped out. Several vacationers at the luxurious Richelieu Apartments there held a hurricane party to watch the storm from their spectacular vantage point. Richelieu Apartments were smashed apart as if by a gigantic fist, and 26 people perished.

Conflict heightens

Writer builds to his climax

19 Seconds after the roof blew off the Koshak house, John yelled, "Up the stairs—into our bedroom! Count the kids." The children huddled in the slashing rain within the circle of adults. Grandmother Koshak implored, "Children, let's sing!" The children were too frightened to respond. She carried on alone for a few bars; then her voice trailed away.

20 Debris flew as the living-room fireplace and its chimney collapsed. With two walls in their bedroom sanctuary beginning to disintegrate, John ordered, "Into the television room!" This was the room farthest from the direction of the storm.

Writer is showing the courage of the individuals in the struggle

21 For an instant, John put his arm around his wife. Janis understood. Shivering from the wind and rain and fear, clutching two children to her, she thought, *Dear Lord, give me the strength to endure what I have to*. She felt anger against the hurricane. *We won't let it win.*

22 Pop Koshak raged silently, frustrated at not being able to *do* anything to fight Camille. Without reason, he dragged a cedar chest and a double mattress from a bedroom into the TV room. At that moment, the wind tore out one wall and extinguished the lantern. A second wall moved, wavered. Charlie Hill tried to support it, but it toppled on him, injuring his back. The house, shuddering and rocking, had moved 25 feet from its foundations. The world seemed to be breaking apart.

Tension increases

23 "Let's get that mattress up!" John shouted to his father. "Make it a lean-to against the wind. Get the kids under it. We can prop it up with our heads and shoulders!"

24 The larger children sprawled on the floor, with the smaller ones in a layer on top of them, and the adults bent over all nine. The floor tilted. The box containing the litter of kittens slid off a shelf and vanished in the wind. Spooky flew off the top of a sliding bookcase and also disappeared. The dog cowered with eyes closed. A third wall gave way. Water lapped across the

Highest point in action

slanting floor. John grabbed a door which was still hinged to one closet wall. "If the floor goes," he yelled at his father, "let's get the kids on this."

Climax

25 *In that moment, the wind slightly diminished, and the water stopped* rising. Then the water began receding. *The main thrust of Camile had passed.* The Koshaks and their friends had survived. (Italics added.)

Time sequence

Effects of the hurricane

With the dawn, Gulfport people started coming back to their homes. They saw human bodies—more than 130 men, women and children died along the Mississippi coast—and parts of the beach and highway were strewn with dead dogs, cats, cattle. Strips of clothing festooned the standing trees, and blown-down power lines coiled like black spaghetti over the roads.

None of the returnees moved quickly or spoke loudly; they stood shocked, trying to absorb the shattering scenes before their eyes. "What do we do?" they asked. "Where do we go?"

By this time, organizations within the area and, in effect, the entire population of the United States had come to the aid of the devastated coast. Before dawn, the Mississippi National Guard and civil-defense units were moving in to handle traffic, guard property, set up communications centers, help clear the debris and take the homeless by truck and bus to refugee centers. By 10 a.m., the Salvation Army's canteen trucks and Red Cross volunteers and staffers were going wherever possible to distribute hot drinks, food, clothing and bedding.

From hundreds of towns and cities across the country came several million dollars in donations; household and medical supplies streamed in by plane, train, truck and car. The federal government shipped 4,400,000 pounds of food, moved in mobile homes, set up portable classrooms, opened offices to provide low-interest, long-term business loans.

Camille, meanwhile, had raked its way northward across Mississippi, dropping more than 28 inches of rain into West Virginia and southern Virginia, causing rampaging floods, huge mountain slides and 111 additional deaths before breaking up over the Atlantic Ocean.

Time element

26 Like many other Gulfport families, the Koshaks quickly began reorganizing their lives. John divided his family in the homes of two friends. The neighbor with her two children went to a refugee center. Charlie Hill found a room for rent. By Tuesday, Charlie's back had improved, and he pitched in with Seabees in the worst volunteer work of all—searching for bodies. Three days after the storm, he decided not to return to Las Vegas, but to "remain in Gulfport and help rebuild the community."

Time element

27 Near the end of the first week, a friend offered the Koshaks his apartment, and the family was reunited. The children appeared to suffer no psychological damage from their experience; they were still awed by the incomprehensible power of the hurricane, but enjoyed describing what they had seen and heard on that frightful night. Janis had just one delayed reaction. A few nights after the hurricane, she awoke suddenly at 2 A.M. She quietly got up and went outside. Looking up at the sky and, without knowing she was going to do it, she began to cry softly.

Characterization

28 Meanwhile, John, Pop and Charlie were picking through the wreckage of the home. It could have been depressing, but it wasn't: each salvaged item represented a little victory over the wrath of the storm. The dog and cat suddenly appeared at the scene, alive and hungry.

But the blues did occasionally afflict all the adults. Once, in a low mood, John said to his parents, "I wanted you here so that we would all be together, so you could enjoy the children, and look what happened."

29 His father, who had made up his mind to start a welding shop when living was normal again, said, "Let's not cry about what's gone. We'll just start all over."

"You're great," John said. "And this town has a lot of great people in it. It's going to be better here than it ever was before."

Purpose of the writer

30 Later, Grandmother Koshak reflected: "We lost practically all our possessions, but the family came through it. When I think of that, I realize we lost nothing important." (Blank's italics except in paragraph indicated.)

STRUCTURE REVIEW THREE/NARRATION

Name _____ Class _____

Answer each question in the space provided below it.

1 Who is the protagonist?

2 What opposing forces make up the conflict?

3 What information in the setting is especially important to the story?

4 What is the dominant point of view (through whose eyes do we see the action)?

5 How does the writer give order and logical movement to the sequence of happenings?

6 Does the writer focus chiefly on developing character, action (plot), or idea (theme)?

7 At what point in the story does the action reach its highest point?

8 At what point would you have ended the story? Why?

9 In what ways does the writer hold his readers in suspense?

10 Why do you think the writer interrupted the narration to present data about the tremendous might of the hurricane? Can you think of a better way to fulfill this purpose?

See answers on page 130.
A writer often tells a story when his interest is something other than a presentation of interesting—and exciting—series of incidents. He will use the happenings and action to develop a *theme*—the dominant idea of the piece of writing. He has a purpose for telling the story, for example, to show the indomitable courage of the Koshaks and their friends in the life-death struggle with hurricane Camille. Oftentimes,

the writer of this kind of narration will clearly reveal his purpose in a concisely stated thesis sentence at the beginning of the story or at its end as in "Face to Face with Hurricane Camille."

GUIDE TO NARRATION

1 *Character(s)* is a term applied to human beings in a story. The leading character in a struggle is called the *protagonist;* his opponent is the *antagonist.* Some stories are termed *stories of character* because the writer's intent is to focus on character delineation.

2 *Climax* is the highest point in a story, the point when tension is greatest. The struggle between the opposing forces has reached a breaking point. The climax brings about a resolution of the struggle.

3 *Conflict* is struggle between opposing forces. Some of the most common conflicts are the following: man against man, man against nature, man against society, man against himself.

4 *Expository narration* is telling a story to explain or inform.

5 *Narration* is telling a story. Narration is a series of connected events or happenings that have a beginning, a middle, and an end. Action is the dominant feature of narration.

6 *Plot* is the plan or arrangement of incidents in time.

7 *Point of view* is the writer's choice of the individual through whose eyes he will tell the story.

8 *Protagonist* is the leading character in a story. *Antagonist* is the opponent or opposing force in a conflict.

9 *Selectivity* applies to the writer's choice of events and happenings in a story plot. Since he cannot tell everything that occurred, he must select those events that will fulfill his purpose.

10 *Theme* is the idea revealing the purpose behind the story.

11 *Time order* is development of a story or piece of writing according to the time that happenings occurred. *Altered time order,* known as the *flashback technique* in motion pictures, is a method of beginning in the middle of the action and returning to the beginning to move forward again. It applies also to beginning the story at other places in the action and returning to continue with the story.

THE DAY SING SING LICKED US
Edwin D. Barton

The finest basketball player I have ever seen was a stumpy, courageous, unknown convict at Sing Sing Prison. For one unforgettable afternoon, his bril-

SOURCE NOTE: Edwin D. Barton, "The Day Sing Sing Licked Us," *Coronet,* (December 1960), 33–37. Copyright © 1960 by Coronet.

liant play pierced the gray gloom of the "Big House" and brought hardened prisoners out of their seats cheering and even weeping, stirred by a college spirit few had ever known. Singlehandedly, he defeated my team—an all-star squad from the Columbia University College of Physicians and Surgeons— but I would not trade that one defeat for all our victories. The story began six year ago, when I became Student Activities Director at the Columbia medical school. Our basketball captain, Howard Nay, urged me to schedule tougher opponents. "The boys would like more of a fight," he said. The request prompted a major change in our policy. For the first time, we played against sterner, nonmedical school competition. Even so, we won with monotonous ease—except for one game. The Sing Sing team held us to a slim six-point margin, our closest call in years.

After the game, Gerald Curtin, the Sing Sing coach and recreation director, approached me. "How about a rematch next year?" he asked. "We still think we can beat you—especially since most of our starters will still be with us next season!"

I called a team meeting and found that the boys were all for another game with Sing Sing.

For one thing, they enjoyed the unique experience of penetrating the forbidden and mysterious prison walls. They also believed that as student doctors they were helping troubled men by providing them with an afternoon of lively recreation.

Once inside Sing Sing, vigilant guards treat even young visiting athletes as potential security risks. Before being loaded into a windowless "paddy wagon" for the short ride to the gym, they are searched thoroughly, and any metal object sharper than a cigarette lighter must be checked at the gatehouse. Then a guard asks for silence and delivers a short speech.

"I am the sergeant assigned to your supervision while you are inside the Prison," he says. "You are in my custody until you are checked back through the gate to the outside. Do not do anything without my specific permission. While you are playing, bear in mind that these men are convicted criminals. If you should see anyone you recognize, do not speak with him. During the game, do not talk with players except where it pertains to the game, and keep such conversation to technical basketball language."

With this, he signals the gateman in the tower, and the team is let through two successive steel gates. The last gate opens only wide enough to allow one man at a time to pass through, and on the other side the players are herded into the wagon, with a guard on each side.

In a few minutes, the truck backs up to the door of a large building. The guards step out and motion for the players to follow. All hustle directly into the building, through a door leading directly to the visiting team's dressing room. Again, the visitors are counted, and two guards remain with them as they put on their uniforms.

As our team trotted on court, I shook hands with Coach Curtin. As we chatted, he pointed to one of his Sing Sing players, a stocky fellow of about 25 who was shooting baskets at the far end of the court. "That's Corwin," Gerry told me. "He gets out tomorrow after serving a term for burglary. Two years ago, when he came to me, he had never played basketball. But he stuck with the game and worked up to a varsity position. Now I believe he's going to be all right on the outside. We won't be seeing him here again." Curtin smiled with satisfaction.

Just before the opening whistle, I called my players together. "Run up a quick lead so we can take it easy in the second half," I told them.

In accordance with our strategy, we rolled up 14 quick points to Sing Sing's two—a basket by Corwin. But the prison's players were beginning to recover from our opening attack. Corwin and their tall, redheaded center, Craft, began to find the range. By the end of the first quarter, our lead had been cut to four points.

Shortly before the half-time intermission, Corwin dribbled through our whole team and curled in yet another driving basket. Abruptly the scoreboard was changed to: Home 26; Visitors 25.

Normally, Sing Sing prisoners cheer for a good play or shot. They are not team conscious, however. But now a ripple of interest swept the stands. There was still little fervent cheering; the change was subtler and unique to Sing Sing.

High above the grandstand is the scoreboard. At floor level at the same end of the gymnasium is a huge blackboard with the word VISITORS in box-car letters. As messages are received that a prisoner has a visitor, the inmate's number is written on the blackboard. When a number went up, the designated man would leave for a rare visit with someone from the outside. But when Corwin sank the shot that put his team ahead, priority visibly shifted from the visitors' board to the scoreboard.

By this time, I sensed that my team was in trouble. Our rigorous medical-school work schedule precludes long practice sessions that would keep the team in top physical condition. Obviously, Gerry Curtin had schooled his players to run us into the floor. At the half, we were 11 points behind. Still, I had no doubt that after a rest we could regain the lead.

But as I returned to my seat in the gym after the intermission, I felt it would be almost impossible to root against Corwin, who not only was a magnificent player but a good sport. Not once during the hard-fought first half did he fail to have a smile on his face. He addressed himself to the contest as though it was a privilege to play. Although there was fierce, unavoidable body contact, he never complained—and often helped a fallen opponent to his feet. To beat Sing Sing, I knew we must stop the relentless attack of this smiling convict—but my heart wasn't in it.

"Corwin is just great this year," I told Coach Curtin as our paths crossed going to our respective benches. "I remember him from a year ago, and I've never seen an athlete develop so fast."

"We're lucky he's here today," answered Curtin. "He didn't want to play because he gets out tomorrow, and if he got badly banged up in the game, he might not be in shape to leave." But Corwin had decided to play. He wanted to help his team beat us—something that they had never done before—and he wanted to show his appreciation to Gerald Curtin, who had helped him find satisfaction in grueling discipline and honest achievement.

Early in the third period, we edged in front once again, but from then on the lead changed hands with every basket. Desperately, I made frequent substitutions in an effort to keep my team fresh. But Corwin remained in the Sing Sing line-up, apparently tireless and releasing bull's-eye shots despite the most careful guarding.

I could hardly believe my eyes. Corwin's legs were knotted and discolored by varicose veins. His calf muscles were lumped up in one spot, his locomotion was uneven and his pivoting jerky and awkward. His dribbling or shooting seemingly qualified him for an intramural basketball team and no more. Yet here he was leading a group of mediocre players in a nip-and-tuck duel with one of the fine graduate school teams in the Ivy League.

With ten minutes to go, the game was still in doubt. I put our first-string team back into the game, hoping that Charlie Bucknam, who had been an all-star player at Bates College, could stop Corwin's spectacular play. Bucknam had scored 34 points against Sing Sing the year before. But Corwin promptly went on a fantastic scoring spree. His teammates fed him the ball constantly, and he never seemed to miss. Inexorably, Sing Sing forged further and further ahead.

With one minute to go, Coach Curtin finally sent in a substitute for Corwin. The weary convict shook hands with Al Moscarella, who had been guarding him, and as he started toward the Sing Sing bench, his fellow inmates awoke to what was happening: Corwin was being taken out for the last time. I had never heard applause for a player at Sing Sing, but when someone yelled, "Corwin's coming out!" spontaneous cheers broke out and spectators began to rise, slowly at first, until every convict, official, guard and visiting player was on his feet. The place rang with a standing ovation for a stoop-shouldered little man who had mastered basketball and fought his heart out to bring inspiration to every inmate.

I knew the rules about not speaking to prisoners, but when the final horn sounded, I asked Coach Curtin if I could congratulate Corwin personally before he headed back to his cell block. But Curtin had anticipated my request. "Mr. Barton," he said. "I want you to meet one of our players." He pushed Corwin forward. I gripped his hand and told him that he had played the greatest game I had ever seen, wished him luck and invited him to visit me at any time.

Behind me all ten of our players had lined up to shake Corwin's hand. Out of the corner of my eye, I saw the sergeant who had ordered us not to speak to prisoners. I stared at him and he winked, a broad smile on his face.

On the way to the shower room, I looked at the stands, which last year had emptied seconds after the game was over. Hundreds of prisoners were still standing fast, a few of them with tears in their eyes, watching the Columbia players congratulate Corwin.

For that one moment, at least, Sing Sing was not a prison but a college of triumph and hope which all could attend.

STRUCTURE REVIEW FOUR/NARRATION

Name _____   Class _____

Answer each question in the space provided below it.

1 What is the function of the first paragraph?

2 What necessary background does the writer give the reader in the first paragraph?

3 Do you consider the title effective? Why? Why not?

4 Why do you think the writer devoted so much space to describing the experience of entering the prison?

5   What was the writer's purpose in discussing the system of announcing visitors?

6   From what point of view is the story told?

7   Who is the protagonist?

8   What do you consider to be the conflict?

9   Where in the story does the writer clearly reveal his theme?

10   What contrast is there between the attitude of the guards at the beginning of the story and at the end? Is this point important to the writer's purpose? Why?

ASSIGNMENT/STRUCTURING NARRATION

List in chronological (time) order the things that happened to you for a short period of time at school, at home, in a sporting event, at a dance or party, etc., that you think might serve later for a personal experience story.

With a definite purpose in mind, eliminate those incidents from your list that are not important to your plan.

Structure a topic outline of your personal experience.

ASSIGNMENT/WRITING NARRATION

1 Write on any one of the following suggested topics or develop a topic of your own, using the material completed for the previous assignment.
2 During your life you must have been frightened by some happening. Write a short expository narration of 200 or 300 words around a thesis that will lend itself to development by informing or explaining.
3 Write a short expository narration that develops any one of the following ideas or any similar idea:

My first lesson in the importance of schooling came about quite accidentally.

My first lesson in prejudice came when I went to camp.

Death had no real meaning for me until my mother died.

My first lesson in politics came when I campaigned for _____ .
4 Write a short expository narration telling how your dream or dreams were shattered.

DESCRIPTION

In describing, a writer paints a verbal picture of some place, thing, or person. In order to enable his reader to perceive the reality of the original, he reproduces an image and evokes that reality essentially by specific and concrete words that appeal to the reader's senses of sight, smell, sound, taste, and touch. A writer will seldom focus on description alone; he will usually blend it so smoothly and unobtrusively with other forms of writing that it is hardly distinguishable.

To create effective description, a writer must carefully select specific details, particular words, and a logical order of development. To describe well, a writer must first be a perceptive observer, noticing details that will reproduce the desired image of the original when he puts words on paper. He cannot hope to record every detail; such a presentation would result in a mere listing rather than a word picture. Instead, he must concentrate on selecting significant details that will suggest the original. In the description that follows, observe how

Washington Irving chose details that would suggest a man who looked like a crane.

The cognomen of Crane was not inapplicable to his person. He was tall, but exceedingly lank, with narrow shoulders, long arms and legs, hands that dangled a mile out of his sleeves, feet that might have served for shovels, and his whole frame most loosely hung together. His head was small, and flat at the top, with huge ears, large green glassy eyes, and a long snip nose, so that it looked like a weathercock perched upon his spindle neck to tell which way the wind blew. To see him striding along the profile of a hill on a windy day, with his clothes bagging and fluttering about him, one might have mistaken him for the genius of Famine descending upon the earth or some scarecrow eloped from a cornfield.[1]

Selection of words

To gain the kind of selectivity to write description like Washington Irving, a writer must learn about words. General and abstract words are of little value in describing. They refer to a class; therefore, they serve the purposes of exposition and argumentation well, where statements of opinions and ideas are important. Words, for example, like "animal," "dwelling," "clothes," "land," and "weather" are much too general to suggest images. Words like "large," "truth," "justice," "beautiful," and "happiness" are too abstract to evoke in the reader sensory perceptions.

Concrete and specific words, on the other hand, are the language of description. They refer to a particular member of a class; therefore, they narrow the reader's focus on a specific person, place, or thing. Along with figures of speech, they appeal to the reader's senses of sight, smell, sound, taste, and touch. In the model paragraph describing Ichabod Crane, Washington Irving writes that Crane "was tall, but exceedingly lank, with narrow shoulders, long arms and legs, hands that dangled a mile out of his sleeves, feet that might have served for shovels, and his whole frame most loosely hung together." Crane had "large green glassy eyes" and "a long snip nose."

In order to further suggest the image of a crane, Irving uses figures of speech—the simile and metaphor. He compares Crane's head to a weathercock—"it looked like a weathercock perched upon his spindle neck to tell which way the wind blew." And he enriches the total image with two metaphors comparing Crane to the "genius of Famine" and "a scarecrow eloped from a cornfield."

[1] Washington Irving, "The Legend of Sleepy Hollow," *Selected Writings of Washington Irving*, ed. Saxe Commins, pp. 23–24. Copyright © 1945 by Random House, Inc.

Figurative language or figures of speech are words and expressions used out of their literal sense to give vividness to writing and suggest pictures and images. Among the most common figures of speech are the following: simile, metaphor, personification, hyperbole, and allusion.

A *simile* states a direct comparison using the word "like" or "as."

Cigars are becoming as old fashioned as chin whiskers. (Keith Monroe)

The joints of their limbs were like knots in a rope. (Joseph Conrad)

A *metaphor* is an implied comparison without "like" or "as."

To the youth, it [the charge by the enemy] was an onslaught of redoubtable dragons. (Stephen Crane)

Personification is giving human characteristics to lifeless things.

It seemed now Nature had no ears. (Stephen Crane)

Hyperbole is emphasis by exaggeration.

. . . hands that dangled a mile out of his sleeves. (Washington Irving)

An *allusion* is a direct or indirect reference to familiar people or happenings, especially from art, history, literature, and mythology.

His whole high, broad form, seemed made of solid bronze, and shaped in an unalterable mold, like Cellini's cast of Perseus. (Thomas Hardy)

ASSIGNMENT/IDENTIFYING FIGURES OF SPEECH
In the blank below the example, identify the figure of speech as a simile, metaphor, personification, hyperbole, or allusion.

1   The seats sagged like the jowls of a bulldog. . . . (Truman Capote)

_____

2   But there is an influence in the light of the morning that tends to rectify whatever errors of fancy, or even of judgment, we may have incurred during the sun's decline, or among the shadows of the night, or in the less wholesome glow of moonshine. (Nathaniel Hawthorne)

_____

3   The elementary school was a big brick cube set in a square of black surfacing chalked and painted with dragons and runes of children's games. (John Updike)

_____

4 "By heavens if I had a thousand wild cats like you I could tear th' stomach outa this war in less'n a week." (Stephen Crane)

---

5 Festival fires to Thor and Woden had followed on the same ground and duly had their day. (Thomas Hardy)

---

6 He had been an animal blistered and sweating in the heat and pain of war. (Stephen Crane)

---

7 Indeed, it is pretty well known that such blazes as this the heathen men were now enjoying are rather the lineal descendants from the Druidical rites and Saxon ceremonies than the invention of popular feeling about Gunpower Plot. (Thomas Hardy)

---

8 Night's candles are burnt out, and jocund day
Stands tiptoe on the misty mountain tops. (William Shakespeare)

---

9 [The abandoned boat] tossed and gaped beneath the ship's bows like a chip at the base of a cataract. . . . (Herman Melville)

---

10 . . . feet that might have served for shovels . . . (Washington Irving)

NOTE: See answers on page 130.

Organizing description

Description is usually organized and developed by space order. The writer's flowing thought follows logically the movement of his eyes as they move over the subject. He first establishes a *point of view;* that is, he takes a fixed position in space or a moving position through space and describes what he sees. He may also establish a mental attitude toward his subject as part of his point of view. He selects details in some kind of logical order; he may concentrate on a dominant impression—the subject's long nose or angry flashing eyes—and then move onward to the other features cf the face and body; he may move from a distance to close up, from close up to a distance, from left to right, from right to left, from bottom to top, from top to bottom, etc. He chooses words that will reproduce the original according to his purpose. If he wishes to be essentially informative so that he can recreate an objective picture of the original, he selects unemotional and concrete words. If his wishes to reproduce an emotional view of the original, he will select words with connotative meanings that will evoke the same feelings he has toward the subject.

In the model description that follows, the writer presents an objective and informative picture of a Roman fortress. He views the structure first from outside to describe its resemblance to the Roman farm-forts, noting its thick walls and one entrance leading to eleven rooms. Then he shifts to a moving description of the interior as the reader follows the archaeologists into the fortress when they first entered it. He describes what they saw—a rectangular chamber with thick walls. Next, he moves to the soil-covered floor and then onward to what was beneath the floor and to another chamber—the tomb of Tin Hinan.

To the practised eye, the appearance of the fortress suggests some of the possible answers. We can see in it, for instance, some resemblances to the Roman farm-forts along the northern frontiers of the desert. The walls, on an average four feet thick, are built of basalt blocks, some of which have been squared off in the Roman manner. There is only one entrance, leading to eleven rooms which open out one from the other—again typical of the farm-houses along the *limes.* The room farthest from the entrance was found sealed off in the Franco-American excavations of 1926. Breaking in, the archaeologists found themselves in a rectangular chamber measuring about sixteen by twelve feet with walls eight feet thick. The floor of this room was covered with soil and, under the debris, a layer of stone chips; and under this flooring six large monoliths, the biggest of which measured nearly seven feet long, a foot wide, and five inches thick. When these stone slabs were removed, the excavators looked down into another chamber, seven feet long, four feet wide, and four feet high. It was the tomb of Tin Hinan, the first "queen" of the Hoggar, the legendary ancestress of the Tuareg. Her skeleton was still *in situ.*[2]

Important to any description, but especially necessary to the model that follows, is a related element of point of view—*scale,* that is, a presentation by the observer of what his eyes can actually see from his physical position in space. In the model description below, for example, it would have been ridiculous if the writer had used the same

[2] James Wellard, "Tin Hinan," *The Great Sahara,* pp. 46–47. Copyright © 1964 by James Wellard. Permission of E. P. Dutton & Company.

kind of small details in describing the islands of Greece from the air as he would have used if he had been describing them as he walked about on foot. From the air, he can present only broad and vague details of the lands below. To him they seem paler, purer, soberer, older, and wilder than anything farther west. The sea is smooth; the islands of all sizes are a dry terra-cotta with little cultivation on them. There are few plainly cut ribbons of roads, and "the haze of the fawn-colored foreground shades away into blue, where the mountains stand dim and serene."

When you look down and see the first Greek islands, you are surprised by the difference from Italy, whose dense plantings of parched yellow fields you have so short a time before left behind. Here is paler, purer, soberer country, which seems both wild and old and quite distinct from anything farther west. The sea is absolutely smooth, sometimes violet, sometimes blue, with a softness of water-color, glistening in patches with a fine grain of silver; and the islands of all sizes in bulbous or oblong shapes—blobs and round-bottomed bottles and the contours of plump roast fowl—seem not to rise out of the water but to be plaqued on it like cuff-links on cuffs or to lie scattered like the fragments of a picture-puzzle on a table with a blue cloth cover. These islands are a dry terra-cotta—quite unlike the deep earthy clay tints to which one has been accustomed in Italy—almost the color of two well-cooked liver, and the vegetation looks like gray lichens. The marblings on the looping beaches set up a feeling of uncanny familiarity which refers itself, as one recognizes in a moment, to the patterns on the ancient Greek vases made out of this very soil. Even on the large islands and the mainland, there are visible little cultivation and few plainly cut ribbons of roads, and the country, after humanized Italy, seems grander and more mysterious. The haze of the fawn-colored foreground shades farther away into blue, where the mountains stand dim and serene. These are the "shadowy mountains" of Homer.[3]

Kinds of description

Description is seldom used alone; it is most frequently found in narration. However, it is convenient to break down description on the basis of the writer's intent or purpose into two types: (1) *objective* or *expository description* and (2) *subjective* or *emotional description.* In writing expository description, a writer's intent is to inform or explain; therefore, he tries to recreate the original as accurately as possible. He paints with words an objective and impersonal picture, selecting factual details and using denotative and concrete words to avoid an emo-

[3] Edmund Wilson, *Europe without Baedeker,* 2d ed., pp. 236–237. Copyright © 1947, 1966 by Edmund Wilson. Permission of The Monday Press, a division of Farrar, Straus and Giroux.

tional or distorted reproduction. In the model expository description that follows, observe the concrete words, the objective tone, the numerous factual details that combine to give a very informative picture of the Sphinx.[4]

The Sphinx seems bigger, more sombre, and more wonderful than ever. Her face is that of a remarkably good-looking Negro girl, though it is said that her complexion was originally of a beautiful pink. All of this pink has now been worn away by the sands of the desert, which have for more than six thousand years been showering their amorous kisses upon it, until all that is left is a little red paint just under the left eye. That figure with the head and bust of a woman upon the body of a lion, carved out of the ages-old rock which stood here upon the desert, has been noted among the peoples of the world as far back as history extends, and those stony eyes have seen civilization after civilization rise and fall.

It would take a good-sized city lot to hold the Sphinx. The body is one hundred and forty feet long, and the paws each measure fifty feet. Her head alone is so big that a vault fourteen feet square and the height of a three-story house would be just large enough to contain it. Though you measure six feet in your stockings and have arms as long as those of Abraham Lincoln, if you stood on the tip of this old lady's ear you could hardly touch the crown of her head. The ear by actual measurement has a length of over four feet, and if that mouth would open it could swallow an ox. The nose is five feet seven inches long, and originally partook of an Ethiopian character. Now, however, it is sadly mutilated, for it has formed a target both for the conquering Mohammedans of the past and the vandal Bedouins of a later day. Tradition says, too, that Napoleon cut off the nose to spite Egypt when he was forced to retreat from the country.

In writing emotional description, a writer tries to evoke in the reader his feelings about the subject; therefore, he selects words rich in connotative meaning and appeals strongly to the senses. He is subjective and personal. In the model description that follows, the writer describes "the haunting presence of the ocean" on the surrounding country. Observe the selection of words, the use of personification, the appeal to the ear that help the writer fulfill his purpose. As he walks about with the writer, the reader hears "a great faint sound of breakers," "the roar of the water," the "voice of the Pacific," and "the sound of the sea." At the summit with the writer, the reader hears "on every hand and with freshened vigor, that same unending, distant, whispering rumble of the ocean." Finally, "the whole woodland is begirt with thundering surges."

[4] Frank G. Carpenter, *Cairo to Kisumu.* Copyright © 1923 by Frank G. Carpenter. Permission of Frances Carpenter and Doubleday & Company, Inc.

The one common note of all this country is the haunting presence of the ocean. A great faint sound of breakers follows you high up into the inland canyons; the roar of water dwells in the clean, empty rooms of Monterey as in a shell upon the chimney; go where you will, you have but to pause and listen to hear the voice of the Pacific. You pass out of the town to the southwest, and mount the hill among pine woods. Glade, thicket, and grove surround you. You follow winding sandy tracks that lead nowhither. You see a deer; a multitude of quail arises. But the sound of the sea still follows you as you advance, like that of wind among the trees, only harsher and stranger to the ear; and when at length you gain the summit, out breaks on every hand and with freshened vigor, that same unending, distant, whispering rumble of the ocean; for now you are on the top of Monterey peninsula, and the noise no longer only mounts to you from behind along the beach towards Santa Cruz, but from your right also, round by Chinatown and Pinos lighthouse, and from down before you to the mouth of the Carmello River. The whole woodland is begirt with thundering surges. The silence that immediately surrounds you where you stand is not so much broken as it is haunted by this distant, circling rumor. It sets your senses upon edge; you strain your attention; you are clearly and unusually conscious of small sounds near at hand; you walk listening like an Indian hunter; and that voice of the Pacific is a sort of disquieting company to you in your walk.[5]

Before moving onward to an analysis of other model descriptions, review what you have learned about the form by studying the information in the guide.

GUIDE TO DESCRIPTION

1 *Abstract* and *general words* are words that refer to a class and express a quality or characteristic rather than a specific object or instance, e.g., "tree," "athlete," "condition."

2 An *allusion* is a direct or indirect reference to familiar people or happenings, especially from art, history, literature, or mythology.

3 *Concrete* or *specific words* are words that refer to a member of a class and to a particular object, person, or thing, e.g., "oak," "golfer," "brain tumor."

4 *Connotative words* are words that strongly suggest meanings that are imaginative and poetic, e.g., "lass," "bower," "casement."

5 *Denotative words* are words that express the meaning that they elicit, e.g., "girl," "house," "window."

6 *Description* is a verbal picture of some place, thing, or person.

[5] Robert Louis Stevenson, "The Old Pacific Capital" in *Across the Plains,* pp. 80–81. Copyright © 1892 by Charles Scribner's Sons.

7 *Dominant impression* is the central feature in a subject of description on which the writer focuses first and then moves to the other details to complete his reproduction of the original. Examples are the following: a long nose, snowcovered mountain peak, flashing eyes, water crashing over a falls.

8 *Emotional description* is a description by which a writer evokes in the reader feelings about the subject.

9 *Expository description* is description by which a writer reproduces as accurately as possible the original for the purpose of informing or explaining.

10 A *figure of speech* uses words and expressions out of their literal sense to give vividness, variety, and emphasis to communication.

11 An *hyperbole* is exaggeration to enrich communication.

12 A *metaphor* is an implied comparison; the word "like" or "as" is not expressed.

13 *Personification* is the giving of human qualities or characteristics to animals, inanimate objects, or abstract ideas.

14 *Point of view* in description is the physical position in space from which a writer views his subject or his mental attitude toward the subject or a combination of both.

15 *Scale* is the presentation by the observer in description of what his eyes can actually see from his physical position in space.

16 A *simile* is a comparison with the word "like" or "as" expressed.

17 *Space order* is development of a writer's reproduction of a subject by movement logically and naturally through space.

Read the model essay that follows. Be prepared to answer questions in Structure Review Five.

TIN HINAN
James Wellard

1 Among all these voiceless mounds and rings of stones which mark either the poor graves or simple shrines of the central Saharan people only one monument speaks to us in a language we can partially understand: that is, the language of the Roman civilization. This monument, certainly the most exciting archaeologically in the desert south of the Roman *limes,* is the fortress and tomb of Tin Hinan, at an oasis called Abelessa near Tamanrasset in the Hoggar. The name Abelessa itself has a Roman sound, which has led some historians, notably Henri Lhote, to go so far as to suggest that it may be a variant of "Balsa", a place actually recorded in written history. Pliny, in fact, mentions a "Balsa" in connection with the African campaign of Cornelius

SOURCE NOTE: James Wellard, "Tin Hinan," *The Great Sahara,* pp. 46–48. Copyright © 1964 by James Wellard. Permission of E. P. Dutton & Company.

Balbus, conqueror of the Fezzan. From this supposition—that Abelessa is Balsa—it is only one step for the more daring, or imaginative, of theorists (that is, those who have no academic prestige to maintain) to suggest that the fortress of Tin Hinan was an actual Roman outpost halfway to Timbuktu. The shadow of the Third Augusta Legion falls at this point on central Saharan history.

2   Be that as it may, there is no doubt at all that the fortress, or castle, is unique; that its architecture bears no relationship to the monuments erected by the savages, or the later barbarians who inhabited the desert wastelands. Tin Hinan, in fact, is the work of quasi-civilized hands, and was certainly occupied by people who had contacts with the civilized world; for when it was excavated, it was found to contain artifacts which we associate with an advanced culture: e.g. a wooden bed, Roman coins, jewelry, lamps, and utensils that were certainly not made by the natives of the surrounding desert. Tin Hinan, therefore, was built and occupied by foreigners. Who were they? And what were they doing a thousand miles away from the centres of the civilized world?

3   To the practised eye, the appearance of the fortress suggests some of the possible answers. We can see in it, for instance, some resemblance to the Roman farm-forts along the northern frontiers of the desert. The walls, on an average four feet thick, are built of basalt blocks, some of which have been squared off in the Roman manner. There is only one entrance, leading to eleven rooms which open out one from the other—again typical of the farmhouses along the *limes.* The room farthest from the entrance was found sealed off in the Franco-American excavations of 1926. Breaking in, the archaeologists found themselves in a rectangular chamber measuring about sixteen by twelve feet with walls eight feet high. The floor of this room was covered with soil and, under the debris, a layer of stone chips; and under this flooring six large monoliths, the biggest of which measured nearly seven feet long, a foot wide, and five inches thick. When these stone slabs were removed, the excavators looked down into another chamber, seven feet long, four feet wide, and four feet high. It was the tomb of Tin Hinan, the first "queen" of the Hoggar, the legendary ancestress of the Tuareg. Her skeleton was still *in situ.*

4   She was lying on her back, with her arms lightly folded. She had evidently been laid to rest on what appeared to be a ceremonial bed of ornamented wood, or perhaps a chair-throne. Only a few pieces of this bier remained. The jewels buried with her had survived: on the right forearm were seven silver bracelets and on the left seven gold bracelets. The number seven may have had some symbolic significance, as it did in classical numerology. Lying beneath the neck of the queen was her pendant of a hundred silver beads. Another pendant of white and red pearls was in place on her ribs; on her right shoulder two safety-clasps with the remains of her dress attached; by her side

several baskets containing date stones, some wheat, wood faggots, a little gold ring, fragments of glass, and the figurine of a good-luck charm. This statuette appears to be of great age, belonging to the dawn of mankind's religious beliefs, for it has a featureless head, a shapeless body, with the whole emphasis placed upon the hips and female pudenda: not an idealistic reproduction of an anthropomorphic divinity, then, such as the Greeks and Romans worshipped, but a fetish whose symbolism is the female counterpart of the phallus, or Priapus of other cults. And just as phallic amulets were, and still are, worn as lucky charms, so no doubt this palaeolithic Venus was worn by Tin Hinan.

STRUCTURE REVIEW FIVE/DESCRIPTION

Name _____ Class _____

Answer each question in the space provided below it.

1 What is the chief function of paragraphs 1 and 2?

2 What is the writer's purpose in describing Tin Hinan?

3 To what does he compare the fortress? Why?

4 In addition to the artifacts found on and close to the Queen's body, what else does the writer describe in some detail? Why?

5 In what way does the writer's purpose affect his selection of descriptive details?

6 Why are the questions at the end of paragraph 2 important in the structural organization of the description?

ASSIGNMENT/EFFECTIVE CHOICE OF WORDS

In the passages below, underline words that you consider effective adjective and adverb modifiers. Circle strong verbs and verbals.

1 The hoofs of the horses splashed and clicked in the water. (James Boyd)

2 Today the sea is a purplish gray; surf foams like thick suds about the treeless islands; the distant Cadillac [mountain] cuts the western sky, sharp and keen as a new knife blade; the spruces of Schoodic are jet-black above the tossing water; and southward the open ocean is ridged with white at the breaking of the swells, uninhabited now, as it is so often even in summer, by a solitary sail. (Mary Ellen Chase)

3 The narrow creek was like a ditch, tortuous, fabulously deep, filled with gloom under the thin strip of pure and shining blue of the heaven. (Joseph Conrad)

4 The car bounced and rushed on, swaying on the curves and up the hills and fleeing down again as if the earth had dropped from under them. (William Faulkner)

5 He looked like a man cut away from the stake, when the fire had overrunningly wasted all the limbs without consuming them, or taking away one particle from their compacted aged robustness. (Herman Melville)

6 At the second shot he [the elephant] did not collapse but climbed with desperate slowness to his feet and stood weakly upright, with legs sagging and head drooping. (George Orwell)

NOTE: See answers on page 131.

ASSIGNMENT/POINT OF VIEW
Briefly discuss the point of view in the following paragraph in the space below the model.

The favorite abode of this Manitou is still shown. It is a great rock or cliff on the loneliest part of the mountains, and, from the flowering vines which clamber about it, and the wild flowers which abound in its neighborhood, is known by the name of the Garden Rock. Near the foot of it is a small lake, the haunt of the solitary bittern, with water-snakes basking in the sun on the leaves of the pond-lilies which lie on the surface. This place was held in great awe by the Indians, insomuch that the boldest hunter would not pursue his game within its precincts. Once upon a time, however, a hunter who had lost his way, penetrated to the Garden Rock, where he beheld a number of gourds placed in the crotches of trees. One of these he seized and made off with it, but in the hurry of his retreat he let it fall among the rocks, when a great stream gushed forth, which washed him away and swept him down precipices, where he was dashed to pieces, and the stream made its way to the Hudson, and continues to flow to the present day; being the identical stream known by the name of the Kaaters-kill.[6]

NOTE: See discussion on page 131.

[6] Irving, "Rip Van Winkle," op. cit., p. 20.

THE BLUE NILE
Alan Moorhead

"Egypt is an acquired country, the gift of the river."
Herodotus.

1   The Blue Nile pours very quietly and uneventfully out of Lake Tana in the northern highlands of Ethiopia. There is no waterfall or cataract, no definite current, nothing in fact to indicate that a part at least of this gently moving flow is embarked upon a momentous journey to the Mediterranean, 2,750 miles away. The actual outlet lies in a bay at the southern end of the lake, and it would be quite possible for a traveller to miss it altogether. The shore line unobtrusively divides into low islands fringed with black lava boulders and overgrown with jungle, and the grey-green water slips in between. There are no villages here, and except for a few fishermen paddling about on their papyrus rafts like water-boatmen in a pond, no sign of civilization at all. The silence is absolute. One sees a few spry grey monkeys on the rocks, and the black and white kingfisher, fluttering ten feet above the water before he makes his dead-straight drop upon a fish. Pythons are said to live in these regions, and they grow to a length of twenty feet or more and are adorned in patterns of black and many colours. If you are very lucky you might catch sight of one of them swimming to new hunting grounds along the shore, but more often they are to be found in the low branches of trees, and from that safe hiding place among the leaves they lash out to grab and demolish a monkey or a small unsuspecting antelope coming down to the river to drink. . . .

2   A few miles downstream from the lake the water begins to boil turbulently over rocks and shallows which are impossible to navigate with any safety; and so he must take to mules and follow the river as close to its banks as the thick scrub will allow him.

3   The landscape is delightful, a combination of tropical and mountainous Africa: acacia trees and the lotus, the banyan and the alien eucalyptus, palms and delicate water-ferns. The baobab in these rain forests is not the smooth bald barrel of a tree which the river will meet far down below in the Sudanese deserts: it puts out broad shady leaves. We are as yet a little too far upstream for the crocodile, but there is an exuberance of birds; the fish eagle calling from the treetop in the morning, white storks with a delicate fringe of black on the wings, starlings that look like anything but starlings since their feathers gleam with an iridescent blue, the black ibis with its scimitar beak, pelicans, darters, hoopoes, rollers and kites; and the giant hornbill which is the size of a young ostrich and rather more ungainly until it lumbers into the air, and then reveals the great sweep of its wings, each tipped with white.

SOURCE NOTE: Alan Moorhead, *The Blue Nile*, pp. 3–12. Copyright © 1962 by Alan Moorhead. Permission of Harper & Row, Publishers.

4   The eastern bank is a succession of rough hills, but on the west black cotton-soil plains spread away to distant mountains which are very strange: their tops are the granite cores of extinct volcanoes and they sprout like vast grey cactuses in the sky.

5   After about twenty miles of this one is aware of some sort of commotion ahead. The murmur of the water grows into a roar, and a low wet cloud hangs over the valley. This is the great object of this stage of your journey, the Tisisat Falls, and it is an extraordinary thing that they should be so little known, for they are, by some way, the grandest spectacle that either the Blue or the White Nile has to offer; in all Africa they are only to be compared with the Victoria Falls on the Zambezi. As with the Victoria Falls, there is the same calm approach past small wooded islands and smooth rocks, and then abruptly the stream vanishes in a tremendous white downpour that thunders as it falls. Looking down from the top one sees far below a narrow gorge filled with racing water, and it twists and turns until it is finally lost to sight in the surrounding cliffs. The spray flung up from this gorge creates a perpetual soft rain which is blown upon the hillside opposite, and here a forest of wet green reeds keeps waving from side to side like seaweed at the bottom of the sea. To stand there just for five minutes means that you will be wet to the skin. For the newcomer it is an alarming sort of place, and he will see with surprise flocks of little black birds with pointed pinkish wings flying directly into the spray and landing on the slippery rocks at the very lip where the water makes its frightful downward plunge. Unconcerned they fly off again through a rainbow which is nearly circular and which hangs in the spray like a whirling firework.

6   The Tisisat Falls are the end of all peace on the Blue Nile. The river now begins to make its great gash through the Ethiopian plateau. For nearly four hundred miles it continues in an immense curve, at first in a southerly direction, then west, then north, until it pours itself out of the mountains into the hot plains of the south Sudan. The further it goes the deeper it cuts; by the time it reaches central Ethiopia the gorge is a mile deep and at places fifteen miles wide, yet still, even at the height of the dry season, it tears and boils along too fast for any boat to live upon the surface. No one has ever made the boat journey down the Blue Nile from Lake Tana to the Sudan, no one as yet has managed to walk or take a mule along the full length of its precipitous banks. . . .

7   The Blue Nile is now a formidable stream, and it flows on with increased force to join the White Nile at Khartoum.

8   The White Nile is a much longer river than the Blue. Already at Khartoum it has come two thousand miles from its source in Lake Victoria in Central Africa, and except for its passage through the great swamp of the Sudd in the

south Sudan its banks are inhabited nearly all the way. But the fall of the White
Nile's water over this vast distance has been barely 2,000 feet (compared to
the Blue Nile's tumultuous drop of nearly 5,000 feet), and so it has a quiet and
sedate appearance. Steamers and feluccas move about comfortably on its
broad expanse of water. It is very much the parent stream. However, the real
strength of the two rivers that now unite and lose their separate identity at
Khartoum lies in the Blue Nile. It provides six-sevenths of the total volume of
water in the combined stream, and for six months of the year it rushes down
from the Ethiopian mountains with the effect of a tidal wave. By June the force
of this flood is so great that the White Nile is dammed back upon itself at
Khartoum; it pauses, as it were, and stands back while the younger, livelier
river pushes past carrying hundreds of thousands of tons of discolouring grit
and soil to Egypt. At last in January the tremendous rush subsides, and the
White Nile begins to assert itself again. Then at Khartoum you can see the two
rivers flowing on quietly side by side, and for a few miles there is a distinct
dividing line between them on the surface of the water; the White Nile not
precisely white but more nearly muddy grey, the Blue seldom absolutely blue
except for certain moments at dawn and in the evening, but more of a brown-
ish-green.

   9   The river still has another 1,750 miles to go before it reaches the Mediterranean, and it will receive only one more tributary, the Atbara—another gift of
the Lake Tana highlands—before it plunges into regions where there is no
rain at all, nothing but this warm, brown, softly-moving flow of water to relieve
the endless sameness of the desert. Here at last, in a region where everything
would seem to conspire to make life a misery—the heat, the duststorms, the
isolation and the lack of any green thing beyond the confines of the river—we
come on the first evidence of ancient civilizations which are a flat denial of the
primitiveness of Africa, indeed, they are hardly African at all. The first adum-
bration of these things occurs about 180 miles downstream from Khartoum, at
Meroë, near Shendy, where there are some two hundred ruined pyramids
standing in the desert, but then, as the river descends towards the Egyptian
border over a series of long but gentle cataracts, more and more temples and
fortresses appear. This is the region of Nubia, which is another frontier of a
kind, or rather a no-man's-land where in ancient times invading armies came
up the Nile in search of slaves, gold and ivory, each conqueror in his turn
raising a new dynasty and new monuments to his own glory, only to be driven
out again by other conquerors, Egyptians, Persians, Greeks, Romans and the
Nubians themselves, and it is strange that so many of them worshipped the
sun, which was their enemy, and not the river which was their only hope of
life. It is also remarkable that in our own era this wild region which was so
eagerly fought for and cultivated in the past should have been so very much
abandoned. Such life as has remained fixes itself upon the Nubian settle-

ments on the river bank, where the brightly painted designs on the houses remind one far more of primitive Africa than ancient Egypt, and upon the caravan routes winding from oasis to oasis across the desert, and the pilgrimage to Mecca which continues to cross these wastes year after year with a kind of ant-like fidelity, a determined search for grace through the awful hardships of travelling in the African heat.

10 At Aswan, which was a great caravan centre in its day, and the most southerly outpost of the Roman Empire, another change overtakes the river valley. For the last few hundred miles all has been stark rock and arid yellow sand, but now as one descends the last cataract past the island temples of Philae plantations of wheat and sugar-cane appear, lines of camels and donkeys move along the river bank among palms and tamarisks, and there is hardly a moment when one is out of sight of a village. On the river itself feluccas slide by with long thin coloured pennants on the masts to show the direction of the wind; and even the wind which was such a terror on the Upper Nile is now beginning to fail. It is the beginning of the softness and lushness of Egypt, and the end of the wildness of the Nile. The very birds have a tame and unhurried air, whether they be the white egrets feeding in the swamps, the pigeons on every rooftop, or the herons and storks standing in the shallows like decorations on a Japanese screen. Even that murderous thrust of the heron's beak, the quick upward jerk of the head and the swallowing of the fish, is a rhythmical and poetic movement as far removed from the image of death as is the frieze on the temple wall where the Pharaoh, with his raised arm, is about to club his cringing enemies to the ground. The buffalo, released at last in the evening from his monotonous circling round the water wheel, comes down to the bank and subsides with a groan of satisfaction into the mud. Both crocodiles and hippopotamuses have now vanished from the river.

11 One after another the great temples next come into view: Kom Ombo dominating a bend in the river, Edfu still intact on the western bank, Karnak and Luxor, Dendera and Abydos. There is a monumental stillness in the warm air, an intimation of past existence endlessly preserved, and day after day one glides on to the north seeing the same things that every traveller has always seen. It is a process of recognition: the pyramids and the Sphinx are prefigured in the mind long before they meet the eye.

12 Now finally the Nile begins to drop its Ethiopian mud at Cairo, a hundred miles from the sea. Confused by flatness and its own tame pace, it spreads out through many different canals and waterways into the green fan of the delta. Little by little with its falling silt it has pushed the land out into the Mediterranean and lost itself in swamps and lakes. Of the seven mouths the ancients knew only two remain, one at Rosetta and the other at Damietta, but still at the height of its flood the river stains the sea for many miles out, and in a storm coming from the north russet waves are driven back on to the Egyptian shore.

13 This then, is the end of the river, the end of a continuous chain of re-creation by which the Blue Nile brings life down from the mountains to the desert and the Delta.

STRUCTURE REVIEW SIX/DESCRIPTION

Name _____   Class _____

Answer each question in the space provided below it.

1 How does the writer give order to this long description of the Blue Nile?

2 In this description, the writer makes effective use of verbs. List some verbs you consider used effectively in the first three paragraphs.

3 How does point of view contribute to the drama of viewing the Tisisat Falls?

4 Good description appeals to the senses. What particular sense appeals are obvious in this description?

5 What is the main idea of paragraph 8? With what kind of materials does the writer support his generalization?

6 Mention two examples of the following:
Simile
a
b
Personification
a
b
Contrasts
a
b

7 Does the writer have a purpose other than simply a description of the Blue Nile?

8 What particular word picture stands out most vividly in your mind after reading about the Blue Nile?

See answers on page 131.

ASSIGNMENT/WRITING DESCRIPTION
Suggested Topics

1 Describe a house or some place that as a child you believed to be haunted by spirits.

2 Describe as clearly and objectively as you can a natural object, such as a mountain, a lake, a seashore, or a valley from a distance.

3 Describe a natural object from a shifting point of view. Select details and words that will create an emotional reaction in the reader.

4 Describe a busy street from a roof, balcony, or window emphasizing the smells and sounds below.

5 Focus on a dominant impression; move toward or away from it until you complete a word picture of the original.

6 Describe a person who looks like a bird, a fish, or some other animal.

ANSWER SECTION

STRUCTURE REVIEW THREE

1 John Koshaks, Jr.

2 The Koshaks and their friends against the hurricane.

3 Time: Sunday, August 17, 1969; place: Gulfport, Mississippi.

4 Although the writer shifts point of view many times, the third person (omniscient) with the "he" for John Koshak, Jr., is possibly the dominant point of view.

5 He presents the happenings in order of time.

6 He emphasizes action—the series of struggles against the might of hurricane Camille.

7 The climax comes at the moment that they decided to put the "kids on a closet door if the floor went"—the identical moment that the main thrust of Camille passed onward.

8 Although I feel that the writer needs to give information about the might of the hurricane and about the aftermath, I think he would have had a stronger narration by ending it much sooner after the climax.

9 The reader is never sure that the Koshaks and friends will survive. Each new happening heightens the suspense, for they seem to be losing the struggle.

10 The writer wished to show what power the hurricane had; thus, he was able to emphasize the valiant struggle against it. He could have presented this information in the introductory paragraphs and given information about what happened after the hurricane much more briefly after the climax.

ASSIGNMENT/IDENTIFYING FIGURES OF SPEECH

1 Simile

2 Personification

3 Metaphor
4 Hyperbole
5 Allusion (to mythology)
6 Metaphor
7 Allusion (to history and religion)
8 Personification
9 Simile
10 Hyperbole and metaphor

ASSIGNMENT/EFFECTIVE CHOICE OF WORDS

1   The hoofs of the horses splashed and clicked in the water.
2   Today the sea is a *purplish gray;* surf foams like *thick* suds about the *treeless* islands; the *distant* Cadillac cuts the *western* sky, *sharp* and *keen* as a *new knife* blade; the spruces of Schoodic are *jet-black* above the *tossing* water; and *southward* the *open* ocean is ridged with white at the breaking of the swells, uninhabited now, as it is so often even in summer, by a *solitary* sail.
3   The *narrow* creek was like a ditch, *tortuous, fabulously deep,* filled with gloom under the *thin* strip of *pure* and shining blue of the heaven.
4   The car bounced and rushed on, swaying on the curves and up the hills and fleeing down again as if the earth had dropped from under them.
5   He looked like a man cut away from the stake, when the fire had *overrunningly* wasted all the limbs without consuming them, or taking away one particle from their *compacted aged* robustness.
6   At the second shot he did not collapse but climbed with *desperate slowness* to his feet and stood *weakly* upright, with legs sagging and head drooping.

ASSIGNMENT/POINT OF VIEW

The writer focuses on a dominant impression—the great rock or cliff on the loneliest part of the mountain. He moves to the flowering vines about it and to the wild flowers in the neighborhood. He moves onward to the foot of the great rock to a small lake and water snakes lying on the leaves on its surface.

STRUCTURAL REVIEW SIX

1   By selecting details that are important to his purpose, which is to show what the Blue Nile is like and to stress the importance of the Nile in bringing life down from the mountains to the desert and the delta.
2   A few of the important verbs are the following: ''pours,'' ''fringed,'' ''embarked,'' ''are adorned,'' ''lash out to grab and demolish,'' ''to boil,'' and ''lumbers.''

3 His physical position is at the top of the falls. This position enables him to describe the narrow gorge below filled with racing water. It gives him also an opportunity to stress that "it is an alarming place." In addition he can emphasize the interesting surroundings at the top of the falls, especially the fact that the river changes abruptly from a calm stream to a tremendous white downpour.

4 Sight and sound.

5 A contrast (differences) between the White Nile and the Blue Nile. He cites facts concerning the length, amount of fall, and strength of the two rivers.

6 There are many in this selection; student's choice.

7 Yes. He wishes to show that the Blue Nile brings life down from the mountains to the desert and the delta.

8 Student's choice.

Comparison, Contrast, and Analogy

As we mentioned in the previous chapter, the purpose or intention of the writer of exposition (informative writing) is to inform or to explain. He appeals to a reader's understanding with verifiable facts and valid information, explaining and interpreting that material so that the reader will accept his point of view or explanation. Thus, he must organize and develop his thought objectively and present it with honesty and completeness so that the reader will have confidence in the discussion. Most important, then, in good exposition is the ability of the writer to organize and present his material in order to fulfill his purpose.

Because the reader needs to know at the beginning what the writer intends to do, certain frames or structures are very effective in organizing this kind of thought. You have met these kinds of structure already in the essays in the book. With a thesis—a statement of the central thought or a statement of your purpose—as your foundation, you can begin building the framework by placing the statement of the central thought or statement of purpose into the organizational pattern in much the same way as you did the topic sentence of the paragraph. If you wish the direction of your thought to flow from a clear expression of the central thought or purpose through the support to a conclusion (the most common method), you will place the unifying idea of the subsequent material at the beginning of the paper. More often than not, this unifying idea is simply a statement of the writer's purpose. In an essay entitled "The American War Game" (see page 138), Thomas B. Morgan states clearly his purpose in the second paragraph; he writes:

It is therefore in the interest of peace that one should inquire into the nature of the "war" game.

In his essay "The Common Cold" (see page 186), Richard Gordon expresses his purpose for writing in the first paragraph; he states:

These home cures generally follow one of these distinct courses and as each reflects the psychology of the sufferer, let us examine them in detail. They are: (1) the Fresh-Air Treatment; (2) the Scientific Attack; (3) the Coddle.

In other pieces of expository writing, the writer expresses the unifying idea in the form of a central thought—a statement sentence that presents a point of view requiring supporting material so that the reader will accept it. In his essay entitled "How to Take the Profit out of Hard Drugs" (see page 210), Peter F. Drucker expresses the central thought in the opening paragraph; it reads:

The greatest threat to our cities is not air pollution, the poor, the blacks, the white racists, the automobile, or the "system." The greatest threat is our present narcotics laws. They make 99 per cent of us who are free from addiction the main victims of this monstrous plague.

In "The Loneliness of the Alcoholic" (page 206), C. A. D'Alonzo states the central thought in the first line of the essay; he writes:

The alcoholic is a lonely man.

This kind of organizational pattern has the advantage of providing the reader with a clear understanding of what the paper is about as well as indicating the direction of the flowing thought of the subsequent discussion. Let us call this frame or pattern the *thesis-support frame.*

If you wish to lead your reader through various kinds of supporting material in order for him to accept the final conclusion based on that material, you will place the thesis statement in the final paragraph. This *support-thesis frame* is more difficult to structure than the previous one since the reader does not know where the supporting material is taking him or why he is moving onward in a certain direction until he reads the unifying central thought. In his essay "On Law and Order" (page 247), Joseph Wood Krutch begins the discussion stating that our time is "a more than usually troubled time." He follows in the next paragraph with the statement, "Why this is so, why all these things are happening to us, we do not know." He then presents a series of paragraphs explaining possible reasons why our time is so troubled—none of them satisfactory answers. He ends the discussion with his point of view—a thesis sentence expressing his point of view.

There will never be a reign of law and order until those engaged in the various protests now epidemic everywhere know with certainty when they have gone beyond the legal limit and, if they have, what penalties will be imposed upon them.

In developing thought within this support-thesis frame, you must organize and present your thought in such a way that the reader can grasp its meaning and sense that you are leading him to a logical conclusion. This frame has certain advantages over the first frame; it creates more suspense, and it gives more emphasis to the central thought since the end position in the final paragraph is a very emphatic position.

If you wish to state clearly the thesis in the first paragraph and emphasize its importance again at the end of the discussion, place the thesis statement in the first paragraph and restate it in slightly different words in the final paragraph. The advantages of this *thesis-support-thesis frame* are obvious.

Another common and effective frame is, of course, the *question-to-answer frame.* It is a simple method for the reader to understand, and it creates immediate interest in the subject. In his essay "What Produced Those Pot-smoking, Rebellious, Demonstrating kids?—Television!" Eliot Daley begins the discussion with four questions.

Whatever happened to some of these kids today?

How come they smoke pot, sleep around, demonstrate, and drop out?

And why won't they study in our schools, work at our jobs, and kill in our wars?

What got into them?

Television did.

Not all papers have a clearly stated thesis or statement of purpose or develop one single unifying idea. There are other frames, but they require considerable experience on the part of the writer. Some experienced writers do not state the thesis or indicate clearly their purpose; they let the reader infer it from the developing thought. Other experienced writers may place the thesis statement in other positions than the first paragraph or final paragraph; the second paragraph and middle paragraph are popular positions. Still other writers place the thesis in parts in various sentences throughout the paper and let the reader construct the central thought in his own mind as he moves onward. Obviously, such frames or lack of frames place a greater burden of organization and development on the writer and a greater burden of understanding of what the writer is saying and doing on the reader.

Within these frames or structures, you can organize and develop the thought in exposition by the variety of methods discussed earlier; let us consider the first three of these methods: comparison, contrast, and analogy.

Showing likenesses *(comparison)* or differences *(contrast)* or both between two or among three or more persons, places, things, or ideas is a common and very effective method of informing and explaining. Mrs. Jones discusses her son Robert with his aunt; she says, "He's so like his father." She then begins to point out a number of similarities between the two in appearance, interests, habits, personality. Edward Smith studies religion. As he learns more about the major religions he begins to note the amazing similarities among them; each has a book, a belief in one God, a flood, a set of rules or commandments, and a prophet or leader on this earth. Peter Carr is certain that Professor Smiley will ask the class to contrast Generals Lee and Grant; therefore, he makes a study plan by first listing under the title General Grant a point and following with a contrasting point under General Lee.

These examples of comparison and contrast tell us much about the methods. A writer should first have a purpose for comparison or contrast. He should make sure that his subjects have a sufficient number of likenesses or differences to warrant development by those methods, and finally, the writer should announce his comparison or contrast clearly so that the reader will have no doubt about the organizational structure and purpose.

COMPARISON

Comparison is a method of developing thought by pointing out likenesses between two or among three or more persons, places, things, or ideas. In structuring comparison, a writer begins with a purpose in mind. He may wish to show likenesses between two subjects because he has discovered that one would not expect them to be alike; for example, Byron and Hemingway, Tokyo and Los Angeles, Christianity and Islam. Still another writer compares two subjects to tell something important about one of the subjects or both subjects. One writer, for example, compares the early organizational structure of Mormon society to a large-scale business organization to explain the success of the Mormon experience and to emphasize their keen sense of business.

When you have your purpose clearly in mind, write down a statement of the central thought in a thesis sentence. Your problem in organizing thought by comparison is that you are dealing with more than one subject—two, three, even four subjects—and that you are involved in establishing the comparable subjects by showing likenesses of a number of characteristics common to these subjects. Thus, you will find that the thesis-support frame helps you unify the comparison that follows. You will observe, therefore, when you read model essays on comparison and contrast by experienced writers that these authors will usually announce the comparison or contrast in the first few sentences of the opening paragraph and reveal also their purpose for writing. In "The American War Game," the model essay that follows, the writer Thomas B. Morgan begins his comparison by stating his thesis: "Football is unique among American sports—its metaphoric relationship to war goes beyond strategic analogies and deathly symbolism to the action itself." In the last sentence of paragraph 2, he reveals his purpose for writing when he states, "It is therefore in the interest of peace that one should inquire into the nature of the 'war' game." Thus, Morgan leaves no doubt in the reader's mind as to his purpose and as to how he will organize and develop his thought to fulfill that purpose. He will compare football to war to reveal the nature of the "war game."

Once you have written down the thesis statement, begin to list characteristics underneath it that make the two or more subjects comparable; for example, a listing of characteristics that enabled Morgan to compare football and war might look something like the following:

FOOTBALL AND WAR
1 Violence
2 Pain and suffering
3 Suicide squads
4 Limits of stoicism
5 Injuries like wounds in battle
6 Anger
7 Persistent torture
8 A young man's game
9 Specialization
10 Field general

In reading the model essay on football and war, observe the clear statement of the comparison, the statement revealing the writer's purpose, the number of characteristics that firmly establish the comparison, and the full development of each point of likeness so that the reader will understand and accept the comparable nature of the two subjects.

THE AMERICAN WAR GAME
Thomas B. Morgan

Statement
of the
compari-
son

1   Football is unique among American sports—its metaphoric relationship to war goes beyond strategic analogies and deathly symbolism to the action itself. Unlike chess or poker or even hockey, football is a game played on a team basis that not only sanctions physical violence but requires it on every play. It is, as Walter Millis says, pseudo war, and, as played by professionals in the past decade, it has replaced baseball as our national sport. We may be trying to tell ourselves something. There has been an eerie parallel in the recent histories of United States politics and pro football. Neutralism changed to war-readiness and the strategy of massive land battles gave way to massive retaliation. The pros simultaneously evolved an open aerial style out of a sluggardly, ground oriented game. Alas, what could be more appropriate for our time than the Sabbath roar, "Throw the bomb!"

2   We are, it seems, guilty about the metaphor. The literature tends to apologize for the pro game, concealing the purgative purpose of it behind learned appraisals of complex plays, strategic patterns, and the point spread. Likewise, the conversation of fans tends to overcompensate, insisting on game technology and the cerebral sphere. Perhaps for one last instant, as we rush from our seats and onto the field after the final gun, we feel the enormity of the stadium, the vastness of the field, and an heroic sense of the mercenary struggle just ended. But like bullfight aficionados (probably for the same reason), we quickly adjust and rejoin the rest of civilization, everyone gabbing about the latest defense and spread formation, shuffling along the turf toward the exit with that straight-arm stuffed in our pocket and those snake hips under firm control. This is a pity because it dislocates the truth about professional football. The surest road to war is a denial of our instinct for it. *It is therefore in the interest of peace that one should inquire into the nature of the "war" game.*

Purpose of
writer

SOURCE NOTE: Thomas G. Morgan, "The American War Game," *Esquire Magazine,* October 1965, 78–79. Reprinted by permission of Esquire Magazine. © 1965 by Esquire, Inc.

Points of
likenesses

3 The players know what it is. "Pro football is the closest thing you can get to all-out war," Baltimore's quarterback, Johnny Unitas, says. "It is physical combat. In place of weapons, they use hands, forearms, shoulders, and anything else they've got to get at you. Thank God they don't have guns out there, but sometimes I wish I had one." The coaches call it "contact." We may define it with a better word, *violence.* Pittsburgh's fullback, John Henry Johnson, for example, once hit the Cardinals' Charley Trippi with a blindside block that fractured Trippi's skull and broke his nose. He tackled a teammate during a practice scrimmage, breaking the man's jaw in two places. And another time, after he had broken the jaw of Les Richter of the Rams, Johnson himself was knocked flat and set upon by four of Richter's teammates. Johnson jumped to his feet, yanked a steel sideline marker out of the ground, and began clubbing his attackers before the referees stopped the fight. Green Bay's middle linebacker, Ray Nitschke, once tackled a halfback so hard that the man lay unconscious for ten minutes after he was carried off the field into the locker room. The Bear's right end, Mike Ditka, has a straight-arm like a jousting pole; a defensive back once grabbed the arm and was dragged twenty-five yards across his own goal line. And the Detroit Lions' defensive tackle Roger Brown, who weighs three hundred pounds, once stopped quarterback Billy Wade of the Chicago Bears by actually throwing a Bear blocker at him. The unfortunate flying Bear weighed two hundred forty-three pounds.

Examples
of violence

Pain and
suffering

4 The corollary of such violence is the stoicism of the players as they suffer it. The Giants' old quarterback, Charley Conerly, who had been knocked out in his first two games as a pro, who suffered lost teeth, a cheek fracture, and countless spinal concussions, and who became known as the "most beat-up man in football," once told me, "It only hurts when you lose." But this is poetry. Pro football hurts, win or lose. The average offensive lineman blocks with a lunging motion toward his opponent, using the right or left forearm as a club against the other man's chest or head. In time, he not only pains the enemy but also beats his own arm to a pulp. A protective pad on one or both forearms helps, but not much. At the same time, the defensive lineman absorbs his would-be blocker's punishment and returns similar blows with the heels of his palms, or, on occasion, his bare knuckles, index finger, or fingernails. After this exchange, he may even be in position for a tackle. He may smash the runner high or low, back, side or front, twisting anything that fits his grasp. Or the runner, with knees driving like pistons and head down for ramming, may kick, butt, or stomp him. Often, it hurts both ways. As Green Bay's ingenious fullback, Jim Taylor, was being battered by the Giants' defensive tackle, Dick Modzelewski, during the 1962 N.F.L. Championship game, Taylor bit him.

5 Some players—usually offensive backs and ends—suffer more than others. Last year, the Dallas quarterback Don Meredith, playing behind a weak line, suffered severe injuries to an ankle, shoulder, and foot, torn abdominal muscles, and knee damage requiring surgery. The Ram's flankerback, Tommy McDonald, one of the tiniest men in the N.F.L. (175 pounds), says he has been knocked unconscious five times in eight years as a pro and, at one time or another, has continued to play with a broken jaw, a shoulder separation, or cracked ribs. Once he recalled, he came to on the field singing the Oklahoma fight song. An offensive end, recently switched to defensive cornerback, told me not long ago that he figured the coach had thereby added five years to his life expectancy in pro football. The end position, as McDonald's experience shows, is that tough.

Suicide
squads

6 Most violent and painful of all may be the clash between the pros' suicide squads, composed for the most part of men who have not made a defensive or offensive unit. They operate as expendables on kickoff plays and punts. "It is the roughest thing in football," the Colts' suicide squad captain, Alex Hawkins, says, "because of our momentum before contact. The team returning the kick gets a thirty-yard run. The team defending gets a forty-yard run. Here come the blockers running top speed in a wedge formation. And here come the defenders with only one thought—make that tackle. Then we hit. It's the time when more injuries occur, especially knee injuries, because the wedge blockers can get you from the side. I'm scared from the time I get on the field until the time I leave it."

Limits of
stoicism

7 The stoicism of the pros has its limits. They may regard a black eye, facial cuts, or gaps in the smile as badges of honor. But their bitterest prospect is an injury that can wreck a man's season or, worse, his career. They are constantly threatened by blindside blocks and occasionally by clipping (a block from the rear), both of which could destroy the knees. An offensive back may even be wiped out in a pileup. In 1961, Green Bay's Jim Taylor narrowly escaped from the bottom of a pile where he lay at the mercy of six Rams. Expert knees hammered at his ribs and powerful hands twisted his ankles. He survived, but his

injuries forced Coach Lombardi to change the Packers' game plans for weeks. The most vulnerable players are backs and ends in their role as pass receivers. When a man leaves his feet and stretches up his hands to make a catch, he is quite defenseless. As San Diego's back, Keith Lincoln, leaped for a pass during last year's A.F.L. Championship, Buffalo's two-hundred-forty-pound linebacker, Mike Stratton, crunched him chest high, ending Lincoln's season with a broken rib.

Fighting on the playing field

8 At any moment, after incidents like these, a fight may break out on the field. Ordinarily, the pros experience a rhythmic pattern of hostility. They accumulate fury as they set themselves for a play, then discharge it in the play itself. In general, this pattern of tension and release constitutes the basic emotional mechanism of the game. But the pattern can be upset by an "unnecessary" injury, by injustice. When, as the sports announcers say, tempers flare, chances are someone has gone beyond the acceptable bounds of brutality.

Football produces anger

9 One may use one's hands during a play, but not after the whistle. One may dig in with one's cleats on an opponent's exposed hand or leg in line of duty, but not when climbing off a pile. According to the rules, one may clip in the line (this tactic is so frustrating and so painful that the victim may swing on his adversary to salve his pride), but a clip anywhere else is the most perfect example of a punishable offense. In any case, the anger of a pro is a poignant thing—he can't really throw a solid punch through his foe's face guard. So, he must contain himself until an opportunity for a sharp elbow in the throat or a vicious sideline block presents itself while the ball is in play. Once while poor Jim Taylor was sitting on the Packer bench with his helmet in his lap, a Minnesota linebacker came over and hit him in the face for a previous offense, real or imagined.

Pain—violently inflicted

10 Although it is rarely discussed on the sports pages, even the fundamental strategy of pro football is a function of pain, violently inflicted. The game, after all, is played not only against time but *over* time. That is, the pain is cumulative; sometimes masquerading as fatigue, sometimes associated with it, pain can become a more effective block than any thrown by an opponent. Sid Gillman, San Diego's coach, has two signs in the Charger locker room inspired by his knowledge of every player's unspoken strategic vulnerability:

GAME STRATEGY
FIRST QUARTER: *Blast! Bewilder them!*
SECOND AND THIRD QUARTERS: *Keep working on them!*
FOURTH QUARTER: *It's ours if we have more courage, more heart, more backbone, better conditioning!*

The other says:

The answer to victory in a tight game is how well you can play in the fourth quarter when you are tired and hurting.

Persistent torture

11 Like inquisitors, then, linemen face each other with the knowledge that persistent torture may pay dividends at any time, most likely in the final period. A man who is blocked hard again and again, perhaps catching a chop on the neck or a jab in the groin from time to time, may at last hesitate a fraction of a second after the ball is snapped. Also a player with a bandaged nose may find his face guard repeatedly pushed in his face. The object is to worry his wound in the hope of encouraging retreat or excessive concentration on self-protection. Since deception in the backfield needs only that instant of weakness to deceive completely, the strategy of pain can decide a game. Conversely, were the sore nose playing offense, exacerbation could lead to the slightest adjustment of a blocking assignment, a leaning away from the torturer that opens a path into the offensive backfield.

Pain as a weapon

12 Pain is a strategic weapon against offensive backs, too. Tackled again and again, twisted, stomped, gouged and repeatedly buried under a half ton of flesh, even the best may be discouraged by the fourth quarter. The pressured quarterback may begin throwing too soon or the aching halfback may falter, especially on faking assignments. Because the success of a play may well depend on how convincingly a back fakes into the line, the slightest reluctance to hit may mean the collapse of an entire sequence of plays. To the point is this unlikely statistic: roughly one-fourth of scoring in N.F.L. championship games since 1933 has occurred in the fourth quarter. If, as may be assumed, players are at their physical peak in the earlier periods, scoring in the fourth quarter probably should be lower. That it isn't indicates, I think, that the strategy of pain works.

13 Effective violence and endurance are the measure of "roughness" of the pro game, rougher today than ever before. To ask why is to go to the heart of the matter. Most likely, every pro at sometime in his life as a football player has experienced a precise moment of understanding, a point in time after which he *knows* the game in a way that releases his body from domination by the mind and enables him to respond creatively to his function. If it hadn't happened, regardless of his native strength or speed, he would be in some other line of work. Once it happens (the result of talent, practice and luck), he plays at a new level of awareness. Football, no matter how complicated it may

seem to the spectators, makes beautiful sense to him. He is able to take on assignments, make adjustments, and react with a felicity that would have been unthinkable before. Usually, understanding occurs in high school. It must occur in college. At any rate, by the time he has been drafted for the pros, he has had this critical experience—after which a number of interrelated factors determine his career.

Young
men play
the game

14 If any one thing has made professional football a rougher game than ever before, as Coach Gillman says, "It is because we have been replacing the potbellies with a new breed of bigger, stronger, quicker, faster young men in top condition—you can't get ready for the season in a steam bath anymore." Gillman has hired a "Strength Coach" who does nothing but "figure out how to make the boys stronger, even if it means borrowing ideas from the Russians." ("Not that we believe in the Russian political doctrine," Gillman adds, hastily.) About eighty-five per cent of the Chargers follow a year-round exercise program. Elsewhere in both leagues at the very least, players must show up for preseason practice in mid-season condition.

Specialization

15 Second only to physical condition, the roughness of the pro game depends on the ability of each man to master an offensive or defensive position. In the late Forties, as crowds began flocking to N.F.L. stadiums, it seemed that specialization, the creature of mass substitution, might make pro football a gentler game than it had been in the days of sixty-minute men like Bronko Nagurski and Mel Turner. This was all right with Jimmy Cannon who pointed out that specialization rescued the athletes from the constant beatings of their predecessors: "You played till you were unconscious," Cannon wrote and, allowing for hyperbole, he was not wrong.

Substitutions

16 But, as it turns out, mass substitution has not made for a less rugged game. We have already noted frequent unconsciousness among contemporary pros. More importantly, the fact is that specialization gives the game a tougher basis— tougher because individual players are *better* at what they do and likely to be better able to do it throughout the game. Nowadays, one is more likely than ever before to see blocking and tackling as crisp and brutal in the last minute of play as in the first. Sixty-minute players, working both offense and defense, would be annihilated in such a game. And it should become even tougher now that college football has reverted to mass substitution rules. In recent years, rookies entering the leagues had been accustomed to both offensive and defensive play.

Learning to specialize took time and often required a certain psychological adjustment—one does not readily give up, say, the pleasures of the block for the joys of the tackle which are separate, distinct, and uniquely satisfying. Better now (for the pros, anyway) that the new men will have specialized early in their college careers and may be expected to reach professional form sooner.

17 There is, by the way, no need to debate the philosophy of specialization as opposed to iron-man football. Obviously, symbolic values are lost through mass substitutions. But the fans are happier. Now it is merely intriguing to wonder what might happen if the old style returned. Certainly it would enable teams to get along with fewer players and might tap new sources of popular interest: it is a thought for the organizers of the proposed Continental League.

Field general

18 At the epicenter of violence in the pro game, the quarterback stands as the most interesting specialist of all. His contribution to the ruggedness of the game is essentially moral. He moves the team, emotionally as well as strategically. He is the maximum leader, often as much a hero to his teammates as to the fans. Linemen protect him as best they can and are depressed when they can't. On the bench, the defensive unit takes inspiration from his efforts. Above all, he is the matador, specifically hated by all the opposing bulls. It is probably not true that quarterbacks are more intelligent today than in the past (the football I.Q. of a Sid Luckman or a Sammy Baugh was surely equal to that of any quarterback playing now). But the game does require them to learn more then ever before. Increasing reliance on deception, on the balanced attack, on split-second adjustments to defensive patterns places an increasing intellectual burden on the quarterback. And this, too, has tended to escalate the roughness of the game. As the Colts' coach, Don Shula, says, "When Unitas passes, our primary concern is to give him time to execute the plays. We feel Berry and Orr can beat the defense if Unitas has time. That means offensive contact must be harder than ever. It means you have to have a running game that keeps the defense from concentrating on Unitas—it all fits if everybody gets off the ball on the count." Of course, it is in the interest of the defense to deprive a Unitas of enough time to get his work done. The resulting conflict is the nexus of the pro game.

Why they play

19 Under these conditions, the *desire* to play pro football must be counted as the individual player's most decisive psychological attribute. Without it, without the hope of some emotional reward, there would be no willingness either to hit or be hit, to maintain physical condition or to master mechanical skills. Among coaches, there is general agreement that desire is inherent. "The love of contact must be there," Green Bay's Vince Lombardi says. "You can't give it to a boy. He has it or he doesn't. He can't play without it." Players are at once more practical and more idealistic about themselves. "I play for enjoyment," Johnny Unitas says, "I enjoy competition. And then, of course, the money enters in." But some pros support the expected view of psychologists that the players' motives are deeply involved with childhood needs. Ray Nitschke, for example, says he enjoyed "belting people" since his earliest days. "My father died when I was three," he explains, "my mother when I was fourteen, so I took it out on all the kids in the neighborhood. What I like about this game is the contact, the man-to-man, the getting it out of your system." But desire is most usefully analyzed by the former New York and Boston quarterback, Paul Governali, whose doctoral thesis on pro football (a) is still unpublished after more than ten years and (b) is still the best work in the field.

Like soldiers in war

20   The pro's reward, Governali says, is his *moment of greatness*—when he owns the crowd and belongs to it, because he has been "the instrument of its ecstatic fulfillment." Having tasted such fruit in college, the men are willing to suffer mightily for more of the same, plus money. They are sad, Governali notes, when they must leave all that glory at the end of their careers. It leads them, like soldiers, into a theater of "war" where they are booed for weakness and cheered for grace, coordination, athletic skill, and brutality. It even leads them into warlike fantasies, imagining the fate of their enemies before the game and reveling in that fate (if they win) after the act of violence is over. Often, they weep in defeat.

Spectators like violence

21   On thinking about the purpose of it all, we are turned back on ourselves. It is our own taste for violence that is ecstatically fulfilled down on the field. Undoubtedly, there are other gratifications as well. Some people hate football and go to the games to spite themselves. Some are crowdlovers and some are baseball refugees. Some are pugs who come for the fight in the bleachers. Some are performing fatherly duties ("Have another hot dog, son?") and some are kidding the Old Man along ("Okay, Dad"). Some—mostly women, I suspect—are merely willing themselves young again in the autumn air (an awful sight for them last year was old Y. A. Tittle on his last legs). And finally, some are filling up a great emptiness in their lives: A fellow named Brownie has been sitting behind me in the upper deck at the Giant games for the past seven years keeping a quarter-by-quarter account in the white space of his scorecard, recording every first down, pass completion, fumble, kick, and score. He used to tabulate downfield tackles as well, but gave it up after a few games. "Too esoteric," he said. Brownie follows his Giants on television, too, correlates his statistics every Sunday night, and commits the cumulative record to memory. He says he doesn't bet. Rather, in the Platonic sense, he is serious about play. One must assume there are hundreds, perhaps thousands, like him whose interest in the game is profoundly *necessary.*

22   Yet, all such exceptions noted, most of us probably come to see something like a war between the pros. A Von Clausewitz writing on our game would paraphrase much of his material from *On War:*

Conclusion   23   "Combat in football is not combat of individual against individual, but an organized whole made up of many parts. The player is paid, clothed and trained, he sleeps, eats, drinks, and practices merely to execute plays at the right place and the right time. All activity is directed to the destruction of the enemy, or rather his ability to fight. If one of the two belligerents is determined to seek victory, he has a high probability of success as soon as he is certain the enemy is not. . . .

24   "Since football is the province of physical exertion and suffering, the province of uncertainty, chance, and danger, the first quality of players is courage. A special direction of the intellect, not meditative, is also supremely important.

25   "There are two kinds of courage. One is moral courage, the courage held in the presence of responsibility. Moral courage is essential to the quarterback or, if I may say, the field general. The other kind of courage is physical, being either indifferent to danger or imbued with team spirit, or both, which is ideal. All in all, courage is the feeling of one's own strength as directed to his moral self-preservation on the football field.

26   "At last, the game is neither art nor science. It belongs to the province of human intercourse, like business and politics. *Pro football is a continuation of war by other means."* (Italics added.)

27   As such, as long as we understand the lethal difference, no apology is necessary.

STRUCTURE REVIEW SEVEN/COMPARISON

Answer each question in the space provided below it.

1 What is the function of paragraph 1?

2 Why does the writer want to "inquire into the nature of the 'war' game"?

3 What parallel does the writer draw between U.S. politics and professional football? How does he tie this information in with his purpose?

4 What characteristic does the writer develop most fully in establishing the comparison between football and war?

5 How does Morgan's discussion of the "suicide squad" help the comparison?

6 Mention some characteristics that develop the comparison other than the "suicide squad" of which the writer discusses only one side—the side related to football.

7 In the parallel between football and war, what part does the quarterback play?

8 Why is the material quoted from Governali important to the writer's purpose?

9 What is the writer's purpose in relating the writing of Von Clausewitz' *On War* to football?

10 Does the writer reach a conclusion? Where is it placed?

ASSIGNMENT/WRITING COMPARISON

1 Write a paragraph or paragraph unit showing similarities between two persons, places, or things. Announce the comparison in the first sentence. Before you begin to write, make a list of the points of likenesses.
2 Research will show amazing similarities between the death of Lincoln and the death of Kennedy. Research this comparison by reading newspapers at the time of the death of President Kennedy. Write a comparison based on your findings.
3 Compare two subjects that people would not ordinarily expect to be similar in order to stress this fact.
4 Compare two subjects with a definite purpose in mind other than to show they are similar. Gather points of likenesses and present the comparison to fulfill this purpose.

CONTRAST

Contrast is a method of developing thought by pointing out differences between two or among three or more persons, places, things, or ideas. In structuring contrast, a writer has a purpose, gathers a sufficient number of differences to firmly establish the contrast and fulfill his purpose, and presents his material in a logical order of development.

An inexperienced writer will find it wise to organize contrast before he puts it on paper. He should first phrase in the form of a topic sentence his contrast if he is developing a paragraph or paragraph unit by contrast in order to alert his reader to his purpose. This statement of purpose in the topic sentence might look something like the following:

In athletic sports, English training is briefer and less severe than American training.

Grant and Lee were oddly different generals.

The differences between Rome and Greece are very clearly marked.

If he is writing a longer paper, he should state clearly his purpose of contrast in the early part of the paper; for example,

Athens and Rome stand side by side as the parents of Western civilization. The parental metaphor is almost irresistible.

In order to be sure than his subjects can be best treated by contrast, he should set up a preliminary plan of the differences by listing points under subject A and following with contrasting points under subject B and subject C (if more than two subjects are involved).

Subject A (Grant)	Subject B (Lee)
1 Son of a tanner on the Western frontier.	**1** Aristocrat from tidewater Virginia.
2 Sees himself in relation to a broader society.	**2** Sees himself in relation to his own region.
3 Grant was a modern man.	**3** Lee was of the age of chivalry.
4 Grant was a long time gaining fame.	**4** Lee was a famous general at the beginning of the Civil war.

In deciding the order of development for contrast that will best suit his purpose, an inexperienced writer has two choices: (1) contrast by point by point *(alternating pattern)* and (2) contrast by wholes (the *subject-at-a-time pattern)*. In developing a contrast by the alternating pattern, a writer will present one point concerning subject A and follow with a contrasting point related to subject B. He may present a point concerning subject A in the first part of a sentence and follow with the contrasting point in the second part of the same sentence. He may decide to present one point concerning subject A in a complete sentence and follow with the contrasting point in the next complete sentence. In the following model paragraph, the writer presents a point concerning Grant and follows with a contrasting point related to Lee.

So Grant and Lee were in complete contrast, representing two diametrically opposed elements in American life. Grant was a modern man emerging; beyond him, ready to come on the stage, was the great age of steel and machinery, of crowded cities and a restless, burgeoning vitality. Lee might have ridden down from the old age of chivalry, lance in hand, silken banner fluttering over his head. . . .[1]

[1] Bruce Catton, "Grant and Lee: A Study in Contrasts," in E. S. Miers (ed.), *The American Story*, p. 204. Copyright © 1956 by Channel Press, Inc., New York. Permission of Broadcast Music, Inc.

In the next model paragraph, observe the point-by-point pattern of contrast.[2]

Lee is usually ranked as the greatest Civil War general, but this evaluation has been made without placing Lee and Grant in the perspective of military developments since the war. Lee was interested hardly at all in "global" strategy, and what few suggestions he did make to his government about operations in other theaters than his own indicate that he had little aptitude for grand planning. As a theater strategist, Lee often demonstrated more brilliance and apparent originality than Grant, but his most audacious plans were as much the product of the Confederacy's inferior military position as of his own fine mind. In war, the weaker side has to improvise brilliantly. It must strike quickly, daringly, and include a dangerous element of risk in its plans. Had Lee been a Northern general with Northern resources behind him, he would have improvised less and seemed less bold. Had Grant been a Southern general, he would have fought as Lee did.

Fundamentally Grant was superior to Lee because in a modern total war he had a modern mind, and Lee did not. Lee looked to the past in war as the Confederacy did in spirit. The staffs of the two men illustrate their outlooks. It would not be accurate to say that Lee's general staff were glorified clerks, but the statement would not be too wide of the mark. Certainly his staff was not, in the modern sense, a planning staff, which was why Lee was often a tired general. He performed labors that no general can do in a big modern army— work that should have fallen to his staff, but that Lee did because it was traditional for the commanding general to do it in older armies. Most of Lee's staff officers were lieutenant-colonels. Some of the men on Grant's general staff, as well as on the staffs of other Northern generals, were major and brigadier generals, officers who were capable of leading corps. Grant's staff was an organization of experts in the various phases of strategic planning. The modernity of Grant's mind was most apparent in his grasp of the concept that war was becoming total and that the destruction of the enemy's economic resources was as effective and legitimate a form of warfare as the destruction of his armies. What was realism to Grant was barbarism to Lee. Lee thought of war in the old way as a conflict between armies and refused to view it for what it had become—a struggle between societies. To him, economic war was needless cruelty to civilians. Lee was the last of the great old-fashioned generals; Grant, the first of the great moderns.

In organizing contrast by wholes, a writer treats subject A in a separate paragraph or the first half of a single paragraph and follows with contrasting points in the same order in the next paragraph or in the

---

[2] T. Harry Williams, *Lincoln and His Generals.* Copyright © 1952 by Alfred A. Knopf, Inc. Permission of the Publisher.

second half of the same paragraph that he presented material about subject A.

And that, perhaps, is where the contrast between Grant and Lee becomes most striking. The Virginia aristocrat, inevitably, saw himself in relation to his own region. He lived in a static society which could endure almost anything except change. Instinctively, his first loyalty would go to the locality in which that society existed. He would fight to the limit of endurance to defend it, because in defending it he was defending everything that gave his own life its deepest meaning.

The Westerner, on the other hand, would fight with equal tenacity for the broader concept of society. He fought so because everything he lived by was tied to growth, expansion, and a constantly widening horizon. What he lived by would survive or fall with the nation itself. He could not possibly stand by unmoved in the face of an attempt to destroy the Union. He would combat it with everything he had, because he could only see it as an effort to cut the ground out from under his feet.[3]

"Athens and Rome"—the model contrast and comparison essay that follows—is an excellent example of the use of comparison and contrast to inform and explain. The writer begins with a point-by-point contrast between masculine Rome and feminine Greece—a metaphor which he considers a serious fallacy. In paragraph 2, the writer notes that "the resemblances between Greece and Rome are clearly marked." He mentions such points of similarity as language, customs, dress, and "a common Mediterranean culture, reposing possibly on a common aboriginal stock which has been variously influenced by intruding tribes and geographical conditions."

In paragraph 3, the writer presents a contrast, announcing it in the first sentence, "But with all these resemblances, one of the most interesting features of ancient history lies in the psychological contrast between Greece and Rome, or rather between Athens and Rome." He then presents points of contrast by wholes.

ATHENS AND ROME
J. C. Stobart

Statement   **1** Athens and Rome stand side by side as the parents of West-
of contrast   ern civilisation. *The parental metaphor is almost irresistible.*

---

[3] Catton, op. cit., p. 204.

SOURCE NOTE: J. C. Stobart, "Athens and Rome," *The Grandeur That Was Rome*, 4th ed., pp. 1–2. Copyright © 1962 by Sidwick & Jackson, Ltd. Permission of Hawthorn Books, Inc., 70 Fifth Avenue, New York, N. Y.

Point-by-point differences	Rome is so obviously masculine and robust, Greece endowed with so much loveliness and charm. Rome subjugates by physical conquest and government. Greece yields so easily to the Roman might and then in revenge so easily dominates Rome itself, with all that Rome has conquered, by the mere attractive-
Limitation of contrast	ness of superior humanity. *Nevertheless this metaphor of masculine and feminine contains a serious fallacy.* Greece, too, had
Likenesses	had days of military vigour. It was by superior courage and skill in fighting that Athens and Sparta had beaten back the Persian invasions of the fifth century before Christ and thus saved Europe for occidentalism. Again it was by military prowess that Alexander the Great carried Greek civilisation to the borders of India, hellenising Asia Minor, Syria, Persia, Egypt, Phoenicia,
Discussion of fallacy in the metaphor	and even Palestine. This he did just at the moment when Rome was winning her dominion over Latium. Instead, then, of looking at Greece and Rome as two coeval forces working side by side, we must regard them as predecessor and successor. Rome is scarcely revealed as a world-power until she meets Greek civilisation in Campania near the beginning of the third century before Christ. The physical decline of Greece is scarcely apparent until Pyrrhus' phalanx returns beaten in battle by the Roman legions at Beneventum. Moreover, in addition to this chronological division of spheres there is also a geographical division. Greece takes the East, Rome the West, and though by the time that Rome went forth to govern her Western provinces she was already pretty thoroughly permeated with Greek civilisation, yet the West remained throughout mediaeval history far more Latin than Greek. When Constantine divided the empire he was only expressing in outward form a natural division of culture.
Statement of comparison	2 The resemblances between Rome and Greece are very clearly marked. In many respects they are visibly of the same family, and though we no longer speak as loosely of "Aryan" and "Indo-European" as did the ethnologists and philologists of the nineteenth century, yet there remains an obvious kinship
Similarities	of language, customs, and even dress. Many of the most obvious similarities, such as those of religion and literature, are now seen to be the result of later borrowing, but there remains a distinct cousinship; both peninsulas may be regarded as exhibiting phases of a common Mediterranean culture, reposing possibly on a common aboriginal stock which has been variously influenced by intruding tribes and by geographical conditions.
Statement of contrast	3 *But with all these resemblances, one of the most interesting features of ancient history lies in the psychological contrast*

Point of
contrast

between Greece and Rome, or rather between Athens and Rome. Athens is rich in ideas, full of the spirit of inquiry, and hence fertile in invention, fond of novelty, worshipping brilliance of mind and body. Rome is stolid and conservative, devoted to tradition and law. Gravity and a sense of duty are her supreme virtues. Here we have the two types that succeed and conquer, set side by side for comparison. *To which is the victory in the end?* (Italics added.)

Read the following model contrast from which we have excerpted examples. As you read, observe how frequently the writer announces the purpose of contrast in the topic sentences of paragraphs. Notice also the way he uses both methods of contrast to develop the differences between Grant and Lee.

GRANT AND LEE: A STUDY IN CONTRASTS
Bruce Catton

1   When Ulysses S. Grant and Robert E. Lee met in the parlor of a modest house at Appomattox Court House, Virginia, on April 9, 1865, to work out the terms for the surrender of Lee's Army of Northern Virginia, a great chapter in American life came to a close, and a great new chapter began.

2   These men were bringing the Civil War to its virtual finish. To be sure, other armies had yet to surrender, and for a few days the fugitive Confederate government would struggle desperately and vainly, trying to find some way to go on living now that its chief support was gone. But in effect it was all over when Grant and Lee signed the papers. And the little room where they wrote out the terms was the scene of one of the poignant, dramatic contrasts in American history.

3   They were two strong men, these oddly different generals, and they represented the strengths of two conflicting currents that, through them, had come into final collision.

4   Back of Robert E. Lee was the notion that the old aristocratic concept might somehow survive and be dominant in American life.

5   Lee was tidewater Virginia, and in his background were family, culture, and tradition . . . the age of chivalry transplanted to a New World which was making its own legends and its own myths. He embodied a way of life that had come down through the age of knighthood and the English country squire. America was a land that was beginning all over again, dedicated to nothing much more complicated than the rather hazy belief that all men had equal rights and should have an equal chance in the world. In such a land Lee stood

SOURCE NOTE: Bruce Catton, "Grant and Lee: A Study in Contrasts," in E. S. Miers (ed.), *The American Story,* pp. 202–205. (New York: Channel Press, Inc., 1956). Permission of Broadcast Music, Inc.

for the feeling that it was somehow of advantage to human society to have a pronounced inequality in the social structure. There should be a leisure class, backed by ownership of land; in turn, society itself should be keyed to the land as the chief source of wealth and influence. It would bring forth (according to this ideal) a class of men with a strong sense of obligation to the community; men who lived not to gain advantage for themselves, but to meet the solemn obligations which had been laid on them by the very fact that they were privileged. From them the country would get its leadership; to them it could look for the higher values—of thought, of conduct, of personal deportment—to give it strength and virtue.

6 Lee embodied the noblest elements of this aristocratic ideal. Through him, the landed nobility justified itself. For four years, the Southern states had fought a desperate war to uphold the ideals for which Lee stood. In the end, it almost seemed as if the Confederacy fought for Lee; as if he himself was the Confederacy . . . the best thing that the way of life for which the Confederacy stood could ever have to offer. He had passed into legend before Appomattox. Thousands of tired, underfed, poorly clothed Confederate soldiers, long since past the simple enthusiasm of the early days of the struggle, somehow considered Lee the symbol of everything for which they had been willing to die. But they could not quite put this feeling into words. If the Lost Cause, sanctified by so much heroism and so many deaths, had a living justification, its justification was General Lee.

7 Grant, the son of a tanner on the Western frontier, was everything Lee was not. He had come up the hard way and embodied nothing in particular except the eternal toughness and sinewy fiber of the men who grew up beyond the mountains. He was one of a body of men who owed reverence and obeisance to no one, who were self-reliant to a fault, who cared hardly anything for the past but who had a sharp eye for the future.

8 These frontier men were the precise opposites of the tidewater aristocrats. Back of them, in the great surge that had taken people over the Alleghenies and into the opening Western country, there was a deep, implicit dissatisfaction with a past that had settled into grooves. They stood for democracy, not from any reasoned conclusion about the proper ordering of human society, but simply because they had grown up in the middle of democracy and knew how it worked. Their society might have privileges, but they would be privileges each man had won for himself. Forms and patterns meant nothing. No man was born to anything, except perhaps to a chance to show how far he could rise. Life was competition.

9 Yet along with this feeling had come a deep sense of belonging to a national community. The Westerner who developed a farm, opened a shop, or set up in business as a trader, could hope to prosper only as his own community prospered—and his community ran from the Atlantic to the Pacific and from Canada down to Mexico. If the land was settled, with towns and highways and accessible markets, he could better himself. He saw his fate in terms of the nation's own destiny. As its horizons expanded, so did his. He had, in other words, an acute dollars-and-cents stake in the continued growth and development of his country.

10 And that, perhaps, is where the contrast between Grant and Lee becomes most striking. The Virginia aristocrat, inevitably, saw himself in relation to his own region. He lived in a static society which could endure almost anything except change. Instinctively, his first loyalty would go to the locality in which that society existed. He would fight to the limit of endurance to defend it, because in defending it he was defending everything that gave his own life its deepest meaning.

11 The Westerner, on the other hand, would fight with an equal tenacity for the broader concept of society. He fought so because everything he lived by was tied to growth, expansion, and a constantly widening horizon. What he lived by would survive or fall with the nation itself. He could not possibly stand by unmoved in the face of an attempt to destroy the Union. He would combat it with everything he had, because he could only see it as an effort to cut the ground out from under his feet.

12 So Grant and Lee were in complete contrast, representing two diametrically opposed elements in American life. Grant was the modern man emerging; beyond him, ready to come on the stage, was the great age of steel and machinery, of crowded cities and a restless, burgeoning vitality. Lee might have ridden down from the old age of chivalry, lance in hand, silken banner fluttering over his head. Each man was the perfect champion of his cause, drawing both his strengths and his weaknesses from the people he led.

13 Yet it was not all contrast, after all. Different as they were—in background, in personality, in underlying aspiration—these two great soldiers had much in common. Under everything else, they were marvelous fighters. Furthermore, their fighting qualities were really very much alike.

14 Each man had, to begin with, the great virtue of utter tenacity and fidelity. Grant fought his way down the Mississippi Valley in spite of acute personal discouragement and profound military handicaps. Lee hung on in the trenches at Petersburg after hope itself had died. In each man there was an indomitable quality . . . the born fighter's refusal to give up as long as he can still remain on his feet and lift his two fists.

15 Daring and resourcefulness they had, too; the ability to think faster and move faster than the enemy. These were the qualities which gave Lee the dazzling campaigns of Second Manassas and Chancellorsville and won Vicksburg for Grant.

16 Lastly, and perhaps greatest of all, there was the ability, at the end, to turn quickly from war to peace once the fighting was over. Out of the way these two men behaved at Appomattox came the possibility of a peace of reconciliation. It was a possibility not wholly realized, in the years to come, but which did, in the end, help the two sections to become one nation again . . . after a war whose bitterness might have seemed to make such a reunion wholly impossible. No part of either man's life became him more than the part he played in their brief meeting in the McLean house at Appomattox. Their behavior there put all succeeding generations of Americans in their debt. Two great Americans, Grant and Lee—very different, yet under everything very much alike. Their encounter at Appomattox was one of the great moments of American history.

STRUCTURE REVIEW EIGHT/CONTRAST

Name _____   Class _____

Answer each question in the space provided below it.

1 What is the purpose of the first two paragraphs?

2 What is the function of paragraph 3?

3 How are paragraphs 4, 5, and 6 organized?

4 How are paragraphs 7, 8, and 9 organized?

5 What purpose does the first sentence of paragraph 10 serve?

6 What is the function and organizational pattern of paragraph 12?

7 How does the plan of development change in paragraph 13?

8 In what position in the essay does the writer state his purpose?

Answers are on page 168.

IRELAND, ISRAEL—ALIKE YET DIFFERENT
Elizabeth C. Winship

1 Ireland and Israel are both very small countries. They are both very old countries

2 Both were late under British rule, winning their respective independence only quite recently. There is still British evidence in either place—both countries use the pound as a monetary unit. Neither country is overloaded with Anglophiles.

3 Agriculture plays a large role in their economies. So do large hordes of roving tourists.

4 In both countries, religion is closely linked to government. They do not insist on separation of church and state as we do. Kosher food is served almost without exception in all public places in Israel. The whole country shuts down Friday afternoon to prepare for the Saturday Jewish Sabbath. In the Irish Free State, the public schools are Catholic.

5 Each country has its grand old man. Eamon de Valera is 88 and still president of his party, the Fianna Fail. He is a man revered and respected throughout the world. So is David Ben-Gurion. Now 84. Ben-Gurion has retired from the Knesset, (the Israeli Parliament) and is writing his memoirs, but he is still the man that all important visitors want to see.

6 Both countries are neat. Both are orderly. Both have their wars. Both begin with "I".

7 So what do all these similarities lead up to? Two countries, just about as different as they could possibly be.

8 Ireland is all greens and soft rain, and the enveloping kindness of the world's most hospitable people.

9 Israel is contrasts—hot sand here, lush green there with quick hot sun and the world's most determined people.

10 The tourists' predominant impression of Israel is new and bustling; of Ireland, ancient and resigned.

11 The climate hits you first. If only Israel could swap a little of her sun for some of Ireland's rain. But then, each country would lose something. Israel without its deserts and her people without their bronzed skins would not be half so attractive. The keynote of Ireland is her drenched green fields, and as for those rumors about the Irish complexions—they are true, and then some!

12 An early impression on a visitor to Ireland is the walls. The country is crisscrossed and crosshatched with them. In Israel there are none, to speak of. Both countries are richly endowed with stones, and the Irish have laid them up into neat grey walls, mile upon mile, separating the fierce green little fields.

SOURCE NOTE: Elizabeth C. Winship, "Ireland, Israel—Alike yet Different," *Boston Sunday Globe,* Aug. 25, 1970. Copyright © 1970 by the *Boston Sunday Globe,* Boston, Mass.

The Israeli, when clearing fields, simply dumps the stones around the edges in heaps. Lazy? No. There's no need for fences because their animals are not pastured but herded. Cheaper for a man to watch a flock than build a wall, and they are in a hurry, too, to get the earth producing food.

13 These walls say something about differences in the concept of property. Ireland has been subdividing her land among sons, and then redividing among grandsons for hundreds, thousands of years. Israel never had these divided fields. Bedouin-type grazing, where anything that grew that an animal could eat, was the fashion, and even when land was privately owned, little of it was tilled until this century when the Jews almost miraculously wrested arable land from desert and swamp.

14 The whole aspect of the farms today is still entirely different. The kibbutz or co-operative farm stresses joint ownership or co-operative action, which enables Israeli farmers to take advantage of modern agricultural methods and equipment. Israel's universities help develop the most efficient techniques to produce the fruits and vegetables and dairy products the country relies on for export.

15 Jaffa oranges come to our supermarkets from the neatest, best tended groves. Gladiolas bloom in the desert, for export. Baby olive trees are growing in nurseries that sprouted only boulders for thousands of years.

16 Irish farms seem unchanged over the centuries. One of the most charming sights is the countryside dotted with small thatch-roofed farms with their neat courtyards. These one-family privately owned farms cannot afford the machinery for modern day operations. The lovely whitewashed houses please the tourist's eye and add hugely to the serenity of the landscape, but will the farmer's wife and children want to continue a hard, old-fashioned way of life?

17 In both countries history is visible everywhere, but the histories are very different.

18 Israel is ancient history, even pre-history. Civilization is thought to have dawned in the land between the Tigris and the Euphrates rivers, not very far northeast. And, of course, you live in the Bible from one end of the country to the other. Stand anywhere in the wasteland areas which cannot be cultivated, and you feel the presence of the past. You can see Abraham riding south towards Egypt, and all the hordes of peoples, Turks, Romans, Crusaders, Egyptians, who have rolled over the land. Stepping into old Jerusalem is a powerful experience, whether, one is Jew, Christian or Moslem.

19 But, and this is a big but, step into modern Jerusalem, or any other part of new Israel, and history flees. You are in a thriving, bustling modern Western culture, and not likely to forget it.

20 In Ireland, too, antiquities are visible at every hand. Though the civilization may not have got underway as early as in Israel, there was a thriving society here in the Bronze Age making Irish gold ornaments so good they were popular in Britain, France and Luxembourg.

kings came, and made their presence felt the length and breadth of the land. And later on the English and Normans.

22 Everywhere you go there is a church or castle, grey granite weathering, like as not falling down. Like the Jews, the Irish know their history, and delight in telling you who lived here, or what battles were fought.

23 These relics of the past are not so old as Nazareth or Bethelem, but curiously, the general atmosphere in Ireland seems to be much more than one of age. People look more to the past. The cities and towns look old. They aren't full of cellar holes for new buildings, or edged with masses of steel and concrete, reaching skyward for high-rise apartments.

24 Compare the Parliament buildings, for instance. The Dail, in Dublin, is traditional Gothic, venerable and dignified. Jerusalem's Knesset is brand new, the most modern of architecture.

25 The governments in these buildings are even more unlike. Israel is, or has been, unified under the pressure of the war from without. Ireland is frac- tionalized by the war from within—the Catholic-Protestant differences, and the division between Irish Free State in the South and the British oriented five counties in the North.

STRUCTURE REVIEW NINE/COMPARISON AND CONTRAST

Name _____ Class _____

Answer each question in the space provided below it.

1 How does the writer organize and develop the thought of the first six paragraphs?

2 Does the writer find it necessary to introduce her subject formally?

3 What is the main function of paragraph 7?

4 Does the writer develop her contrasts point by point or by wholes?

5 In this section, there are many short paragraphs. What is the advantage of short paragraphing?

LOVE STUFF, COPS-AND-ROBBERS STYLE
Donald E. Westlake

The gangster is coming back. To the movies, that is; in real life, he never went away. But in the motion picture, after dominating the screen throughout the 30s and on into the 40s, the mob departed, muscled out by—something, I forget what. And now at last they're coming back.

But with a difference. The crooks are no longer quite what they used to be. The crime movies way back when were built on the headlines of the time, of course, based on the Dillingers and the Capones of that era, but somehow the people were altered in translation and came out totally unlike anybody who had ever trod this earth. Something Runyonesque occurred, and both the crooks and the society they lived in became jauntier, stronger, better.

You could always trust a deathbed confession, for instance; if Humphrey Bogart said the kid wasn't in on the jailbreak, the warden took his word for it and the kid went free. Edward G. Robinson might try to bump off a tough DA, but it would never even occur to him to try to buy him off. And James Cagney might rob banks for a living, but he'd die before he'd turn over secret military information to a foreign power; he was a crook, yes, but he was an American crook.

And, like all the rest of the movie crooks of that time, he had a tough line of patter and a fast right hand and a lot of self-reliance, and if he finally had to walk that Last Mile he did it with his head up and his shoulders back.

But not only the crooks were better than life in those movies; the whole world was. The DA really didn't take bribes. Reporters loved their jobs so much they constantly risked death to bring in the story. Justices of the peace would put on a ratty bathrobe and marry a sweet young couple on the lam at any hour of the night. And when the bank robbers got to the bank there was a parking space out front.

The people in those movies also had a language all their own, never heard anywhere other than a sound stage. All their sentences, for instance, began with the word say, as in, "Say, you can't get away with that." Or, "Say, that's a pretty snazzy heap you got there." Or, at particularly important plot turns, "Say, don't I know you from someplace?"

Well, all things do come to an end, and sometime around World War II the boys all turned legit. Robinson suddenly showed up as an insurance investigator, Cagney metamorphosed into Yankee Doodle Dandy, and Bogart came twitching back as—an assistant district attorney.

Be that as it may. Wherever they went, and for whatever reasons, something broke up that old gang of ours, and the screen was a blander place without them. But now, at long last, they do seem to be coming back.

SOURCE NOTE: Donald E. Westlake, "Love Stuff, Cops-and-Robbers Style," *Los Angeles Times Calendar*, p. 14, Sunday, May 7, 1972. Copyright © 1971 by the Los Angeles *Times*.

Though with a difference. Things never do return exactly as they were before. What would Edward G. Robinson's Rico, for instance, think of Warren Beatty's Clyde? Akim Tamiroff once played a syndicate boss named Steve Recka, who played the organ in moments of stress, who lived with his Oriental mistress (Anna May Wong), and whose downfall was caused by his futile love for a girl from the upper classes; the level of romance in Don Corleone is pretty well summed up by his style of overcoat.

The fact is, the romance has gone out of our lives, and we aren't going to believe anybody who claims otherwise. For example, I wrote a comic robbery novel a couple of years ago called "The Hot Rock," which was recently turned into a movie. At one point in the film the crooks use a helicopter, and director Peter Yates had a grand time showing the helicopter moving among the skyscrapers of Manhattan.

Most of the people who've talked to me about the picture say they loved that sequence, and I think I know why. It's almost the only romantic moment in the whole film, and by the time it comes along the audience already knows these crooks are simply ordinary shmos trying to make a living like anybody else; romance when it does happen is accidental and incidental and a happy surprise, as in life. The audience is pleased for the characters because they've been a given a good moment, which is still possible for any of us, and therefore both hopeful and believable.

So although the crooks are coming back, they aren't quite the same breezy glib semi-indestructible crew they were the last time around. Organized crime, whether treated seriously as in "The Godfather" or comically as in "The Gang That Couldn't Shoot Straight," is simply a business these days, operated by businessmen with business problems to resolve; nothing at all like the Cagney-Bogart business partnership in "The Roaring Twenties," brought to an end by trouble over a girl singer (a "chantoozie," as the boys used to say).

And the big robbery, too, has changed. Whether done seriously as in "The Split" or comically as in "The Hot Rock," the boys are no longer anything at all like the tough loner of "High Sierra" who was pulling one last job to get the money for a crippled girl's operation. The thieves, too, are businessmen these days, small independent businessmen trying to survive in the era of the major corporation.

Does the return of the crook to the motion picture mean that America is becoming more crooked than it used to be, or that Americans will start to turn crooked by the thousands after seeing these movies? I think just the reverse is true; we have more laws this year than we had last year, and several thousand more laws are on the books now than existed before World War II. We're so law-abiding we're strangling in all the rules and regulations, and it's a respite and a relief for all of us to see contemporaries of ours who survive somehow outside the law's crushing grip.

So even in a deromanticized world, even as a businessman among businessmen, the crook still has one advantage over most heroes of fiction. Stepping outside society, operating without regard for those proliferating rules that hem in the rest of us, he is in one of the few businesses where romance can still happen. Not as frequently as when gang members were putting their kid brothers through medical school, but sometimes; they do get that occasional helicopter ride. And we get to ride along with them.

ASSIGNMENT/CONTRAST
Write a brief analysis of the essay "Love Stuff, Cops-and-Robbers Style," showing how in many places in the essay the writer implies the points of contrast with subject A.

DISCUSSION TWO/FILMS

1 What was the "gangster" of the 1930s and 1940s like, according to the films of that era?
2 Do you think that the gangster films of the 1930s and 1940s truly reflect the society of that era?
3 In your opinion is America "more crooked" than it used to be?
4 Do you agree with the writer's conclusion?

ASSIGNMENT/WRITING CONTRAST AND COMPARISON

1 Write a four- or five-paragraph essay in which you compare and then contrast high school and college. Prepare a preliminary plan and outline the material gathered before writing.
2 Write a contrast developed by wholes of an American and an Englishman.
3 Contrast point by point a campus conservative with a campus radical.
4 Select two subjects that seem quite similar and show that they are actually different in many ways.
5 Select two subjects that seem quite different and show that they are actually similar in many respects.
6 Contrast two "isms" like capitalism and communism or socialism. Have a purpose for the contrast.

ANALOGY

An analogy implies a comparison. A simple analogy is nothing more than a metaphor. But, the *extended analogy* is a special kind of comparison used to make clear the unfamiliar by pointing out likenesses between it and a subject familiar to the reader. Some common extended analogies are the following:

1 The structure of the atom and the structure of the solar system
2 Life and a game of chess
3 The function of the heart and the function of a pump
4 The function of the eye and the function of a camera
5 Undesirable social structure and a stagecoach

Analogies give a vividness to the writing. A writer, however, does not sit down with the purpose of writing an analogy; it arises out of his thinking about a subject and organizing and developing the material. In the model analogy that follows, the writer explains the foreign policy of a government by comparing it to the national game of the individual nation.

THE GAMES NATIONS PLAY
Max Lerner

When Mr. Nixon meets the successive heads of states between now and May, he will be bringing his game plan (to use his

Statement
of the
analogy

favorite term) to counter theirs. *But each nation has its own characteristic national game or pastime.* Is it too crazy a notion to think that the games nations play in their leisure time may do much to shape the game plans they use in their foreign policies?

United
States and
football

The American game is, of course, football. Grown men look back to their football days as days of glory, and Mr. Nixon has a sharply nostalgic memory of them. His current political power is probably linked in his mind with that memory, and he sees his diplomatic strategy, his economic strategy and even his Supreme Court strategy in terms of a football game plan.

Additional
support of
point one

There is an interview with George Sauer (in the current Intellectual Digest) in which the former star of the New York Jets sees the essence of the game as one of aggression and domination: You regard your opponent not as a human being but as a depersonalized obstacle to be blotted out. Mr. Nixon's conservative critics, who fear and hate his new foreign policy, probably feel he has gone soft not only on Chinese and Russian communism but also on the aggressive side of American

SOURCE NOTE: Max Lerner, "The Games Nations Play," *Los Angeles Times,* Dec. 5, 1971, sec. L, 6.
Copyright © 1971 by the Los Angeles *Times.*

football. His liberal critics feel that he still has plenty of aggression in his domestic policy. For any adequate view, one would have to know also what Henry Kissinger's favorite sport is—probably dancing, where the idea is not to overthrow anyone, but for both to keep moving and stay on their feet. In short, equilibrium theory.

British and cricket

Of the others in the power struggle, *the British with their historic addiction to cricket* seem resigned to the long-scoring sequence of their rivals, as they once boasted a scoring sequence of their own in the days when they had their vaunted empire.

The two greatest nations (aside from the United States) who were touched by the British heritage of a virtuous it-isn't-cricket

India and the dance

stance are India and Canada. *The Indians* have largely inherited the British sports, but their real expressiveness *lies rather in their dance.* Mrs. Gandhi's speeches in Parliament on the war with Pakistan have all the multimeanings of a dance of Shiva, with arms reaching out in all directions.

Canada and ice hockey

As for Canada, if its national game is ice hockey, Prime Minister Pierre Trudeau expresses it well in the sharp glacial edge of his remark that he has done everything Mr. Nixon is doing in foreign policy toward China and Russia, only earlier. One would have to add that he also has less of a power base than Mr. Nixon, and has been skating on thinner ice.

France and bicycle race

The French game style may come from the lonely rider in the grueling cross-country bicycle race (Tour de France), seemingly a team but in fact highly individualist, with a flare for the rough terrain: as witness Gen. Charles de Gaulle.

Spain and bullfights

The foreign policy of the Spanish over the centuries has been showy, ritualistic and decadent, as in their *bullfights.* It is hard to find a continuing symbol for the *Germans* that would include Bismarck, Hitler and Brandt. Perhaps the *Wagnerian*

Germans and Wagnerian opera

opera (if we can stretch the idea of games) comes closest, in its combining of the thrust to power with the touch of grandiosity.

The *Russians* have been, of course—until the wild accident of Bobby Fischer—*the chess masters of the world,* and their

Russia and chess

diplomacy from Lenin and Chicherin has shown it, with its feints of cunning and its naked assertion of power.

Although they share between them the great power-mass of the Communist world, the game styles of the Russians and Chinese are very different. If the *Chinese national* passion is for

China and Ping-Pong

Ping-Pong rather than chess, the thrust and counterthrust of Chinese diplomacy shows it with its action-and-reaction sequences—each of them all-out—in one direction or another while the Russian style is more veiled and indirect. It is zig-and-zag, rather than ping-and-pong.

Japan—contradic-tions

I leave *Japan* for the end because it is the most puzzling, with its blend of the traditional No plays and the modern Western game of baseball. Japanese policy can contain these *contra-dictions,* of the highly disciplined with the imitative, because in a sense Japan has no policy game plan which is distinct from its society: The point is that the teamwork structure of the soci-ety itself is built into the decisions the leaders make.

No game for Israel—stark real-ity

Something of the sort, in a very different way, can be said for the tiny state of Israel. *The Israelis have no game separate from politics,* since their survival depends on policy. As David Ben-Gurion put it, the Israelis are a nation of several million prime ministers. But from the start danger has been built into their game plan, since *it isn't a game at all but a stark reality.* (Italics added.)

ANSWER SECTION

STRUCTURE REVIEW EIGHT

1 The first two paragraphs introduce the subject and gain reader interest.
2 In paragraph 3, the writer states his purpose of contrast.
3 Paragraphs 4, 5, and 6 constitute a paragraph unit that includes points concerning General Lee.
4 Paragraphs 7, 8, and 9 constitute a paragraph unit including opposite points related to General Grant. The contrast is developed by wholes.
5 The first sentence serves to summarize and emphasize the major differ-ence between Grant and Lee.
6 It serves as a summarizing paragraph for the whole contrast. It is orga-nized by an alternating pattern.
7 The writer begins the organization by comparison. He finishes the essay by showing likenesses between the two men.
8 In the next to the last line of the essay, Bruce Catton states his purpose: Grant and Lee were two great Americans—"very different, yet under every-thing very much alike."

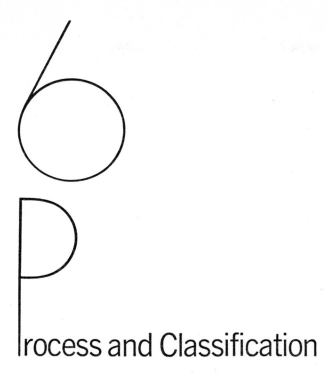

rocess and Classification

In organizing and developing thought by process, a writer breaks down his subject into steps or divisions in order to explain how to do something or how something is done. There are two kinds of processes: *instructional* and *informational.*

INSTRUCTIONAL PROCESS

In writing an instructional process, the writer's purpose is to show his reader how to do something. He knows the process thoroughly; therefore he can describe it in detail. In time order, he breaks the operation or procedure down into a series of orderly steps. If it is possible, he will group related steps into stages or logical divisions. He will explain each step clearly and completely enough so that the reader can duplicate that step before moving onward to the next one. He will define any terms that he feels the reader may not know and will tell the reader what tools and materials are essential for the operation. He will describe each step in simple language and repeat any instructions if he considers the step to be complicated. He will caution the reader not to do certain things that may prevent him from completing the operation successfully. In the model instructional process that follows, the writer recommends a basic method to teach swimming that is favored by many famous swimming coaches.

A BASIC METHOD TO TEACH SWIMMING

1 If a youngster can paddle the length of an ordinary swimming pool, it may save his life. According to the National Safety Council, more than 2,500 youngsters died of accidental drowning last year, *the majority within 50 feet of safely.* With a rudimentary knowledge of swimming, most of these deaths could have been avoided.

Introduction

2 For a variety of reasons, many parents feel that a child's introduction to swimming is best left to organizations like the Red Cross, YMCA, YWCA or the Boy Scouts, who specialize in group learn-to-swim classes. Yet any parent can teach his child the fundamentals of water safety, provided he has confidence in his own ability as a swimmer, plus a fair amount of patience.

Where?

3 Where and when should a child learn? Almost any body of water will do—bay, lake, pond, indoor community swim club or a neighbor's backyard pool. (Teaching a youngster in the ocean should be attempted only under ideal weather conditions, if at all.) There is no best age to start. However, the consensus of experts polled by The Better Way is: the sooner the better.

When?

4 Philip Moriarty, coach of the championship Yale University swimming team, for example, begins teaching children to swim between the ages of three and five. Here is the approach recommended by Moriarty and other authorities:

Process Steps

1 Preparing the child to enter water.

5 Prepare the child psychologically. Don't say, "Tomorrow morning at 10 o'clock you are going to learn to swim." Do say, "I saw Billy out swimming the other day. He's your age, isn't he? Would you like to give it a try?" Appealing to the naturally competitive instinct in children will achieve faster results than the stiff, authoritarian approach.

2 Moving into water

6 Get the child wet all over before he enters the water. Rub arms, legs and torso. Then, holding the child securely, take him into water sufficiently shallow so he can touch bottom. Bob up and down together at eye level, making it a play period.

Flotation devices

7 Many instructors believe it advisable to equip the beginner

SOURCE NOTE: "A Basic Method to Teach Swimming," *Good Housekeeping,* August 1969, pp. 44–46. Copyright © 1969 by Good Housekeeping.

with some sort of a flotation device. Their reasoning is that it reassures the child that he will stay on top of the water. Opponents of these devices say that flotation gear gives a false sense of security—the security should come from the mother or father during the training period.

3 Vary routine

8 Vary the bobbing routine by pushing the child away from your body, while at the same time retaining a firm grip. If the youngster becomes tired, stop and begin again tomorrow. "A parent must be very patient at the beginning," remarks Charles Hickcox, winner of three Olympic gold medals in 1968. "It's not something that can be done right away." Never force a child to swim.

4 Placing face in water

9 Have a child place his face in the water. (For the reluctant or fearful youngster, have him practice by blowing bubbles in the bathtub—"making a sound like a motorboat.") Then, standing in waist-high water, have him retrieve objects from the bottom.

5 Prone float

10 Face the child at arm's length to teach him the prone, or face-down, float. Hold his hands. Tell him to take a deep breath, put his face in the water, and stretch out his legs as far as he can. With steady practice, he will soon be able to float by himself. The next step is the prone glide. In chest-high water, the child leans forward, arms extended and hands together, and pushes off from the bottom or side of the pool. In both these exercises, move toward the shallow end of the pool or inshore.

6 Prone glide

7 Arm and leg movements

11 Start the arm and leg strokes by having him use his arms as if he were "digging in the sand." Elbows should be bent and fingers closed. Kicking is somewhat like riding a bicycle; it is largely hip action. Keep the legs out straight, knees close together, feet extended. In kicking, the feet should not rise above the surface, nor should the knee bend.

8 Home exercises

12 Between water sessions, try an at-home drill, using the child's bed and a full-length mirror. To perfect his leg stokes, the child lies on the bed, the lower part of his legs hanging over the end, and kicks. Standing directly in front of the mirror, or to one side, he practices the propelling motions of the arm strokes.

STRUCTURE REVIEW TEN/INSTRUCTIONAL PROCESS

Name _____   Class _____

Answer each question in the space provided below it.

1 Why doesn't the writer begin discussing the actual process until the third paragraph?

2 Where does the writer state his thesis?

3 Into how many stages can the process be logically divided? What are the separate stages?

4 Mention some specific things the writer cautions the teacher of swimming not to do (negative directions).

5 What is the simple subject of most sentences in the essay? Why is this point of view especially appropriate for the instructional process?

See answers on page 190.

The instructional process that follows differs from that of "A Basic Method to Teach Swimming" primarily because the writer is dealing with a different kind of process—the writing of a short story. Because not many people are interested in writing a short story and because many people feel that they cannot write, Millie McWhirter must not only describe the process but capture the reader's interest as well if she is going to be successful. Therefore, she tells a story in which she informs the reader how to write a short story. She uses her own experiences in writing the short story "Four Little Words" to hold the reader's interest while, at the same time, using the story itself as example material for the steps in the process.

On the surface, this process seems to be more complicated and less simply organized than the process on swimming, yet it is actually more skillfully organized and as clearly developed as the previous essay. She breaks down the process into ten stages: (1) seeking sources for stories, (2) discovering the theme and planning the plot, (3) beginning the story, (4) developing character, (5) creating suspense, (6) triggering the flashback, (7) using and developing minor characters, (8) moving toward the climax, (9) reaching the highpoint or climax, (10) ending the story or denouement.

In making clear the steps, she uses example material from her own story to show how she does it. She makes sure that the reader is aware of this technique by such guide phrases as "here's the way 'Four Little Words' begins," "so here we begin developing the theme," or "here's the paragraph describing Fran." In addition she tells the reader what not to do; for example, she writes:

"Remember that Sally mustn't indulge in self-pity."

"Characterize with a few words without stopping the story-action."

"She is not given a name because the story emphasis would shift to her problems."

"Don't tell the reader, show him."

Millie McWhirter's language is simple, and the organization is according to the time sequence of the steps.

THE SHORT-SHORT STORY
Millie McWhirter

It all starts with awareness, with knowing that there are story ideas all around us, no matter what we're doing or where we are. Even if we happen to be flat on our backs in a hospital, there's an idea for a story, an article, somewhere out there in the corridor, or maybe here in the bare, white room.

Now there may be some way of dramatizing *your* surgery so that your friends will sit still, enchanted, when you begin "Well, when I had *my* operation . . ." But if you can do it, you're much better than I! However, my stay in the hospital did provide me with an idea which finally became a short-short. It was titled "Four Little Words" and appeared in the Feb. '68 issue of *St. Anthony Messenger.*

The idea for the story came about, basically, like this:

Most patients, I noticed, tend to "put on a happy face" during visiting hours. When family or friends came to ask how they were feeling, they would say, "Oh, fine . . . just fine." But later, when the lights were dimmed and patients visited with each other, they expressed their fears over tomorrow's surgery, worried about results of lab tests. I remember one woman whose husband was unable to get over to see her the night before her surgery. He telephoned to tell her that something vital to his business had delayed him but that if she needed him he'd walk out on the meeting and come anyway. "I told him he mustn't even think of coming," she said to me. "I certainly don't want him to be worried about *me!* And yet . . ." And she started to cry.

So here was the theme for a story. There's always a certain ambivalence to our emotions. In truth, we don't want our loved ones to worry. But this is the old story about be careful what you wish for, you might get it. The plot, then, was about a woman's struggle to appear bright, cheerful as she's rolled to surgery. She truly doesn't want a single soul to be worried about her. And yet . . .

One rule of the short-short is: start the story as near the ending as possible. The first paragraph should give a feeling of immediacy, some suspense, and, hopefully, the who, when, what, where. Here's the way "Four Little Words" begins:

Now that the moment was near, Sally Harter was grasping for just the right words, the words that would make it possible to exit smiling.

Until now, she'd managed to appear serene, even cheerful. But now the doctor was saying, "Sorry about the delay. It won't be much longer."

In one of the first drafts of this story (before the endless rewrites), I'd written that Sally Harter was "grasping for just the right words to say." But, as

Source note: Millie McWhirter, "The Short-Short Story," *Writer's Digest,* January 1969, pp. 39–41.

it turns out, it wasn't what Sally wanted to say, but what she wants to *hear* said. She doesn't know that, of course, and neither does the reader, but the denouement comes when her husband says the four little words I'll tell you about a little later. So this must be planted early in the story.

Remember that Sally mustn't indulge in self-pity. Let the reader feel sorry for her, but admire her attempts to keep smiling no matter what. Then the reader will keep turning the pages (we hope!) to see if she succeeds.

Concise Characterization

Another rule of the short-short: Characterize with a few words, without stopping the story-action. Here's the third paragraph, when we see the doctor, the time of day, and know that Sally's going to surgery:

> His bald head reflected the bright morning sun outside the hospital window. His brown suit belied the fact that soon he'd be thrusting his arms into a surgeon's gown, tying a mask over his face.

The story is told entirely from Sally's viewpoint, third person. Throughout the story, the reader always knows what Sally is thinking, knows that she keeps trying to smile, to make light chatter with her husband, her doctor, even though the words uppermost in her mind are: *Hurry. Hurry! Hurry, before my face wears out.*

The delay in the surgery schedule, mentioned in the beginning, is a device for creating suspense. We all know that we can do most anything for a time, but not indefinitely. There's bound to be a breaking point. Also, while Sally is waiting, there is time for her to be thinking about what has happened prior to this moment, and to make use of the flashback.

The reader learns that Tom, her husband, has come early to the hospital, planning to stay with Sally until she is taken to surgery. Tom has an important meeting this morning, but he'd have time to get there if the original schedule was kept. But now there's a delay and Sally says, "Tom, you really must go on. You mustn't be late for your meeting."

Tom said now, "Quit worrying. I'm not."

So here we begin developing the theme. Sally thinks Tom is worried, but not about her. She's seen him glancing at his watch, and thinks he's worried about meeting the important client.

Triggering the Flashback

Sally, Tom, the Doctor, continue to wait. Sally thinks how pale she must look, and tries to nibble some color into her lips. This provides a device for going into flashback. Sally is thinking about her pale mouth and then thinks: *Last night, when the nurse came into her room to tell her to remove her nail polish, to not wear lipstick in the morning . . .* And then we are into the scene of what happened last night.

The reader learns that last night Sally had walked out into the corridor, and seen the girl in the room across the hall.

This minor character is described only as "a blond girl in a pink robe, who looked to be about 18." She is not given a name because then the story emphasis would shift to her problems, and, in the short-short, there isn't time. The blond girl is used here only to contrast Sally's emotions.

Sally notices that the blond's room is filled with flowers, cards, and thinks how different it looks from her own room. She thinks the girl must have been here for some time. "No, only two days," the girl says, "but time enough to call everyone I know!" But Sally has called almost no one, only her mother to ask her to stay with the children during her "very minor surgery." She'd told no one else, she thinks, "unless you counted Fran Wilkins."

Fran is also a minor character, but she is given a name because the reader is supposed to remember Fran later in the story. Here's the paragraph that first describes Fran.

Fran was president of PTA, and Sally had phoned her only to say she'd be entering the hospital and unable to help with the rummage sale. Fran was not a close friend, and had said only, "Well, too bad. But we'll count on you for the spring tea," and rung off.

Here, we're back to the theme again. Fran was not worried about Sally. And Sally thinks this is the way she'd intended it. Later, Sally realizes what she really had wanted from Fran.

While we're still in this flashback of last night, the reader learns that the blond girl has told Sally that she can't sleep, she's afraid. Sally tries to comfort her, takes hold of her cold hands. Sally thinks that she, herself, is not afraid. But after she's in her own bed, she "rings for an extra blanket." So, though Sally thinks she isn't afraid, the reader knows she is. This is that old rule: don't tell the reader, show him.

As the story progresses, the time is drawing closer. Finally, the nurse comes in, gives Sally a shot. Now, in a few minutes, she'll be taken to surgery. All during the story action, Sally has been making light chatter with Tom, the nurse, etc. There have been times when she almost fails, but always she manages to regain her composure, to find some words to say. Now, with this medication, she feels herself slipping toward sleep, but she fights it. *Not yet,* she thinks, *I'm not ready yet* . . . For a moment, her eyes have closed, but she forces them open. It's then she sees Tom sitting by her bed, his head in his hands. She says, "Tom?" and he looks up, startled. There are tears in his eyes.

In the space of this article, there isn't room to give the details of the final paragraphs, but to sum up: Tom tells Sally that he never intended to leave her, that he had called his client and said he'd been delayed. He'd tried to be cheerful, because he thought that was what she wanted, but finally he says. "I'm worried about you!" and Sally realizes now that these are the words she's been searching for. The medication has relaxed her now, and she can admit to her emotions. "Oh, Tom," she says, "I've wanted to shout to the whole world . . . worry about me, weep with me!"

Tom doesn't understand, because Sally seemed to be the one who'd not wanted anyone to know. Sally, being truthful now, says, "But I did tell Fran Wilkins. She's the one who tells everything she knows. But this time she didn't tell a soul about me. Not a single soul."

The story ends as Sally is able to laugh at herself, as she realizes that no matter how we protest we still want others to care about us. In the final paragraph, Sally does exit smiling, which is what she'd wanted to do all the time.

So there it is, start to finish. I hope Sally's saga will be of some help to you in earning those other words which you and I long to hear: "Your manuscript is accepted!"

STRUCTURE REVIEW ELEVEN/INSTRUCTIONAL PROCESS

Name _____ Class _____

Answer each question in the space provided below it.

1 How does the writer's beginning help fulfill her purpose?

2 Into what logical steps is it possible to break down the process of writing a short-short story?

3 Why doesn't Millie McWhirter explain more fully the theme and the plot of "Four Little Words" at the beginning?

4 What instructions tell the reader what not to do?

5 Is it important to the writer's purpose that the reader get interested in "Four Little Words"? Why?

6 Why does Millie McWhirter use the first person plural "we" point of view?

7 When she states a rule for the short story, she shifts to the "you" point of view. Why?

8 Why does she also use the first person "I" point of view?

INFORMATIONAL PROCESS

In writing the informational process, a writer's purpose is to inform or explain how something is done or how it happened. He does not intend that his readers duplicate the process. He may show how an engine works or how a political party, a big business, or a university is organized. He may explain how the New York Mets won the World Series in 1969 or present steps necessary for a ship to pass through the Panama Canal. Still other writers may be concerned with how the Battle of Britain was won, the manner in which the Great Pyramid was built, the way earthquakes are measured, or the birth of an island like Bermuda.

A very common method of organizing the informational process is to use the same step-by-step plan of the instructional process. Many writers, however, break down a process into parts in order to show a cause-and-effect or effect-and-cause relationship. Such a process is called a *causal process.* In the model informational process that follows, the writer discusses causes and effects that result from those causes.

THE HIDDEN LANDSCAPE
Edith Raskin

<table>
<tr><td valign="top">

Introductory sentence

Statement of process

Step

Step

Time

Result

Examples

</td><td>

1 *The hidden landscape shaped by ground water has its own fantastic beauty which we can observe in explored caverns.* Within these caves, dripping rain water, underground streams, and waterfalls have carved a weird architecture. Ground water makes an admirable chisel in sculpturing the subterranean passages when it combines with carbon dioxide to form carbonic acid. The acid dissolved in water etches away at limestone, a rock which has little resistance to this chemical combination. *So slow a process must have required millions of years to form the immense caverns under the limestone formations in the world.* Such caves as the Mammoth Cave of Kentucky, the Howe Caverns in New York, the Luray Caverns in Virginia, the Carlsbad Caverns in New Mexico, and the Pierre St. Martin Caves of the Pyrenees had their beginnings far back across the ages. From nature's point of view, the Rock of Gibraltar is not a sturdy fortress but a limestone mass riddled with underground passages and caves.

</td></tr>
<tr><td valign="top">

Process

Steps

</td><td>

2 Countless raindrops seeping through the limestone rock gradually gather into a pool. The pool flows and a stream is underway, dissolving its own channel as best it may. Where the bedrock dissolves readily, hollows form and where more resistant rock stands, narrow, winding alleys remain. Thus, as the underground stream curves its path, it leaves behind chambers, galleries, and passageways, sometimes spacious, sometimes cramped. On the roofs, floors, and walls, the constantly replenished ground water decorates the hidden chambers.

</td></tr>
<tr><td valign="top">

Process continues

Result

Description of stalactites

</td><td>

3 Drip by drip, the ground water deposits its liquid lime load. The water evaporating from the cavern roof leaves behind a small drop of limestone which it had picked up on its journey down. The limey drops slowly form stone pendants, frozen lace, cones, and fringed drapes hanging from the cave ceiling. Not all the water evaporates; some falls to the floor to build its own distinctive designs. *Slender columns, doomed upshoots, huge drip candles take shape as the stone drops accumulate.* The hanging formations are called stalactites; those rising from the floor are stalagmites.

4 While both types form in all caves, some caves have beauti-

</td></tr>
</table>

SOURCE NOTE: Edith Raskin, "The Hidden Landscape," *Many Worlds: Seen and Unseen*, pp. 100–101. Copyright © 1954 by Edith Raskin. Permission of David McKay Company, Inc.

and stalag-
mites

Explana-
tion for dif-
ferent pro-
cess

ful stalactites dominating the scene with their petrified pen-
dants. Other caves have magnificent stalagmites which reach
upward in overpowering number, dwarfing the dainty stone fingers suspended above. Often, the stalactites and stalagmites
meet to create impressive columns stretching from floor to ceiling. The difference in cave architecture may be accounted for
partly by how fast the seepage of ground water proceeds. With
rapid seepage the drops fall to the floor with most of the lime
load and the stalagmites are favored. Where the water perco-
lates more slowly the stalactites cast their stony grace more
abundantly. The joined stalactites and stalagmites are likely to
result from a uniform rate of formation, an equal division of the
water drops and the minerals. (Italics added.)

STRUCTURE REVIEW TWELVE/INFORMATIONAL PROCESS

Name _____ Class _____

Answer each question in the space provided below it.

1 What do the first two sentences of this selection tell the reader about the process?

2 What is the result of the slow process described in paragraph 1?

3 What results from the natural events that are discussed in paragraph 2?

4 In paragraph 3, the writer continues her discussion of the process discussed in paragraphs 1 and 2. What is the result of the process at this stage?

5 Into what stages does the writer divide the process?

6 What is the function of paragraph 4?

ASSIGNMENT/WRITING THE INSTRUCTIONAL PROCESS

Write a process in which you explain how to do something in simple language. Listed below are some suggested topics.

How to row a boat

How to ski

How to built a _____

How to train a pet

How to study efficiently

How to hit a baseball

ASSIGNMENT/WRITING THE INFORMATIONAL PROCESS

Write a process based on how something was done or how something happened. Listed below are some suggested topics.

What happens when it rains

An eclipse of the sun or moon

The rise of Hitler

The structure of the medieval church

The formation of petroleum

The end of an era

Structure of a university

CLASSIFICATION

In organizing and developing thought by classification, a writer breaks down his subject into groups, classes, types, sorts, or kinds. He places persons, places, things, and ideas together in a particular group on some basis and identifies the members of each group by presenting similar characteristics. People, for example, are classified in a number of different ways; they may be grouped into races, religions, nationalities, political parties, or social levels in society. By classifying, a writer is able to give order to a seemingly disorganized and confused mass of information. Writers of textbooks like this one, for instance, feel that their readers will better understand the whole writing process if they treat each type separately; therefore, they break the writing process down into four traditional major classes or types: narration, description, exposition, and argumentation. A major class like exposition is further divided and subdivided. Exposition is broken down into eight subclasses: (1) comparison, (2) contrast, (3) process, (4) classification, (5) partition, (6) causal analysis, (7) definition, and (8) a combination of methods. Process is further divided into the two sub-subclasses of (a) instructional process and (b) informational process.

The preceding discussion also illustrates the two systems of classifying: simple classification and complex classification. In *simple classification,* a writer divides his subject into the major classes. In *complex classification,* a writer breaks down the subject into classes and subclasses.

To make his classifying informative and significant, a writer must first have a basis for the classification. Written discourse, for example, was divided and subdivided on the basis of the writer's purpose or intent. To simply group students on campus into males and females is hardly informative and certainly not significant. But to place the twenty-five students in your English writing class into groups on the basis of their major field of interest is informative and somewhat significant because the grouping will probably reveal that few of the students taking the course are English majors. This grouping raises some perplexing questions. How much interest in writing do these students have? Do they really need the course? Should it be elective? Is the course meeting the needs of all students or only those of the English major?

Frequently a writer will state clearly the basis for classifying in the first paragraph of the essay. The opening sentence of a Congressional Report read as follows:

Each campus contained a spectrum of opinion and activity that divided roughly into four groups: extremists, radicals, moderates, and the uninvolved.

ASSIGNMENT/BASIS FOR CLASSIFICATION

Read the statements below. In the blanks to the right, place the basis for classification. Underneath the classification basis, write the classes or groups into which the subject will be divided.

Clouds are classified cumulus and stratus according to how they are formed.

——————————————   ——————————
——————————————
——————————————
——————————————

Clouds are classified by altitude into four families: high clouds, middle clouds, low clouds, and towering clouds.

——————————————   ——————————
——————————————
——————————————
——————————————

The marijuana user, on any given campus, may be placed in one of three categories: a dabbler, a user, a head.

——————————————   ——————————
——————————————
——————————————
——————————————

What we see growing around us is a sort of social stratification in which the highbrows are the elite, the middlebrows are the bourgeoisie, and the lowbrows are *hoi polloi.*

———————————————   ———————————————
———————————————
———————————————
———————————————

In the subsurface component of any terrestrial habitat the organisms are divisible into three groups on the basis of their size. The groups are (1) the microbiota, (2) the mesobiota, and (3) the macrobiota.

———————————————   ———————————————
———————————————
———————————————
———————————————

In the following essay, "The Common Cold," the writer divides cold sufferers into three types on the basis of how they treat a cold. The three types of treatment are (1) the Fresh-Air Treatment, (2) the Scientific Treatment, and (3) the Coddle. As do most writers developing by classification, he organizes his material by wholes, presenting in separate paragraphs characteristics that identify each type.

In paragraph 2, he discusses the first type. This group is made up of "large red-faced men in check suits." They are fresh-air buffs who have never been to a doctor in their lives. All illness to them is "psychological." Yet, at the first sneeze, they jump into a cold bath, do breathing exercises all night, and spread the cold germs freely about them.

He next discusses the "Scientific sufferer" who is a "precise, clerkish man" with a much calmer view of the cold. He reads avidly medical articles and patent-medicine advertisements. During the winter he gargles with antiseptic for five minutes every night and morning; he wears wool next to his skin, and makes sure that he gets sufficient calcium. As soon as his nose starts running, he races to the drug store and buys all kinds of cold remedies. When he arrives home, he places them on a shelf and takes each one, following the directions exactly. He does not take his cold lightly.

The "Coddler," the third type, is usually a woman. She has been told since girlhood that she must take care of a cold or it could develop into something worse. Thus, she is terrified of germs. At first signs of a cold, she phones her husband and her friends to announce her misfortune. She retires to her bedroom and makes preparations to enjoy the illness. She goes to bed for a fortnight, and her family cares for her every need.

THE COMMON COLD
Richard Gordon

Statement of classification
These home cures generally follow one of three distinct courses, and as each reflects the psychology of the sufferer, let us examine them in detail. They are: (1) the Fresh-Air Treatment; (2) the Scientific Attack; (3) the Coddle.

Group one characteristics
The Fresh-Air Treatment is practiced only by those large red-faced men in check suits who look you in the eye, slap their chests, and declare they've never owned an overcoat or been to a doctor in their lives, as if claiming freedom from original sin. They have a simple attitude to illness: it's all "psychological," from smallpox to fractured femurs. But they are only human, and in time claimed by both death and colds. The first sneeze affects them like a starter's pistol: they tear off their ties and waistcoats, stamp around the house throwing open the windows, jump into a cold bath, and upset their wives by doing breathing exercises all night in bed. The discomfort in which they wallow for a fortnight makes no difference to the course of the disease, but by rendering their surroundings unfit for human habitation, they rarely manage to infect anyone else.

Group two characteristics
The Scientific sufferer takes a much calmer view of his cold. He is generally a precise, clerkish man, who files the medical articles from the *Reader's Digest* and reads the patent-medicine advertisements like a girl looking into a bride-shop window. During the winter he gargles for five minutes with antiseptic night and morning, wears wool next to the skin, and eats sufficient calcium to keep a schoolroom in chalks. As soon as his nose starts to run he calls at the druggist's and arrives home with his brief case clinking gently with small bottles. He announces to his wife: "Think I'm getting a touch of a cold, m'dear," as though he were having a baby. He makes for the bathroom and unpacks his bag, which is filled with cough mixtures, fever pills, throat lozenges, nose drops, eye lotions, gargles, and liniments. He sets the bottles carefully on the shelf and works his way through them thoughtfully and solemnly, like a sailor trying out the drinks in a strange port.

SOURCE NOTE: Richard Gordon, "The Common Cold," *The Atlantic,* February 1951, pp. 50–51. Permission of the author and The Atlantic Company.

This type of invalid follows the directions on the label with scientific precision: if it orders "An egg-cupful four-hourly," he fetches an eggcup; if it says "Rub on the chest till it stings," he scrapes away until his skin begins to peel. He then has a mustard bath, soaks his feet in salt water, puts on two pairs of flannel pajamas, and goes to bed with *The Household Doctor.* No physician ever watched the recovery of a wealthy patient more sadly than he notices his own returning health. For, once he has caught his cold, he does not lightly let it go. From October to May he richly justifies the famous mistranslation of *voici l'anglais avec son sangfroid habituel*—here comes the Englishman with his usual bloody cold.

Group three characteristics The Coddler is usually a woman, with a far more fuzzy idea of her internal organs than the Scientific sufferer. Since girlhood she has been told that she must Take Care of a Cold or it will turn into Something Else; her life passes in a terror of Germs, which she imagines as small green animals, with red eyes and long teeth, that hide under the dustbin. Before she has blown her nose twice, the Coddler has phoned her husband's office and all her friends to explain that she has a cold, in the tone of someone announcing that smallpox has just broken out. She then pours herself a large Scotch, lights a fire in her bedroom, piles extra eiderdowns on the bed, shuts the windows, rubs herself all over with camphorated oil, phones out for grapes, calf's-foot jelley, chicken essence, barley water, Eau de Cologne, and the other prerogatives of illness, shifts the television upstairs, collects all the magazines in the house, and goes to bed. She stays there for a fortnight, her family fetching her egg-and-milk, lightly sprinkled with nutmeg, every hour.

Study the structure of the model selection that follows in preparing to answer questions in the next Structure Review.

TYPES OF VOLCANOES
Edith Raskin

1 Submarine and subterranean volcanoes are activated by the same forces. Either type may eject its volcanic materials in a number of ways, depending on the nature of its lava and the kind of opening it finds. Where the long narrow fissures occur,

SOURCE NOTE: Edith Raskin, "Types of Volcanoes," *Many Worlds: Seen and Unseen,* pp. 96–98. Copyright © 1954 by Edith Raskin. Permission of David McKay Company, Inc.

the melted rock spreads out to form lava plains or plateaus. The melted rock erupting through round holes or craters piles up lava mountains.

2   The melted rock, or lava, varies from a syrupy consistency to a thick, gummy state. The gummy lava is more highly charged with gases. Struggling to bubble out from the thick lava, the gases build up enormous pressure. When they do burst forth, they erupt a billowing black cloud with a fiery inferno concealed in its midst. The burning cloud, containing superheated steam, carbon, sulfur, and hydrogen compounds,

Explosive type

suffocates and scorches everything in its path. Two notorious examples of this *extremely explosive type* of volcano are Mt. Pelée and Krakatoa. . . .

3   In gentle contrast the thin lava, less gas-filled and easily boiling off its steam and sulfur fumes, flows quietly out upon the

Gentle type

surface. Mauna Loa and Kilauea, the two famous volcanoes on the island of Hawaii, *exemplify this type* of lava flow. Compared to the explosive volcanoes, the Hawaiian brand is fireworks in the grand manner rather than destructive holocausts. . . .

Intermediate type

4   Most volcanoes are an *intermediate type* combining both explosive and quiet behavior. In these eruptions the lava is moderately thick and the gases escape with mild explosions which hurl solid cinders skyward followed by lava flows. A good part of the ejected material piles up near the central opening,

Repetition of types on a new basis

forming a cone-shaped mountain. The quiet volcanoes build gently sloping cones with wide bases, while the violent types pile up steep cones and the intermediate ones have mixed cones with moderate slopes. (Italics added.)

STRUCTURE REVIEW THIRTEEN/CLASSIFICATION

Name _____ Class _____

Answer each question in the space provided below it.

1   Does the writer state clearly the classification that will follow? What confusion on the part of the reader can result from the writer not announcing the classification?

2   What is the function of the last sentence of the selection?

3   What, then, is the function of the first paragraph?

4   In what sentence does the writer tell the reader what paragraph 2 is about?

5   How does the writer develop her thought concerning the second type of volcano?

6   Why did the writer discuss the "intermediate type" last?

7 On what does the writer base her classification?

8 What basis for classifying volcanoes does the last sentence of the selection suggest?

See answers on page 191.

ASSIGNMENT/WRITING CLASSIFICATION

1 Write a paragraph or paragraph unit classifying physical objects, such as trees, shrubs, houses, or automobiles.

2 Research types of clouds. Decide on a basis of classification. Using a complex system of classifying, write a theme dividing and subdividing clouds. Prepare a plan before you begin writing.

3 Students and teachers may be classified into many different types. Select a basis for classifying, and divide students or teachers into types in order to fulfill some purpose other than merely establishing classes. Make a plan of the classification before writing.

4 Write a theme on any one of the following topics using classification as the dominant form of developing the thesis: communities, social systems, forms of governments, languages.

5 Listed below are some possible subjects for classification essays.

TV commercials	Student protestors
Films	Ideas or philosophies
Books	Athletes
Compact cars	Job opportunities
Campus housing	Rocks

ANSWER SECTION

STRUCTURE REVIEW TEN

1 He introduces the subject, showing why any parent can and should teach his child to swim. In this way he hopes to capture reader interest.

2 In the last sentence of the second paragraph.

3 About seven, in addition to the background (when and where):
   a Preparing the child psychologically
   b Getting the child into the water
   c Using the bobbing routine
   d Placing the face in the water
   e Learning to float—prone or face-down float
   f Learning the prone glide
   g Beginning the arm and leg strokes

4 Avoid stiff, authoritarian approach (step 1). Never force a child to swim (step 3). In kicking, the feet should not rise above the surface, nor should the knee bend (step 7). Teaching a youngster in the ocean should be attempted only under ideal weather conditions, if at all (background).

5 "You." In this way the writer is speaking directly to the individual who is performing the operation. It is the point of view best suited for the instructional process.

STRUCTURE REVIEW THIRTEEN

1 No. The reader of this selection may become confused by the failure to announce the classification that will follow although the title indicates the subject. He may think that the writer will discuss submarine and subterranean volcanoes as the types.

2 To state the classification and mention that volcanoes may also be classified on the basis of type of cones.

3 This is background material for understanding how the types of volcanoes are formed.

4 The final sentence. In that sentence the writer names the first class of volcanoes.

5 By contrast.

6 It is easier to explain it since her discussion includes facts concerning the explosive type and the quiet-behavior type.

7 The kind (severity) of the explosion.

8 By kinds of cones.

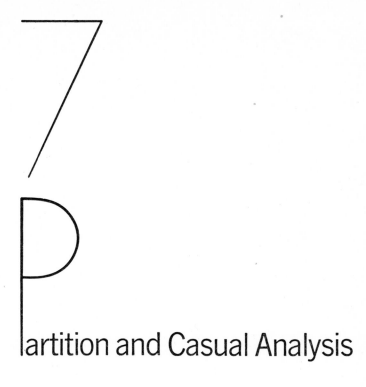

Partition and Casual Analysis

In analysis by partition, a writer breaks down a subject into its parts in order to convey some discovery about the whole. He develops thought by partition because this method enables him to treat each part separately, showing its relationship to the other parts and to the whole. A writer, for example, wishes to establish the greatness of Winston Churchill as a wartime prime minister; therefore he treats each quality, showing its role in contributing to Churchill's ability and fame. Another writer wants to explain the structure of the earth; he breaks his subject down into a series of layers or shells, taking his readers from the outer layer deep into the inner core of the earth, discussing each layer as he moves downward.

Analysis by partition is simply organized and developed, usually in the thesis-support frame. The writer, in much the same manner as he did in organizing comparison, contrast, and classification, will announce the partition in the first paragraph—often in the first sentence of the opening paragraph; for example:

Geologists conceive the earth ball as a series of shells with an inner core.

Tax monies in this community are wasted in six ways.

Before constructing an imaginary life history of a typical wave, we need to become familiar with some of its physical characteristics.

The national seashore does have two spectacular features.

We feel that certain general features will be necessary in an organization of states designed to preserve the peace in a disarmed world.

Next, he treats each part in some kind of logical order—by time, by space, by importance, by order of appearance, by position. He often designates the separate parts or divisions with "1," "2," "3," etc., or "first," "a second," "a third," etc. If he were writing a formal partition, he would divide and subdivide and divide further until all parts were discussed. In most informative writing, however, the writer partitions only to a degree necessary to fulfill his purpose.

Analysis by partition does not mean a mere enumeration of the parts that make up a whole. As we saw in the thesis sentences above, the writer of partition uses the method for a purpose; he breaks a subject down to show its complexity, the problem or problems connected with it, the understanding of the whole. Do not confuse partition, then, with the process where the writer breaks the operation into steps to show the reader how to do something or how something is done.

There are two kinds of partition—*physical partition* and *conceptual partition*.

PHYSICAL PARTITION

A physical partition is so named because the writer treats a real or tangible entity. He may break down the ear, a carburetor, or an electric motor into its component parts to show something about the nature of the mechanism, not to show how it operates *(process analysis)*. In the model partition that follows, Edith Raskin explains the nature of the earth by conceiving it as an earth ball with a series of shells and an inner core.

THE EARTH BALL
Edith Raskin

Statement   *Geologists conceive the earth ball as a series of shells with an*
of partition   *inner core.* To take an imaginary look inside the earth, they
               conveniently cut the rock ball in half. The average distance
               from the outermost shell to the core or center of the earth is

SOURCE NOTE: Edith Raskin, "The Earth Ball," *Many Worlds: Seen and Unseen,* pp. 81–83. Copyright © 1954 by Edith Raskin. Permission of David McKay Company, Inc.

First division

First subdivision

Discussion

Second subdivision

Discussion

Name of second layer

Second division

Third division

Subdivisions

about 3,960 miles. The rock ball begins with *a two-layered crust* about 60 miles deep. *The top layer* of the crust is a thin, light shell like a membrane covering the earth ball. Granite, the basic rock of the surface continents, comprises the earth's top layer, too. The first layer descends to a relatively shallow depth, only 30 miles down.

Below the granite is *the second layer* containing crystalline basalt rock. Basalt is heavier than granite but like it igneous in origin. The Pacific Ocean, with its great depths, has a basalt rock floor, while the other ocean bottoms have a granite icing, so to speak, on their basalt bottom layer. Fifty miles down in the earth's interior the crystalline basalt changes to a glassy basalt. The granite and basalt layers are called *the earth's crust,* indicating their outer marginal nature.

The rock ball continues with the shell that lies between the crust and the core, *termed the mantle.* Considered to be about 1,800 miles thick, this intermediate zone is a wide, unexplored area. Increasingly denser than the rocks above, the mantle rocks are supposed to be heavy metal oxides. Olivine, a mineral commonly found in dark caves and many meteorites, is the geologists' current choice for the mantle rocks. These rocks possessing both rigid and elastic properties will yield slightly to pressure but also return to their original form.

The last shell is the inner core, about 2,100 miles thick, and in its heart lies the center of the earth. Some scientists believe that this inner core is made of melted iron and nickel. Others suggest *a core with two regions,* an inner and outer part. The outside is assumed to be a very heavy form of molten silicate rock, while the innermost core consists mainly of solid iron and nickel. Whether the core be all molten or only partly so, agreement as to its great density is universal. (Italics added.)

STRUCTURE REVIEW FOURTEEN/PHYSICAL PARTITION

Name _____ Class _____

Answer each question in the space provided below it.

1 What does the first sentence of the selection tell the reader about the development of thought that follows?

2 Into how many parts does the writer break down the earth ball?

3 How much subdividing of parts does the writer do?

4 How does analogy help the explanation?

5 What is the writer's purpose?

In organizing and developing the thought in the next selection, a complete unit excerpted from a larger discussion entitled "Thine Alabaster Cities," the writer, Peter Blake, uses partition very effectively. He breaks down his discussion into three elements that made for "good" communities throughout the history of Western civilization. He then shows that these three elements are not present in today's suburbia. Thus, he says, modern cities are without character and form. In the last two paragraphs, Peter Blake explains the meaning of his partition into those three elements by stating that we do not seem to possess common faiths, especially a consciousness of the physical symbols of democratic government, that shaped cities like Florence.

He opens his discussion by stating clearly the partition: three elements that made up good communities throughout the history of Western civilization. He discusses each element in turn, beginning with the most important element—outdoor spaces—moving to the few truly symbolic buildings, and then onward to the shopping centers and other utilitarian buildings like schools, police stations, fire houses, and "even a town hall." He shows how each element is without character and form; thus, modern suburbia is so ridiculously planned that no city builder of the Middle Ages or the Renaissance would have dared propose what modern suburbia looks like.

Read the model partition with the following questions in mind.

1 What is the purpose of the writer?
2 How does partitioning help him fulfill that purpose?
3 Does the writer clearly indicate the parts of his partition?
4 Does he develop each part sufficiently?
5 In what order does he discuss the parts?

TODAY'S SUBURBIA
Peter Blake

Statement of partition
1 In architectural terms, throughout the history of Western civilization, good communities have been made up of three elements: utilitarian buildings (places where people live and work), which may be entirely plain and unpretentious in character; symbolic buildings (places that form some sort of focal points in a community), which are likely to have a much more distinctive appearance, size, and location, depending, of course, on what they are meant to symbolize; and finally (and most importantly), outdoor spaces of different size and character.

Outdoor spaces

Characteristics
2 In today's Suburbia, it is virtually impossible to create outdoor spaces of *any* character. Individual little houses plonked down on individual little lots do not form continuous "walls" of the sort we still find along the cobblestone streets of Beacon Hill. Our little houses form, at best, a ragged fence, full of gaps; they face each other across wide streets and deep front yards,

SOURCE NOTE: Peter Blake, "Today's Suburbia," *God's Own Junkyard,* pp. 20–21. Copyright © by Peter Blake. Permission of Holt, Rinehart and Winston.

so that the distances between them are likely to measure at least 100 feet; and because our little houses are generally low-slung, the "ragged fences" created by them, together with the wide distances between parallel "fences," add up to absolutely nothing in terms of definable, outdoor space. For any "outdoor room," just like any indoor room, depends for its success upon the proportions of height to width to length. Suburbia's streets are "outdoor rooms" 100 feet wide, lined (if you look closely) with ragged walls that may be 12 feet high, and completed at each end by an intersection or, possibly, a fire hydrant. No city builder of the Middle Ages or the Renaissance would have dared to propose anything so ridiculously amorphous; if he had, his fellow citizens would have run him out of town.

Symbolic buildings

3 As for symbolic buildings, what do we see in Suburbia? It is true that there are probably some churches along the nearest highway. But while the churches of our early New England towns and villages were tall enough (and sufficiently close by) to be visible from almost everywhere, the sprawl of today's Suburbia has pushed the churches so far out that their spires are no longer visible farther than a block away. (The Howard Johnson spire, more often than not, is more visible.) This condition may, of course, be an accurate reflection of today's relative values, but it is also a further contribution to the formlessness of modern Suburbia. One of the important functions of a tall building in any community is to serve as a point of reference, to permit people to find their way about without trouble, much as a lighthouse helps a ship's captain to chart his route.

4 Suburbia's other "symbolic" buildings are those of the shopping center, which is certainly symbolic of *some*thing—though perhaps not of anything we would particularly want to symbolize. (Some new shopping centers have tried to become "community centers" in a broader sense, and perhaps there is

Utilitarian buildings

some validity in this.) Then there are schools, police stations, fire houses and, indeed, somewhere, there may even be a town hall.

Conclusion

5 *The meaning of all this is twofold:* first, we do not seem, at this time, to possess the sort of common faiths that shaped cities like Florence (whose only tall buildings were the symbols of religion and of government) or, at least, we do not seem to

Meaning of this poor planning

be very strongly committed to any common faiths; and, second, one reason we are not so committed is, quite clearly, that nobody living in Suburbia (and very few people living in Urbia) is conscious of the physical symbols of democratic government—the one faith we do claim to hold in common.

Conclusion   **6** This is not merely an esthetic problem, or even primarily an esthetic problem, because Suburbia, in its present form, is incapable of generating significant outdoor spaces and is so spread out that its few, symbolic buildings are lost among the forests of telephone poles; moreover, we find ourselves with 50 million suburbanites most of whom are totally disinterested in local government, refuse to participate in it, and frequently don't even know what community (if that is the appropriate word) they belong to. The only local issue that arouses any degree of passion is taxes—and that one tends to generate more furore than constructive illumination.

ASSIGNMENT/PHYSICAL PARTITION
Break down into its component parts some tangible entity in order to inform your reader about some problem or discovery you uncovered in your investigation of it. Some suggested subjects are the following:

1   A volcano
2   An atoll
3   A sailboat
4   A power lawnmower
5   A uniform
6   A chapter in a textbook
7   An income tax form
8   A short story
9   A film
10   A newspaper or a news program on television

CONCEPTUAL PARTITION

In writing the conceptual partition, a writer treats something intangible like a concept by breaking it down into its parts in order to reveal a discovery or a conclusion concerning it. A writer may wish to alert the reader to the fact that the university is in danger; therefore, he breaks the university down into six groups, showing how each group is endangering the university. Another writer wishes to explain how inflation is a problem; he breaks inflation down into undesirable characteristics, explaining how each one contributes to the problem. Still another writer in explaining the course of events for the last one hundred years breaks his subject down into three principal forces that shaped the history of that period.

In the next model selection, the writer reminds the reader that it might be well to "think again before sending your child to college."

He organizes and develops his thought by partitioning his subject into four reasons, explaining the reasons in some detail in four separate paragraph units. He ties his reasons into the thesis as he moves along by writing conclusions to two of the reasons and ends the paper with a statement of the thesis in slightly different words; thus, he frames his thought in the thesis-support-thesis structure.

THINK AGAIN BEFORE SENDING YOUR CHILD TO COLLEGE
James D. Hodgson

Statement of thesis

1 The time has come for parents and students to reassess the need for a college education and perhaps to look elsewhere for rewarding career opportunities.

Paragraph unit 1—financial angle

2 Why? First, let's look at it from the financial angle. Five years ago, the average cost of a school year at a public university in a student's own state was $1,199. Next year, it is expected to average $1,621. That comes to nearly $6,500 in four years for tuition, required fees, room and board only.

3 A comparable increase has occurred in the cost of private colleges—from $2,104 per year to $3,022 annually. Therefore, the bill for four years at a liberal arts college can run more than $12,000 just for the basic expenses.

4 And that is by no means the total cost of a college education. To the out-of-pocket expense must be added lost wages. Even starting at the minimum wage and receiving annual increases, the student will have *lost some $16,000 in a four-year period!*

Repeat of his thesis

5 In view of these sacrifices, and the diminishing return on the investment, I think that parents and young people should *stop to ask themselves, "Is college really the best answer?"*

Transition sentence

6 In the coming decade, it may well not be. For while the net increase in the supply of new college-educated workers during the 1970's is estimated at 9.8 million, the increase in demand is expected to total only 9.6 million, clearly changing the situation from a "sellers' market" to a "buyers' market."

Paragraph unit 2—job opportunities

7 Nor is this just temporary. We foresee no return to the condition of the '50's and '60's, in which employers were forced to bid against each other for the services of new graduates. The earnings gap between college graduates and non-graduates is

SOURCE NOTE: James D. Hodgson, "Think Again Before Sending Your Child to College," *Family Weekly,* Sept. 17, 1972, p. 14.

Conclusion of paragraph unit 2	expected to narrow. Conclusion? *The student whose talents and interests are rooted in other than academic fields might be well advised to consider alternatives.*
Paragraph unit 3— education and white-collar jobs as symbols of success and status	**8** For several generations now, the college education and the white-collar job have been considered the symbols of success and status. And yet I wonder whether these are not artificial symbols—symbols that have forced young people to strive for a status that they didn't really want? **9** For if you look down your block or around your neighborhood, I think you'll find skilled craftsmen living next door to professionals—living the same kind of life, enjoying the same luxuries, and in many instances bringing home larger paychecks. And while the harried executive comes home with a bulging briefcase, his neighbor is free to relax, enjoying the pride of accomplishment that comes to the skilled artisan who works with his hands.
Conclusion for thesis based on discussion in paragraph unit 3	**10** Therefore, although a college education can be intellectually and socially stimulating for those young men and women whose interests lie in that direction, it is certainly not logical to encourage *all* high school students to continue their education in a four-year college or university.
Paragraph unit 4— presentation of alternatives to college	**11** For some, a two-year community college might be an excellent alternative. For others, training or apprenticeship in an expanding field could be the best solution. The latter offers an immediate income, with high wages upon completion of training. For still others, a combination of job training in the daytime and education courses in the evening might be the best answer.
Examples of job opportunities in alternative fields	**12** Occupations in which the demand is greater than the supply pay well for competent help. For example, a computer operator with only a few years experience can easily earn $160 a week. The average for a worker skilled in any of the offset-printing specialties is well over $6 per hour. An automobile mechanic can make about $5 an hour—more in large cities. **13** A draftsman preparing architectural drawings can earn $150 or more weekly with a little experience. An electrician in a metropolitan area commands more than $8 an hour. And a skilled executive secretary can almost write her own ticket—in a large firm, the salary is often more than that of the junior executives.
Conclusion to essay	**14** Of course you can't view an education merely from an economic standpoint. Attending college can be a most worthwhile and enriching experience, intellectually and socially.

15   On the other hand, *many youths should not be pushed into college just for the sake of taking a degree. For the marginal student who is pushed into college may never earn substantially more than he would have with only a high school education.* For this individual, it could take a lifetime to return his investment—a lifetime that might have been spent much more happily working at a well-paid job better suited to his individual skills. (Italics added.)

Read the partition that follows. Be prepared to answer questions in a Structure Review.

THE NEXT INDUSTRIAL REVOLUTION
Athelstan Spilhaus

1   We must have a new industrial revolution even if a few of us have to generate it. Other industrial revolutions have come about unplanned. The first was hailed as a way of ennobling human beings by substituting steam and electrical power for their muscles. This it undoubtedly did, but the generation of power brought with it side effects—including air pollution—which, far from being ennobling, were and continue to be degrading to human existence. In the second revolution the multiplication of "things" came about—"things" that at last could be mass-produced, so that people could have more and more of them. Thus was generated the solid-waste problem.

2   A third revolution was the tremendous growth in industrial chemistry, and the ability to tailor-make chemicals in vast quantities very cheaply, for all kinds of purposes—for example, pesticides intended to selectively destroy forms of life inimical to various groups of human beings. But these turned out not to be so selective; they have upset the little-understood ecological balance, and have polluted and poisoned the waters.

3 · In preparation for the next industrial revolution, I suggest that we revise our vocabulary. For instance, there is no such thing, no such person, as a consumer. We merely *use* "things"; and, according to the law of the conservation of matter, exactly the same mass of material is discarded after use. Thus, as the standard of living goes up, the amount of waste and consequent pollution must go up.

4   I believe we must base the next industrial revolution—a planned one—on the thesis that there is no such thing as waste, that waste is simply some useful substance that we do not yet have the wit to use. Industry so far is

SOURCE NOTE: Athelstan Spilhaus, "The Next Industrial Revolution," *Science,* Mar. 27, 1970, p. 1273. Copyright © 1970 by the American Association for the Advancement of Science, 1515 Massachusetts Ave., N.W., Washington, D.C. This editorial was adapted from a lecture presented at a National Industry Conference Board conference on Management and Man in the Computer Age, held in New York. The complete text appeared in the February 1970 issue of *The Conference Board Record.*

doing only half its job. It performs magnificent feats of scientific, technological, and managerial skill to take things from the land, refine them, and mass-manufacture, mass-market, and mass-distribute them to the so-called consumer; then the same mass of material is left, after use, to the so-called public sector, to be "disposed of." By and large, in our society, the private sector makes the things *before* use and the public sector disposes of them *after* use.

5   In the next industrial revolution, there must be a loop back from the user to the factory, which industry must close. If American industrial genius can mass-assemble and mass-distribute, why cannot the same genius mass-collect, mass-disassemble, and massively reuse the materials? If American industry should take upon itself the task of closing this loop, then its original design of the articles would include features facilitating their return and remaking. If, on the other hand, we continue to have the private sector make things and the public sector dispose of them, designs for reuse will not easily come about.

6   We industrial revolutionaries must plan to move more and more into the fields of human service, and not leave such concerns to the so-called public sector. We have seen our food supply grow to abundance in the United States, with fewer and fewer people needed to grow it. We are seeing the automation of factories, with an abundance of "things" provided by fewer and fewer people. On the other hand, we have a shortage of human services and a shortage of people providing these services. It follows quite simply that, if private enterprise is not to dwindle, while the public sector grows to be an all-embracing octopus, then private enterprise must go into the fields of human service.

7   The next industrial revolution is on our doorstep. Let us be the revolutionaries who shape it, rather than have it happen—and shape us. (Spilhaus's italics.)

STRUCTURE REVIEW FIFTEEN/CONCEPTUAL PARTITION

Name _____   Class _____

Answer each question in the space provided below it.

1 Read the first paragraph; mention two things about its organization and development.

2 Into what parts does the writer break down his subject?

3 To what part does he devote most space? Why?

4 In your opinion is the conclusion especially fitting for the material? Why? Why not?

5 How is the organization and development of the first three paragraphs similar? What is the purpose?

6 Discuss briefly the writer's purpose for writing the essay.

7 Why does the writer not consider it necessary to more fully support his thesis with effects of each revolution?

8 Does the language suit the writer's purpose?

See answers on page 227.

ASSIGNMENT/ANALYZING THE CONCEPTUAL PARTITION

Read the model conceptual partition that follows. Write a brief paragraph or paragraph unit analyzing its structural organization. Develop your analysis by partition.

DANGERS FACING THE UNIVERSITY
Theodore Sorenson

The university is in danger.

It is endangered by those members of the student body whose only consistent program is to wreck a virtually defenseless institution through violence, coercion, threats and arbitrary interference with the rights of other students.

SOURCE NOTE: Theodore Sorenson, "Dangers Facing the University," *Columbia Journal*, November 1969.

It is endangered by those members of the faculty who place their passion for popularity among the students and their desire to be in the avant-garde ahead of their obligation to the university's integrity and future.

It is endangered by those administrators whose refusal to heed the peaceful protests, to negotiate just grievances, to listen to reason, or to accept change, thereby makes violence predictable, however unjustifiable.

It is endangered by those trustees who seek to suppress dissent and non-conformity on the campus, who refuse to grant students any voice in their own affairs and who, thereby, invite an escalation of protest tactics and an enlargement of the protesting group.

It is endangered by those public officials, law enforcement officers and politicians who respond to popular dismay over student behavior by unleashing a host of hard measures and methods, ranging from swinging billy clubs to cutting off financial aid; methods that do not discriminate between just and unjust student objectives, between peaceful and violent demonstrators or between those who are committing outrages against the university and those who are protesting outrages by the university.

The university is endangered, finally, by those members of the general public whose reaction to continued disorder is all too likely to be one of repression instead of reform, thereby increasing the power and popularity of those already committed, even in the absence of disorder, to cutting back on university funds and freedom, to holding back the rights of the young and the black, and to boosting the very causes of militarism, racism and bossism that most protestors struggle to end.

Read the next model partition. Remember to prepare for the Structure Review found on page 209.

THE LONELINESS OF THE ALCOHOLIC
C. A. D'Alonzo

1 The alcoholic is a lonely man. He is lonely when he is alone, and being an alcoholic he must be alone a great deal of the time. He has difficulty tolerating himself. He thinks he has to drink, so he does—then he hates himself for his drinking. He is, in other words, lonely in his Jekyll and Hyde role: one is the guy who drinks and tries to rationalize to himself a reason or need for doing so. The other is the fellow who realizes he shouldn't drink, and is aware that alcohol is ruining him.

2 The alcoholic is lonely even when he is among "friends." For who are his friends? Those closest to him should be his family, but the alcoholic notoriously shuns and avoids his family. Then, are his friends those who drink with him continuously? Are they people with a similar problem who likewise are

SOURCE NOTE: C. A. D'Alonzo, "The Loneliness of the Alcoholic," in *The Drinking Problem—And Its Control*, pp. 13–16. Copyright © 1959 by the Gulf Publishing Company, Houston, Tex.

lonely? Are they perhaps those who may be capitalizing on another drink? Or are they friends who must sooner or later either wear out their welcome, or have the victim wear out his?

3 Perhaps the alcoholic realizes all this, and is, therefore, more acutely aware of his loneliness than is suspected. With these facts, and his hidden or apparent awareness of them, his loneliness grows in intensity as it feeds on itself. It becomes obvious in his every move, as he is lonely when alone, and lonely when he is with others. He has a forlorn expression in his eyes and on his face as the loneliness adds to his fears and his fears to his loneliness. He fundamentally resents his friends who give him drink, yet he dares not lose them.

4 The roughness of day and the stillness of night irritate this lonely feeling. He appreciates that as long as he drinks he will be basically lonely, and as long as he is lonely, he will be bedeviled with the need of drinking. He cannot cultivate desirable friends when he is drinking, and he cannot bear to meet new friends when he isn't drinking because of his phobias, fears, shaking, nervousness, and loneliness. His is truly a vicious cycle. Little wonder that he has difficulty getting off the merry-go-round! And little wonder that he is a sick as well as a lonely man—and that he needs help, comfort, guidance, and understanding.

5 His spiritual loneliness can be cold and penetrating; it can be malignant. To be lonely is to be deprived of the warmth and satisfaction of good friendship and fellowship; the companionship and sharing of those better off than we, and the privilege and comfort of assisting those not as well off. Without this friendship and sharing of the joys and woes, a person changes—bitterness appears. Guilt complexes, rationalization, "the false front," and infantile behavior are the results.

6 Watch the alcoholic at the bar. Watch as a group crowds around him, but also watch how quickly they grow tired of him. Then finally watch the expression on the victim's face as his new "acquaintances" move on. He must then seek "new friends," and the cycle is repeated. As the friendships evaporate, his loneliness and bitterness increase. It is a horrible existence.

7 The more his own family attempts to help and reach him, the more he resents and separates from them. He is a lonely man to his family. It seems both strange and unfortunate that the victim here is unwilling to accept the aid and warmth of those closest and dearest to him. But it is a fact.

8 The loneliness of the alcoholic is of the pernicious type. It spreads and molds into his every thought, his every deed, his work, his social contacts. It creates fewer successes and stimulates additional failures. It moves him to despair and hopelessness. His fears and phobias are intensified, and his burdens are increased.

9 These are the facts which you must know and appreciate when approaching the alcoholic. You must realize these points before you can help and guide these victims and win their trust. A lack of really good friends, together with loneliness, bitterness, and darkness, are fertile breeding grounds for despondency, dejection, and despair. There is little wonder that there are so many suicidal attempts among these individuals, and there are more of these attempts than we all realize.

10 The combination of alcohol and loneliness are potent adjuncts in contributing to spiritual and physical sickness. In his attempted rest, the alcoholic finds only restlessness, and even when he sleeps long periods, it is accompanied by weird and fearful dreams and leads to little peace and comfort.

11 Understanding the extreme and widespread loneliness of the alcoholic is indeed vital to a full appreciation of the physical and mental makeup of these individuals. You must penetrate that shell of loneliness, however, in order to reach the core of despair. The alcoholic is in dire need of sympathetic understanding, appreciation, and warmth, and those generally best equipped to render it are recovered alcoholics themselves—members of Alcoholics Anonymous.

STRUCTURE REVIEW SIXTEEN/CONCEPTUAL PARTITION

Name _____ Class _____

Answer each question in the space provided below it.

1 Discuss the organizational pattern of paragraph 1.

2 What is the main idea of paragraph 2?

3 Other than to discuss "the loneliness of the alcoholic," what is the writer's purpose?

4 In paragraph 6, the writer changes point of view from "he" to "you." Why do you think he shifted his point of view?

5 What is the writer's conclusion concerning the alcoholic?

6 What is the point of view of the final paragraph—the third person (he) or second person (you)? Why the shift again?

7 Is the writer developing two central thoughts? If so, what are they? Does the writer tie the two trends of thought in the discussion into a unified whole? In other words, is the essay well organized?

HOW TO TAKE THE PROFIT OUT OF HARD DRUGS
Peter F. Drucker

The greatest threat to our cities is not air pollution, the poor, the blacks, the white racists, the automobile, or "the system." The greatest threat is our present narcotics laws. They make the 99 per cent of us who are free from addiction the main victims of this monstrous plague.

SOURCE NOTE: Peter F. Drucker, "How to Take the Profit out of Hard Drugs," *Saturday Review,* May 13, 1972, pp. 26–27. Copyright © 1972 by the Saturday Review.

It is fear that is destroying our big cities: fear of the mugger, the holdup man, the petty burglar—knife in hand, half-crazed by an uncontrollable drug need. There are only a few, a very few of them. Even in New York, which, we are told, harbors half of all the hard-drug addicts in the United States, they amount, at most, to one in fifty, a mere 2 per cent of the city's population. But this handful of desperately sick people makes the cities unlivable for the rest of us.

A city is not livable if people are afraid to walk the streets, if the parks have become places to be dreaded rather then enjoyed, and if even the well-to-do cower at night behind barred doors. And so everyone who can flees, leaving behind only a very few rich and the very many poor who have no place to go. Yet this flight is self-defeating. Just as the nobles who fled plague-stricken medieval Florence carried the infection with them to the countryside, so the panic-stricken who flee from our cities to the suburbs take with them today's epidemic—to Scarsdale and the Oranges, to Winnetka and Palo Alto, to Wellesley and Philadelphia's Main Line. And the suburbs are threatened with rapidly becoming as unlivable as the inner cities—and for precisely the same reason.

It is not addiction that makes the drug taker violent. On the contrary, the drugs themselves, and especially the opiates such as heroin, induce apathy, docility, listlessness. The drug addict becomes violent for one reason only: the need, the overpowering need, to get the $75, $100, or $150 it takes every day, day in and day out, to pay for his fixes. Virtually all of this is profit to the drug traffic. Incredible though it seems, the true cost of a kilogram of heroin is approximately the same as the cost of a kilogram of potatoes. But when the kilogram of heroin reaches the streets of our cities, it fetches as much as $50,000. And as long as there is this fantastic profit to be made by a whole galaxy of "middlemen"—processors, smugglers, wholesalers, and small dealers—the narcotics laws must remain self-defeating.

There is only one way out: Take the profit out of hard drugs. And this means making them available to the addict free or at cost. I am concerned here with only the opiate drugs, especially heroin. I am arguing neither for nor against "legalizing" marijuana or the amphetamines. I detest and distrust all "mind-stretching" drugs, addictive or not. In view of the severe personality deformations that have been caused by hashish throughout the Middle East and India for 2,000 years or more, I am unimpressed by all the studies purporting to prove that pot is harmless. And the amphetamines are at least as toxic to the user as the opiates (though far less addictive). But these drugs harm the user alone; the opiates and only the opiates maim the nonaddict and threaten the fabric of city and community.

If our narcotics laws kept the opiates out—as those of Japan still do, for instance—I would be all for their vigorous enforcement. But the narcotics laws, despite strenuous efforts, have failed in the United States, at least for the present. All they do now is make the traffic in opiates irresistibly profitable.

And it is the consequence of this failure against which the innocent, healthy nonaddict needs to be protected.

The legalization of drugs is, of course, not a new proposal. But in the past all proposals regarding the treatment of drug addiction focused on the addict or, as our laws do, on the pusher. It is time to realize that this is looking at the problem through the wrong end of the telescope.

The problem is not the curing of the addict; the problem is the protection of the healthy. The priority is not to stop the drug traffic; it is to save our cities. Subordinating the welfare of the addict may be callous. But it is far more callous to punish the 99 per cent of our population who are not addicts for a disease from which they do not suffer. Permitting narcotics to be dispensed legally may be immoral. But it is far more immoral to permit the existence of a legal situation that so royally rewards trafficking in drugs and, as a result, threatens the destruction of our cities by making life unbearable for so many of their inhabitants.

Hard-drug addiction is the leprosy of this civilization. Like leprosy, it is a loathsome, horrible disease. Like leprosy, it makes no distinction between rich and poor, white and black. Indeed, by now it may well be a disease more of the young, middle-class white than of the poor black in the inner-city ghetto. As with leprosy 700 years ago, we neither understand the cause nor know a cure.

But we do know the right policy for an epidemic. The first requirement is to protect the healthy. And the second is to contain the epidemic's spread. Our narcotics laws have failed to do either. What is more, they make the healthy suffer, and they abet the epidemic's spread. Indeed, they make its spread inevitable, for they generate the profits of drug addiction and at the same time force the addict to spread his disease to the healthy.

Figures are notoriously untrustworthy on so emotion-laden an issue as the drug problem, which involves a criminal activity as well. Of course, there are no published, audited reports, but there is little doubt that one hard-drug addict is "worth" something like $5,000 a year to the pusher and probably a good deal more to the higher-ups in the drug traffic. Recently, narcotics agents caught the man who reputedly had headed the drug ring in a large industrial complex in an eastern city for a little over two years. In this short time he is said to have made profits of $2-million. Even if the real figure is only one-tenth of this, it is more than enough to tempt any gangster to take the risk of a few years in jail. And the drug ring in the area was back in business within a few weeks, as active as before.

With so much money as bait, it takes only a handful of professional criminals to keep the traffic booming. But it is not only the professionals who find such profit irresistible. It is far too great a temptation for the decent but weak: the airline stewardess who can earn a year's salary by putting into her flight bag a small, neatly wrapped, brown-paper parcel; the nineteen-year-old student who runs out of money on a European trip; the Florida fisherman who finds deep-sea charters scarce in a recession winter.

Above all, with so much money to be made so easily, creating new addicts becomes irresistibly attractive, especially to the addict who desperately needs a considerable amount of money to satisfy his own craving. Much, perhaps most, of the alarming invasion of the schools, down to the elementary-school level, by hard drugs is through "induced addiction"—that is, the deliberate "creation of customers" by means of purposeful, systematic attempts to lure children into "getting hooked" and thereby becoming significant revenue and profit producers for older addicts.

Paradoxically, every "victory" in the "war against narcotics" increases the profitability of this trade and soon creates new pushers, more addicts, and bigger profits. When the narcotics agents "smash a drug ring" and confiscate fifty kilograms of heroin, the drug temporarily becomes scarce around Manhattan, in downtown San Francisco, or on Harvard Square. The price goes up—and with it the profit for the drug rings whose sources of supply are still intact. Addicts becomes more desperate. Crime and violence—and with them, fear—rise more sharply. More people are lured by their own need and by the high profits into becoming peddlers and pushers, producing still more addicts.

Making narcotics legally available to the addicted is unlikely to unleash a drug epidemic. It may even be the one way to contain and control it. If it is not profitable to make an addict out of a teen-ager, there won't be many pushers around the schools talking students into "trying" the stuff. There won't be many part-time or amateur smugglers. And crime syndicates are unlikely to have much interest in a trade that no longer produces big payoffs. Drug education in schools may have a chance if the addicts themselves, who know only too well the danger and torture in which they live, warn youngsters off. The victims of bad LSD trips did just that and were largely responsible for the decline in the use of that drug on the campuses.

But, above all, the addicts' need for money will diminish, and with it the muggings, the burglaries, and the robberies for the sake of a few dollars. And when this occurs, the fear that is sapping our cities and is beginning to sap the suburbs will also begin to diminish.

I am not a public health expert and do not pretend to know how narcotics should best be made available. Undoubtedly, there will have to be strict supervision. Undoubtedly, we should experiment with several modes of delivery—in the neighborhood mental health center, in special outpatient departments in the community hospital, through such programs as New York's methadone experiment, and so on. There will have to be control lest supplies be diverted to the black market—though as profits disappear, so do black markets.

But all this, bluntly, is completely secondary. The first and overriding concern now must be the nonaddicts. The first task is to make the city livable again.

The first prescription for the survival of our cities is not "Law and Order"; it must be "Freedom from Fear."

DISCUSSION THREE/DRUGS

1 Do you agree that our narcotics laws are the greatest threat to our cities?
2 In your opinion, why do many young people turn to drugs?
3 Drucker advises that "we take the profit out of hard drugs." Do you think this solution will work?
4 "Drugs are no worse than alcohol." How would you refute this as a reason for taking drugs?
5 How would you solve the drug problem on a national scale? on the local level?

ASSIGNMENT/WRITING THE CONCEPTUAL PARTITION [Suggested Topics]

1 Using the essay "Dangers Facing the University" as a model, write a brief essay of your own concerning the dangers facing your own particular school.
2 Write a short essay developed by conceptual partition for your student newspaper. State clearly the thesis. Select a subject of your own choosing or limit any one of the following subjects so that you can treat it adequately for your purpose.

The drug problem

Crime today

Athletes and campus politics

The black student minority

The elective system

Loss of identity in a large university

Student apathy

Social change and violence

The radical left

Students and administration

3 Write an essay on "the new morality" explaining some discovery about it that you consider important for the older generation to understand.

4 Write a conceptual partition developing any one of the following subjects; limit the topics further if it is necessary.

I live in a period of great social change.

Americans are destroying their natural environment.

The rise of some famous man like John F. Kennedy, Adolf Hitler, or Napoleon (break down his political, military, or social career into stages).

CAUSAL ANALYSIS

In developing thought by *causal analysis,* a writer breaks down his subject into cause-and-effect or effect-and-cause relationships or both. He answers two questions: What happening, condition, or circumstance caused this? Given a set of happenings, conditions, or circumstances, what will be the effect? Thus, in structuring thought by causal analysis, a writer establishes specific relationships in time, explaining why something happened (cause) or predicting what will happen from a certain set of circumstances (effects).

Establishing causal relationships is important because one cannot solve certain problems, such as crime, alcoholism, violence, unrest on campus, drug abuse, the generation gap, unless he finds out what causes them. In addition, predicting effects and studying effects of things that have happened are essential to the reasoning process. Rachel L. Carson wrote forcefully of the effects of DDT and other harmful insecticides on plant and animal life in her classic book *Silent Spring.* One need only think of the effects in this country today of our part in the war in Vietnam to be convinced of how vital are these kinds of relationships.

Cause-and-effect relationships, however, are not easily established. First, one seldom finds a single cause or a single effect in this kind of relationship. More often than not, one finds multiple causes and effects. Think of the many causes of the American Civil War, the defeat of Richard Nixon for President in 1960, the disenchantment of the modern student with education and society. Consider the many effects of inflation, an economic depression, the eighteen-year-old vote, or the establishment of an all-volunteer army.

Second, one must be able to distinguish between true causes and effects and signs that are not verifiable. A writer of causal analysis cannot assume that simply because an event follows another event in time, the first event is the cause of the second; this fallacy, known as the *post hoc fallacy,* is the source of much false reasoning and superstition. Moreover, one must distinguish between important and unimportant causes and effects and between remote and immediate causes and effects. He must select those causes that will best fulfill his purpose. How would you treat Hitler's invasion of Poland in discussing the causes of World War II, Hoover's role in causing the Great Depression, or the Democratic Party as the cause of American participation in the wars of the twentieth century?

A writer may organize causal analysis in a variety of ways. He may begin by simply announcing the causal relationship; for example, "As I grew older, I discovered why the Chinese are quite indifferent to the suffering of animals. The Chinese believe that an evil person after death becomes an animal in his next incarnation." He may begin with a question and answer it; for example, "Why are so many men waiting on Death Row?" "What are the effects of inflation?" Still another writer may organize and develop his causal analysis by time sequence. Other writers simply announce the causal relationship in the first paragraph or first sentence and consider each cause or each effect separately, showing the relationship to the thesis.

In the essay that follows, T. K. Irwin states one cause—noise pollution—and shows the various effects resulting from it.

NOISE POLLUTION: DESPITE FUROR, THE PROBLEM STILL GROWS
T. K. Irwin

1 If you're afflicted with a throbbing headache, frayed nerves or a flareup of peptic ulcer, it could be blamed on noise pollution. Whether you have been bombarded by the din of a bulldozer, power mower, rock music, or a combination of other clangorous assaults, you show symptoms of being "noiseated."

2 That we have become the most cacophonous nation in the world has been recognized for several years. It was even mentioned by President Nixon in his State of the Union message, when he proposed "a strong new set of initiatives to combat noise." Yet, despite all the publicity, the problem continues to mushroom: the over-all loudness of environmental noise is doubling every decade. Because of industrial noise alone, an estimated $4-billion is spent each year on worker inefficiency, loss of work time, accidents and compensation. Off the job and at home, noise makers threaten our sanity.

3 The findings of medical experts on the physiological and psychological damage wrought by excessive noise are disquieting. Obviously, all investigators agree that prolonged exposure to extreme noise will result in definite hearing loss. As many as 16 million U.S. industrial workers may be partially or

SOURCE NOTE: T. K. Irwin, "Noise Pollution: Despite Furor, the Problem Still Grows," *Family Weekly*, Nov. 21, 1971, p. 10. Permission of Family Weekly Magazine Corporation.

totally deafened by factory noise. What happens is that the cilia (hairlike out-growth) in the inner ear are destroyed, resulting in nerve-sensation hearing deficiency.

4 Generally, for most people, the danger level for hearing loss is above 80 decibels. One decibel (db) is the least sound detected. Many plants, such as textile mills, produce 120 dbs. At home, a power mower emits 107 dbs; a kitchen food blender, 93. You know when you hit 80 because talking on the phone becomes virtually impossible.

5 Besides deafness, noise can cause other bodily harm. According to the U.S. Public Health Service, "physiological changes include glandular, cardio-vascular and respiratory effects reflecting a generalized stress reaction." Some doctors believe there's a direct link between noise and heart disease, peptic ulcer, colitis, high blood pressure and migraine.

6 Dr. Samuel Rosen, the noted ear specialist who has tested his ideas on noise around the world, from the Arctic to raucous city discothèques, de-scribes the impact of sudden noise:

"Adrenalin is shot into the blood, as during anxiety. The heart beats rapidly, blood vessels constrict, pupils dilate, the skin pales, and the stomach, esophagus and intestines are seized by spasms. In a word, the biological organism is disturbed."

7 Just as air pollution is a threat to people with asthma and emphysema, studies have shown that prolonged or sudden noise adversely influences the digestive, vascular and nervous systems. Long-term experiments with labora-tory animals demonstrated that high noise boosted cholesterol levels and in-creased hardening of the arteries.

8 Mental and emotional damage is harder to measure, though it's apparent to all of us that constant noise impairs peace of mind. "People exposed to prolonged loud noise," says Doctor Rosen, "are more inclined to argue, fight or fly off the handle suddenly." At the National Institute of Mental Health, one scientist commented that a startling sound could very likely propel an excit-able person over the line into irrational behavior. A recent study showed that people living near a busy airport have a higher incidence of mental illness.

9 Evidently there's still more to sound pollution than meets the ear. It's been held responsible for everything from fatigue to the high divorce rate, social conflict and even loss of sexual desire. And medical authorities don't entirely rule out these possible consequences. Just as many people are allergic to nuts or pollen, others may be particularly sensitive to certain clamor and clat-ter.

10 Some of the effects emerging are surprising. Until recently, for instance, scientists believed that unborn babies were insulated from noise. Evidence now indicates that noise can have a profound effect on them, perhaps retard-ing development of the fetus.

11 Thus far, little more than skirmishes have been waged against environmental noise. What's needed are many more civic action groups like Citizens for a Quieter City in New York. Although Manhattan is still the noisiest community in the country, by working closely with city governments and private industry, public pressure has at least brought about antinoise ordinances and has persuaded manufacturers to make quieter compressors and garbage trucks.

12 Ideally, noise can be muffled, if not eliminated, in a variety of ways:
- Construction of soundproof buildings.
- Federal standards for quieter engines in planes and helicopters.
- More efficient mufflers for construction equipment, trucks, motorcycles and garbage removal.
- In industry, instead of having workers wear ear muffs, research should develop quieter machines.
- The FCC should forbid overloud T.V. commercials.

13 Also, you can do your part at home. Put up an acoustical ceiling in your kitchen and other noisy rooms. Draperies and carpeting soften sounds in the living room. Use rubber treads or carpeting on stairs. If a dishwasher, washing machine or dryer causes noise problems, mount it on a felt or rubber mat to absorb vibrations. Weatherstrip windows and doors to prevent rattling. Pneumatic spring door-closers eliminate slamming.

While you may not achieve precisely a heavenly hush, at least at home you'll be able to hear yourself think—about the insidious menace of noise pollution.

STRUCTURE REVIEW SEVENTEEN/CAUSAL ANALYSIS

Name _____ Class _____

Answer each question in the space provided below it.

1 How does Irwin begin his discussion? It it effective?

2 In what paragraph does the writer state his thesis? Where does the writer repeat this thought?

3 What is the function of the first sentence in paragraph 3?

4 What is the topic sentence in paragraph 3?

5 What are the paragraphs that make up the paragraph unit held together by the main idea, "noise can cause other bodily harm"?

6 How does the direction of the writer's flowing thought change after paragraph 10?

See answers on page 228.

The following selection was originally a series of remarks spoken by a Midwestern judge in sentencing two boys who borrowed automobiles to go joy riding. His words were printed in *The Clinton Herald,* Clinton, Iowa, in 1945.

HAVE YOU EVER BEEN CONVICTED OF A FELONY?

1 You come from good homes, both of you. Yet now you have been convicted of a felony—a crime for which you might be sent to the penitentiary. In this case I do not have to send you to the penitentiary. I am permitted to give you a parole.

2 But even if you never see the inside of a penitentiary or jail, you will not have escaped the penalties of your crime. The record of your conviction will be here as long as the courthouse stands. No amount of good conduct in the future can ever erase it.

3 Next year, or ten years from now, or when you are old men, if you are ever called to be witnesses in any court of law, some lawyer will point his finger at you and ask: "Have you ever been convicted of a felony?" You will hang your head and admit that you have, because if you deny it, the records of these proceedings will be brought from the vaults and read to the jury.

4 The question will be asked for the sole purpose of casting doubt on your testimony. Convicted felons are not believed as readily as other persons.

5 Someday you may have a chance to live and work in one of the expanding countries of South America, and you will apply for a passport. You may not get it. You might enter Canada for a fishing trip, but you would not be allowed to stay. No country will allow you to become a resident. Your world is so much smaller than it was.

6 Someday you may seek a position in the civil service of your state or nation. On the application blank you will find this question: "Have you ever been convicted of a felony?"

7 Your truthful answer will bar you from appointment. An untruthful answer will be detected because appointments are made only after investigation. The record is here to be found by anyone interested.

8 In a few years you will be 21, and others your age will have the right to vote—but you will not. You will be a citizen of your state and country, but you will have no voice in public affairs.

9 Someday the governor may pardon you and restore your rights, but it is going to be humiliating to ask him. He'll want to know your whole record. It is a bad one.

10 I am granting you a parole. A parole is in no sense a pardon. You will report to the men who have accepted your parole as often as they may ask. Your convenience is not a matter of importance. You will also obey your parents. If your parents send you to bed at nine o'clock, you will go without complaint. You will perform such tasks as are assigned to you. Your parole is a fragile thing.

SOURCE NOTE: "Have You Ever Been Convicted of a Felony," *The Clinton Herald,* Clinton, Iowa, 1945. Copyright © 1945 by the Clinton Herald Co., Sixth Avenue, S. Clinton, Iowa.

11 Should the slightest complaint of your conduct reach this court, your parole will be revoked immediately and you will begin serving your sentence. You will not be brought back here for questioning and/or explanations. You will be picked up and taken to prison—without notice to you and without delay.

DISCUSSION FOUR/YOUTH AND CRIME

1 Do you think that if young people knew the effects of crime, as the judge points them out, they would be as ready to commit crimes?
2 In your opinion, why has crime by young people increased?
3 Should the youth who commits a violent crime, such as armed robbery and murder, be tried as an adult?
4 What can be done to decrease crime by young people?
5 Is punishment the answer to the youth crime problem?
6 Do you consider the judge's sentence just?

Be prepared to answer the questions in the Structure Review that follows the next model causal analysis.

WHY SO FEW CONSERVATIVES ON CAMPUS?
John P. East

1 Today in American colleges and universities political "liberalism" is the established *Weltanschauung.* This is hardly a new or startling finding, and in fact it is so commonly known that, in the words of the lawyer, we need not "prove" it, we may simply take "judicial notice" that it is so. The noted sociologist Seymour Lipset has written recently, "Intellectuals, academics . . . in the United States tend as a group to be disproportionately on the left. They are either liberal Democrats or supporters of left-wing minor parties."
2 In those academic disciplines where the discussion of politics is central, political science and history, the liberal-left dominance is greater than it is in the whole of academe. In my discipline of political science, and to a lesser extent it is true of history departments, conservatism, either of traditional or libertarian strains, is represented by an exceedingly small group of professors.
3 The most crucial effect of faculty liberalism is upon the students. There are studies indicating that colleges and universities have a liberalizing effect on young people. As Seymour Lipset puts it, "Universities clearly do have a liber-

SOURCE NOTE: John P. East, "Why So Few Conservatives on Campus?" *The New Guard,* May 1970. Copyright © by The New Guard. Permission of the author and publisher.

alizing effect, so that there is a gradual shift to the left." It is hardly surprising that liberal faculties would produce liberal students.

4 Liberal dominance of the faculties means a shutting out of conservative thought and ideas. Students are likely to know who Arthur Schlesinger, Jr., and John Kenneth Galbraith are, and they are almost certain to know of Che, Fidel, Ho, Malcolm X, Goodman, Sartre, Cleaver and Marcuse. Their teachers have prepared them well. On the other hand ask them about Kirk, Burnham, Voegelin, Strauss, Hazlitt, Tonsar, Molnar, Herberg, Possony, Kinter, or any figure affiliated with contemporary conservative thought, and the likelihood is great they will have never heard of them. At best they may know of Buckley (who doesn't?), but the image they will have of him is usually unfavorable.

Conservative Thought Manhandled

5 One of the most appalling manhandlings of conservative thought I have encountered of late is the statement by Professor Thomas Greer in his widely used paperback text, "A Brief History of Western Man." Greer informs his student readers, "Drawing upon the political tradition of Edmund Burke, the Fascists asserted that the state is a living entity, transcending the individuals who compose it." One could weep silently at philosophical illiterates who cannot distinguish between Burke and Mussolini, but we must cry out with anguish that they should write our textbooks.

6 A further effect of liberal dominance and the absence of conservative voices on the campus is to frame the discussion of political issues for the students in terms of liberal versus radical. No conservative alternative is offered.

7 A profound effect of faculty liberalism has been, in the words of Russell Kirk, the growth of "Behemoth University" in America with all of its ugly side effects. With liberal faith in mass education the emphasis in higher education has too often been on size rather than quality with the resulting impersonality and IBM syndrome of the modern campus. This has been a contributing factor to student radicalism, for it fosters rootlessness and alienation. Conservative guidance would have stressed quality over quantity, the personal over the impersonal, it would have kept research and teaching in proper balance, and because of this emphasis it is doubtful that anomie and alienation would have blossomed so extensively on the modern campus.

8 Under liberal guidance "Behemoth University" has tended, in its lust for quantity over quality, to emphasize "things," whereas under conservative influence the emphasis would more likely have been on ideas and "the life of the mind." Where the campus liberal has encouraged direct political "action and involvement," the conservative, if present, would have encouraged thought, contemplation and reflection, and he would have resisted the politicizing of the campus for any point of view.

Why The Imbalance?

9 One is still plagued, however, with the nagging question of why liberal dominance is so utterly disproportionate in academe compared with American thought and life in general. We have conservatives in journalism, the professions, business, practical politics and throughout American culture generally. Indeed, a broadly defined conservatism may well be the dominant theme of American life. Certainly it is clear that the liberal-left professoriate is hardly representative of "mainstream" America. Why is the imbalance so great and so pronounced?

10 The problem is more fruitfully approached not by concentrating on why liberals move into academic work (why shouldn't they? It is an honorable and challenging profession), but rather by focusing on why conservatives shy away from college and university teaching.

11 To begin with, the graduate schools, which train our future faculties, are overwhelmingly liberal and they attract and reproduce their own kind. This vicious circle is difficult to break. At best the graduate school environment for the conservative is usually a neutral one, and sometimes it can be hostile. Too often liberal academe equates liberalism with intelligence, and conservatism with lack of same. The end result is to discourage conservative students from entering graduate work in such crucial disciplines as political science and history where this formula is more likely to be honored.

12 Furthermore, the academic world is heavily bureaucratized and socialized, and unappealing to the conservative. It may be questionable whether college and university organizations are any more bureaucratized than the modern business corporations, but it is true that they can be highly socialized in terms of economic rewards. The difference between "top" and "bottom" salaries at a given institution is often not great, and salaries overall are held at levels lower than comparable jobs in private industry. If college and university salaries were based upon a "free market," they would increase dramatically, for clearly today a college education is a "service" or "commodity" in great demand. But the libertarian spirit of the free market is anathema to the liberal professoriate, and it would prefer lower salaries to a breach of faith regarding its sacred economic theories. This is not an economic setting sufficiently challenging to many conservatives.

13 Part of the blame for conservative absence on the campus must be placed upon American conservatism itself, which is heavily rooted in the narrow confines of economic conservatism or laissez-faire capitalism, and its growth beyond those roots has been qualitatively but not quantitatively impressive. Many of our most talented conservatives in America have been caught up in either creating or servicing the great industrial-technological revolution that has preoccupied America over the past century. This point was personally brought home to me by a close and brilliant conservative friend who is now a partner in one of America's leading law firms. He was a Phi Beta

Kappa undergraduate in history, and graduated first in his law school class. He told me, "I would rather be a third-rate lawyer than a first-rate history professor."

A Frenzied Life Style

14 I find my non-teaching conservative friends in their frenzied lives of maintaining and servicing the great American industrial-technological apparatus (I agree that someone must do it, but why not make the liberals do some of this dirty work?) live almost wholly in a world of "action" in which "the life of the mind" is at best a remote dream. In this regard their life style is not much different from the liberal world where action takes priority over thought, contemplation and reflection. There can even be a subtle anti-intellectualism in which books and "ideas" are considered hallmarks of the effete to the "dynamic" young executive "on the go."

15 In short, too much of American conservatism is an intuitive, narrowly based economic conservatism with at best an additional exposure to popular conservative editorial writers. But when it comes to the cultural conservatives of the stature of Kirk, et al., American conservatives know little. "Getting and spending" exacts a heavy toll. Because it lacks cultural breadth and depth, American conservatism itself is partially to blame for the dearth of conservative teachers on our campuses. Unfortunately to a considerable extent it lacks the intellectual content to nurture potential young teachers.

16 We need to encourage our talented undergraduate conservatives to enter college teaching. Why not? It is an honorable profession, the financial rewards in it have improved significantly in recent years and, above all, opportunity for service to the country and conservative principles in general is unexcelled.

17 Unfortunately there is evidence that some leading conservatives no longer feel the struggle on the campus is worth the effort. Russell Kirk has recently written, ". . . wild horses couldn't drag me back to permanent residence on the typical campus." Similarly, prior to his recent entry into the partisan political arena, former Professor Philip M. Crane wrote, "If there were a genuine hope of reforming the university from within, conservative professors could take the lack of promotions, minimal pay raises, cramped offices, paper work, committee overloads, suppression in the journals, prejudice in the reviews as a small price to pay to achieve the restoration of the academy. But the prospect of internal reform appears remote."

18 Is American conservatism willing to concede the loss of higher education to the liberals and radicals? If so, a great and tragic watershed in the history of this Republic has been passed. The struggle today on our campuses for the minds of the young is spirited and vital. If you will, this is where the action is. If conservatives are willing to concede this crucial battle, I fear they will ultimately lose the war.

STRUCTURE REVIEW EIGHTEEN/CAUSAL ANALYSIS

Name _____ Class _____

Answer each question in the space provided below it.

1 In what paragraph does John P. East express his thesis?

2 What is the purpose of paragraphs 1 and 2?

3 What does the writer tell the reader in paragraph 10 about his flow of thought?

4 How does the discussion in paragraph 2 relate to the writer's purpose at this stage of the development?

5 The first logical structural division of the paper may be broken down into two paragraph units; complete the frame below indicating the organization of this section.

Paragraph unit 1 consists of the following paragraphs: _____ .

Main idea is _____ .

Paragraph unit 2 consists of these paragraphs: _____ .

Main idea is _____ .

6 What is the main idea of paragraph 4? With what kind of support does the writer develop the topic sentence?

7 What is the effect of the cause discussed in paragraph 11?

8 In paragraph 12, what does the guide word indicate about the flow of thought?

9 What is the effect of the cause discussed in paragraph 12?

10 What is the main idea of paragraph 13?

11 What action does the writer suggest?

12 How is the whole essay organized?

See answers on page 228.

ASSIGNMENT/WRITING CAUSAL ANALYSIS [Suggested Topics]

1 Write a paragraph or paragraph unit explaining the causes of the student protests on your campus or a campus that you have read about.

2 Research the causes of World War I. Write a theme explaining the causes. Distinguish between immediate and remote causes, and between important and less important causes.

3 Explain why you think man is still faced with any one of the following tragedies: war, inequality, injustice, poverty, suicide.

4 Write a paragraph unit on the causes of one of the following: inflation, a strike, smog in your area, loss of a championship, or an accident.

5 Write a paragraph or paragraph unit explaining the effects of any one of the subjects listed in the assignment above.

6 Write an essay in which you describe the effects upon society of any one of the following: the war in Vietnam, the death of John F. Kennedy, the airplane, the landing on the moon, labor unions, voting rights for 18-year-olds, a 25-hour work week, or the present long weekends.

7 Write a causal analysis explaining some happening or event, such as a curfew in a town or city, the abolition of competitive athletics, the control of a government by a few, police violence or mob violence, industrialization, or the rise in the cost of living.

ANSWER SECTION

STRUCTURE REVIEW FIFTEEN

1 The first sentence suggests the thesis. Since the writer begins at once to discuss the first and second revolutions, the reader can assume that he will develop by partition.

2 Into revolutions.

3 The next revolution. He states his thesis in paragraph 4: "I believe we must base the next industrial revolution—a planned one—on the thesis that there is no such thing as waste. . . ." It is necessary, therefore, to explain the new revolution, supporting his thesis.

4 It is a very effective conclusion. The pattern is the thesis-support-thesis frame. Thus, the writer emphasizes his central thought in the final sentence; he also suggests future action.

5 He mentions a kind of revolution—explains it briefly and emphasizes its shortcomings. Such a brief treatment hints that each revolution really did not contribute much to progress, but had disastrous results. Thus, he builds up his case for the next revolution—a planned one.

6 The answer is in the thesis statement in paragraph 4 and the repetition of that idea in the final paragraph.

7 The effects are obvious to people living today.

8 Yes. He does not involve the reader in needless details, and he writes for the layman, not the sociologist. We must all be responsible for shaping our future.

STRUCTURE REVIEW SEVENTEEN

1 The writer begins his discussion by mentioning the effects of noise pollution. This kind of information should gain reader interest, for its impact is great. The reader's health is being seriously threatened.
2 Paragraph 2: "Yet, despite all the publicity, the problem continues to mushroom. . . ." In the last sentence of the essay: "at least at home you'll be able to hear yourself think—about the insidious menace of noise pollution."
3 The first sentence introduces the direction of the writer's flowing thought for the next part of the essay—the effects of noise pollution.
4 "Obviously, all investigators agree that prolonged exposure to extreme noise will result in definite hearing loss."
5 Paragraphs 5, 6, and 7.
6 He begins to discuss ways that noise pollution can be controlled and people protected against noise.

STRUCTURE REVIEW EIGHTEEN

1 Paragraph 9.
2 He establishes the fact that in American colleges and universities the faculties are politically liberal.
3 He will focus on the reasons (causes) why conservatives "shy away from college and university teaching."
4 He presents examples to support the generalization expressed in paragraph 1.
5 Paragraphs 1 and 2. Main idea: "Today in American colleges and universities political 'liberalism' is the established *Weltanschauung*." Paragraphs 3 through 8. Main idea: Effects of liberalism.
6 "Liberal dominance of the faculties means a shutting out of conservative thought and ideas." Examples are given of outstanding conservatives and liberals.
7 Conservative students are discouraged from "entering graduate work in such crucial disciplines as political science and history where this formula is more likely to be honored."
8 "Furthermore" indicates a discussion of another cause-effect relationship.
9 The academic world is heavily bureaucratized and socialized (cause). Thus, it is unappealing to the conservative (effect).

10 "Part of the blame for conservative absence on the campus must be placed upon American conservatism itself, which is heavily rooted in the narrow confines of economic conservatism or laissez-faire capitalism, and its growth beyond those roots has been qualitatively but not quantitatively impressive."

11 In paragraph 16, the writer suggests that we need "to encourage our talented undergraduate conservatives to enter college teaching."

12 Paragraph unit 1 (paragraphs 1 and 2) establishes that faculties are liberal. Paragraph unit 2 (paragraphs 3 through 8) gives effects of liberalism on campus. Paragraph unit 3 (paragraphs 9 and 10) gives statement of thesis and method of organization. Paragraph unit 4 (paragraphs 11 through 15) gives causes for lack of conservatives on campus. Paragraph 16 gives a suggested course of action. Paragraph 17 repeats reason why conservatives are not on campus. Paragraph 18, the conclusion, alerts the reader to what might happen if conservatives do not take action.

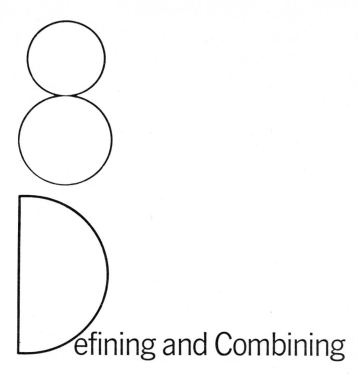

8 Defining and Combining

Definition is a method of developing thought by which a writer explains the meaning of a word or term so that his reader will understand its usage in much the same way as he does. In defining, a writer answers the question: What is this, or what does it mean? By defining, a writer is actually limiting the use of the word by placing boundaries around it. *Webster's New World Dictionary* (Second College Edition, 1970) gives eight separate meanings for the word "culture."

cul·ture (kul'chər) *n.* [ME. < L. *cultura* < *colere:* see CULT] **1.** cultivation of the soil **2.** production, development, or improvement of a particular plant, animal, commodity, etc. **3.** *a)* the growth of bacteria or other microorganisms in a specially prepared nourishing substance, as agar *b)* a colony of microorganisms thus grown **4.** *a)* development, improvement, or refinement of the mind, emotions, interests, manners, taste, etc. *b)* the result of this; refined ways of thinking, talking, acting, etc. **5.** development or improvement of physical qualities by special training or care [body *culture,* voice *culture]* **6.** the ideas, customs, skills, arts, etc. of a given people in a given period; civilization—*vt.*

-tured, -tur·ing 1. to cultivate **2.** to grow (microorganisms) in a specially prepared medium.[1]

Thus, when a writer says "culture" means "cultivation of the soil" (definition 1), he is limiting the word "culture" by saying that he means only this. But when he uses the same word in another sentence, he means it to be something else; e.g., in the sentence "Greek culture contributed much to Roman culture," the writer means "culture" to be "the ideas, customs, skills, arts, etc. of a given people in a given period; civilization" (definition 6). There are three types of definitions: the *dictionary,* the *formal,* and the *extended definition.*

DICTIONARY DEFINITION

The dictionary definition gives much information about a word. It presents variant spellings and pronunciations, the part of speech, current meanings, past meanings, and meanings in specialized fields like science, physics, law, music, history; it also gives the history of the word (etymology), synonyms, antonyms, and syllabication. The form, however, is too mechanical and structured for use in writing. Simple definitions, based on the dictionary meaning, therefore, must be worked smoothly into the writer's flowing thought. A writer can present the meaning of a word or term in a variety of ways. He can define a word or a term directly by giving its meaning in a separate sentence or follow the word immediately with its meaning in the same sentence.

Richard Jones was a *misogynist,* a hater of women.

A most striking feature of the Cuna Indians is the high percentage of *albinos* (persons with pale, milky skin, light hair, and pink eyes) among them.

He may let the reader infer the meaning of a word or term by its context, the surrounding words that give meaning to the word to be defined.

Spartacus struck his opponent a *mortal* blow over the heart with the short sword, ending quickly the gladiatorial contest.

His *arbitrary* decision angered the committee members, and they called for impeachment of the dictatorial chairman.

He may define the word or term indirectly by placing the meaning in the structure of the sentence.

Followers of his *unorthodox* political philosophy *refused to conform to the established and conventional practices and ideas* of the two other parties.

---

[1] *Webster's New World Dictionary of the American Language,* Second College Edition, p. 345. Copyright © 1970 by World Publishing Company, Cleveland, Ohio.

The Cuna Indian's *view* of the world is sustaining because his *conception* of things gives him a strong sense of rightness and security.

He may make the meaning of the word or term clear by using a simile.

Many in the courtroom felt that the defendant was as much of a *libertine* as the notorious Don Juan.

The owner of the mill and most of the town, like Scrooge, was a *parsimonious, cantankerous,* old relic.

In writing the simple definition, the writer must be careful to avoid the common errors in defining. He should not define the word with the word itself; this error is called the *circular definition.*

Sophistic is pertaining to a *Sophist,* the art or method of *Sophists.*

Sophistic means great skill in subtle argumentation under logical forms.

Exclamation is the art of *exclaiming.*

An *exclamation* is an abrupt or emphatic utterance, outcry, etc.; an interjection.

He should define the word or term in simpler terms than the original word.

A *eulogy* is an *encomium* or a *panegyric.*

A *eulogy* is a spoken or written piece of great praise, such as a funeral oration.

Acumen means *discernment* or *perspicacity.*

Acumen is quickness of insight or keenness of intellect.

He should not give an example as a definition. Examples are valuable in aiding the reader to understand the meaning of the word; they are not definitions.

Barbiturates are sleeping pills.

Barbiturates are derivatives of barbituric acid; they act as depressants on the central nervous system.

A *crustacean* is a lobster or a shrimp.

A *crustacean* is any of a class (Crustacea) of arthropods, including shrimps, crabs, barnacles, and lobsters, that usually live in water and breathe through gills; they have a hard outer shell and jointed appendages and bodies.

He should avoid the expressions "is where" and "is when" in structuring the definition. It is better to use "means" or "is" followed directly by the key word in the definition.

A *usurer* is when one lends money at an illegal rate.

A *usurer* is one who lends money, especially at an exorbitant or illegal rate.

A *symposium* is where people meet to discuss a particular subject.

Symposium means a meeting for discussion of a particular subject.

ASSIGNMENT/DICTIONARY DEFINITION

Using the dictionary entry below, write the synonym or synonyms that best explain the meaning of "irritable" in the following sentences.

ir·ri·ta·ble (ir′i tə b′l) *adj.* [L. *irritabilis* < *irritare,* to IRRITATE] **1.** easily annoyed or provoked; impatient; fretful **2.** *Med.* excessively or pathologically sensitive to a stimulus **3.** *Physiol.* able to respond to a stimulus—**ir′ri·ta·bil′i·ty, ir′ri·ta·ble·ness** *n.*—**ir′ri·ta·bly** *adv. SYN.*—irritable implies quick excitability to annoyance or anger, usually resulting from emotional tension, restlessness, physical indisposition, etc.; **irascible** and **choleric** are applied to persons who are hot-tempered and can be roused to a fit of anger at the slightest irritation; **splenetic** suggests a peevish moroseness in one quick to vent his malice or spite; **touchy** applies to one who is acutely irritable or sensitive and is too easily offended; **cranky** and **cross** suggest moods in which one cannot be easily pleased or satisfied, **cranky** because of stubborn notions or whims, and **cross** because of ill humor.[2]

1 Because John was still recovering from the flu, he became irritable when they asked him personal questions.

_____

2 Since he missed the winning basket, he grew irritable whenever one mentioned the championship game.

_____

3 They attributed his irritable disposition to his hot temper.

_____

4 When things weren't going exactly as he wished, he was irritable with everyone around him.

_____

5 If anyone mentioned her humble beginnings, she grew irritable and became uncooperative.

_____

ASSIGNMENT/SIMPLE DEFINITIONS AND ERRORS IN DEFINING

Listed below are letters of the alphabet identifying kinds of definitions and errors in defining. Read the statements below them and identify each definition by placing in the blank to the right the correct letter of the alphabet.

[2] Ibid., p. 746.

a   Meaning in a statement sentence
b   Explanation immediately following the word
c   A simile
d   By context
e   Circular definition
f   Use of "is where" or "is when"
g   Use of a more complicated and less familiar term

1   His appearance was as *grotesque* as the gargoyles on a _____
medieval church.

2   Scientists measure the impact of noise in terms of *decibels* _____
(*deci* for the value of ten, and *bel* after Alexander Graham Bell,
who is responsible for the telephone and its ring). Decibels,
which are based on the faintest noise that can be heard,
measure vibrations of sound numerically.

3   A *cupola* is where there is a small dome or similar structure _____
on a roof.

4   *Noise* is unwanted sound. _____

5   *Indigence* is the condition of being indigent. _____

6   *Extenuation* is a mitigation of the seriousness of a crime or _____
offense.

7   The criminal crept up behind the bank guard and strangled _____
him with a *garrote*.

8   *Pousette* is when a couple or couples dance round and _____
round with hands joined.

9   A *curator* is a person in charge of a museum or library. _____

10   *Extenuation* is a thing that extentuates. _____

11   According to speakers at a *symposium,* a conference _____
organized to discuss a subject, the environmental din is
doubling every ten years.

12   John was *recalcitrant* like a spoiled child who doesn't get _____
his own way; therefore, he refused to play.

13   *Itinerant* means peripatetic. _____

14   His conservative parents would not *condone* his radical _____
behavior.

15   *Extenuation* is a lessening of the seriousness of a crime or _____
offense.

FORMAL DEFINITION

Defining by formal or analytic definition, a writer places a word or term
into a class or genus and then shows properties or characteristics that
are peculiar to the term itself. He is actually structuring an equation:

Definition = genus + differentiae

In other words, he places the term in a class and next distinguishes it clearly from the other members in the class by showing differences. Study the following examples.

Word		Genus	Differentiae
Psychology	is the	science	of human and animal behavior.
Meteorology	is the	science	of weather and climate.
Identification	is a	defense mechanism	in which we imagine that we are like another person.
Regression	is a	defense mechanism	in which we retreat to early or primitive forms of behavior.
A doctor	is a	person	who is a physician or surgeon.
A doctor	is a	person	on whom a university has conferred one of its highest degrees.
A doctor	is a	person	licensed to practice any one of the healing arts.
A doctor	is a	person	who is a medicine man or witch doctor.

In the formal definition that follows, Carl Becker defines the term "democracy" by placing it in the genus government and then with contrast shows how it differs from government by one person.

Democracy [term to be defined] refers primarily to a form of government [genus] by the many [difference] as opposed to government by one—government by the people [clarification of the difference] as opposed to government by a tyrant, or an absolute monarch.

In order to discuss democracy intelligently it will be necessary, therefore, to define it, to attach to the word a sufficiently precise meaning to avoid the confusion which is not infrequently the chief result of such discussions. All human institutions, we are told, have their ideal forms laid away in heaven, and we do not need to be told that the actual institutions conform but indifferently to these ideal counterparts. It would be possible then to define democracy either in terms of the ideal or in terms of the real form—to define it as government of the people, by the people, for the people; or to define it as government of the people, by the politicians, for whatever pressure groups can get their interests taken care of. But as a historian I am naturally disposed to be satisfied with the meaning which, in the history of politics, men have commonly attributed to the word—a meaning, needless to say, which derives partly from the experience and partly from the aspirations of mankind. So regarded, the term democracy refers primarily to a form of government by the many as opposed to government by the one—government by the people as opposed to government by a tyrant, a dictator, or an absolute monarch. This is the most general meaning of the word as men have commonly understood it.[3]

EXTENDED DEFINITION

Writers also present the meaning of the word or term by extending the simple dictionary-based definition into a paragraph, a paragraph unit, a chapter, or even a longer piece of writing. Such a definition is called an *extended definition.* A writer may organize and develop his definition by a variety of methods; he will most frequently combine a number of methods in defining. Thus, he may distinguish the word or term from another by comparison, contrast, or analogy. He may use classification or partition or causal analysis. In the model definition that follows, observe the various methods for making clear the meaning of the term "Renaissance."

WHAT WAS THE RENAISSANCE?
T. Walter Wallbank and Alastair M. Taylor

Definition

Meaning in the past

Reasons for change in its meaning

1   The term "Renaissance" means literally rebirth. Until recent times, men have looked upon the age which bears the name as a "sudden turning on of the light after some centuries of darkness." Today we know that the Middle Ages were anything but "dark ages" because, as we have seen, medieval thought and art made rich contributions to our modern culture. Furthermore, we know that there was no revolutionary change in the development of European culture from the fourteenth to the sixteenth centuries. But these centuries did witness the gradual shift from a purely medieval viewpoint to a modern one and saw the quickening of human activity in nearly every phase of man's life.

Narrow meaning of term

2   In a narrow sense, the Renaissance was a new and intense interest in the art and learning of Greece and Rome, to the disparagement of the Middle Ages. The Renaissance scholars,

[3] Carl Becker, *What Is Democracy?*

SOURCE NOTE: T. Walter Wallbank and Alastair M. Taylor, "What Was the Renaissance?" *Civilization: Past and Present,* 3d ed., vol. 1, pp. 485–486. Copyright © 1954 by Scott, Foresman and Company, Glenview, Ill.

called Humanists, imitated everything classical, loved the past, "were less interested in the present, and not at all in the future." This phase of the Renaissance was really regressive, for

Broad meaning of term it looked backward in history toward antiquity. But the Renaissance in its broader aspects was a stimulation of interest in discoveries by explorers and scientists, a new urban culture of the rising middle class, new advances in statecraft and the growth of the national states, new concepts in literature and art, and a lively interest in secular affairs as contrasted with the otherworldliness of the Middle Ages. In its broad sense the Renaissance was progressive, for it looked forward in history and laid the foundations of our modern civilization.

Age of transition 3   The Renaissance was an age of transition, a transition from medievalism with its emphasis on Scholasticism, church authority, and asceticism to modernism with its emphasis on science, skepticism, and individualism. The Renaissance was also a transition from a relatively static to a dynamic culture, from a society based on feudal, rural, and monastic ideals to one based on an individualistic, urban, and secular pattern. The

Contrast Middle Ages tended to look upon the world as sinful and human nature as destined to be repressed; the modern age looks upon the world as vital and invites human nature to be expressed. In the Renaissance we find an intermingling of the two ideals. The common people remained illiterate and clung to the ways of their forefathers; the relatively few who had acquired education and the new culture revolted from medievalism.

The writer may feel that words like "freedom," "orientation," or the expression "the generation gap" have been distorted by misuse and wish to discuss more fully the true meaning as he sees it. In the definition of "nobility" that follows, Ortega y Gasset defines with this method.

It is annoying to see the degeneration suffered in ordinary speech by a word so inspiring as "nobility." For, by coming to mean for many people hereditary "noble blood," it is changed into something similar to common rights, into a static, passive quality which is received and transmitted like something inert. But in the strict sense, the *etymon* of the word nobility is essentially dynamic. Noble means the "well known," that is, known by everyone, famous, he who has made himself known by excelling the anonymous mass. It implies an unusual effort as the cause of his fame. Noble, then, is equivalent to effortful, excellent. The nobility or frame of the son is pure benefit. The son is known because the father made himself famous. He is known by reflection, and in fact, hereditary nobility has an indirect character, it is mirrored light, lunar nobility, something derived from the dead. The only thing left to it of living, authentic, dynamic is the impulse it stirs in the descendant to maintain the level of effort reached by the ancestor. Always, even in this altered sense, *noblesse oblige.* The original noble lays an obligation on himself, the noble heir receives the obligation with his inheritance. But in any case there is a certain contradiction in the passing-on of nobility from the first noble to his successors.[4]

A writer may state the meaning of the word or term and clarify it by example. In the model definition that follows, Robert Gorham Davis defines in this manner.

This [Ignoratio Elench] means, in idiomatic English, "arguing off the point," or ignoring the question at issue. A man trying to show that monarchy is the best form of government for the British Empire may devote most of his attention to the charm of Elizabeth II and the affection her people felt for her. In ordinary conversational argument it is almost impossible for disputants to keep to the point. Constantly turning up are tempting side-issues through which one can discomfit an opponent or force him to irrelevant admissions that seem to weaken his case.[5]

A writer may clarify the meaning by presenting an historical account of the word's meaning and show how ideas related with it in history color the meaning of the word today.

The word chivalry comes from *chevalier,* meaning horseman, and it refers to a code of etiquette connected with knighthood. It did not appear until quite late in the Middle Ages. It developed from three sources: The German tribal custom of investing adolescent youth with military arms, the Christian religious and moral ideas, and the Saracenic concepts of poesy and heraldry. Chivalry as an institution reached its zenith in the twelfth and thirteenth centuries.

The chivalric code of conduct was strict. It demanded fidelity to one's lord and to one's vows, championship of the Church against her enemies, protection of women, children, and the infirm, generosity, courtesy, reverence toward womanhood, and service to God by warring against the infidel and the heretic. Unfortunately, chivalry was quite different in practice. While he might cloak his motives under high-sounding words, the average knight continued to plunder, fight, and abuse women, especially if they were not of the noble class. With the decline of chivalry, its code became fantastic and even ridiculous. But the ideals of chivalry definitely affected the conduct of later society.

---

[4] Jose Ortega y Gasset, *The Revolt of the Masses,* p. 64. Copyright © 1932 by W. W. Norton & Company, Inc. Permission of W. W. Norton & Company, Inc.
[5] Robert Gorham Davis, *Handbook for English.* Reprinted by permission of Robert Gorham Davis, Theodore Morrison, and the President and Fellows of Harvard University.

They seeped down into middle-class life and today color our own conception of a true "gentleman."[6]

A writer may present a common definition of the word or term and follow it with a definition that he considers better as in the model that follows.

Noise has been defined as one or more loud, harsh nonharmonious sounds or vibrations that are unpleasant and irritating to the ear. A better definition of noise is "unwanted sound."

A writer may make clear the meaning of a word or term by presenting etymological information showing from what language or situation it was derived.

Billingsgate means coarse, vulgar, violent, abusive language. The term is derived from the fact that the fishwives in Billingsgate fish market in London used foul, vulgar language.

Pseudonymous means having a false name. It goes back to the French *pseudonyme,* which is derived from the Greek *pseudōnymous* consisting of the root *pseudēs,* meaning "false," plus *onyma,* meaning "name." A writer who adopts a fictitious name for professional use or to disguise his true name chooses a *pseudonym.* Sidney Porter, for example, chose the name "O. Henry" as a pen name and Madame Amantine Lucile Aurore Dudevant is far better known by her *nom de plume* of George Sand.

In the next model definition, the writer shows how the word "aristocracy" has been used in various ways and then defines the word "as comprehensively as possible."

The want of a feeling for aristocracy, among the rich as well as the poor, among the intelligentsia and among artists, constitutes the most signal failure of the American spirit. To the death of this spirit we can attribute too the gradual recession of European culture or, to use the Europeans' unflattering term, its Americanization. The word "aristocracy" itself has been used in various familiar ways: to refer to a social or political caste, or, in a figurative and etymologically more dubious sense, to moral, intellectual or aesthetic excellence. But let us use the term as comprehensively as possible, intending not only moral and intellectual distinction, and not only aesthetic elevation, but also a distinct social group ideally embodying these qualities, and possessing in addition that much despised virtue known as manners, or good breeding. Thus the *feeling* for aristocracy is the desire for, or the picturing of, a harmonious nobility which expresses itself by moral, intellectual, aesthetic and so-

---

[6] Wallbank and Taylor, op. cit., p. 360.

cial distinctiveness, and in that division of mankind known as class conscious-ness. This feeling is traditionally the possession of an actual (and, of course, imperfect) aristocracy and of its intellectual allies.[7]

Read the next model essay. Be prepared to answer questions in Structure Review Nineteen on page 244.

CONSERVATIVES TAKE PRACTICAL TACK SEEKING ORDER, CHANGE
Russell Kirk

1   During the 1930s, '40s, and early '50s, most American politicians desired to be known as liberals. Nowadays, practical political advantage often lies in being considered conservative; and public men who formerly called them-selves liberals feel more at ease if the press refers to them as "moderates." What do these labels really mean?
2   My favorite definition occurs in Ambrose Bierce's "Devil's Dictionary"—"Conservative: A statesman who is enamored of existing evils, as distin-guished from the liberal, who wishes to replace them with others."
3   More gravely, Abraham Lincoln put it thus: "What is conservatism? Is it not preference for the old and tried, over the new and untried?" By that definition, Lincoln continued, he was a true conservative himself.
4   Historically speaking, the words are derived from "conservator," an official guardian of public liberties in certain medieval cities of Italy. A conservative, then, in the root sense of the word, is a guardian: one who tries to preserve order, justice, and freedom.
5   As terms of modern politics, these words first were used in France, very early in the 19th century, by men of politics and letters who were strongly influenced by the writings of Edmund Burke. In Burke's spirit, they were en-deavoring to combine the best in the old order of European civilization with the necessities of modern society, after the disasters of the French Revolution and the Napoleonic wars.
6   During the 1820s, these words became part of the British political vocabu-lary; during the 1840s, they were incorporated into American political termi-nology. (Both John C. Calhoun and Abraham Lincoln thought of themselves as conservatives.) In the beginning, at least, "conservatism" implied a middle path, between the extremes of tyranny and anarchy: it meant moderation in politics.

[7] Oscar Mandel, "Nobility and the United States," *The American Scholar*, Spring 1958, p. 197.

SOURCE NOTE: Russell Kirk, "Conservatives Take Practical Tack Seeking Order, Change," *San Gabriel Valley Tribune*, Covina, Calif., Sept. 23, 1969, sec. B, p. 3.

7 Generally speaking, a conservative is a person who would neither reject the old merely because it is old, nor yet oppose reform merely because it is new. If an institution or a custom has worked well for a long while, says the conservative, we would be foolish to abandon it merely for the sake of novelty.
8 But as Edmund Burke declared, "Change is the means of our preservation." Society must change if it is to live, much as the human body must slough off some old tissue and take on new flesh. The chief necessity is to keep this change within bounds: to maintain the norms of order and justice and freedom even while the outward aspect of society alters. The good statesman, again in Burke's phrase, is one who combines a disposition to preserve with an ability to reform.
9 This description of the conservative mind may seem strange to people who have heard these words often as terms of abuse, hurled by liberal or radical publicists. There are, of course, various types of conservatives, quite as there are various types of liberals or radicals. The vice of selfishness afflicts some conservatives, for instance, rather as the vice of envy afflicts some liberals.
10 But if we examine political labels dispassionately, we find that words like "conservative" and "liberal" are not (or should not be) simply god-terms or devil-terms. Instead, they are categories of particular ways of looking at the civil social order.
11 Conservative opinions are founded upon a certain understanding of human nature and society. The conservative believes that man is not perfect or perfectible; therefore no society can be perfect. We never will achieve Utopia, because Utopia does not exist, and cannot. Politics is the art of the possible. What we should strive for is the maintenance of order and justice and freedom, within institutions and beliefs that a nation has slowly and painfully developed over many generations.
12 If you will, a conservative is a man who prefers the devil he knows to the devil he doesn't know. Devils—that is, bad men and bad ideas—always are abroad in the world. If we preserve the continuity of a society, we may succeed in restraining or even defeating the devil we know. But if we cast away our historical experience, we don't abolish devils; we only find ourselves confronted by a new devil, who may be dreadfully difficult to restrain, because we don't understand him.
13 The American conservative is strongly attached to political structures and to a way of life developed during more than three centuries of social existence in America, and rooted moreover in thousands of years of European experience. He believes, for instance, in the rule of law, not of men; in slow beneficial change, not in hasty radical experimentation; in local liberties and constitutional guarantees.

He believes in private property and honest competition, not in centralized economic direction or concentration of power and wealth; he believes in freedom of choice, under moral and positive law; he believes that social variety, rather than social uniformity, is the spice of life.

14 He believes that we moderns owe a debt to our ancestors, who gave us life and wisdom, and that we have obligations toward the generations which will follow us in time. He believes that the principle of order has primacy: that is, we cannot achieve freedom or justice until order has been secured. Or, to put it another way, he believes that the claims of order and the claims of freedom should be in a healthy balance, for only then is it possible to attain justice.

He believes that society is held together by love and common interests, not by force or fraud. He believes that personal morality is the foundation of a decent society; for without good men, there cannot be a good state.

STRUCTURE REVIEW NINETEEN/DEFINITION

Name _____   Class _____

Answer each question in the space provided below it.

1 What is the purpose of paragraph 1?

2 How do the definitions in paragraphs 2 and 3 help Kirk fulfill his purpose? What method of defining does he use?

3 What kind of definition does Kirk use in paragraphs 4, 5, and 6? How does this kind of defining help his purpose?

4 Why does Kirk define the word again in paragraphs 7 and 8?

5 Where does Kirk begin his definition of "conservative"?

6 In addition to defining the term, what is the writer's purpose?

See Answers on page 249.

ASSIGNMENT/WRITING DEFINITION [Suggested Topics]

1 Make a diagram of defining by formal definition for three words or terms with which you are familiar. Write an extended definition for one of the words or terms by beginning with the formal definition and making its meaning clear by examples.

2 Define a word or term negatively; then develop its meaning with more than one definition, e.g., "school spirit," "freedom," "body contact in basketball."

3 Write a definition making clear the meaning of some abstraction, such as "civil rights," "justice," "love," "friendship," or "wisdom."

4 Look up in your dictionary a word that has more than one level of meaning, such as "naïve," "financial," or "meander." Explain the various meanings and settle on a specific meaning that you will use for purposes of making some point of view clear.

5 Using special dictionaries like the *Oxford English Dictionary,* define a word like "gentleman," "university," "essay," or "colloquialism," making clear its meaning by the historical method of defining. Refer to its origin, etymology, and changes in meaning.

6 In the fields of sociology or political science search for some words or terms that have a meaning different from their general use. Write an extended definition making clear the specialized meaning and the general usage.

7 Define some words that have taken on a derogatory meaning, such as "intellectual," "radical," "ivory tower," "capitalist," explaining the change in meaning.

COMBINATION OF METHODS

You have learned now a variety of methods of effectively structuring your thoughts when your purpose is to inform and explain. You have probably become aware that many essays by experienced writers are developed by more than one expository method and that the intent of the writer determines which method dominates. In other words, in informing and explaining, a writer does not begin by deciding that he will structure his thoughts concerning violence, volcanoes, or the generation gap by comparison, contrast, or classification. He has the ability to develop his thought about these subjects in a variety of ways and uses the method or methods that will best fulfill his purpose and best shape the material with which he is working.

In the essay that follows, "On Law and Order" by Joseph Wood Krutch, you will find that the writer states clearly his thesis in the final paragraph of the essay: "There will never be a reign of law and order until those engaged in the various protests now epidemic everywhere know with certainty when they have gone beyond the legal limit and, if they have, what penalties will be imposed upon them." The direction of his flowing thought, then, is through the particulars to a final statement—the thesis—expressing his point of view (support-thesis frame).

Krutch knows, however, that before his reader will accept his conclusion, he must be convinced that it is valid. He knows also that he must gain reader interest and present sufficient background material so the reader will understand why his point of view is correct and necessary. Krutch, therefore, begins his essay by mentioning effects of our troubled times and emphasizing that "ours really is a more than usually troubled time."

This conclusion leads him logically into the causes for "why this is so" and a warning that the disorders of the present "will get worse unless we make up our minds what we should do about them." Later we shall see that this introductory material is a perfect setting for his solution to the problem.

In paragraphs 4 and 5, Krutch touches more directly on his thesis by presenting two points of view regarding law and order that are prevalent today. He explains the permissive view in paragraph 4 and in paragraph 5 points out to the reader the resulting "most rigidly repressive" reaction to it.

Paragraph 6 moves the reader further along in the same direction since Krutch states that neither of these extremes has worked very well. He then stresses the urgency for defining clearly "what laws and what kind of order."

He further establishes the necessity for formulating definitions by contrasting today's troubled times with less troubled times when many of today's unanswerable questions "never arose in any serious form." His main point is that "where there is a consensus, the problem of definition does not arise." Today, "no comfortable consensus exists."

In paragraph 9, he asks questions that involve answers based on legal limits. And he concludes that there are no generally accepted answers to those questions, "nor any consistent method of dealing with them." By this time, Krutch has firmly established that today's troubled times are the result of our not making up our minds what we should do about them. The two opposite views have not worked. "There will never be a reign of law and order until those engaged in the various protests now epidemic everywhere know with certainty when they have gone beyond the legal limit and, if they have, what penalties will be imposed upon them."

Although the structural organization of this essay is movement from particulars to the final statement of the thesis—the writer's point of view—analysis by causes and effects, contrast, question to answer, and definition are also methods that play an important part in developing the thought.

ON LAW AND ORDER
Joseph Wood Krutch

1 All times are troubled times—but some, like ours, are more troubled than others. There is always a generation gap; there are always dissatisfactions with social inequalities; there are always crimes of violence. But the generation gap does not always result in open rebellion; dissatisfaction with social equality does not always lead to riots; the crime rate is not always climbing steadily. Ours really is a more than usually troubled time.

2 Why this is so, why all these things are happening to us, we do not know. Or, at least half a dozen different answers are given by those who are sure they do know. One of them, possibly correct, is that we brought today's troubles on ourselves. We did not inquire what youth wanted; we did not recognize the extent of social inequalities; we did not attempt to remove the causes of crime. And, say some, we shall never win our way back to a more normally troubled time until we have corrected all these mistakes.

3 Perhaps. But with the best will in the world they cannot all be corrected overnight. We are certainly in for many more months, probably many more years of trouble before our world will seem as settled as it did even two decades ago. Meanwhile we cannot wait until all the abuses are corrected before deciding what we ought to do about the disorders which certainly will get worse unless we make up our minds what we shall do about them.

4 Unfortunately we are still very far from having made up our minds, and the options given vary all the way from the most boundlessly permissive to the most rigidly repressive. If a minority of students take over the college, why, say

SOURCE NOTE: Joseph Wood Krutch, "On Law and Order," *This Week Magazine* Oct. 19, 1969, p. 2. Copyright © 1969 by United Newspapers Magazine Corporation, 485 Lexington Avenue, New York, N.Y. 10017.

some, let them. They know better than their teachers what they need to learn. If deprived slum dwellers riot and loot, treat them gently because they are at least as much sinned against as sinning.

5 But such permissiveness soon begins to seem intolerable to most people, and they call for "Law and Order." If necessary, answer violence with equal violence. Club the students into submission; shoot looters in the act of looting.

6 At certain times and places, both of these extremes have recently been tried, and neither works very well. Nor will anything work very well as long as no rebellious student, no slum rioter, or, for that matter, no simple criminal, knows how he will be treated. "Law and order" means nothing unless we know what laws and what kind of order. It is this that no advocate and no opponent of the get-tough principle has ever clearly defined. In times of uncertainty like the present, society is always threatened by the opposite evils of anarchy on the one hand and the police state on the other. Today we are uncomfortably close to being seriously threatened by one or the other.

7 In less troubled times, many of the questions which now seem unanswerable never arose in any very serious form. Consider, for example, the present problem of nudity or the obsession of writers and other artists with explicit representations of sexual activity. What is and what is not pornography? Complete submissiveness seems to threaten a sort of anarchy; any censorship a sort of police control of art and thought.

8 The permissible limits of free speech in this respect were not a serious problem in the 19th century because the vast majority of people took it for granted that everybody knew what the permissible limits were, and only a few extremists, like the generally ridiculed Anthony Comstock, were dissatisfied with the prevailing manners. Where there is a consensus, the problem of definition does not arise. But no comfortable consensus exists today, and we are faced with the necessity of formulating definitions very difficult to formulate.

9 What are the limits of free speech? At what point does the right of peaceful assembly cease to be peaceful in fact? When does protest become rebellion or revolution? There is no generally accepted answer to any of these questions, nor any consistent method of dealing with them.

10 It has long been recognized that the effectiveness of any punitive legislation depends less upon the severity of the penalty imposed than upon the probability that the penalty will be visited, actually and promptly, upon the offender. And this condition cannot be met unless the offenses are clearly defined. At the present moment no rioter, no rebellious student, no purveyor of what some call pornography has any way of knowing what he can "get away with" and what he cannot.

11 There will never be a reign of law and order until those engaged in the various protests now epidemic everywhere know with certainty when they have gone beyond the legal limit and, if they have, what penalties will be imposed upon them.

DISCUSSION FIVE/LAW AND ORDER

1 What reasons does Krutch give for stating that our time is more troubled than others?
2 What reasons do you believe explain our troubled times?
3 According to Krutch, why is our time so troubled?
4 Does Krutch believe in answering violence with violence?
5 Why were the permissible limits of free speech not a serious problem in the nineteenth century?
6 What answer does Krutch give to the problem?
7 Do you believe the many problems of today can be solved? How?

ANSWER SECTION

ASSIGNMENT/DICTIONARY DEFINITION

1 Irritable because of physical indisposition
2 Touchy
3 Irascible and choleric
4 Cranky or cross
5 Splenetic

ASSIGNMENT/SIMPLE DEFINITIONS AND ERRORS IN DEFINING

1	c	**7**	d	**13**	g
2	b	**8**	f	**14**	d
3	f	**9**	a	**15**	a
4	a	**10**	e		
5	e	**11**	b		
6	g	**12**	c		

STRUCTURE REVIEW NINETEEN

1 To gain interest and introduce the terms.
2 He gains humor by the first definition and gains prestige by telling his readers that Lincoln was a conservative. His purpose was to define the term "conservative" and show that this view was the best one. Kirk is a well-known leader of the conservative cause. By example.
3 Historical definitions. By history he shows that the conservative view was held by many famous men and that it was a very sound view.

4 He presents a general definition of the word, emphasizing two points that help his purpose: (1) a conservative will not reject the old merely because it is old, (2) a conservative will not oppose reform merely because it is new. He cites Burke to support his view.

5 Beginning with paragraph 11 and moving onward through paragraph 14.

6 To support his belief that conservatism is the best political philosophy.

ersuasion

Today, the formal arguments of Madison and Hamilton, Lincoln and Douglas, and the debates of the early twentieth century are no longer popular. Even presidential candidates who agree to debate the issues on television, such as did Nixon and Kennedy, discard many of the formal rules and practices of argumentation in order to make their discussion more appealing to the modern audience so effectively conditioned by the informality of the "fireside chat"—the friendly President speaking to the nation from his home—the White House. The formal argumentation paper likewise has changed, becoming an opinion paper or a persuasion paper mixing certain procedures of classical argumentation with the popular style and approach of the editorial in the current periodicals. This new form appeals to the reader because it is brief, informal in style, less intellectually demanding, and probably more interesting.

Nevertheless, the purpose of the writer of the persuasion paper or the "modern orator," however subtle or novel his approach, is the same as that of the persuader of old in his formal argumentation. He presents his position and interprets the facts in order to convince his reader to accept or at least seriously consider his conclusion or conclusions.

Persuasion, then, is the art of convincing a person, usually a group of persons, to accept a conclusion or conclusions that you have reached concerning somebody, something, or some belief. It can be as simple and trivial as changing your friend's mind so that he will go with you to a football game when he has other plans or as complex and important as convincing the people of this nation that you should be the next President. Learning the strategies of persuasion will not only enable you to participate in discussion of important issues of the day on and off campus, but it will also train you to become a critical listener and reader of the views of others.

The knowledge that you have gained about organizing and developing the forms of discourse—especially the importance of phrasing the thesis and developing it with sound reasoning so that the reader will understand and accept your point of view—will serve you well in structuring the persuasion paper. Therefore, it is learning the strategies of persuasion—both honest and dishonest devices—that will demand your attention in this discussion. Persuasion is more than a logical and honest presentation of evidence. Sound reasoning and a cogent presentation of your position based on honest fact, you will discover, are not enough to win the case.

How do you reach people that studies have shown do not really "know what they want," will not tell the truth about their likes and dislikes even if they know them, and do not behave "in a rational way"? (See Vance Packard, *The Hidden Persuaders,* David McKay Co., New York, 1957, pp. 15–16.) How do you propose a solution to a problem or voice a belief that you have reached by honest evaluation of the evidence to a people who do not want their illusions destroyed, resent the obvious, and will resist, even at times with violence, any threat to their well-being.

One way—perhaps, at first glance, the easiest way—is to manipulate them by emotionally appealing to their love of freedom and country; by playing on their guilt, fears and greed; by deceiving them with distortions of fact, exaggerations, omissions, false analogies; by any means—honest or dishonest—that will achieve your end.

Another way—in the long run, the best way—is by honest persuasion without deception and insincerity. This kind of persuader admits his purpose, eliminates opposing views without attacking those who hold them, avoids excessive appeals to emotions, presents cogently but fairly his position, and allows the reader or listener to draw his own conclusions or accept the conclusion advanced in the paper on the basis of the evidence as well as the power of the persuader.

This kind of persuader, however, must know the strategies of persuasion, both dishonest and honest, if he is to be successful. Moreover, the informed citizen of this country must be able to recognize deception and sham in advertising, marketing, politics, education, labor, and industry if he is to make free and reliable choices. Let us consider, then, the strategies of dishonest persuasion first.

STRATEGIES OF DISHONEST PERSUASION

Perhaps the most complex and controversial of the strategies of persuasion is the use and misuse of *emotional appeals*. It is important at the beginning of this discussion to distinguish between emotional appeals and the emotional impact of a persuasive paper on the audience. It is also important to note that there exists a very thin line between the legitimate use of emotional appeals and the excessive use and abuse of these persuasive devices.

No one who has read the speeches of Thomas Paine, Patrick Henry, Abraham Lincoln, or Daniel Webster will question the power of emotion as an effective persuader. Anyone today who has listened to any of the memorable speeches of Franklin D. Roosevelt, Winston S. Churchill, or John F. Kennedy will not soon forget those experiences. The crux of the controversy lies in the kinds of emotional appeals that the persuader uses and in the honesty of his intent. It is the ethics of persuasion, then, that is the real issue.

Some of the most common dishonest strategies of persuasion with emotional appeals are the following:

1 Writers or speakers who appeal to hate, jealousy, envy, greed—any of the baser passions of man—and not to his reason are dishonest persuaders.

My black opponent for mayor of this great city who now pledges to represent all of you regardless of race, color, or religion was the leader of those racists who just a few months ago burned and looted our fair city and murdered three policemen in the name of equality.

If candidate X is elected President, the Pope in Rome will make the important decisions.

Any person born with a silver spoon in his mouth cannot understand the problems of the working man.

2 Writers or speakers who abuse the appeals to love of freedom, country, and fellow man are dishonest persuaders. This kind of persuader demeans such ideals when he uses them to glorify and make heroic beliefs and situations that have little or nothing ennobling about them.

Progress is the American way, from the early frontiersmen who opened up the great Western lands to the modern adventurers in space who placed the flag of the United States on the moon. We cannot let a bunch of crazy nature lovers stop the building of a plant which means 3,000 jobs for our city.

3 Writers or speakers who appeal to the fears of man, such as infamy, oppression, and loss of personal security.

America has never lost a war; we are not going to lose this one.

If you elect him mayor, he will appoint his black friends to key positions in government. Soon we will become a black state.

His program of social reform will bankrupt this state in six months.

The real danger of appeals to emotions, even when used by honest persuaders, is that they conceal the true issues and prejudice objective inquiry and rational decision making so necessary for the success and perpetuation of a free and open society.

Distortion by omission

When a writer or speaker selects from various sources only those points that strengthen his position and omits any details that would weaken his case, he is slanting his evidence. Thus, he prevents the reader or listener from reaching the proper conclusion on the basis of all the facts. In distortion by omission, it is not what the persuader presents that reveals the dishonesty of his persuasion; it is what he omits.

An article in a newspaper in a town close to a college in Southern California attacked the program of studies offered the students of that district. The reporter's view was that the courses were of little value— even ridiculous. Thus, the college was wasting the taxpayer's money. He cited as evidence such courses as Farm Tractors, Children's Clothing, Flight Food Service, Oral Interpretation of Literature, Sport Officiating, Camp Leadership, and Body Building (Advanced). The resulting furor was hardly unexpected by school officials. Hours were spent on the telephone by administrators, faculty members, and students explaining the omissions to irate citizens. The college was a community college with over 6,000 students in a two-year program of studies and approximately 10,000 students in a transfer program qualifying them to enter a four-year college in their junior year. Thus, Farm Tractors, one of over sixty courses offered in agriculture science, was necessary for a certain kind of agriculture major. Children's Clothing was one of approximately fifteen courses offered in home economics. Flight Food Training was an essential course for a girl training to be an airline stewardess in that program of studies. Oral Interpretation of Literature, an elective, was one of twenty speech courses. And the physical education courses were three of over a hundred courses, many leading to a degree in physical education.

Distortion by flattery

Writers or speakers who use flattery to manipulate their audience are dishonest persuaders. This kind of persuader is usually "a common man" like those to whom he appeals. He shares their views and feelings because he is one of them. He recognizes their ability to "see the true issues." He has supreme faith in their "intelligence," "ability to discriminate," "sense of fair play," and "Christian values." He like them despises "deception," "authority," "demagogy," and "pressure tactics." Because he was poor, he understands better the problems of the ghetto and the disadvantaged. Because he is in the business of making a living, he knows the problems of the working man. Because he too pays taxes, he knows how much of that hard-earned paycheck goes to the state and federal governments in taxes. Because he is a father, he understands the difficulties of parenthood. He is able, therefore, to flatter any group because he is one of them; he praises them instead of presenting the issues and letting them decide for themselves. He writes or speaks to his audience in a manner something like the following:

Discriminating voters have only one choice.

People like you and me raised in a Christian home with Christian values must refuse that kind of atheistic proposal.

I have come here not to tell you what is needed, but to listen to what you have to say about the great issues of our time.

No individual who knows the insidious aim of communism will accept such reforms.

Distortion by superlatives and connotative words

SUPERLATIVES

The dishonest persuader knows, as do the propagandist, the advertiser, the publisher, and the agent, that emotive language rich in superlatives and connotative words will sell his product. Superlatives not only help the seller to say that his product is the best; they enable him to claim that is it better than the best. At one time in the history of sports, there were "stars," but today, the "real greats" are the "superstars." *Ben Hur,* a film of the past, was advertised as a "great spectacular." Today, a similar film is advertised as a "gigantic," "colossal" spectacular, "unparalleled" in the history of film making. Superlatives work negatively also. Not long ago, a social problem was "detrimental" to our society; today, the same social problem "threatens us with annihilation," or "is fatal to our future."

CONNOTATIVE WORDS

Words may be classified according to meaning as *denotative* or *connotative* words. *Denotation* gives the direct, explicit reference of the word; for example, "a dog is any of a large and varied group of domesticated animals related to the fox, wolf, and jackal." But when we refer to a dog as "man's best friend," "man's faithful servant," "a cur," "a mongrel," or call a man a dog or call an unattractive person a dog (slang), we are using the connotative meaning—what the word suggests to the reader or listener, that is, those various meanings that have been associated with the word through its use in our language. In the lists below, note the power of suggestion each word carries:

dwelling	public defender
house	official
home	politician
cottage	statesman
mansion	
shack	

Well aware of the emotional value of superlatives and the connotative words, the dishonest persuader blasts out any chance for reasonable interpretation of the facts with his carefully chosen rhetoric. If he were a candidate for public office, he might present his case on pollution in the following manner:

With many years of experience as a faithful public servant, I will face courageously yet firmly the problems of pollution that threaten us with extinction. I believe our children deserve clean air above this great land of ours, and rivers, lakes, and streams as fresh and invigorating as when God created them. Therefore, I will inaugurate a massive and dynamic program unparalleled in our time to eliminate those killers in the air and the wastes in our waters that are fatal to our society.

I will bring about this revolution to restore nature's balance without using the hard-earned money of the taxpayers of this glorious state. I will pay for these long-needed reforms with taxes and fines justifiably levied on those most responsible for this catastrophe—the owners of those plants and factories.

My vacillating opponent, the incumbent, is a bureaucrat spending government funds recklessly—spending your money, for the government, my dear friends, is the people—in an aimless and confused attempt to straddle the fence between the well-meaning but impractical environmentalists who stand inflexible on one side of that invisible though rigid barrier to progress and the selfish, profit-motivated industrialists who face them on the other side. His hopeless policy of appeasement has blackened the blue sky above us and stagnated the pure waters of our beloved state, leaving you and me the victims of our own waste.

Distortion by the rhetorical question

A rhetorical question is a question that requires no answer, for the question is so worded that the answer lies in the question itself. It can be phrased so that the reader or listener really has no choice, for example:

Question: Would you deny your children the chance to improve their grade in school?
Answer: No. Of course not.
Then you must buy a set of *Adam's Encyclopedia.*

Question: Would you deprive your wife of the convenience that is essential to her comfort and health on those sweltering summer days when you are in your comfortable air-conditioned office?
Answer: No. Of course not.
Then you must purchase a new, modern Knott's Air Conditioner at our sale price.

The rhetorical question can be used by the dishonest persuader to attack the man, not the issues he defends:

Would you elect a man to such an office of trust who has been known to associate with some of the lowest criminal elements in the state?

Distortion by false analogy

An analogy is an extended comparison (a simile or metaphor) of two persons, places, things, or ideas. It is effective for making the unknown clear by comparing it to the known. It also gives vividness to writing and serves well for illustration and example. However, an analogy proves nothing. No matter how many points of likeness exist between two persons, places, things, or ideas, ultimately any comparison will break down, for there are always differences. The eye, for example, is like a camera and the heart like a pump in the way they function. But the differences are obvious.

In persuasion, analogy is used inductively; the persuader reasons that because two things are alike in certain respects there are other and sometimes important parallels between the two that he can use to support his point of view. An analogy, then, to be logical and acceptable to the reader or listener must be established by a sufficient number of similarities between the two subjects and any differences must be explained.

The dangers in using analogy in persuasion are two: (1) a true parallel does not exist between two subjects; therefore, any analogy will break down if carried far enough; and (2) if the differences are greater than the likenesses, the conclusion reached may not be true. Suppose a writer or speaker were to develop an extended analogy on each of the metaphors below and reach the conclusion that follows it.

1 Football is a war game. Therefore, football should be played to win regardless of the rules.
2 A hospital is a big business. Therefore, it should be run like one.
3 The state is a ship. Therefore, the governor must have absolute authority.

ASSIGNMENT/ANALOGY
Read the selection below; then write a paragraph or paragraph unit explaining the use of analogy by the persuader.[1]

1 This false philosophy that has brought Europe into this war will, in my judgment, bring into war any nation that adopts it. Europe has built its hope of peace upon a false foundation, upon the foundation of force and fear and terrorism; the only hope of peace that these European nations have had rested in the belief that each could terrorize the other in peace.
2 It is a false philosophy; if you want to see how false it is try it on a neighborhood. The big questions between nations are settled by the very same rules that we apply to neighborhoods. I will show you what this philosophy is, and then you can judge whether it can be expected to bring anything else except war.
3 Suppose nearby you have two farmers, living side by side, good farmers, well-meaning farmers who wanted to be friends, and suppose they tried to maintain peace on the European plan, how would they go at it? One would go to the nearest town and buy the best gun he could find, and then he would put a notice in the paper saying that he loved his neighbor and that he had no thought of trespassing upon his neighbor's rights; but that he was determined to protect his own rights and protect his honor at any cost, that he had secured the best gun in the market, and that if his neighbor interfered with him, he would shoot him. Then suppose the neighbor went to town the next day and got him a better gun and, with the same frankness, consulted the newspaper and put in a similar notice explaining that he loved peace as well as his neighbor did but that he was just as determined to defend his own rights and protect his honor and that he had a better gun than his neighbor and that, if his neighbor crossed his line, he would kill him. And suppose then the first man, when he read that notice, went to town and got two guns and advertised that fact in the paper, and the second man, when he read it, went to town and got three guns, and so on, each alternately buying guns. What would be the

[1] From William Jennings Bryan.

result? Every undertaker in that vicinity would go out and become personally acquainted with the two men, because he knew there would be at least one funeral in that neighborhood. That is the European plan. One country gets a battleship and announces that it can blow any other battleship out of the water; then a rival nation gets a dreadnaught that can sink the battleship; then the first nation ·gets a super-dreadnaught; then they go to the dictionary and look for prefixes for the names of their battleships as they build them larger and larger; and they make guns larger and larger and they equip armies larger and larger, all the time talking about how much they love peace and all the while boasting that they are ready for a fight.

4   Go back to the time when they commenced to pass laws against the carrying of concealed weapons and you can get all the material you want for a speech on preparedness, because the arguments made in favor of carrying revolvers can be put into the speeches made today in favor of preparedness, without changing a word. Did you ever hear of a man who wanted to carry a revolver to be aggressive? No, it was just to protect his rights and defend his honor, especially his honor, but they found by experience that the man who carried a revolver generally carried it with a disposition to use it on slight provocation and a disposition to provoke its use by others. For the promotion of peace, every state in this union has abolished preparedness on the part of individuals because it did not preserve peace. It provoked trouble, and unless we can convince ourselves there is a moral philosophy applicable to nations that is just the opposite of the moral philosophy applied to individuals, we must conclude that, as the pistol-toting man is a menace to the peace of a community, so the pistol-toting nation is a menace to the peace of the world.

HONEST PERSUASION

Persuasion is honest if the persuader uses the strategies of persuasion honestly, leaving the reader a choice based on the truth of the presentation and its effectiveness. Persuasion is honest if the persuader himself is honest. After carefully examining the evidence, he has reached reasonable conclusions. Because he believes that the issues are of vital concern to others as well as himself, he wants to convince others that his beliefs or courses of action are worth consideration. The honest persuader is no different from anyone else in certain respects; he will appreciate the plaudits of the crowd and receive satisfaction if others believe him right. But personal gain and profit are not his motivations.

Read the excerpt below, taken from a speech by Winston Churchill given to the House of Commons on June 4, 1940, after the glorious but tragic evacuation of 335,000 French and British soldiers at Dunkirk. The result of the defeat was that British soldiers were driven from the continent of Europe and an invasion of the British Isles by German forces appeared imminent.

CHURCHILL'S SPEECH TO HOUSE OF COMMONS,
JUNE 4, 1940

1   Meanwhile, the Royal Air Force, which had already been intervening in the battle, so far as its range would allow, from home bases, now used part of its main metropolitan fighter strength, and struck at the German bombers and at the fighters which in large numbers protected them. This struggle was protracted and fierce. Suddenly the scene has cleared, the crash and thunder has for the moment—but only for the moment—

Emotional
appeals
died away. *A miracle of deliverance, achieved by valor, by perseverance, by perfect discipline, by faultless service, by resource, by skill, by unconquerable fidelity, is manifest to us all.* The enemy was hurled back by the retreating British and French troops. He was so roughly handled that he did not hurry their departure seriously. The Royal Air Force engaged the main strength of the German Air Force, and inflicted upon them losses of at least four to one; and the Navy, using nearly 1,000 ships of all kinds, carried over 335,000 men, French and British, out of the jaws of death and shame, to their native land and to

Conces-
sion
the tasks which lie immediately ahead. *We must be very careful not to assign to this deliverance the attributes of a victory. Wars are not won by evacuations.* But there was a victory inside this deliverance, which should be noted. It was gained by the Air Force. Many of our soldiers coming back have not seen the Air Force at work; they saw only the bombers which escaped its

Counter-
proposals
protective attack. They underrate its achievements. I have heard much talk of this; that is why I go out of my way to say this. I will tell you about it.

2   This was a great trial of strength between the British and German Air Forces. Can you conceive a greater objective for the Germans in the air than to make evacuation from these beaches impossible, and to sink all these ships which were displayed, almost to the extent of thousands? Could there have been an objective of greater military importance and significance for the whole purpose of the war than this? They tried

SOURCE NOTE: Winston S. Churchill, "Dunkirk," speech to House of Commons, June 4, 1940, in *Blood, Sweat and Tears* by Winston S. Churchill, G. P. Putnam's Sons, New York, pp. 292–297. Copyright © 1941 by Winston S. Churchill.

hard, and they were beaten back; they were frustrated in their task. We got the Army away; and they have paid fourfold for any losses which they have inflicted. Very large formations of German aeroplanes—and we know that they are a very brave race—have turned on several occasions from the attack of one-quarter of their number of the Royal Air Force, and have dispersed in different directions. Twelve aeroplanes have been hunted by two. One aeroplane was driven into the water and cast away by the mere charge of a British aeroplane, which had no more ammunition. All of our types—the Hurricane, the Spitfire, and the new Defiant—and all our pilots have been vindicated as superior to what they have at present to face.

3   When we consider how much greater would be our advantage in defending the air above this island against an overseas attack, I must say that I find in these facts a sure basis upon which practical and reassuring thoughts may rest. I will pay my tribute to these young airmen. The great French Army was very largely, for the time being, cast back and disturbed by the onrush of a few thousands of armored vehicles. May it not also be that the cause of civilization itself will be defended by the skill and devotion of a few thousand airmen? There never has been, I suppose, in all the world, in all the history of war, such an opportunity for youth. The Knights of the Round Table, the Crusaders, all fall back into the prosaic past: not only distant but prosaic; but these young men, going forth every morn to guard their native land and all that we stand for, holding in their hands these instruments of colossal and shattering power, of whom it may be said that

Praise or flattery?

> Every morn brought forth a noble chance
> And every chance brought forth a noble knight,

deserve our gratitude, as do all of the brave men who, in so many ways and on so many occasions, are ready, and continue ready, to give life and all for their native land.

4   I return to the Army. In the long series of very fierce battles, now on this front, now on that, fighting on three fronts at once, battles fought by two or three divisions against an equal or somewhat larger number of the enemy, and fought fiercely on some of the old grounds that so many of us knew so well, in these battles our losses in men have exceeded 30,000 killed, wounded and missing. I take occasion to express the sympathy of the House to all who have suffered bereavement or who are still anxious. The President of the Board of Trade is not here

today. His son has been killed, and many in the House have felt the pangs of affliction in the sharpest form. But I will say this about the missing. We have had a large number of wounded come home safely to this country—the greater part—but I would say about the missing that there may be very many reported missing who will come back home, some day, in one way or another. In the confusion of this fight it is inevitable that many have been left in positions where honor required no further resistance from them.

Admission
of great
losses

5 *Against this loss of over 30,000 men, we can set a far heavier loss certainly inflicted upon the enemy. But our losses in material are enormous.* We have perhaps lost one-third of the men we lost in the opening days of the battle of 21st March, 1918, but we have lost nearly as many guns—nearly 1,000 guns—and all our transport, all the armored vehicles that were with the Army in the north. This loss will impose a further delay on the expansion of our military strength. That expansion had not been proceeding as fast as we had hoped. The best of all we had to give had gone to the British Expeditionary Force, and although they had not the number of tanks and some articles of equipment which were desirable, they were a very well and finely equipped Army. They had the first-fruits of all that our industry had to give, and that is gone. And now here is this further delay. How long it will be, how long it will last, depends upon the exertions which we make in this island. An effort the like of which has never been seen in our records is now being made. Work is proceeding everywhere, night and day, Sundays and week days. Capital and Labor have cast aside their interests, rights, and customs and put them into the common stock. Already the flow of munitions has leapt forward. There is no reason why we should not in a few months overtake the sudden and serious loss that has come upon us, without retarding the development of our general program.

6 Nevertheless, our thankfulness at the escape of our Army and so many men, whose loved ones have passed through an agonizing week, must not blind us to the fact that what has happened in France and Belgium is a colossal military disaster. The French Army has been weakened, the Belgian Army has been lost, a large part of those fortified lines upon which so much faith had been reposed is gone, many valuable mining districts and factories have passed into the enemy's possession, the whole of the Channel ports are in his hands, with all the tragic consequences that follow from that, and we must

expect another blow to be struck almost immediately at us or at France. We are told that Herr Hitler has a plan for invading the British Isles. This has often been thought of before. When Napoleon lay at Boulogne for a year with his flat-bottomed boats and his Grand Army, he was told by someone, "There are bitter weeds in England." There are certainly a great many more of them since the British Expeditionary Force returned.

7 The whole question of home defense against invasion is, of course, powerfully affected by the fact that we have for the time being in this island incomparably more powerful military forces than we have ever had at any moment in this war or the last. But this will not continue. We shall not be content with a defensive war. We have our duty to our Ally. We have to reconstitute and build up the British Expeditionary Force once again, under its gallant Commander-in-Chief, Lord Gort. All this is in train; but in the interval we must put our defenses in this island into such a high state of organization that the fewest possible numbers will be required to give effective security and that the largest possible potential of offensive effort may be realized. On this we are now engaged. It will be very convenient, if it be the desire of the House, to enter upon this subject in a secret session. Not that the Government would necessarily be able to reveal in very great detail military secrets, but we like to have our discussions free, without the restraint imposed by the fact that they will be read the next day by the enemy; and the Government would benefit by views freely expressed in all parts of the House by Members with their knowledge of so many different parts of the country. I understand that some request is to be made upon this subject, which will be readily acceded to by His Majesty's Government.

Future action

8 We have found it necessary to take measures of increasing stringency, not only against enemy aliens and suspicious characters of other nationalities, but also against British subjects who may become a danger or a nuisance should the war be transported to the United Kingdom. I know there are a great many people affected by the orders which we have made who are the passionate enemies of Nazi Germany. I am very sorry for them, but we cannot, at the present time and under the present stress, draw all the distinctions which we should like to do. If parachute landings were attempted and fierce fighting attendant upon them followed, these unfortunate people would be far better out of the way for their own sakes as well as for ours. There is, however, another class, for which I feel not the

slightest sympathy. Parliament has given us the powers to put down Fifth Column activities with a strong hand, and we shall use those powers, subject to the supervision and correction of the House, without the slightest hesitation until we are satisfied, and more than satisfied, that this malignancy in our midst has been effectively stamped out.

Invasion

9 Turning once again, and this time more generally, *to the question of invasion,* I would observe that there has never been a period in all these long centuries of which we boast when an absolute guarantee against invasion, still less against serious raids, could have been given to our people. In the days of Napoleon the same wind which would have carried his transports across the Channel might have driven away the blockading fleet. There was always the chance, and it is that chance which has excited and befooled the imaginations of many Continental tyrants. Many are the tales that are told. We are assured that novel methods will be adopted, and when we see the originality of malice, the ingenuity of aggression, which our enemy displays, we may certainly prepare ourselves for every kind of novel stratagem and every kind of brutal and treacherous maneuver. I think that no idea is so outlandish that it should not be considered and viewed with a searching, but at the same time, I hope, with a steady eye. We must never forget the solid assurances of sea power and those which belong to air power if it can be locally exercised.

10 I have, myself, full confidence that if all do their duty, if nothing is neglected, and if the best arrangements are made, as they are being made, we shall prove ourselves once again able to defend our island home, to ride out the storm of war, and to outlive the menace of tyranny, if necessary for years, if necessary alone. At any rate, that is what we are going to try to do. That is the resolve of His Majesty's Government—every man of them. That is the will of Parliament and the nation. *The British Empire and the French Republic, linked together in their cause and their need, will defend to the death their native soil, aiding each other like good comrades to the utmost of their strength.* Even though large tracts of Europe and many old and famous States have fallen or may fall into the grip of the Gestapo and all the odious apparatus of Nazi rule, we shall not flag or fail. We shall go on to the end. We shall fight in France, we shall fight on the seas and oceans, we shall fight with growing confidence and growing strength in the air, we shall defend our island, whatever the cost may be. We shall fight on the beaches, we

Purpose of this appeal

shall fight on the landing grounds, we shall fight in the fields and in the streets, we shall fight in the hills; we shall never surrender, and even if, which I do not for a moment believe, this island or a large part of it were subjugated and starving, then our Empire beyond the seas, armed and guarded by the British Fleet, would carry on the struggle, until, in God's good time, the New World, with all its power and might, steps forth to the rescue and the liberation of the old. (Italics added.)

ASSIGNMENT/PERSUASION

Write a paper analyzing Churchill's speech explaining why you consider it effective persuasion or why you do not. In your analysis, be guided by the following questions.

1 Is the speech honest persuasion? Why? Why not?
2 What is his purpose?
3 Does his praise of the Royal Air Force and the defeated British and French armies degenerate into flattery?
4 Does he present evidence to support the "miracle of deliverance"?
5 Does he admit to tragic losses on the Continent?
6 What are his proposals for future action?
7 How does he use emotional appeals? Mention some emotional appeals in your answer.
8 How does the occasion affect the tone and presentation of the speech?

STRUCTURING THE PERSUASION PAPER

In structuring the persuasion paper, you can develop the thesis—the controversial topic—by any one or any combination of methods that you learned earlier. In addition, you must learn certain techniques and skills that are important to the success of your persuasion. Make use, therefore, of the following suggestions.

Know your purpose

Before you begin writing a persuasion paper or preparing a persuasive speech, have clearly in mind the thesis around which you will develop the issues—the main points of the argument. Gather as many issues as possible including those that are favorable to the opposition's case. Eliminate any issues that are weak or irrelevant. Study those issues in your opponent's case that may be refuted or must be accepted as valid. Have in mind what you desire from the audience.

Are you interested in informing them about a problem or situation so that they will become aware of it? Do you want them to take a certain course of action? Are you seeking to shake them up so that in thinking about the topic they will begin to doubt the case of the opposition? Do you want to change their beliefs or feelings about the topic?

Know your audience

Learn as much as you can about who makes up your audience. How familiar are they with the topic? How strongly do they feel about it? What are their fears and desires? How strong is the opposition?

Let us assume that you are convinced that new members of the drama club should have equal rights in the decisions and activities of the organization. Let us assume also that you are concerned with how the bookstore should be run. You are convinced that it should be operated by students as a nonprofit business.

In presenting your case in the form of a paper for the school newspaper or a paper to be read before the members of the drama club, you will be addressing an emotional opposition from the senior members of the club who resent deeply giving new members rights and privileges that seniority has rightfully earned. They will be well informed because they have had much experience in club activities. Your task will not be easy.

In presenting your views on the operation of the bookstore, you will be writing for a different audience, but an equally formidable one. It will consist of students, faculty, and administration; some individuals will care little about the discussion; others will be deeply concerned; still others will wish to maintain the status quo. You will find that some individuals care but wish to express views of their own different from yours. Certain members of the student body, faculty, and administration will fear a loss of power or welcome an increase in their power. Others may fear for their jobs. You may find the discussion resulting from your presentation breaking down into important side issues, such as who should run the school, the high cost of textbooks, or the inefficiency of the bookstore in serving faculty and student needs. Many that read your paper will be well informed; others will have little knowledge of the subject.

Know the issues

An issue is a point that supports the thesis in a persuasion paper. It will probably be a statement of fact or an interpretation of fact with which the opposition will disagree. In the structure of the paper, the statement of an issue is the topic sentence of a paragraph or paragraph unit. In planning your persuasion paper, as with the other forms of discourse, your next step, after phrasing the thesis, is to list as many issues as you can, including those that are contrary to your point of view. Listing contradictory issues is very important because the process will give you an opportunity to think through the argument, recognize the strength of the opposition, identify weak, false, or irrelevant points in the opponent's position, and consider the kind of approach and structure for your own persuasion. Once you have finished listing issues, set the paper aside for a time. Come back later and add any important issues that you may have omitted, eliminate any weak or irrelevant issues, and separate those issues related to your opponent's case into (1) strong issues that you may have to concede and (2) weak issues which you can refute (attack and show that they are not valid).

ASSIGNMENT/THE ISSUES

Study the following issues. Then separate them into valid and weak issues for your case and valid and weak issues for the case of your opponent by listing the numbers of the issues under the appropriate headings.

New Members Should Be Admitted into the Drama Club with All Rights

Issues

1 New members were admitted into the club in the first place because they were involved in dramatic activities, making sets, selling tickets and advertising, performing in plays, etc.

2 Decisions made by the club affect the new members as well as the senior members.

3 They will bring new enthusiasm and new ideas to the club.

4 New members are among the hardest workers and deserve recognition for their labor.

5 If the new members leave the club, all members will suffer.

6 The Drama Club is not a club just for upperclassmen; it is a club for all drama students.

7 New members want too much too soon.

8 New members have not had to earn the right to privilege.

9 New members have not enough experience to make wise decisions.

10 Upperclassmen are selfish and domineering.

11 The advisors are weak; thus we need strong leadership.

12 Upperclassmen are lazy and refuse to do many tasks because they feel such work is beneath them.

13 There are more new members than old members.

14 Veterans have earned the right to certain privileges because they have been in the club longer and served their period of apprenticeship.
15 The club is more important than any of its members.

Note: Add any issues that you wish.

Your Case

Weak Issues   Valid Issues

Case of Opposition

Weak Issues (Will Refute)   Valid Issues (Will Concede)

Organizing and developing the issues

The most logical frame for organizing and developing the persuasion paper is the *thesis-support-thesis frame.* Using this frame gives you the opportunity to introduce the controversy and state clearly your position and to repeat that position for emphasis in the last paragraph. However, you may modify the form or use another pattern if the topic and material dictate it. You can develop the thesis with any method you have previously studied with certain modifications and new approaches that will enable you to present the issues more convincingly.

In beginning the paper, do not antagonize your audience. Keep these facts in mind. Some of the people in the audience will share views similar to yours. Other members of the audience will feel so deeply about contrary views that you will not be able to change their minds. You must concentrate, then, on winning to your side those individuals who are unfamiliar with the topic, those who have not yet made up their minds, and those who hold contrary views but still doubt the rightness of their position. Adopt, therefore, a conciliatory manner. Try to impress the audience with your sincerity, calmness, and reasonableness, rather than irritate and probably lose them by an opening paragraph full of bombast, invective, and alarm. Seek first a common ground on which all can agree and go on from there. In proposing equal rights for the new members of the drama club, you could begin your presentation after the introductory paragraph by pointing out how much the club means to all members and that it would be a tragedy to destroy it when a reasonable and unemotional consideration of the issues might result in action acceptable to the majority of members.

Present the issues cogently but honestly. Admit that in certain respects the opponents have good reason for being emotional about the proposal. The senior members of the club, for example, have every right to feel that their years of apprenticeship and experience are worthy of special privilege. Be willing to concede certain disadvantages in your suggested course of action if there are any. If there are more new members than senior members, they could vote as a unit and control the club. But, be quick to follow any concession with a counterproposal that establishes the validity of your original course of action. By voting as a unit, the new members would destroy the club as surely as the senior members are now doing. In addition, point out that such unit action on most controversial issues before the club is doubtful since this kind of action requires individual rather than unit action for solution. By making certain concessions, you show that you are willing to listen to reason. You will also discover that by making concessions concerning the disadvantages in your proposal you will not suffer as much as you would have if they were first pointed out by your opponent.

Refute the claims of your opponent, especially those that are weak, false, or irrelevant. You may place the refutation at the beginning of the paper or at the end, or you may answer each of the opponent's claims point by point as you move onward.

Each of these strategies of persuasion—conciliation, concession, refutation—enables you to better present your case. In presenting your position, be honest with the evidence, the facts, the analogies, the testimony of competent witnesses or authorities, the reasoning by induction and deduction, and the conclusions drawn from the evidence and your own experiences or you will leave yourself open to attack from your opponents. In addition, if you do not present your case fairly, your readers will doubt your sincerity and honesty.

Read the model persuasion that follows. Be prepared to answer questions in Structure Review Twenty.

SCHOOLBOY SPORTS A BONE-CRUSHING FINANCIAL PROBLEM
David L. Martin

1 The quarterback takes the snap and drops back. Suddenly, he's in a predicament. The four opposing linemen rushing him have a combined weight that is 40 pounds more than a prize-winning steer's; their demeanor makes the Four Horsemen of the Apocalypse look like the Lennon sisters; and the sneers on their saliva-dripping mouths indicate that, next to cracking their knuckles, the thing they love best is squashing quarterbacks.

2 For protection, the quarterback has one 127-pound halfback who poses part-time for the "before" pictures in those body-building ads. The quarterback's primary pass receiver is being covered by a couple of sticky-fingered defensive backs who have formed an Arc de Triomphe over the receiver's head.

3 The quarterback decides to keep the ball, and nobody's happy with the decision. Not only is his team thrown for a loss, but in the process the quarterback has all his bones (except those in the inner ear) crushed by the linemen.

4 Mercy, says the quarterback.

5 Mercy, say school board members and superintendents who participate in similar types of bone-crushing, yard-losing plays called controversies. Often the boardmen and administrators in the middle of these nasty situations can be sure of only one thing: The decision they make will be dismissed as wrong, immoral or stupid by nearly everyone affected.

6 The Great Competitive Athletic Debate is that type of controversy. It is all about the amount of money the public schools are spending on interscholastic sports and whether those expenditures can be justified against: (a) the often meager number of dollars spent by school boards on nonsport extracurricular activities, and (b) the near-poverty level at which more school districts each year are finding themselves forced to operate.

7 Regardless of the conclusion a school board ultimately might reach, the mere hint that it is considering a reevaluation of its reasons for spending relatively large sums of public monies on competitive sports sometimes is more than enough to rile any town—from a hamlet to, as recently was the case, a vast metropolitan community such as Philadelphia. The result often is far more than a debate ending with clear-cut winners.

SOURCE NOTE: David L. Martin, "Schoolboy Sports a Bone-crushing Financial Problem," *The Los Angeles Times,* Sunday, July 9, 1972, sec. J, 3. Copyright © 1972 by *The Los Angeles Times.*

8 It can turn into a mindless extravaganza that has been known to spawn more controversy in some communities than Vietnam and Teapot Dome combined. Yet, as one school district upon another encounters financial tumult, the incumbency to examine the substantial dollar expenditures seemingly lavished by some school districts on competitive interscholastic athletics weighs formidably on conscientious school boards and their superintendents.

9 Just wait until you hear what you're called when you and your board decide to review the interscholastic athletic programs in your schools. Such a review, nevertheless, looms necessary for many school boards if for no other reason than the fact that good management techniques usually indicate that any dollar-fat program (interscholastic sports programs seem routinely to have entered that category) needs continued scrutiny.

10 The first response evoked by your district's reassessment of its sports program probably will be: Get rid of competitive athletics. Here's the second: Don't you dare.

11 You're on your way.

12 Clearly, carefully devised and carefully administered high school athletic programs constitute a worthwhile extracurricular activity, and in most cases it would be a mistake to disband them at a time when more people are trying to find more ways to keep teen-agers off the streets, off the drugs and on projects that are enjoyable and constructive.

13 Let's assume, then, that a school board has made the relatively easy decision to retain sponsorship of competitive sports teams. Now the more difficult question: How much emphasis in terms of time and money and energy should be spent on a district's interscholastic sports programs?

14 Because of the nearly universal popularity of sports, it is not impossible for a school district's athletic program to grow out of proportion in a way that is reminiscent of a horror movie, like "The Blob That Ate Philadelphia."

15 Speaking of Philadelphia, school board members there must have suffered mild indigestion trying to swallow what happened last fall after they cut 600 teaching jobs and all extracurricular activities (including varsity sports) because of a lack of funds. Citizens didn't say much about the teaching jobs, but cut out varsity football? Not on your letterjacket.

16 Citizen groups, high school students, professional football players, even mayoral candidates rallied to save the city's high school football teams from being clipped by "stuffy people who are antisport" as the board members were called by one Philadelphia lawyer. In this case, community interest saved the teams but not the necessity to make cuts *somewhere* in the school budget.

17 Sometime during its review of interscholastic sports, a school board probably will hear competitive athletics charged with a crime too serious and too basic to be remedied by a cut in expenditures or a simple reordering of priorities. The charge: Competitive athletics do more harm than good to participants. The crime: Building children with strong bodies and corrupt characters.

18   This concern has won some support from San Jose State College Professors Bruce C. Ogilvie and Thomas A. Tutko. The pair evaluated 15,000 athletes and found "no empirical support for the tradition that sports build character."

19   Indeed, say Ogilvie and Tutko, "there is some evidence that athletic competition limits growth in some areas. It seems that the personality of the ideal athlete is not the result of any molding process, but comes out of the ruthless selection process that occurs at all levels of sport. Athletic competition has no more beneficial effects than intense endeavor in any other field."

20   Criticism like that is made to order for setting off the sports fans who insist that competitive high school athletics are, at the very least, a clear path to strong character and, at their shining best, a highway to health, happiness and heaven. But, notwithstanding such loyal if mindless sports fervor, the attack on competitive sports does seem to have validity when it is applied—not to the basic concepts of athletics—but to the way athletic games are sometimes conducted.

21   It is no fun that your neighbor's son (remember that happy, little sandlot baseball player?) was turned into a vomiting, nervous, second-string shortstop because of the overcompetitiveness and overorganization of the Little League. Sadly, that is the no-fun way some sports are being played today.

22   Plainly, then, a school board review of athletics should include an analysis of the philosophy of the athletic program—and how that philosophy is being practiced on the field—along with pragmatic considerations such as cost.

23   School board members can do themselves a favor by making it clear to all parties involved that the board is not out for blood but is determined to evaluate the athletic program and, if necessary, to nudge it back in line with the education goals of the school district.

24   Here are some categories in which school boards may have to nudge:

25   1—Coaches. The school board should hire coaches who are teachers first and athletic chauvinists second, and who may be expected to exert a positive influence on the attitudes and ideals of youngsters. Board members should not be swayed by community sports fans who are interested mainly in a coach's win-loss record.

26   Often the most effective and popular coaches are those with a healthy sense of the place of athletics—in a high schooler's life, in the schools, and in society. But some coaches haven't managed to pass the mental age of 15 (an accusation offered by a coach), and they often don't see far beyond their nose-guards when considering how sports fit into the overall scheme of things.

27   One eye-opening example: During a debate about cutting athletic expenditures so that more money could be saved to rescue a district's faltering education program, one coach asked the big question: "When a student gets to high school, are reading, writing and mathematics more important than extracurricular activities?" You might not want him on your team.

28   2—Education priorities. The attitudes, appreciations and ideals of players and spectators should improve as a result of their experience with high school competitive athletics; and interscholastic sports programs should—in addition to providing educational and recreational values to players and spectators—be consistent with the general aims of a district's education program.

29   This doesn't mean that school boards should be asking: What did the kids learn in football today? It's probably enough if sports are great fun and wholesome diversions for the players, schools and communities. School boards, however, should demand that school athletic programs not turn playful pups into insensitive mastiffs nor fun-seeking fans into bloody rioters.

30   3—Individual rights. A district's sports program may be ripe for a penalty call from the courts if those programs deny participation to an individual because of dress or hair styles, marital status or sex. At least, that appears to be the trend in recent court rulings.

31   Surely, one of the saddest of all failures of school sports programs must be the denial of equitable athletic opportunities to girls. Patently, there is little excuse for denying participation to females, either in separate programs or in the same sports programs that are open to boys.

32   For proof that the walls won't come tumbling down when there's a boy-versus-girl situation on the playing field, consider this: In 100 New York high schools, girls competed with boys in 10 noncontact sports. Most of the girls, boys and coaches approved of the experiment, and one boy displayed a healthy attitude about the whole thing: "If a guy gets beat, so what? If he can't admit a girl is better, he has a problem."

33   As may the school board that puts up with coaches who believe that individual rights should be left at the sidelines.

34   A study of Florida public school coaches found that 93% of the coaches who had been in the business for 20 or more years claimed the right to prescribe dress and hair styles for their athletes. Things may be getting better, though: The same study found that only 66% of coaches with fewer than five years experience agreed with the old pros.

35   4—Perspective. Youngsters are discovering that the halls of athletic fame are being tread by some clay feet. Exposes in form of books, magazine articles and interviews with sports figures are telling us all something we knew but wouldn't say out loud: Star athletes, like the rest of us, are sometime-heroes, sometime-villains, full-time humans.

36 In the high school arena, young athletes know full well that one isn't necessarily struck bald for the act of disobeying the coach. Some high school heroes are wearing long hair in defiance of the coach's orders, others divide their attention among sports and other interests, and today's sophisticated young athlete might react with a red face to a "win one for the Gipper" pep talk—not because he's fired up but because he's embarrassed for the speaker.

37 These trends of independence, this questioning the worth and place of athletics have brought sports down to the real world. Well, sports fans, it probably never belonged on a pedestal in the first place, and putting it up there may have been setting it up for a fall—from which all the coaches and all the coaches' men may not be able to recover again.

38 That may be why those who love athletics are among the most eloquent critics of the overcommercialism, artificial priorities and dry competitivism that take the fun out of fun and games. Says one critic:

39 "I love athletics. What I do object to is the do-or-die attitude that has taken the joy and the recreation out of athletics."

40 Who in the world is the blasphemer who said that a few months ago in an article published by the American Medical Assn.? Jesse Owens, that's who.

STRUCTURE REVIEW TWENTY/PERSUASION

Name _____ Class _____

Answer each question in the space provided below it.

1 What is the function of the first five paragraphs (paragraph unit 1)?

2 How does the material in paragraph unit 2 (paragraphs 6 through 11) help the writer's case?

3 What kind of concession does he offer in paragraph 12?

4 In what paragraph does the writer state his thesis?

5 What is the first issue he considers after stating the thesis? How does he support the issue? What conclusion was reached?

6 What is issue number 2? How many paragraphs make up the paragraph unit discussing this issue? How does the conclusion he reaches help his case?

7 What is the purpose of paragraph 23?

8 Into how many divisions does he divide his recommended action?

9 How does he conclude his discussion?

10 What is your opinion of this paper as persuasion?

See answers on page 286.

MEN, WOMEN—AND POLITICS
Lenore Romney

1 Historian Mary Beard once said, "The dogma of woman's complete historical subjection to men must be rated as one of the most fantastic myths ever
created by the human mind."
2 Mary Beard never ran for public office, and her opinion does not apply to
the male-dominated world of politics. In my bid to become the first woman
senator from the state of Michigan, that so-called myth helped to doom my
campaign from the start. And so, the Ninety-Second Congress convened . . .
with just one women—Maine's Margaret Chase Smith—in the United States
Senate, a tiny one percent of its total membership.
3 I found in my campaign that many men and women openly resented the
idea that a woman would even try to unseat a man. Some bluntly asked me,
"You mean you have the nerve to challenge a United States Senator?"
4 I think the rawest example of prejudice came from a farmer who told me,
"Ma'am, we don't vote for women or niggers in this county."
5 In factories, I encountered men standing in small groups, laughing, shouting, "Get back in the kitchen. George needs you there. What do you know
about politics?"
6 Many wouldn't even listen to my credentials or to my discussion of the
issues. Yet for 30 years I have worked at all levels of community endeavor—

SOURCE NOTE: Lenore Romney, "Men, Women—and Politics," *Look,* Apr. 16, 1971, p. 11. Permission
of the author.

for the adoption of a new state constitution, for community schools, educational reform, the Council for Human Resources, and with ghetto problems.

7 I was especially discouraged by women themselves saying that women don't know enough to be public officials. Obviously, they were not ready to rally around one who would have represented them in our most important forum.

8 Some women, as well as men, obviously felt a woman would come out second best in the rough give-and-take of politics. Nonsense. We "give and take" with our husbands and children and acquaintances every day and, without being abrasive, come out very well, thank you. We often can do better than men in getting things out of people.

9 At home, both father and mother are needed. In the nation, our collective home, when we place our faith in men and exclude the voice of women, we are shutting out those who, for example, are especially able to communicate with the young.

10 I feel very strongly that women need to be liberated from the belief that they are not pertinent, not relevant. They want equal pay with men, equal jobs, but women are not willing to help one another get elected to deal with the problems of the day. Equal earnings should have been gained back in the Stone Age. Women should not have to be fighting that battle now, and it's too bad they have to. Instead, they should be using their talents in the social and human areas. If they understood their true role, I think they could attain it.

11 It seems so much more important to me for women to communicate effectively. The problems are mounting, but we stay in the background. The few who do step forward are batted down.

12 Who has the gilt-edged credentials to set our children straight? We do. We have the sensitivity, insight, experiences with youngsters that could be invaluable in understanding the emotional and psychological needs of our kids. But first we must understand this, and concentrate our efforts in these areas. For if women and society in general continue to ignore this special feminine understanding in dealing with our human problems and values, we are missing the boat.

13 Unfortunately, the Women's Liberation Movement is not erasing prejudice against women because many members are abrasive and resentful of their own roles in society, and that attitude simply turns people off. Women can be effective by being magnificent figures in their own right rather than small facsimiles of men.

14 Women, for example, could make a unique contribution in the welfare area. Men in government have decided that only impoverished mothers who have been deserted by their husbands may receive welfare checks. This is grossly inadequate. Women of America know that a man cannot be equated with simply a meal ticket. A woman needs her husband in the home; children need their father. Why can't we encourage families to stay together? Why do they have to be driven apart by a Federal program that often forces husbands to desert the home so their wives and children can be eligible for some welfare money?

15 No woman would have written such a law. No woman would see a home destroyed by a dole, a family made rootless, disinherited spiritually and emotionally.

16 American housewives sometimes remind me of Nora in Ibsen's *A Doll's House.* Treated by her husband like a doll and never like a human being, she slammed the door on her family. Like Nora, women are often regarded as ting-a-ling things. Well, I admire ting-a-ling, or sex appeal, as much as anyone, but if that's all a woman has, she will never have real confidence, because there will always be some other gal who will have more ting-a-ling.

17 Lack of confidence is what women suffer from most, and they therefore lack stature, status and any feeling that they can be just as effective as men. Often, they feel their opinions are not valuable. Some are lazy, and others, who have cooked, cleaned and worked all day, are just plain tired. They sit down at night, pick up the newspaper and read only the women's page, by-passing politics, finance, community affairs—the real world.

18 Many women today are college graduates, but after marriage and children, they give up intellectual pursuits. They lose their political acumen and awareness. Too often, the bridge game, clothes and the maid become the main topics of conversation.

19 Compared with her sister overseas, the typical U.S. woman is a poor second, politically. It's silly to ask if women are capable of leading. Look at Golda Meir of Israel.

20 In this country, women are too often placed on an illusory pedestal. What concerned, intelligent woman wants a pedestal when her country is in crisis? To me, that pedestal is used to indicate that women are things to look at and adore but not to converse with, to counsel or deal with.

21 Nowhere in my campaign did I find prejudice stronger than in some male members of the press, who regarded me as nothing more than a stand-in candidate for my husband. Far from being a stand-in for George, I divorced myself from the Administration in that I made my own decisions and discussed the issues as I saw them. But none of this came through to the public.

22 Often, male journalists have had no experience with the type of woman who knows and cares about public affairs, and instead they see women only as people relegated to the tearooms, the style shows and, yes, the kitchens. When they indicate that women have no business in politics because it's dirty, I take exception. It's the real world, and women have every right—and duty—to be in it.

23 The most gratifying experiences in my campaign were the many direct meetings with our young people, and I will repeat now what I told them then: a revolution against the system is not realistic. It isn't the Government but the people who are in it and who run our institutions, who cause the bottlenecks, who block reform, and delay desegregation. Don't abolish the system: let's change ourselves. Don't our kids realize that regardless of the system, they will have to deal with the Wallaces and the Maddoxes in our country? Not until we can deal with human beings and change their attitudes can we even begin to solve some of our pressing problems. I will continue to work for progress, but I realize only too well that without a forum like the Senate, my task will be more difficult.

24 As for sex discrimination, I say to the men: for goodness' sake, turn the searchlight inward. Are *you* solving our problems adequately? Accept talent wherever you find it, especially if it comes from the experience and humanity of mature women.

DISCUSSION SIX/WOMEN'S LIBERATION

1 What is Lenore Romney trying to tell her readers in this persuasion paper?
2 Do you consider her position on the question, "Who has the gilt-edged credentials to set our children straight?" a strong one?
3 How does she feel women would come out in "the rough give-and-take of politics"? Do you agree?
4 Is her argument about women's contribution to the welfare area a valid one?
5 For what does she criticize women?
6 Do you feel women should hold important offices in government? business? education?
7 What are your feelings about the Women's Liberation Movement?
8 Do the children and husband of a career woman suffer?

WHY WE NEED A WOMAN PRESIDENT IN 1976
Gloria Steinem

1 Five or six years ago, I wouldn't have written anything with this title. In fact, I might have ridiculed the idea of a female Chief of State, all the while feeling that special glow of virtue and safety that comes from conforming to society's notion of a Real Woman.

2 But the last few years have changed women even more than the rest of the country. Students, suburban housewives, welfare mothers, black activists and the millions of divorced women who are heads of families—all of them have played a vital part in the movements against racism, poverty, inflation or the war in Vietnam. And all of them have learned two lessons that Conventional

SOURCE NOTE: Gloria Steinem, "Why We Need a Woman President in 1976," *Look*, Jan. 13, 1970, p. 58. Copyright © 1970 by Gloria Steinem. Permission of The Sterling Lord Agency.

Wisdom never taught. First, that women can exercise power constructively and well in "masculine" areas that have nothing to do with the kitchen or the nursery. And second, that this country's existing power structures—including many of the crusading movements themselves—are not about to let them do it.

3 I learned these lessons ("got radicalized," as the student Left would say) by watching and interviewing gifted, industrious women as they were turned away, limited in scope, denied equal pay and promotion or simply ridiculed by the institutions that needed their talents most. There was the New York political leader, for instance, whom even Robert Kennedy couldn't get promoted to the powerful Democratic post she deserved. Or the brilliant premed student who got pressured by family and professors into becoming a nurse. Or the production assistant who trained each new young producer, watching him get the credit and the cash for a television series that she had created. Or the student leader who was beaten by the police, jailed in sit-ins and given a Ph.D. side by side with her male counterparts, only to find that she was expected to make coffee, not policy, at meetings; that the young men were revolutionary on every subject except women.

4 But these women were still trying. They hadn't completely succumbed to the deepest handicap of second-class groups: believing the myths of their own inferiority. (Which is why, I'm afraid, I once scoffed at the notion of a woman President. Even women with hopes for themselves often believe that females as a group are inferior.) The sadder ones were the conventional wives who were guilty, bewildered or bitter at their inability to find total identity in biological functions and housekeeping, as society had told them they should. Or the unmarried girls who weren't taught to feel responsible for their own lives, and so spent their time going from man to man, restricting their development to the demands of the marriage market.

5 What finally comes from looking at both groups, those learning to love their chains and those still struggling, is an overwhelming sense of waste. A dozen Bernadette Devlins could be buried in the ranks of the SDS, or male-chauvinist unions, or the women's-page ghetto in journalism, and the country would never know. Potential Indira Gandhis are stymied by Washington's time-honored policy of keeping all but one or two females (usually powerless; ambassadors to musical-comedy countries, etc.) out of top Government jobs.

6 There are Golda Meirs in both parties, but their function is limited to winning elections for men. (Rep. Shirley Chisholm, the first black woman to be elected to Congress, says she has always found politicians more prejudiced against her as a woman than as a black.) And the number of college degrees buried in suburban role-playing is legendary.

7 Meanwhile, the country, God knows, needs all the human talent that it can get.

8 A woman President couldn't solve all the problems. The amount of law reform and enforcement necessary to give women an even start isn't likely to get done in four years, much less the changing of consciousness involved. But people will go on supposing the current social order reflects some natural order until the visible one changes. Because the particular is less frightening than the abstract, the real woman candidate will be acceptable to males who would protest wildly at the idea if questioned first. Finally, in this country of heroes and personal charisma, one good heroine—one woman who is truly honored in authority—is worth a thousand court cases, arguments and books. She could free the talent and human aspirations of half the population.

9 And that would help to free the other half. Fewer boring women, childlike wives; no more unearned alimony (think of the votes for that issue); no more responsibility for the identity of a semi-adult human being; fewer lady parasites attached to rich and gifted men; shared responsibility for work and children and running the country. All those rewards await a man's realization that the authoritarian family system—which Engels said was the model for capitalism, and would change only as capitalism changed—has evolved into an egalitarian partnership.

10 Men and women progress together, or not at all.

11 There have been arguments that a woman President would be not only equal, but better; that her mother role makes her closer to the earth, more peaceful, more moral. It seems to me that's a romantic hangover from the days when church and state glorified motherhood beyond all reality as a way of getting the population increased. Women leaders in other countries have often proved it wrong. The truth probably is that women are not more moral, they are only uncorrupted by power.

12 But the female experience of second-classness *has* produced a special sympathy and understanding for others in the same boat. Historically, women have always been in the forefront of movements for humanitarian reform, including the abolitionist movement 70 years before they themselves endured prison and ridicule to get the vote. They've proved their sympathies again in the '60's. (White and black women have common causes that survive racism, and are important bridges across the gulf created by white and black men.) By 1976, what we are likely to need most is a President who can understand the dispossessed enough to keep the country together.

13 Of course, six years aren't enough to change our 19th-century sexual role-playing. And, that being the case, a woman who is not more moral than a man might still be safer. We've suffered through enough Presidents whose masculinity got attached to the military, brinkmanship, face-saving in Vietnam and the imposition of will at home. Wouldn't we be safer with a woman with nothing to prove?

14 In fact, the male-female role-playing problem is probably the greatest threat to peace. Anthropologists have found that the few societies without war are those in which sex roles are clear but not polarized. Women needn't be submissive semi-adults to be women, and men don't have to go to war or dominate their surroundings to be men. Members of society are born male or female, and don't feel much of life must be spent in proving it. A lot of the under-30 generation is already secure enough to prefer this cooperative, un-polarized life-style. And by 1976, that's where 40 percent of the votes are going to be.

15 Of course, there's a long way to go, and six years is optimistic. Women trying to step out of their 19th-century roles will be punished with ridicule, just as Negroes who refused to act like Negroes were greeted with violence and fear.

16 Indeed, if the current pattern continues, the first woman President and the first black one may be the same: blackness has saved recent women candidates from ridicule, and their femaleness has reduced the fear. A black *woman* in the White House; now, that might be more politically likely.

17 If all this seems mind-bending and impossible, think back to the beginning of the '60's. What seemed impossible to us then? Men on the moon? Assassinations? Tanks in our streets? Demonstrations the size of cities?

18 Surely, a woman in the White House is not an impossible feminist cause. It's only a small step in the humanist revolution.

STRUCTURE REVIEW TWENTY-ONE/PERSUASION

Name _____   Class _____

Answer each question in the space provided below it.

1 What does Gloria Steinem remind the reader of in the first paragraph?

2 What are the first two issues that Gloria Steinem presents?

3 Does she offer sufficient evidence to make valid those issues?

4 What issue results from her dividing women into two groups?

5 Gloria Steinem takes a long time before getting to issues related to a woman President. Why was a presentation of these earlier issues necessary for her persuasion?

6 What is the main point discussed in paragraph 8?

7 On what do the rewards discussed in paragraph 9 depend?

8 Why does she refute the arguments in paragraph 11?

9 What issue does Gloria Steinem present in paragraph 12?

10 With what kind of a statement does she close paragraph 13?

11 What is the main point she makes in paragraph 14? What important additional point does she present in this paragraph?

12 What is your opinion of this persuasion paper?

ASSIGNMENT/WRITING PERSUASION [Suggested Topics]

1 Write a persuasion paper on some campus controversy that you feel deeply enough about to take sides and convince your readers to accept or seriously consider your point of view.
2 Write a persuasion paper on a subject of your choice.
3 Write a persuasion paper on any one of the following broad topics. Limit them and research them if necessary to develop them in the time and space requirements of the assignment.

The High Cost of Dying

The High Cost of Hospitalization

Commercialism in Sports

The Olympic Games—1972

The Olympic Games—1976

The Selecting of a Vice President

The Grading System in Schools and Colleges

Our Foreign Policy

Cars and Safety

Campus Politics

Student Government

Religion Today

Higher Education

Modern Music

Pollution

STRUCTURE REVIEW TWENTY

1 The function of the first five paragraphs (paragraph unit 1) is introductory, that is, to gain reader interest and move smoothly into the main discussion. In paragraph 5, he provides the transition: "Mercy, say school board members and superintendents who participate in similar types of bone-crushing, yard-losing plays called controversies."

2 This paragraph unit stresses the emotional tone of the controversy and the unreasonable attitude of the opposition. Yet, he maintains that "such a review, nevertheless, looms necessary for many school boards." He presents an issue: "any dollar-fat program needs continued scrutiny."

3 He concedes that "carefully devised and carefully administered high school athletic programs" are worthwhile. He admits that "it would be a mistake to disband them." But, he is quick to present a counterproposal in the next paragraph by posing the question, "How much emphasis in terms of time and money and energy should be spent on a district's interscholastic sports programs?"

4 The question the writer asks in paragraph 13 is probably the thesis. Yet, in his conclusion he emphasizes that athletics is taking the fun out of sport. In paragraph 23, he mentions that his objective is for school boards to evaluate the athletic program and nudge it back into line with the education goals of the district. In paragraph 22 he states that a school board review of athletics should include an analysis of the philosophy of the athletic program. These statements, however, seem to me to be part of the recommended action.

5 In paragraph 14, he states that "it is not impossible for a school district's athletic program to grow out of proportion. . . ." He supports this first issue with an example from Philadelphia. "Community interest saved the teams but not the necessity to make cuts *somewhere* in the school budget." Paragraphs 14 through 16.

6 "Competitive athletics do more harm than good to participants." Paragraphs 17 through 22 constitute the paragraph unit. "Plainly, then, a school board review of athletics should include an analysis of the philosophy of the athletic program—and how that philosophy. . . ."

7 He makes a concession and then recommends action.

8 Four.

9 In my opinion, his conclusion is weak. He really presents another issue—the fun is taken out of athletics.

10 Individual answer by student.

Contentemporary Literature

POETRY

SHORT STORIES

POETRY

SONGS OF DAWN BOY

1

Where my kindred dwell,
> *There I wander.*

The Red Rock House,
> *There I wander.*

Where dark kethawns are at the doorway,
> *There I wander.*

With the pollen of dawn upon my trail,
> *There I wander.*

At the yuni, the striped cotton hangs with pollen.
> *There I wander.*

SOURCE NOTE: "Songs of Dawn Boy," in George W. Cronyn (ed.), *American Indian Poetry*. Permission of Liveright Publishing Corp. Copyright © 1934 by Liveright Publishing Corp.

Going around with it.
> *There I wander.*

Taking another, I depart with it.
> *With it I wander.*

In the house of long life,
> *There I wander.*

In the house of happiness,
> *There I wander.*

Beauty before me,
> *With it I wander.*

Beauty behind me,
> *With it I wander.*

Beauty below me,
> *With it I wander.*

Beauty above me,
> *With it I wander.*

Beauty all around me,
> *With it I wander.*

In old age traveling,
> *With it I wander.*

On the beautiful trail I am,
> *With it I wander.*

2

In Kininaéki.
In the house made of dawn.
In the story made of dawn.
On the trail of dawn.
O, Talking God!
His feet, my feet, restore.
His limbs, my limbs, restore.
His body, my body, restore.
His mind, my mind, restore.
His voice, my voice, restore.
His plumes, my plumes, restore.
With beauty before him, with beauty before me.
With beauty behind him, with beauty behind me.
With beauty above him, with beauty above me.
With beauty below him, with beauty below me.
With beauty around him, with beauty around me.
With pollen beautiful in his voice, with pollen beautiful in my voice.
It is finished in beauty.
It is finished in beauty.

In the house of evening light.
From the story made of evening light.
On the trail of evening light.
O, House God![1]
3
To the house of my kindred,
                    There I return.
Child of the yellow corn am I.

DISCUSSION

Write the thoughts expressed in this poem in prose. In your opinion, what is poetry?

POETRY
Marianne Moore

I, too, dislike it: there are things that are important beyond all this
        fiddle.
    Reading it, however, with a perfect contempt for it, one discovers
            in
        it after all, a place for the genuine.
            Hands that can grasp, eyes
            that can dilate, hair that can rise
                if it must, these things are important not because a
    high-sounding interpretation can be put upon them but because they
                are
        useful. When they become so derivative as to become unintellig-
            ible,
        the same thing may be said for all of us, that we
            do not admire what
            we cannot understand: the bat
                holding on upside down or in quest of something to
    eat, elephants pushing, a wild horse taking a roll, a tireless wolf
                under
        a tree, the immovable critic twitching his skin like a horse that feels
            a flea, the base-

SOURCE NOTE: Marianne Moore, "Poetry," *Collected Poems.* Copyright © 1935 by Marianne Moore; renewed 1963 by Marianne Moore and T. S. Eliot. Permission of The Macmillan Company.

[1] The rest as in 1, except that lines 12 and 13 are transposed.

ball fan, the statistician—
    nor is it valid
        to discriminate against "business documents and
school-books"; all these phenomena are important. One must make
        a distinction
    however: when dragged into prominence by half poets, the result
        is not poetry,
    nor till the poets among us can be
        "literalists of
        the imagination"—above
        insolence and triviality and can present
for inspection, "imaginary gardens with real toads in them," shall we
        have
    it. In the meantime, if you demand on the one hand,
    the raw material of poetry in
        all its rawness and
        that which is on the other hand
        genuine, you are interested in poetry.

DISCUSSION

1 What is important about poetry?
2 In what ways can poetry be useful?
3 Why does Marianne Moore consider some poetry bad?
4 What must a poet become to succeed?
5 What do you think Marianne Moore means by "imaginary gardens with real toads in them"?
6 Define the terms "rawness" and "genuine" as you think Marianne Moore uses them.

THE LOVE SONG OF J. ALFRED PRUFROCK
T.S. Eliot

S'io credesse che mia risposta fosse
A persona che mai tornasse al mondo,
Questa fiamma staria senza piu scosse.
Ma perciocche giammai di questo fondo
Non torno vivo alcun, s'i'odo il vero,
Senza tema d'infamia ti rispondo.[1]

Let us go then, you and I,
When the evening is spread out against the sky

SOURCE NOTE: T. S. Eliot, "The Love Song of J. Alfred Prufrock, *Collected Poems 1909–1962*. Copyright © 1963 by Harcourt, Brace & World, Inc. Copyright © 1964 by T. S. Eliot. Permission of the Publisher.

[1] The epigraph (from Dante's *Inferno*, XXVII, 61–66) is the first six lines of Guido da Montefeltro's answer to Dante's question about his identity: "If I thought that my answer were given to anyone who would ever return to the world, this flame would stand still; but because no one ever returned from this pit, if what I hear is true, I will answer you without fear of infamy."

Like a patient etherised upon a table;
Let us go, through certain half-deserted streets,
The muttering retreats
Of restless nights in one-night cheap hotels
And sawdust restaurants with oyster-shells:
Streets that follow like a tedious argument
Of insidious intent
To lead you to an overwhelming question . . .
Oh, do not ask, "What is it?"
Let us go and make our visit.

In the room the women come and go
Talking of Michelangelo.

The yellow fog that rubs its back upon the window-panes,
The yellow smoke that rubs its muzzle on the window-panes
Licked its tongue into the corners of the evening,
Lingered upon the pools that stand in drains,
Let fall upon its back the soot that falls from chimneys,
Slipped by the terrace, made a sudden leap,
And seeing that it was a soft October night,
Curled once about the house, and fell asleep.

And indeed there will be time
For the yellow smoke that slides along the street,
Rubbing its back upon the window-panes;
There will be time, there will be time
To prepare a face to meet the faces that you meet;
There will be time to murder and create,
And time for all the works and days of hands
That lift and drop a question on your plate;
Time for you and time for me,
And time yet for a hundred indecisions,
And for a hundred visions and revisions,
Before the taking of a toast and tea.

In the room the women come and go
Talking of Michelangelo.

And indeed there will be time
To wonder, "Do I dare?" and, "Do I dare?"
Time to turn back and descend the stair,
With a bald spot in the middle of my hair—
[They will say: "How his hair is growing thin!"]

My morning coat, my collar mounting firmly to the chin,
My necktie rich and modest, but asserted by a simple pin—
[They will say: "But how his arms and legs are thin!"]
Do I dare
Disturb the universe?
In a minute there is time
For decisions and revisions which a minute will reverse.

For I have known them all already, known them all:—
Have known the evenings, mornings, afternoons,
I have measured out my life with coffee spoons;
I know the voices dying with a dying fall
Beneath the music from a farther room.
    So how should I presume?

And I have known the eyes already, known them all—
The eyes that fix you in a formulated phrase,
And when I am formulated, sprawling on a pin,
When I am pinned and wriggling on the wall,
Then how should I begin
To spit out all the butt ends of my days and ways?
    And how should I presume?

And I have known the arms already, known them all—
Arms that are braceleted and white and bare
[But in the lamplight, downed with light brown hair!]
Is it perfume from a dress
That makes me so digress?
Arms that lie along a table, or wrap about a shawl.
    And should I then presume?
    And how should I begin?

Shall I say, I have gone at dusk through narrow streets
And watched the smoke that rises from the pipes
Of lonely men in shirt-sleeves, leaning out of windows? . . .

I should have been a pair of ragged claws
Scuttling across the floors of silent seas.

And the afternoon, the evening, sleeps so peacefully!
Smoothed by long fingers,
Asleep . . . tired . . . or it malingers,
Stretched on the floor, here beside you and me.

Should I, after tea and cakes and ices,
Have the strength to force the moment to its crisis?
But though I have wept and fasted, wept and prayed,
Though I have seen my head [grown slightly bald] brought in upon a
    platter,
I am no prophet—and here's no great matter;
I have seen the moment of my greatness flicker,
And I have seen the eternal Footman hold my coat, and snicker,
And in short, I was afraid.

And would it have been worth it, after all,
After the cups, the marmalade, the tea,
Among the porcelain, among some talk of you and me,
Would it have been worth while,
To have bitten off the matter with a smile,
To have squeezed the universe into a ball
To roll it toward some overwhelming question,
To say: "I am Lazarus, come from the dead,
Come back to tell you all, I shall tell you all"—
If one, settling a pillow by her head,
    Should say: "That is not what I meant at all.
    That is not it, at all."

And would it have been worth it, after all,
Would it have been worth while,
After the sunsets and the dooryards and the sprinkled streets,
After the novels, after the teacups, after the skirts that trail along the
    floor—
And this, and so much more?—
It is impossible to say just what I mean!
But as if a magic lantern threw the nerves in patterns on a screen:
Would it have been worth while
If one, settling a pillow or throwing off a shawl,
And turning toward the window, should say:
    "That is not it at all,
    That is not what I meant, at all."

No! I am not Prince Hamlet, nor was meant to be;
Am an attendant lord, one that will do
To swell a progress, start a scene or two,
Advise the prince; no doubt, an easy tool,
Deferential, glad to be of use,
Politic, cautious, and meticulous;

Full of high sentence, but a bit obtuse;
At times, indeed, almost ridiculous—
Almost, at times, the Fool.

I grow old . . . I grow old . . .
I shall wear the bottoms of my trousers rolled.

Shall I part my hair behind? Do I dare to eat a peach?
I shall wear white flannel trousers, and walk upon the beach.
I have heard the mermaids singing, each to each.

I do not think that they will sing to me.

I have seen them riding seaward on the waves
Combing the white hair of the waves blown back
When the wind blows the water white and black.

We have lingered in the chambers of the sea
By sea-girls wreathed with seaweed red and brown
Till human voices wake us, and we drown.

DISCUSSION

1 Who is the speaker?

2 What kind of person is he?

3 Explain how *imagery*—"the representation through language of sense experience"—enriches Eliot's appeal to the reader's emotions.

4 How do Eliot's images of the outer world, such as the circuitous streets, the yellow fog, the light brown hair, and the perfume from the dress reveal the turmoil within Prufrock?

5 An *allusion* is a reference to something in history or previous literature. Explain the meaning to the poem of the following allusions:

    a The excerpt from Dante's *Inferno*

    b The reference to John the Baptist

    c The reference to Lazarus

    d The reference to Hamlet

6 A simile is a stated comparison indicated by a word or word group such as "like," "as," "similar to," "seems," etc.; a metaphor is a comparison that is implied. Discuss the effectiveness in the poem of two similes and two metaphors.

7 Does J. Alfred Prufrock ever ask the "overwhelming question"?

8 What line best sums up Prufrock's life?
9 Why does Prufrock believe the mermaids will not sing for him?
10 What is the meaning of the poem?

WHEN YOU HAVE FORGOTTEN SUNDAY: THE LOVE STORY
Gwendolyn Brooks

That the war would be over before they got to you;
—And when you have forgotten the bright bedclothes on a
    Wednesday and a Saturday,
And most especially when you have forgotten Sunday—
When you have forgotten Sunday halves in bed,
Or me sitting on the front-room radiator in the limping afternoon
Looking off down the long street
To nowhere,
Hugged by my plain old wrapper of no-expectation
And nothing-I-have-to-do and I'm-happy-why?
And if-Monday-never-had-to-come—
When you have forgotten that, I say,
And how you swore, if somebody beeped the bell,
And how my heart played hopscotch if the telephone rang;
And how we finally went in to Sunday dinner,
That is to say, went across the front-room floor to the ink-spotted
    table in the southwest corner
To Sunday dinner, which was always chicken and noodles
Or chicken and rice
And salad and rye bread and tea
And chocolate chip cookies—
I say, when you have forgotten that,
When you have forgotten my little presentiment

And how we finally undressed and whipped out the light and
    flowed into bed,
And lay loose-limbed for a moment in the week-end
Bright bedclothes,
Then gently folded into each other—
When you have, I say, forgotten all that,
Then you may tell,
Then I may believe
You have forgotten me well.

SOURCE NOTE: Gwendolyn Brooks, "When You Have Forgotten Sunday: The Love Story," *A Street in Bronzeville.* Copyright © 1944 by Gwendolyn Brooks Blakely. Permission of Harper & Row, Publishers, Inc.

DISCUSSION

1   Who is the speaker?
2   To whom is she speaking?
3   What kind of details does the poet use to show how important their love was?

FOR HETTIE
LeRoi Jones

My wife is left-handed.
which implies a fierce determination. A complete other
worldliness. ITS WEIRD, BABY.
The way some folks
are always trying to be
different. A sin & a shame.

But then, she's been a bohemian
all of her life . . . black stockings
refusing to take orders. I sit
patiently, trying to tell her
whats right. TAKE THAT DAMN
PENCIL OUTTA THAT HAND, YOU'RE
RITING BACKWARDS. & such. But
to no avail. & it shows
in her work. Left-handed coffee,
Left-handed eggs; when she comes
in at night . . . it's her left hand
offered for me to kiss. Damm.
& now her belly droops over the seat.
They say it's a child. But
I ain't quite so sure.

DISCUSSION

1   Poets use *hyperbole* (conscious exaggeration or overstatement) to heighten effect or to produce comic effect. How does the poet use hyperbole in this poem?
2   Who is the speaker?
3   What is the husband's attitude toward his wife?

SOURCE NOTE: LeRoi Jones, "for hettie," *Preface to a Twenty Volume Suicide Note.* Copyright © 1961 by LeRoi Jones. Permission of Corinth Books.

since feeling is first
e. e. cummings

since feeling is first
who pays any attention
to the syntax of things
will never wholly kiss you;

wholly to be a fool
while Spring is in the world

my blood approves,
and kisses are a better fate
than wisdom
lady i swear by all flowers. Don't cry
—the best gesture of my brain is less than
your eyelids' flutter which says

we are for each other: then
laugh, leaning back in my arms
for life's not a paragraph

And death i think is no parenthesis

DISCUSSION

1 What does the poet mean by the expression "the syntax of things"?
2 How do the metaphors "life's not a paragraph" and "death i think is no parenthesis" contribute to the poet's meaning?
3 To whom is the poet speaking?

AZTEC ANGEL
Luis Omar Salinas

I

I am an Aztec angel
      criminal
          of a scholarly
              society

SOURCE NOTE: e. e. cummings, "since feeling is first," Copyright © 1926 by Horace Liveright; renewed 1954 by e. e. cummings. Reprinted from e. e. cummings, *Poems 1923–1954*. Permission of Harcourt, Brace & World, Inc.
SOURCE NOTE: luis omar salinas, "Aztec Angel," *Crazy Gypsy*, Origenes Publication, Universidad de Aztlan, Box 3173, Fresno, Calif. 93766, 1970, pp. 50–51. Permission of the author.

I do favors
   for whimsical
     magicians
where I pawn

   my heart
     for truth
   and find
     my way
through obscure
   streets
   of soft spoken
     hara-kiris

II

I am an Aztec angel
   forlorn passenger
     on a train
   of chicken farmers
     and happy children

III

I am the Aztec angel
   fraternal partner
     of an orthodox
       society
where pachuco children
     hurl stones
   through poetry rooms
and end up in a cop car
   their bones itching
     and their hearts
busted from malnutrition

IV

I am the Aztec angel
   who frequents bars
spends evenings
   with literary circles

and socializes
    with spiks
niggers and wops
    and collapses on his way
        to funerals

V

Drunk
    lonely
    bespectacled
the sky
        opens my veins
        like rain
        clouds go berserk
            around me
        my Mexican ancestors
            chew my fingernails
I am an Aztec angel
    offspring
of a woman
    who was beautiful

DISCUSSION

1   Who is "the Aztec Angel"?
2   What is the tone of this poem?

I, TOO, SING AMERICA
Langston Hughes

I, too, sing America.

I am the darker brother.
They send me to eat in the kitchen
When company comes,
But I laugh,

SOURCE NOTE: Langston Hughes, "I, TOO, SING AMERICA." Copyright © 1926 by Alfred A. Knopf, Inc. and renewed 1954 by Langston Hughes. Reprinted from *Selected Poems* by Langston Hughes. Permission of the publisher.

And eat well,
And grow strong.

Tomorrow,
I'll sit at the table
When company comes.
Nobody'll dare
Say to me,
"Eat in the kitchen,"
Then.

Besides,
They'll see how beautiful I am
And be ashamed—

I, too, am America.

DISCUSSION

1 Who sings of America in this poem?
2 Who is "they" in line 3?
3 Why will "they" be ashamed?
4 What is the writer's purpose?

STOPPING BY WOODS ON A SNOWY EVENING
Robert Frost

Whose woods these are I think I know.
His house is in the village, though;
He will not see me stopping here
To watch his woods fill up with snow.

My little horse must think it queer
To stop without a farmhouse near
Between the woods and frozen lake
The darkest evening of the year.

SOURCE NOTE: Robert Frost, "Stopping by Woods on a Snowy Evening," *Complete Poems of Robert Frost.* Copyright © 1916, 1921, 1923, 1930, 1934, 1939 by Holt, Rinehart and Winston, Inc. Copyright © 1944, 1951, 1958, 1962 by Robert Frost; renewed by Lesley Frost Ballantine.

He gives his harness bells a shake
To ask if there is some mistake.
The only other sound's the sweep
Of easy wind and downy flake.

The woods are lovely, dark, and deep,

But I have promises to keep,
And miles to go before I sleep,
And miles to go before I sleep.

DISCUSSION

1 At a literal level, what takes place in this poem?
2 Who is the speaker?
3 What is a symbol?
4 What might the owner of the woods stand for?
5 What is the horse a symbol of?
6 Could one read meaning into the "woods . . . lovely, dark and deep"?
7 Does the poet tell us what kind of journey the man is on?
8 Why doesn't he remain and enjoy further or forever the woods?

THE MAN HE KILLED
Thomas Hardy

  "Had he and I but met
    By some old ancient inn,
We should have sat us down to wet
    Right many a nipperkin!

  "But ranged as infantry,
    And staring face to face,
I shot at him as he at me,
    And killed him in his place.

  "I shot him dead because—
    Because he was my foe,
Just so—my foe of course he was;
    That's clear enough; although

SOURCE NOTE: Thomas Hardy, "The Man He Killed," *Collected Poems*. Copyright © 1925 by The Macmillan Company.

"He thought he'd 'list, perhaps,
  Off-hand like—just as I—
Was out of work—had sold his traps—
  No other reason why.

"Yes; quaint and curious war is!
  You shoot a fellow down
You'd treat if met where any bar is,
  Or help to half-a-crown."

DISCUSSION

1 Who is the speaker?
2 How much do we know about him?
3 What reason does the speaker give for shooting the man?
4 What word tells you that he is not sure of his reason for killing in war?
5 What do you consider the writer's purpose?

EIGHTH AIR FORCE
Randall Jarrell

If, in an odd angle of the hutment,
A puppy laps the water from a can
Of flowers, and the drunk sergeant shaving
Whistles *O Paradiso!*—shall I say that man
Is not as men have said: a wolf to man?

The other murderers troop in yawning;
Three of them play Pitch, one sleeps, and one
Lies counting missions, lies there sweating
Til even his heart beats: One; One; One.
O murderers! . . . Still, this is how it's
  done:

This is war. . . .But since these play, before
  they die,
Like puppies with their puppy; since, a man,
I did as these have done, but did not die—
I will content the people as I can
And give up these to them: Behold the
  man!

SOURCE NOTE: Randall Jarrell, "Eighth Air Force," *The Complete Poems of Randall Jarrell.* Permission of Farrar, Straus & Giroux, Inc.

I have suffered, in a dream, because of him,
Many things; for this last saviour, man,
I have lied as I lie now. But what is lying?
Men wash their hands, in blood, as best they
    can:
I find no fault in this just man.

DISCUSSION

1 Who is the speaker?

2 If we consider him a dramatic character, where does the scene take place?

3 Who are the murderers?

4 Benjamin Franklin stated: "O that . . . men would cease to be as wolves to one another." If the hutment is a wolf den, does the writer think of the men as wolves, murderers?

5 As one of the murderers, what is the dilemma the writer is in?

6 Is man a wolf (murderer) or a savior of man? How does the poet use the Pontius Pilate metaphor in answering this question?

7 Pilate's wife said: "I have suffered, in a dream, because of him." How does this statement emphasize the speaker's dilemma?

8 If you read the last few lines as irony, what will be the meaning of the poem?

9 What do you think is the meaning of the line: "Men wash their hands, in blood, as best they can"?

10 What do you think is the meaning of the poem?

PORTRAIT
Kenneth Fearing

The clear brown eyes, kindly and alert, with 12–20 vision, give
    confident regard to the passing world through R. K. Lam-
    pert & Company lenses framed in gold;
His soul, however, is all his own;
Arndt Brothers necktie and hat (with feather) supply a touch
    of youth.

With his soul his own, he drives, drives, chats and drives,
The first and second bicuspids, lower right, replaced by bridge-
    work, while two incisors have porcelain crowns;

(Render unto Federal, state and city Caesar, but not unto time;

SOURCE NOTE: Kenneth Fearing, "Portrait." Permission of Ira Koenig, Executor of the estate of Kenneth Fearing; originally published in *The New Yorker*.

Render nothing unto time until Amalgamated Death serves final
   notice, in proper form;

The vault is ready;
The will has been drawn by Clagget, Clagget, Clagget & Brown;
The policies are adequate, Confidential's best, reimbursing for
   disability, partial or complete, with double indemnity
   should the end be a pure and simple accident)

Nothing unto time,
Nothing unto change, nothing unto fate,
Nothing unto you, and nothing unto me, or to any other known
   or unknown party or parties, living or deceased;

But Mercury shoes, with special arch supports, take much of the
   wear and tear;
On the course, a custombuilt driver corrects a tendency to slice;
Love's ravages have been repaired (it was a textbook case) by
   Drs. Schultz, Lightner, Mannheim, and Goode,
While all of it is enclosed in excellent tweed, with Mr. Baumer's
   personal attention to the shoulders and the waist;
And all of it now roving, chatting amiably through space in a
   Plymouth 6,
With his soul (his own) at peace, soothed by Walter Lippmann,
   and sustained by Haig & Haig.

DISCUSSION

1 Who is the speaker?
2 To whom is he speaking?
3 What is irony?
4 What word group, in particular, gives an ironic twist to the speaker's
words?
5 What is the poet's purpose?

ex-basketball player
John Updike

Pearl Avenue runs past the high-school lot,
Bends with the trolley tracks, and stops, cut off

SOURCE NOTE: John Updike, "ex-basketball player," *The Carpentered Hen and Other Tame Creatures.* Copyright © 1957 by John Updike. Originally appeared in *The New Yorker.* By permission of Harper & Row, Publishers, Inc.

Before it has a chance to go two blocks,
At Colonel McComsky Plaza. Berth's Garage
Is on the corner facing west, and there,
Most days, you'll find Flick Webb, who helps Berth out.

Flick stands tall among the idiot pumps—
Five on a side, the old bubble-head style,
Their rubber elbows hanging loose and low.
One's nostrils are two S's, and his eyes
An E and O. And one is squat, without
A head at all—more of a football type.

Once Flick played for the high-school team, the Wizards.
He was good: in fact, the best. In '46
He bucketed three hundred ninety points,
A county record still. The ball loved Flick.
I saw him rack up thirty-eight or forty
In one home game. His hand were like wild birds.

He never learned a trade, he just sells gas,
Checks oil, and changes flats. Once in a while,
As a gag, he dribbles an inner tube,
But most of us remember anyway.
His hands are fine and nervous on the lug wrench.
It makes no difference to the lug wrench, though.

Off work, he hangs around Mae's Luncheonette.
Grease-grey and kind of coiled, he plays pinball,
Sips lemon cokes, and smokes those thin cigars;
Flick seldom speaks to Mae, just sits and nods
Beyond her face towards bright applauding tiers
Of Necco Wafers, Nibs, and Juju Beads.

DISCUSSION

1 How does the poet's description of Pearl Avenue set the tone of the poem?
2 Pearl Avenue "stops, cut off" after two blocks. What significance does this have to the entire poem?
3 Flick "sits and nods . . . towards bright applauding tiers." What does this tell us about Flick and his future?

RICHARD CORY
Edwin Arlington Robinson

Whenever Richard Cory went down town,
  We people on the pavement looked at him:
He was a gentleman from sole to crown,
  Clean favored, and imperially slim.

And he was always quietly arrayed,
  And he was always human when he talked;
But still he fluttered pulses when he said,
  "Good-morning," and he glittered when he walked.

And he was rich—yes, richer than a king,
  And admirably schooled in every grace:
In fine, we thought that he was everything
  To make us wish that we were in his place.

So on we worked, and waited for the light,
  And went without the meat, and cursed the bread;
And Richard Cory, one calm summer night,
  Went home and put a bullet through his head.

DISCUSSION

1 What kind of a "gentleman" is Richard Cory?
2 What do you think is the meaning of the line: "In fine, we thought that he was everything"?
3 What is the purpose of the surprise ending?
4 The poet achieves his purpose by an ironic contrast; what is this contrast?

WOMEN
May Swenson

Women should be pedestals
moving pedestals
moving to the motions of men

SOURCE NOTE: Edwin Arlington Robinson, "Richard Cory," *The Children of the Night.* Permission of Charles Scribner's Sons.

SOURCE NOTE: May Swenson, "Women," from *Iconographs.* Copyright © 1969 by May Swenson. Permission of Charles Scribner's Sons. "Women" first appeared in *New American Review* No. 3.

Or they should be little horses
those wooden sweet oldfashioned painted rocking horses
the gladdest things in the toyroom
The pegs of their ears so familiar and dear
to the trusting fists
To be chafed feelingly
and then unfeelingly
To be joyfully ridden
until the restored egos dismount and the legs stride away
Immobile sweetlipped sturdy and smiling
women should always be waiting
willing to be set into motion
Women should be pedestals to men

DISCUSSION

1 The word "pedestal" may be defined as follows: "any foundation, base, or support, either material or immaterial"; "to hold in high estimation." With what meaning does the writer use the word in this poem?
2 Do you believe that the poet is serious or does she reveal her true feelings with irony?
3 How does the poet see woman's role in sex?

her kind
Anne Sexton

I have gone out, a possessed witch,
haunting the black air, braver at night;
dreaming evil, I have done my hitch
over the plain houses, light by light:
lonely thing, twelve-fingered, out of mind.
A woman like that is not a woman, quite.
I have been her kind.

I have found the warm caves in the woods,
filled them with skillets, carvings, shelves,
closets, silks, innumerable goods;
fixed the suppers for the worms and the elves:
whining, rearranging the disaligned.

SOURCE NOTE: Anne Sexton, "her kind," *To Bedlam and Part Way Back.* Copyright © 1960 by Anne Sexton. Permission of Houghton Mifflin Company.

A woman like that is misunderstood.
I have been her kind.

I have ridden in your cart, driver,
waved my nude arms at villages going by,
learning the last bright routes, survivor
where your flames still bite my thigh
and my ribs crack where your wheels wind.
A woman like that is not ashamed to die.
I have been her kind.

DISCUSSION

1 What image plays an important role in this poem?
2 Explain the image in stanza 3, not its meaning.
3 What are the three kinds of women portrayed?
4 Which kind of woman do you think the poet favors, if any?

ELEGY FOR JANE
(My student, thrown by a horse)
Theodore Roethke

I remember the neckcurls, limp and damp as tendrils;
And her quick look, a sidelong pickerel smile;
And how, once startled into talk, the light syllables leaped for
    her.
And she balanced in the delight of her thought,
A wren, happy, tail into the wind,
Her song trembling the twigs and small branches.
The shade sang with her;
The leaves, their whispers turned to kissing,
And the mould sang in the bleached valleys under the rose.

Oh, when she was sad, she cast herself down into such a pure
    depth,
Even a father could not find her:
Scraping her cheek against straw,
Stirring the clearest water.

SOURCE NOTE: Theodore Roethke, "Elegy for Jane," *The Collected Poems of Theodore Roethke.* Copyright © 1950 by Theodore Roethke. Permission of Doubleday & Company, Inc.

My sparrow, you are not here,
Waiting like a fern, making a spiney shadow.
The sides of wet stones cannot console me,
Nor the moss, wound with the last light.

If only I could nudge you from this sleep,
My maimed darling, my skittery pigeon.
Over this damp grave I speak the words of my love:
I, with no rights in this matter,
Neither father nor lover.

DISCUSSION

1 What is the speaker's relationship with the girl?
2 What images (word pictures) give the poem its beauty?
3 Define the word "elegy."
4 How does the poet's diction help this poem?

THE BALL POEM
John Berryman

What is the boy now, who has lost his ball,
What what is he to do? I saw it go
Merrily bouncing, down the street, and then
Merrily over—there it is in the water!
No use to say "O there are other balls":
An ultimate shaking grief fixes the boy
As he stands rigid, trembling, staring down
All his young days into the harbour where
His ball went. I would not intrude on him,
A dime, another ball, is worthless. Now
He senses first his responsibility
In a world of possessions. People will take balls,
Balls will be lost always, little boy,
And no one buys a ball back. Money is external.
He is learning, far behind his desperate eyes,
The epistemology of loss, how to stand up.
Knowing what every man must one day know
And most know many days, how to stand up.

SOURCE NOTE: John Berryman, "The Ball Poem," *Short Poems.* Copyright © 1948 by John Berryman. Reprinted with permission of Farrar, Straus & Giroux, Inc.

And gradually light returns to the street,
A whistle blows, the ball is out of sight,
Soon part of me will explore the deep and dark
Floor of the harbour. I am everywhere,
I suffer and move, my mind and my heart move
With all that move me, under the water
Or whistling, I am not a little boy.

DISCUSSION

1 Is the boy an actual character or a character in the mind of the poet?
2 What has the boy learned from the losing of the ball?
3 What is the "deep and dark floor of the harbour" a symbol of?
4 What does the speaker tell the reader about life?

FERN HILL
Dylan Thomas

Now as I was young and easy under the apple boughs
About the lilting house and happy as the grass was green,
       The night above the dingle starry,
          Time let me hail and climb
       Golden in the heydays of his eyes,
And honoured among wagons I was prince of the apple towns
And once below a time I lordly had the trees and leaves
          Trail with daisies and barley
       Down the rivers of the windfall light.

And as I was green and carefree, famous among the barns
About the happy yard and singing as the farm was home,
       In the sun that is young once only,
          Time let me play and be
       Golden in the mercy of his means,
And green and golden I was huntsman and herdsman, the calves
Sang to my horn, the foxes on the hills barked clear and cold,
          And the sabbath rang slowly
       In the pebbles of the holy streams.

SOURCE NOTE: Dylan Thomas, "Fern Hill," *Collected Poems.* Copyright 1953 by Dylan Thomas; © 1957 by New Directions. Reprinted by permission of the publisher New Directions Publishing Corporation, J. M. Dent & Sons, Ltd., London, and the Literary Executors of the Dylan Thomas Estate.

All the sun long it was running, it was lovely, the hayfields
High as the house, the tunes from the chimneys, it was air
   And playing, lovely and watery
     And fire green as grass.
   And nightly under the simple stars
As I rode to sleep the owls were bearing the farm away,
All the moon long I heard, blessed among stables, the nightjars
   Flying with the ricks, and the horses
     Flashing into the dark.

And then to awake, and the farm, like a wanderer white
With the dew, come back, the cock on his shoulder: it was all
   Shining, it was Adam and maiden,
     The sky gathered again
   And the sun grew round that very day.
So it must have been after the birth of the simple light
In the first, spinning place, the spellbound horses walking warm
   Out of the whinnying green stable
     On to the fields of praise.

And honoured among foxes and pheasants by the gay house
Under the new made clouds and happy as the heart was long,
   In the sun born over and over,
     I ran my heedless ways,
   My wishes raced through the house-high hay
And nothing I cared, at my sky blue trades, that time allows
In all his tuneful turning so few and such morning songs
   Before the children green and golden
     Follow him out ot grace,

Nothing I cared, in the lamb white days, that time would take me
Up to the swallow thronged loft by the shadow of my hand,
   In the moon that is always rising,
     Nor that riding to sleep
   I should hear him fly with the high fields
And wake to the farm forever fled from the childless land.
Oh as I was young and easy in the mercy of his means,
     Time held me green and dying
   Though I sang in my chains like the sea.

DISCUSSION

1 Who is the speaker?
2 Give some examples of Thomas's ability to combine words in fresh and surprising ways.

3 What Biblical allusions enrich the poem?
4 Explain how time is very important in the poem.
5 What will happen to the speaker's world with the coming of manhood?
6 What is the fern a symbol of?
7 What is the meaning of the poem?

SHORT STORIES

THE GIRLS IN THEIR SUMMER DRESSES
Irwin Shaw

Fifth Avenue was shining in the sun when they left the Brevoort and started walking toward Washington Square. The sun was warm, even though it was November and everything looked like Sunday morning—the buses, and the well-dressed people walking slowly in couples and the quiet buildings with the windows closed.

Michael held Frances' arm tightly as they walked downtown in the sunlight. They walked lightly, almost smiling, because they had slept late and had a good breakfast and it was Sunday. Michael unbuttoned his coat and let it flap around him in the mild wind. They walked, without saying anything, among the young and pleasant-looking people who somehow seem to make up most of the population of that section of New York City.

"Look out," Frances said, as they crossed Eighth Street. "You'll break your neck."

Michael laughed and Frances laughed with him.

"She's not so pretty, anyway," Frances said. "Anyway, not pretty enough to take a chance breaking your neck looking at her."

Michael laughed again. He laughed louder this time, but not as solidly. "She wasn't a bad-looking girl. She had a nice complexion. Country-girl complexion. How did you know I was looking at her?"

Frances cocked her head to one side and smiled at her husband under the tip-tilted brim of her hat. "Mike, darling . . ." she said.

Michael laughed, just a little laugh this time. "O.K.," he said. "The evidence is in. Excuse me. It was the complexion. It's not the sort of complexion you see much in New York. Excuse me."

Frances patted his arm lightly and pulled him along a little faster toward Washington Square.

"This is a nice morning," she said. "This is a wonderful morning. When I have breakfast with you it makes me feel good all day."

SOURCE NOTE: Irwin Shaw, "The Girls in Their Summer Dresses." Copyright 1939, and renewed 1967 by Irwin Shaw. Reprinted from *Selected Short Stories of Irwin Shaw* by permission of Random House, Inc. First appeared in *The New Yorker.*

"Tonic," Michael said. "Morning pick-up. Rolls and coffee with Mike and you're on the alkali side, guaranteed."

"That's the story. Also, I slept all night, wound around you like a rope."

"Saturday night," he said. "I permit such liberties only when the week's work is done."

"You're getting fat," she said.

"Isn't it the truth? The lean man from Ohio."

"I love it," she said, "an extra five pounds of husband."

"I love it, too," Michael said gravely.

"I have an idea," Frances said.

"My wife has an idea. That pretty girl."

"Let's not see anybody all day," Frances said. "Let's just hang around with each other. You and me. We're always up to our neck in people, drinking their Scotch, or drinking our Scotch, we only see each other in bed . . ."

"The Great Meeting Place," Michael said. "Stay in bed long enough and everybody you ever knew will show up there."

"Wise guy," Frances said. "I'm talking serious."

"O.K., I'm listening serious."

"I want to go out with my husband all day long. I want him to talk only to me and listen only to me."

"What's to stop us?" Michael asked. "What party intends to prevent me from seeing my wife alone on Sunday? What party?"

"The Stevensons. They want us to drop by around one o'clock and they'll drive us into the country."

"The lousy Stevensons," Mike said. "Transparent. They can whistle. They can go driving in the country by themselves. My wife and I have to stay in New York and bore each other tête-à-tête."

"Is it a date?"

"It's a date."

Frances leaned over and kissed him on the tip of the ear.

"Darling," Michael said. "This is Fifth Avenue."

"Let me arrange a program," Frances said. "A planned Sunday in New York for a young couple with money to throw away."

"Go easy."

"First let's go see a football game. A professional football game," Frances said, because she knew Michael loved to watch them. "The Giants are play-ing. And it'll be nice to be outside all day today and get hungry and later we'll go down to Cavanagh's and get a steak as big as a blacksmith's apron, with a bottle of wine, and after that, there's a new French picture at the Filmarte that everybody says . . . Say, are you listening to me?"

"Sure," he said. He took his eyes off the hatless girl with the dark hair, cut dancer-style, like a helmet, who was walking past him with the self-conscious strength and grace dancers have. She was walking without a coat and she looked very solid and strong and her belly was flat, like a boy's, under her skirt, and her hips swung boldly because she was a dancer and also because she knew Michael was looking at her. She smiled a little to herself as she went past and Michael noticed all these things before he looked back at his wife. "Sure," he said, "we're going to watch the Giants and we're going to eat steak and we're going to see a French picture. How do you like that?"

"That's it," Frances said flatly. "That's the program for the day. Or maybe you'd just rather walk up and down Fifth Avenue."

"No," Michael said carefully. "Not at all."

"You always look at other women," Frances said. "At every damn woman in the City of New York."

"Oh, come now," Michael said, pretending to joke. "Only pretty ones. And, after all, how many pretty women *are* there in New York? Seventeen?"

"More. At least you seem to think so. Wherever you go."

"Not the truth. Occasionally, maybe, I look at a woman as she passes. In the street. I admit, perhaps in the street I look at a woman once in a while . . ."

"Everywhere," Frances said. "Every damned place we go. Restaurants, subways, theaters, lectures, concerts."

"Now, darling," Michael said, "I look at everything. God gave me eyes and I look at women and men and subway excavations and moving pictures and the little flowers of the field. I casually inspect the universe."

"You ought to see the look in your eye," Frances said, "as you casually inspect the universe on Fifth Avenue."

"I'm a happily married man." Michael pressed her elbow tenderly, knowing what he was doing. "Example for the whole twentieth century, Mr. and Mrs. Mike Loomis."

"You mean it?"

"Frances, baby . . ."

"Are you *really* happily married?"

"Sure," Michael said, feeling the whole Sunday morning sinking like lead inside him. "Now what the hell is the sense in talking like that?"

"I would like to know." Frances walked faster now, looking straight ahead, her face showing nothing, which was the way she always managed it when she was arguing or feeling bad.

"I'm wonderfully happily married," Michael said patiently. "I am the envy of all men between the ages of fifteen and sixty in the State of New York."

"Stop kidding," Frances said.

"I have a fine home," Michael said. "I got nice books and a phonograph and nice friends. I live in a town I like the way I like and I do the work I like and I live with the woman I like. Whenever something good happens, don't I run to you? When something bad happens, don't I cry on your shoulder?"

"Yes," Frances said. "You look at every woman that passes."

"That's an exaggeration."

"Every woman." Frances took her hand off Michael's arm. "If she's not pretty you turn away fairly quickly. If she's halfway pretty you watch her for about seven steps . . ."

"My lord, Frances!"

"If she's pretty you practically break your neck . . ."

"Hey, let's have a drink," Michael said, stopping.

"We just had breakfast."

"Now, listen, darling," Mike said, choosing his words with care, "it's a nice day and we both feel good and there's no reason why we have to break it up. Let's have a nice Sunday."

"I could have a fine Sunday if you didn't look as though you were dying to run after every skirt on Fifth Avenue."

"Let's have a drink," Michael said.

"I don't want a drink."

"What do you want, a fight?"

"No," Frances said so unhappily that Michael felt terribly sorry for her. "I don't want a fight. I don't know why I started this. All right, let's drop it. Let's have a good time."

They joined hands consciously and walked without talking among the baby carriages and the old Italian men in their Sunday clothes and the young women with Scotties in Washington Square Park.

"I hope it's a good game today," Frances said after a while, her tone a good imitation of the tone she had used at breakfast and at the beginning of their walk. "I like professional football games. They hit each other as though they're made out of concrete. When they tackle each other," she said, trying to make Michael laugh, "they make divots. It's very exciting."

"I want to tell you something," Michael said very seriously. "I have not touched another woman. Not once. In all the five years."

"All right," Frances said.

"You believe that, don't you?"

"All right."

They walked between the crowded benches, under the scrubby city park trees.

"I try not to notice it," Frances said, as though she were talking to herself. "I try to make believe it doesn't mean anything. Some men're like that, I tell myself, they have to see what they're missing."

"Some women're like that, too," Michael said. "In my time I've seen a couple of ladies."

"I haven't even looked at another man," Frances said, walking straight ahead, "since the second time I went out with you."

"There's no law," Michael said.

"I feel rotten inside, in my stomach, when we pass a woman and you look at her and I see that look in your eye and that's the way you looked at me the first time, in Alice Maxwell's house. Standing there in the living room, next to the radio, with a green hat on and all those people."

"I remember the hat," Michael said.

"The same look," Frances said. "And it makes me feel bad. It makes me feel terrible."

"Sssh, please, darling, sssh . . ."

"I think I would like a drink now," Frances said.

They walked over to a bar on Eighth Street, not saying anything, Michael automatically helping her over curbstones, and guiding her past automobiles. He walked, buttoning his coat, looking thoughtfully at his neatly shined heavy brown shoes as they made the steps toward the bar. They sat near a window in the bar and the sun streamed in, and there was a small cheerful fire in the fireplace. A little Japanese waiter came over and put down some pretzels and smiled happily at them.

"What do you order after breakfast?" Michael asked.

"Brandy, I suppose," Frances said.

"Courvoisier," Michael told the waiter. "Two Courvoisier."

The waiter came with the glasses and they sat drinking the brandy, in the sunlight. Michael finished half his and drank a little water.

"I look at women," he said. "Correct. I don't say it's wrong or right, I look at them. If I pass them on the street and I don't look at them, I'm fooling you, I'm fooling myself."

"You look at them as though you want them," Frances said, playing with her brandy glass. "Every one of them."

"In a way," Michael said, speaking softly and not to his wife, "in a way that's true. I don't do anything about it, but it's true."

"I know it. That's why I feel bad."

"Another brandy," Michael called. "Waiter, two more brandies."

"Why do you hurt me?" Frances asked. "What're you doing?"

Michael sighed and closed his eyes and rubbed them gently with his fingertips. "I love the way women look. One of the things I like best about New York is the battalions of women. When I first came to New York from Ohio that was the first thing I noticed, the million wonderful women, all over the city. I walked around with my heart in my throat."

"A kid," Frances said. "That's a kid's feeling."

"Guess again," Michael said. "Guess again. I'm older now, I'm a man getting near middle age, putting on a little fat and I still love to walk along Fifth Avenue at three o'clock on the east side of the street between Fiftieth and Fifty-seventh Streets, they're all out then, making believe they're shopping, in their furs and their crazy hats, everything all concentrated from all over the world into eight blocks, the best furs, the best clothes, the handsomest women, out to spend money and feeling good about it, looking coldly at you, making believe they're not looking at you as you go past."

The Japanese waiter put the two drinks down, smiling with great happiness. "Everything is all right?" he asked.

"Everything is wonderful," Michael said.

"If it's just a couple of fur coats," Frances said, "and forty-five-dollar hats . . ."

"It's not the fur coats. Or the hats. That's just the scenery for that particular kind of woman. Understand," he said, "you don't have to listen to this."

"I want to listen."

"I like the girls in the offices. Neat, with their eyeglasses, smart, chipper, knowing what everything is about, taking care of themselves all the time." He kept his eye on the people going slowly past outside the window. "I like the girls on Forty-fourth Street at lunch time, the actresses, all dressed up on nothing a week, talking to the good-looking boys, wearing themselves out being young and vivacious outside Sardi's waiting for producers to look at them. I like the salesgirls in Macy's, paying attention to you first because you're a man, leaving lady customers waiting, flirting with you over socks and books and phonograph needles. I got all this stuff accumulated in me because I've been thinking about it for ten years and now you've asked for it and here it is."

"Go ahead," Frances said.

"When I think of New York City, I think of all the girls, the Jewish girls, the Italians girls, the Irish, Polack, Chinese, German, Negro, Spanish, Russian girls, all on parade in the city. I don't know whether it's something special with me or whether every man in the city walks around with the same feeling inside him, but I feel as though I'm at a picnic in this city. I like to sit near the women in the theaters, the famous beauties who've taken six hours to get ready and look it. And the young girls at the football games, with the red cheeks, and when the warm weather comes, the girls in their summer dresses . . ." He finished his drink. "That's the story. You asked for it, remember. I can't help but look at them. I can't help but want them."

"You want them," Frances repeated without expression. "You said that."

"Right," Michael said, being cruel now and not caring, because she had made him expose himself. "You brought this subject up for discussion, we will discuss it fully."

Frances finished her drink and swallowed two or three times extra. "You say you love me?"

"I love you, but I also want them. O.K."

"I'm pretty, too," Frances said. "As pretty as any of them."

"You're beautiful," Michael said, meaning it.

"I'm good for you," Frances said, pleading. "I've made a good wife, a good housekeeper, a good friend. I'd do any damn thing for you."

"I know," Michael said. He put his hand out and grasped hers.

"You'd like to be free to . . ." Frances said.

"Sssh."

"Tell the truth." She took her hand away from under his.

Michael flicked the edge of his glass with his finger. "O.K.," he said gently. "Sometimes I feel I would like to be free."

"Well," Frances said defiantly, drumming on the table, "anytime you say . . ."

"Don't be foolish." Michael swung his chair around to her side of the table and patted her thigh.

She began to cry, silently, into her handkerchief, bent over just enough so that nobody else in the bar would notice. "Some day," she said, crying, "you're going to make a move . . ."

Michael didn't say anything. He sat watching the bartender s ,wly peel a lemon.

"Aren't you?" Frances asked harshly. "Come on, tell me. Talk. Aren't you?"

"Maybe," Michael said. He moved his chair back again. "How the hell do I know?"

"You know," Frances persisted. "Don't you know?"

"Yes," Michael said after a while, "I know."

Frances stopped crying then. Two or three snuffles into the handkerchief and she put it away and her face didn't tell anything to anybody. "At least do me one favor," she said.

"Sure."

"Stop talking about how pretty this woman is, or that one. Nice eyes, nice breasts, a pretty figure, good voice," she mimicked his voice. "Keep it to yourself. I'm not interested."

"Excuse me." Michael waved to the waiter. "I'll keep it to myself."

Frances flicked the corner of her eyes. "Another brandy," she told the waiter.

"Two," Michael said.

"Yes, ma'am, yes, sir," said the waiter, backing away.

Frances regarded him coolly across the table. "Do you want me to call the Stevensons?" she asked. "It'll be nice in the country."

"Sure," Michael said. "Call them up."

She got up from the table and walked across the room toward the telephone. Michael watched her walk, thinking, what a pretty girl, what nice legs.

DISCUSSION

1 How is the mood at the beginning of the story related to the day? the couple?

2 What kind of a Sunday does Frances plan for them?

3 What complicates the action?

4 Has this obstacle to their happiness occurred before?

5 In what kind of a setting does the argument take place?
6 Describe some contrasts in the action that reveal the tension?
7 Are Michael's arguments reasonable?
8 What does marriage mean to Frances? to Michael?
9 Do they spend the day as Frances originally planned it? Why not?
10 What is Shaw saying about today's attitude toward marriage?

SIXTEEN
Jessamyn West

The steam from the kettle had condensed on the cold window and was running down the glass in tear-like trickles. Outside in the orchard the man from the smudge company was refilling the pots with oil. The greasy smell from last night's burning was still in the air. Mr. Delahanty gazed out at the bleak darkening orange grove; Mrs. Delahanty watched her husband eat, nibbling up to the edges of the toast, then stacking the crusts about his tea cup in a neat fence-like arrangement.

"We'll have to call Cress," Mr. Delahanty said, finally. "Your father's likely not to last out the night. She's his only grandchild. She ought to be here."

Mrs. Delahanty pressed her hands to the bones above her eyes. "Cress isn't going to like being called away from college," she said.

"We'll have to call her anyway. It's the only thing to do." Mr. Delahanty swirled the last of his tea around in his cup so as not to miss any sugar.

"Father's liable to lapse into unconsciousness any time," Mrs. Delahanty argued. "Cress'll hate coming and Father won't know whether she's here or not. Why not let her stay at Woolman?"

Neither wanted, in the midst of their sorrow for the good man whose life was ending, to enter into any discussion of Cress. What was the matter with Cress? What had happened to her since she went away to college? She, who had been open and loving? And who now lived inside a world so absolutely fitted to her own size and shape that she felt any intrusion, even that of the death of her own grandfather, to be an unmerited invasion of her privacy. Black magic could not have changed her more quickly and unpleasantly and nothing except magic, it seemed, would give them back their lost daughter.

Mr. Delahanty pushed back his cup and saucer. "Her place is here, Gertrude. I'm going to call her long distance now. She's a bright girl and it's not going to hurt her to miss a few days from classes. What's the dormitory number?"

"I know it as well as our number," Mrs. Delahanty said. "But at the minute it's gone. It's a sign of my reluctance, I suppose. Wait a minute and I'll look it up."

Source note: From *Cress Delahanty.* Copyright 1948 by Jessamyn West. Reprinted by permission of Harcourt Brace Jovanovich, Inc.

Mr. Delahanty squeezed out from behind the table. "Don't bother. I can get it."

Mrs. Delahanty watched her husband, his usually square shoulders sagging with weariness, wipe a clear place on the steamy windowpane with his napkin. Some of the green twilight appeared to seep into the warm dingy little kitchen. "I can't ever remember having to smudge before in February. I expect you're right," he added as he went toward the phone. "Cress isn't going to like it."

Cress didn't like it. It was February, the rains had been late and the world was burning with a green fire; a green smoke rolled down the hills and burst shoulder-high in the cover crops that filled the spaces between the trees in the orange orchards. There had been rain earlier in the day and drops still hung from the grass blades, sickle-shaped with their weight. Cress, walking across the campus with Edwin, squatted to look into one of these crystal globes.

"Green from the grass and red from the sun," she told him. "The whole world right there in one raindrop."

"As Blake observed earlier about a grain of sand," said Edwin.

"O.K., show off," Cress told him. "You know it—but I saw it." She took his hand and he pulled her up, swinging her in a semicircle in front of him. "Down there in the grass the world winked at me."

"Don't be precious, Cress," Edwin said.

"I will," Cress said, "just to tease you. I love to tease you, Edwin."

"Why?" Edwin asked.

"Because you love to have me," Cress said confidently, taking his hand. Being older suited Edwin. She remembered when she had liked him in spite of his looks; but now spindly had became spare, and the dark shadow of his beard—Edwin had to shave every day while other boys were still just fuzzy—lay under his pale skin; and the opinions, which had once been so embarrassingly unlike anyone else's, were now celebrated at Woolman as being "Edwinian." Yes, Edwin had changed since that day when she had knocked his tooth out trying to rescue him from the mush pot. And had she changed? Did she also look better to Edwin, almost slender now and the freckles not noticeable except at the height of summer? And with her new-found ability for light talk? They were passing beneath the eucalyptus trees and the silver drops, falling as the wind shook the leaves, stung her face, feeling at once both cool and burning. Meadow larks in the fields which edged the campus sang in the quiet way they have after the rain has stopped.

"Oh, Edwin," Cress said, "no one in the world loves the meadow lark's song the way I do!"

"It's not a competition," Edwin said, "you against the world in an "I-love-meadow-larks' contest. Take it easy, kid. Love 'em as much as in you lieth, and let it go at that."

"No," she said. "I'm determined to overdo it. Listen," she exclaimed, as two birds sang together. "Not grieving, nor amorous, nor lost. Nothing to read into it. Simply music. Like Mozart. Complete. Finished. Oh, it is rain to listening ears." She glanced at Edwin to see how he took this rhetoric. He took it calmly. She let go his hand and capered amidst the fallen eucalyptus leaves.

"The gardener thinks you've got St. Vitus' dance," Edwin said.

Old Boat Swain, the college gardener whose name was really Swain, was leaning on his hoe, watching her hopping and strutting. She didn't give a hoot about him or what he thought.

"He's old," she told Edwin. "He doesn't exist." She felt less akin to him than to a bird or toad.

There were lights already burning in the dorm windows. Cress could see Ardis and Nina still at their tables, finishing their *Ovid* or looking up a final logarithm. But between five and six most of the girls stopped trying to remember which form of the sonnet Milton had used or when the Congress of Vienna had met, and dressed for dinner. They got out of their sweaters and jackets and into their soft bright dresses. She knew just what she was going to wear when she came downstairs at six to meet Edwin—green silk like the merman's wife. They were going to the Poinsettia for dinner, escaping salmon-wiggle night in the college dining room.

"At six," she told him, "I'll fly down the stairs to meet you like a green wave."

"See you in thirty minutes," Edwin said, leaving her at the dorm steps.

The minute she opened the door, she began to hear the dorm sounds and smell the dorm smells—the hiss and rush of the showers, the thud of the iron, a voice singing, "Dear old Woolman we love so well," the slap of bare feet down the hall, the telephone ringing.

And the smells! Elizabeth Arden and Cashmere Bouquet frothing in the showers; talcum powder falling like snow; *Intoxication* and *Love Me* and *Devon Violet;* rubber-soled sneakers, too, and gym T-shirts still wet with sweat after basketball practice, and the smell of the hot iron on damp wool.

But while she was still listening and smelling, Edith shouted from the top of the stairs, "Long distance for you, Cress. Make it snappy."

Cress took the stairs three at a time, picked up the dangling receiver, pressed it to her ear.

"Tenant calling Crescent Delahanty," the operator said. It was her father: "Grandfather is dying, Cress. Catch the 7:30 home. I'll meet you at the depot."

"What the matter—Cressie?" Edith asked.

"I have to catch the 7:30 Pacific Electric. Grandfather's dying."

"Oh, poor Cress," Edith cried and pressed her arm about her.

Cress scarcely heard her. Why were they calling her home to watch Grandpa die, she thought, angrily and rebelliously. An old man, past eighty. He'd never been truly alive for her, never more than a rough, hot hand, a scraggly mustache that repelled her when he kissed her, an old fellow who gathered what he called "likely-looking" stones and kept them washed and polished, to turn over and admire. It was silly and unfair to make so much of his dying.

But before she could say a word, Edith was telling the girls. They were crowding about her. "Don't cry," they said. "We'll pack for you. Be brave, darling Cress. Remember your grandfather has had a long happy life. He wouldn't want you to cry."

"Brave Cress—brave Cress," they said. "Just frozen."

She wasn't frozen. She was determined. She was not going to go. It did not make sense. She went downstairs to meet Edwin as she had planned, in her green silk, ready for dinner at the Poinsettia. The girls had told him.

"Are you wearing that home?" he asked.

"I'm not going home," she said. "It's silly and useless. I can't help Grandfather. It's just a convention. What *good* can I do him, sitting there at home?"

"He might do you some good," Edwin said. "Had you thought about that?"

"Why, Edwin!" Cress said. "Why, Edwin!" She had the girls tamed, eating out of her hand, and here was Edwin who loved her—he said so, anyway—cold and disapproving. Looking at herself through Edwin's eyes, she hesitated.

"Go on," Edwin said. "Get what you need and I'll drive you to the station."

She packed her overnight bag and went with him; there didn't seem—once she'd had Edwin's view of herself—anything else to do. But once on the train her resentment returned. The Pacific Electric was hot and smelled of metal and dusty plush. It clicked past a rickety Mexican settlement, through La Habra and Brea, where the pool hall signs swung in the night wind off the ocean. An old man in a spotted corduroy jacket, and his wife, with her hair straggling through the holes in her broken net, sat in front of her.

Neat, thought Cress, anyone can be neat, if he wants to.

Her father, bareheaded, but in his big sheepskin jacket, met her at the depot. It was after nine, cold and raw.

"This is a sorry time, Cress," he said. He put her suitcase in the back of the car and climbed into the driver's seat without opening the door for her.

Cress got in, wrapped her coat tightly about herself. The sky was clear, the wind had died down.

"I don't see any sense in my having to come home," she said at last. "What good can I do Grandpa? If he's dying, how can I help?"

"I was afraid that was the way you might feel about it. So was your mother."

"Oh, Mother," Cress burst out. "Recently she's always trying to put me . . ."

Her father cut her off. "That'll be about enough, Cress. Your place is at home and you're coming home and keeping your mouth shut, whatever you think. I don't know what's happened to you recently. If college does this to you, you'd better stay home permanently."

There was nothing more said until they turned up the palm-lined driveway that led to the house. "Here we are," Mr. Delahanty told her.

Mrs. Delahanty met them at the door, tired and haggard in her Indian design bathrobe.

"Cress," she said, "Grandfather's conscious now. I told him you were coming and he's anxious to see you. You'd better go in right away—this might be the last time he'd know you."

Cress was standing by the fireplace holding first one foot then the other toward the fire. "Oh, Mother, what am I to say?" she asked. "What can I say? Or does Grandfather just want to see me?"

Her father shook his head as if with pain. "Aren't you sorry your grandfather's dying, Cress? Haven't you any pity in your heart? Don't you understand what death means?"

"He's an old man," Cress said obstinately. "It's what we must expect when we grow old," though she, of course, would never grow old.

"Warm your hands, Cress," her mother said. "Grandfather's throat bothers him and it eases him to have it rubbed. I'll give you the ointment and you can rub it in. You won't need to say anything."

Cress slid out of her coat and went across the hall with her mother to visit her grandfather's room. His thin old body was hardly visible beneath the covers; his head, with its gray skin and sunken eyes, lay upon the pillow as if bodiless. The night light frosted his white hair but made black caverns of his closed eyes.

"Father," Mrs. Delahanty said. "Father." But the old man didn't move. There was nothing except the occasional hoarse rasp of an indrawn breath to show that he was alive.

Mrs. Delahanty pulled the cane-bottomed chair a little closer to the bed. "Sit here," she said to Cress," and rub this into his throat and chest." She opened her father's nightshirt so that an inch or two of bony grizzled chest was bared. "He says that this rubbing relieves him, even if he's asleep or too tired to speak. Rub it in with a slow steady movement." She went out to the living room leaving the door a little ajar.

Cress sat down on the chair and put two squeamish fingers into the jar of gray ointment; but she could see far more sense to this than to any talking or being talked to. If they had brought her home from school because she was needed in helping to care for Grandpa, that she could understand—but not simply to be present at his death. What had death to do with her?

She leaned over him, rubbing, but with eyes shut, dipping her fingers often into the gray grease. The rhythm of the rubbing, the warmth and closeness of the room, after the cold drive, had almost put her to sleep when the old man startled her by lifting a shaking hand to the bunch of yellow violets Edith had pinned to the shoulder of her dress before she left Woolman. She opened her eyes suddenly at his touch, but the old man said nothing, only stroked the violets awkwardly with a trembling forefinger.

Cress unpinned the violets and put them in his hand. "There, Grandpa," she said, "there. They're for you."

The old man's voice was a harsh and faltering whisper and to hear what he said Cress had to lean very close.

"I used to—pick them—on Reservoir Hill. I was always sorry to—plow them up. Still—so sweet. Thanks," he said, "to bring them. To remember. You're like her. Your grandmother," he added after a pause. He closed his eyes, holding the bouquet against his face, letting the wilting blossoms spray across one cheek like a pulled-up sheet of flowering earth. He said one more word, not her name but her grandmother's.

The dikes about Cress's heart broke. "Oh, Grandpa, I love you," she said. He heard her. He knew what she said, his fingers returned the pressure of her hand. "You were always so good to me. You were young and you loved flowers." Then she said what was her great discovery. "And you still do. You still love yellow violets, Grandpa, just like me."

At the sound of her uncontrolled crying, Mr. and Mrs. Delahanty came to the door. "What's the matter, Cress?"

Cress turned, lifted a hand toward them. "Why didn't you tell me?" she demanded. And when they didn't answer, she said, "Edwin knew."

Then she dropped her head on to her grandfather's outstretched hand and said something, evidently to him, which neither her father nor her mother understood.

"It's just the same."

DISCUSSION

1 What exposition does the writer present at the beginning?

2 What do the actions and conversation of the parents tell us about the personality of Cress?

3 What does the incident with the gardener tell us about Cress's character?

4 Explain the following lines: "She wasn't frozen. She was determined."

5 What did Edwin mean by "He might do you some good"?

6 How does Cress view death, especially the death of older people?

7 What does Cress do at the death bed that makes sense to her?

8 What does Cress mean by "Edwin knew"?

9 Why were her parents unable to give Cress the answer?

10 Why is the point of view important in this story?

THE CHASER
John Collier

Alan Austen, as nervous as a kitten, went up certain dark and creaky stairs in the neighborhood of Pell Street, and peered about for a long time on the dim landing before he found the name he wanted written obscurely on one of the doors.

He pushed open this door, as he had been told to do, and found himself in a tiny room, which contained no furniture but a plain kitchen table, a rocking-chair, and an ordinary chair. On one side of the dirty buff-colored walls were a couple of shelves, containing in all perhaps a dozen bottles and jars.

An old man sat in the rocking-chair, reading a newspaper. Alan, without a word, handed him the card he had been given. "Sit down, Mr. Austen," said the old man very politely. "I am glad to make your acquaintance."

"Is it true," asked Alan, "that you have a certain mixture that has—er— quite extraordinary effects?"

"My dear sir," replied the old man, "my stock in trade is not very large—I don't deal in laxatives and teething mixtures—but such as it is, it is varied. I think nothing I sell has effects which could be precisely described as ordinary."

"Well, the fact is—" began Alan.

"Here, for example," interrupted the old man, reaching for a bottle from the shelf. "Here is a liquid as colorless as water, almost tasteless, quite imperceptible in coffee, milk, wine, or any other beverage. It is also quite imperceptible to any known method of autopsy."

"Do you mean it is a poison?" cried Alan, very much horrified.

"Call it a glove-cleaner if you like," said the old man indifferently. "Maybe it will clean gloves. I have never tried. One might call it a life-cleaner. Lives need cleaning sometimes."

"I want nothing of that sort," said Alan.

"Probably it is just as well," said the old man. "Do you know the price of this? For one teaspoonful, which is sufficient, I ask five thousand dollars. Never less. Not a penny less."

"I hope all your mixtures are not as expensive," said Alan apprehensively.

"Oh dear, no," said the old man. "It would be no good charging that sort of price for a love potion, for example. Young people who need a love potion very seldom have five thousand dollars. Otherwise they would not need a love potion."

"I am glad to hear that," said Alan.

SOURCE NOTE: Copyright 1941, 1968 by John Collier. Reprinted by permission of Harold Matson Company, Inc. Originally appeared in *The New Yorker*.

Note: Pell Street is in New York's Chinatown.

"I look at it like this," said the old man. "Please a customer with one article, and he will come back when he needs another. Even if it *is* more costly. He will save up for it, if necessary."

"So," said Alan, "you really do sell love potions?"

"If I did not sell love potions," said the old man, reaching for another bottle, "I should not have mentioned the other matter to you. It is only when one is in a position to oblige that one can afford to be so confidential."

"And these potions," said Alan. "They are not just—just—er—"

"Oh, no," said the old man. "Their effects are permanent, and extend far beyond casual impulse. But they include it. Bountifully, insistently. Everlastingly."

"Dear me!" said Alan, attempting a look of scientific detachment. "How very interesting!"

"But consider the spiritual side," said the old man.

"For indifference," said the old man, "they substitute devotion. For scorn, adoration. Give one tiny measure of this to the young lady—its flavor is imperceptible in orange juice, soup, or cocktails—and however gay and giddy she is, she will change altogether. She will want nothing but solitude, and you."

"I can hardly believe it," said Alan. "She is so fond of parties."

"She will not like them any more," said the old man. "She will be afraid of the pretty girls you may meet."

"She will actually be jealous?" cried Alan in a rapture. "Of me?"

"Yes, she will want to be everything to you."

"She is, already. Only she doesn't care about it."

"She will, when she has taken this. She will care intensely. You will be her sole interest in life."

"Wonderful!" cried Alan.

"She will want to know all you do," said the old man. "All that has happened to you during the day. Every word of it. She will want to know what you are thinking about, why you smile suddenly, why you are looking sad."

"That is love!" cried Alan.

"Yes," said the old man. "How carefully she will look after you! She will never allow you to be tired, to sit in a draught, to neglect your food. If you are an hour late, she will be terrified. She will think you are killed, or that some siren has caught you."

"I can hardly imagine Diana like that!" cried Alan, overwhelmed with joy.

"You will not have to use your imagination," said the old man. "And, by the way, since there are always sirens, if by any chance you *should*, later on, slip a little, you need not worry. She will forgive you, in the end. She will be terribly hurt, of course, but she will forgive you—in the end."

"That will not happen," said Alan fervently.

"Of course not," said the old man. "But, if it did, you need not worry. She would never divorce you. Oh, no! And, of course, she herself will never give you the least, the very least, grounds for—uneasiness."

"And how much," said Alan, "is this wonderful mixture?"

"It is not as dear," said the old man, "as the glove-cleaner, or life-cleaner, as I sometimes call it. No. That is five thousand dollars, never a penny less. One has to be older than you are, to indulge in that sort of thing. One has to save up for it."

"But the love potion?" said Alan.

"Oh, that," said the old man, opening the drawer in the kitchen table, and taking out a tiny, rather dirty-looking phial. "That is just a dollar."

"I can't tell you how grateful I am," said Alan, watching him fill it.

"I like to oblige," said the old man. "Then customers come back, later in life, when they are rather better off, and want more expensive things. Here you are. You will find it very effective."

"Thank you again," said Alan. "Good-by."

"*Au revoir*," said the old man.

DISCUSSION

1   What kind of atmosphere or mood does the writer create in the opening sentence?

2   How does the description of the room add to the mood?

3   Who is the protagonist? Why is he so nervous?

4   How does the writer build suspense in the early part of the story? Does the suspense increase or lessen as the action moves onward?

5   What is the peculiar situation that we learn about from the conversation between Alan and the old man?

6   What is the point of view?

7   How does Alan change in the story? Is this change important to the action?

8   What is the conflict? the climax? How complicated is the plot?

9   What is the significance to the meaning of the story of "the life-cleaner"? "the chaser"? the words "*au revoir*"?

10   What is the theme?

A CLEAN, WELL-LIGHTED PLACE
Ernest Hemingway

It was late and every one had left the café except an old man who sat in the shadow the leaves of the tree made against the electric light. In the daytime

SOURCE NOTE: Ernest Hemingway, "A Clean, Well-lighted Place" (Copyright 1933 Charles Scribner's Sons; renewal copyright © 1961 Ernest Hemingway) is reprinted with the permission of Charles Scribner's Sons from *Winner Take Nothing* by Ernest Hemingway.

the street was dusty, but at night the dew settled the dust and the old man liked to sit late because he was deaf and now at night it was quiet and he felt the difference. The two waiters inside the café knew that the old man was a little drunk, and while he was a good client they knew that if he became too drunk he would leave without paying, so they kept watch on him.

"Last week he tried to commit suicide," one waiter said.

"Why?"

"He was in despair."

"What about?"

"Nothing."

"How do you know it was nothing?"

"He has plenty of money."

They sat together at a table that was close against the wall near the door of the café and looked at the terrace where the tables were all empty except where the old man sat in the shadow of the leaves of the tree that moved slightly in the wind. A girl and a soldier went by in the street. The street light shown on the brass number on his collar. The girl wore no head covering and hurried beside him.

"The guard will pick him up," one waiter said.

"What does it matter if he gets what he's after?"

"He had better get off the street now. The guard will get him. They went by five minutes ago."

The old man sitting in the shadow rapped on his saucer with his glass. The younger waiter went over to him.

"What do you want?"

The old man looked at him. "Another brandy," he said.

"You'll be drunk," the waiter said. The old man looked at him. The waiter went away.

"He'll stay all night," he said to his colleague. "I'm sleepy now. I never get into bed before three o'clock. He should have killed himself last week."

The waiter took the brandy bottle and another saucer from the counter inside the café and marched out to the old man's table. He put down the saucer and poured the glass full of brandy.

"You should have killed yourself last week," he said to the deaf man. The old man motioned with his finger. "A little more," he said. The waiter poured on into the glass so that the brandy slopped over and ran down the stem into the top saucer of the pile. "Thank you," the old man said. The waiter took the bottle back inside the café. He sat down at the table with his colleague again.

"He's drunk now," he said.

"He's drunk every night."

"What did he want to kill himself for?"

"How should I know."

"How did he do it?"

"He hung himself with a rope."

"Who cut him down?"

"His niece."

"Why did they do it?"

"Fear for his soul."

"How much money has he got?"

"He's got plenty."

"He must be eighty years old."

"Anyway I should say he was eighty."

"I wish he would go home. I never get to bed before three o'clock. What kind of hour is that to go to bed?"

"He stays up because he likes it."

"He's lonely. I'm not lonely. I have a wife waiting in bed for me."

"He had a wife once too."

"A wife would be no good to him now."

"You can't tell. He might be better with a wife."

"His niece looks after him. You said she cut him down."

"I know."

"I wouldn't want to be that old. An old man is a nasty thing."

"Not always. This old man is clean. He drinks without spilling. Even now, drunk. Look at him."

"I don't want to look at him. I wish he would go home. He has no regard for those who must work."

The old man looked from his glass across the square, then over at the waiters.

"Another brandy," he said, pointing to his glass. The waiter who was in a hurry came over.

"Finished," he said, speaking with that omission of syntax stupid people employ when talking to drunken people or foreigners. "No more tonight. Close now."

"Another," said the old man.

"No. Finished." The waiter wiped the edge of the table with a towel and shook his head.

The old man stood up, slowly counted the saucers, took a leather coin purse from his pocket and paid for the drinks, leaving half a peseta tip.

The waiter watched him go down the street, a very old man walking unsteadily but with dignity.

"Why didn't you let him stay and drink?" the unhurried waiter asked. They were putting up the shutters. "It is not half-past two."

"I want to go home to bed."

"What is an hour?"

"More to me than to him."

"An hour is the same."

"You talk like an old man yourself. He can buy a bottle and drink at home."

"It's not the same."

"No, it is not," agreed the waiter with a wife. He did not wish to be unjust. He was only in a hurry.

"And you? You have no fear of going home before your usual hour?"

"Are you trying to insult me?"

"No, hombre, only to make a joke."

"No," the waiter who was in a hurry said, rising from pulling down the metal shutters. "I have confidence. I am all confidence."

"You have youth, confidence, and a job," the older waiter said. "You have everything."

"And what do you lack?"

"Everything but work."

"You have everything I have."

"No. I have never had confidence and I am not young."

"Come on. Stop talking nonsense and lock up."

"I am of those who like to stay late at the café," the older waiter said. "With all those who do not want to go to bed. With all those who need a light for the night."

"I want to go home and into bed."

"We are of two different kinds," the older waiter said. He was now dressed to go home. "It is not only a question of youth and confidence although those things are very beautiful. Each night I am reluctant to close up because there may be some one who needs the café."

"Hombre, there are bodegas open all night long."

"You do not understand. This is a clean and pleasant café. It is well lighted. The light is very good and also, now, there are shadows of the leaves."

"Good night," said the younger waiter.

"Good night," the other said. Turning off the electric light he continued the conversation with himself. It is the light of course but it is necessary that the place be clean and pleasant. You do not want music. Certainly you do not want music. Nor can you stand before a bar with dignity although that is all that is provided for these hours. What did he fear? It was not fear or dread. It was a nothing that he knew too well. It was all a nothing and a man was nothing too. It was only that and light was all it needed and a certain cleanness and order. Some lived in it and never felt it but he knew it all was nada y pues nada y nada y pues nada. Our nada who are in nada, nada be thy name thy kingdom nada thy will be nada in nada as it is in nada. Give us this nada our daily nada and nada us our nada as we nada our nadas and nada us not into nada but deliver us from nada; pues nada. Hail nothing full of nothing, nothing is with thee. He smiled and stood before a bar with a shining steam pressure coffee machine.

"What's yours?" asked the barman.

"Nada."

"Otro loco mas," said the barman and turned away.

"A little cup," said the waiter.

The barman poured it for him.

"The light is very bright and pleasant but the bar is unpolished," the waiter said.

The barman looked at him but did not answer. It was too late at night for conversation.

"You want another copita?" the barman asked.

"No, thank you," said the waiter and went out. He disliked bars and bodegas. A clean, well-lighted café was a very different thing. Now, without thinking further, he would go home to his room. He would lie in the bed and finally, with daylight, he would go to sleep. After all, he said to himself, it is probably only insomnia. Many must have it.

DISCUSSION

1 What is the appeal of the cafe?

2 How does the waiter of the story view old age?

3 Because of the economy of descriptive and narrative details by Hemingway, what does the reader's interest focus on?

4 What contrasts help the reader with meaning?

5 Who is the narrator?

6 How does the tone of the speeches by the characters clue the reader to meaning?

7 Who is the main character?

8 Why must the cafe be clean and well-lighted?

9 What does the old waiter mean by saying "Many must have it"?

10 What is the meaning of the story?

THE JOCKEY
Carson McCullers

The jockey came to the doorway of the dining-room, then after a moment stepped to one side and stood motionless, with his back to the wall. The room was crowded, as this was the third day of the season and all the hotels in the town were full. In the dining-room bouquets of August roses scattered their petals on the white table linen and from the adjoining bar came a warm, drunken wash of voices. The jockey waited with his back to the wall and

SOURCE NOTE: *The Ballad of the Sad Cafe.* Copyright 1955 by Carson McCullers. Reprinted by permission of the publisher, Houghton Mifflin Company.

scrutinized the room with pinched, crêpy eyes. He examined the room until at last his eyes reached a table in a corner diagonally across from him, at which three men were sitting. As he watched, the jockey raised his chin and tilted his head back to one side, his dwarfed body grew rigid, and his hands stiffened so that the fingers curled inward like grey claws. Tense against the wall of the dining-room, he watched and waited in this way.

He was wearing a suit of green Chinese silk that evening, tailored precisely and the size of a costume outfit for a child. The shirt was yellow, the tie striped with pastel colours. He had no hat with him and wore his hair brushed down in a stiff, wet bang on his forehead. His face was drawn, ageless, and grey. There were shadowed hollows at his temples and his mouth was set in a wiry smile. After a time he was aware that he had been seen by one of the three men he had been watching. But the jockey did not nod; he only raised his chin still higher and hooked the thumb of his tense hand in the pocket of his coat.

The three men at the corner table were a trainer, a bookie, and a rich man. The trainer was Sylvester—a large, loosely built fellow with a flushed nose and slow blue eyes. The bookie was Simmons. The rich man was the owner of a horse named Seltzer, which the jockey had ridden that afternoon. The three of them drank whisky with soda, and a white-coated waiter had just brought on the main course of the dinner.

It was Sylvester who first saw the jockey. He looked away quickly, put down his whisky glass, and nervously mashed the tip of his red nose with his thumb. "It's Bitsy Barlow," he said. "Standing over there across the room. Just watching us."

"Oh, the jockey," said the rich man. He was facing the wall and he half turned his head to look behind him. "Ask him over."

"God no," Sylvester said.

"He's crazy," Simmons said. The bookie's voice was flat and without inflection. He had the face of a born gambler, carefully adjusted, the expression a permanent deadlock between fear and greed.

"Well, I wouldn't call him that exactly," said Sylvester. "I've known him a long time. He was O.K. until about six months ago. But if he goes on like this, I can't see him lasting another year. I just can't."

"It was what happened in Miami," said Simmons.

"What?" asked the rich man.

Sylvester glanced across the room at the jockey and wet the corner of his mouth with his red, fleshy tongue. "An accident. A kid got hurt on the track. Broke a leg and a hip. He was a particular pal of Bitsy's. An Irish kid. Not a bad rider, either."

"That's a pity," said the rich man.

"Yeah. They were particular friends," Sylvester said. "You would always find him up in Bitsy's hotel room. They would be playing rummy or else lying on the floor reading the sports page together."

"Well, those things happen," said the rich man.

Simmons cut into his beefsteak. He held his fork prongs downward on the plate and carefully piled on mushrooms with the blade of his knife. "He's crazy," he repeated. "He gives me the creeps."

All the tables in the dining-room were occupied. There was a party at the banquet table in the centre, and green-white August moths had found their way in from the night and fluttered about the clear candle flames. Two girls wearing flannel slacks and blazers walked arm in arm across the room into the bar. From the main street outside came the echoes of holiday hysteria.

"They claim that in August Saratoga is the wealthiest town per capita in the world." Sylvester turned to the rich man. "What do you think?"

"I wouldn't know," said the rich man. "It may very well be so."

Daintily, Simmons wiped his greasy mouth with the tip of his forefinger. "How about Hollywood? And Wall Street—"

"Wait," said Sylvester. "He's decided to come over here."

The jockey had left the wall and was approaching the table in the corner. He walked with a prim strut, swinging out his legs in a half-circle with each step, his heels biting smartly into the red velvet carpet on the floor. On the way over he brushed against the elbow of a fat woman in white satin at the banquet table; he stepped back and bowed with dandified courtesy, his eyes quite closed. When he had crossed the room he drew up a chair and sat at a corner of the table, between Sylvester and the rich man, without a nod of greeting or a change in his set, grey face.

"Had dinner?" Sylvester asked.

"Some people might call it that." The jockey's voice was high, bitter, clear.

Sylvester put his knife and fork down carefully on his plate. The rich man shifted his position, turning sidewise in his chair and crossing his legs. He was dressed in twill riding pants, unpolished boots, and a shabby brown jacket— this was his outfit day and night in the racing season, although he was never seen on a horse. Simmons went on with his dinner.

"Like a spot of seltzer water?" asked Sylvester. "Or something like that?"

The jockey didn't answer. He drew a gold cigarette case from his pocket and snapped it open. Inside were a few cigarettes and a tiny gold penknife. He used the knife to cut a cigarette in half. When he had lighted his smoke he held up his hand to a waiter passing by the table. "Kentucky bourbon, please."

"Now listen, Kid," said Sylvester.

"Don't Kid me."

"Be reasonable. You know you got to behave reasonable."

The jockey drew up the left corner of his mouth in a stiff jeer. His eyes lowered to the food spread out on the table, but instantly he looked up again. Before the rich man was a fish casserole, baked in a cream sauce and garnished with parsley. Sylvester had ordered eggs Benedict. There was asparagus, fresh buttered corn, and a side dish of wet black olives. A plate of French-fried potatoes was in the corner of the table before the jockey. He didn't look at the food again, but kept his pinched eyes on the centre-piece of full-blown lavender roses. "I don't suppose you remember a certain person by the name of McGuire," he said.

"Now, listen," said Sylvester.

The waiter brought the whisky, and the jockey sat fondling the glass with his small, strong, callused hands. On his wrist was a gold link bracelet that clinked against the table edge. After turning the glass between his palms, the jockey suddenly drank the whisky neat in two hard swallows. He set down the glass sharply. "No, I don't suppose your memory is that long and extensive," he said.

"Sure enough, Bitsy," said Sylvester. "What makes you act like this? You hear from the kid today?"

"I received a letter," the jockey said. "The certain person we were speaking about was taken out from the cast on Wednesday. One leg is two inches shorter than the other one. That's all."

Sylvester clucked his tongue and shook his head. "I realize how you feel."

"Do you?" The jockey was looking at the dishes on the table. His gaze passed from the fish casserole to the corn, and finally fixed on the plate of fried potatoes. His face tightened and quickly he looked up again. A rose shattered and he picked up one of the petals, bruised it between his thumb and forefinger, and put it in his mouth.

"Well, those things happen," said the rich man.

The trainer and the bookie had finished eating, but there was food left on the serving dishes before their plates. The rich man dipped his buttery fingers in his water glass and wiped them with his napkin.

"Well," said the jockey. "Doesn't somebody want me to pass them something? Or maybe perhaps you desire to re-order. Another hunk of beefsteak, gentlemen, or—"

"Please," said Sylvester. "Be reasonable. Why don't you go on upstairs?"

"Yes, why don't I?" the jockey said.

His prim voice had risen higher and there was about it the sharp whine of hysteria.

"Why don't I go to my god-damn room and walk around and write some letters and go to bed like a good boy? Why don't I just—" He pushed his chair back and got up. "Oh, foo," he said. "Foo to you. I want a drink."

"All I can say is it's your funeral," said Sylvester. "You know what it does to you. You know well enough."

The jockey crossed the dining-room and went into the bar. He ordered a Manhattan, and Sylvester watched him stand with his heels pressed tight together, his body hard as a lead soldier's, holding his little finger out from the cocktail glass and sipping the drink slowly.

"He's crazy," said Simmons. "Like I said."

Sylvester turned to the rich man. "If he eats a lamb chop, you can see the shape of it in his stomach a hour afterward. He can't sweat things out of him any more. He's a hundred and twelve and a half. He's gained three pounds since we left Miami."

"A jockey shouldn't drink," said the rich man.

"The food don't satisfy him like it used to and he can't sweat it out. If he eats a lamb chop, you can watch it tooching out in his stomach and it don't go down."

The jockey finished his Manhattan. He swallowed, crushed the cherry in the bottom of the glass with his thumb, then pushed the glass away from him. The two girls in blazers were standing at his left, their faces turned toward each other, and at the other end of the bar two touts had started an argument about which was the highest mountain in the world. Everyone was with somebody else; there was no other person drinking alone that night. The jockey paid with a brand-new fifty-dollar bill and didn't count the change.

He walked back to the dining-room and to the table at which the three men were sitting, but he did not sit down. "No, I wouldn't presume to think your memory is that extensive," he said. He was so small that the edge of the table top reached almost to his belt, and when he gripped the corner with his wiry hands he didn't have to stoop. "No, you're too busy gobbling up dinners in dining-rooms. You're too—"

"Honestly," begged Sylvester. "You got to behave reasonable."

"Reasonable! Reasonable!" The jockey's grey face quivered, then set in a mean, frozen grin. He shook the table so that the plates rattled, and for a moment it seemed that he would push it over. But suddenly he stopped. His hand reached out toward the plate nearest to him and deliberately he put a few of the French-fried potatoes in his mouth. He chewed slowly, his upper lip raised, then he turned and spat out the pulpy mouthful on the smooth red carpet which covered the floor. "Libertines," he said, and his voice was thin and broken. He rolled the word in his mouth, as though it had a flavour and a substance that gratified him. "You libertines," he said again, and turned and walked with his rigid swagger out of the dining-room.

Sylvester shrugged one of his loose, heavy shoulders. The rich man sopped up some water that had been spilled on the tablecloth, and they didn't speak until the waiter came to clear away.

DISCUSSION

1 What kind of atmosphere does the writer create?

2 How do the three men at the corner table fit in with the atmosphere?

3 How do the life-styles of the three men differ from the life-style of the jockey? How does the writer make clear the differences?

4 What is the point of view? How does the point of view help the writer with meaning?

5 Cite evidence of Bitsy's isolation and loneliness.

6 Is Barlow a rich or poor jockey? Why is this fact important to meaning?

7 How complicated is the plot? What is the climax?

8 What is the jockey attacking?

9 What is the meaning of the story?

10 Why does Barlow spit the greasy potatoes on the rug?

FOOTBALL BANQUET AFFAIR
Ruth Pintar

Girls have all kinds of problem fathers, and in my 15 years I've heard of ways to handle most of them, from the overprotective tyrants to the kind that are too busy to give a girl any time or attention. But what do you do with one who thinks he's a dead ringer for Napoleon Solo—and acts like it?

Dad works at a bookstore-publishing house, one of those ultra scholarly musty places that scares you into wearing a pious look even if you're just walking past it. But last summer the store got into some kind of import jam and had to hire high school vacation help. The kids started working on Dad right away, calling him "Mr. Solo" and then explaining the whole U.N.C.L.E. bit when he smiled his quizzical look at them. They had him sold in no time. Can you imagine a grown man falling for a line like that? I mean, if anybody wants an objective opinion, Dad's about as much Napoleon Solo as I am "That Girl."

I hit Mom with it first chance I had. "Dad's making a fool of himself, that's all. Even if there was some basis for it, I mean—he's at least 40 years old. It's ridiculous."

"Calm down, Cindy," Mom said. "Forty isn't terribly old, but it is sort of crucial as ages go. If it's what your father needs, let him have it. Besides, the resemblance is there. You're just too close to him to see it. He has the voice and the mannerisms, the color and the fundamental facial structure. The rest is mostly determination, and you don't want to take that away from him."

"You're as bad as he is!" I groaned. "You're worse. You're encouraging him."

Mom smiled. "Give it time," she said.

I guess we both really expected the whole thing to blow over once the summer help went back to school. Only it didn't work out that way. In mid-September Dad started doing the Royal Canadian Air Force exercises with isometrics on the side. I expected him to sort of collapse after a week, but he just gave up breakfast and lunch instead and substituted a dietary supplement. He also bought a sunlamp to keep his summer tan from fading away.

SOURCE NOTE: From 'Teen, October 1967, pp. 67, 82–85, © 1967 by 'Teen Publications Inc., Los Angeles, Calif. 90069.

I appealed to Mom again. "Can't you make him stop? If the news gets around that he's a Solomaniac—I mean do you want us to be a laughing stock?"

"They may laugh at us, Cindy," Mom said, "but they won't laugh at him. He looks fine. You've just got to admit it."

"I don't care what he looks like. I just want him to be himself."

"Maybe he is being himself," Mom said. "For the first time in a long time. Maybe." But her tone wasn't very convincing.

And then Dad really shook us up when he put aside the stereophones and Wagner operas and joined the rest of us in front of the TV set one Friday night. "They tell me I was in good form last week," he said casually. "May as well see for myself."

My two sisters (younger) just giggled, and Mom tried to smile, but I wasn't having any of it. "You must have decided you have a 12-year-old mind," I said. "You've told us often enough that's all these programs were good for."

Dad had long been critical of our taste in television, but I suppose I'd have challenged any statement he happened to make. It was kind of a reflex I'd developed over the years—whenever he voiced an opinion on anything, I automatically took the opposing view.

"There's no rule," he said lightly, "you can't find some exception to." He raised one eyebrow the tiniest fraction. "How would you like to go to bed—" still that light almost amused tone, "very, very early?"

I knew I didn't dare even twitch after that. It was hard, but I managed somehow.

I had a sinking feeling that judo and karate were going to be Dad's next active interests. It wouldn't do for Napoleon to be anything less than expert, even in a little sleepy out of the way town like ours. Three days after seeing his first program Dad brought home a wild set of instruction books and two days after that he'd broken every pencil in the house practicing one-finger karate chops. And he wasn't the least bit ashamed of himself either.

The only bearable thing about the whole mess was that it hadn't affected any one of us directly. For the most part, Dad sort of blended into the background around home. He had always said the only way to survive the constant girl-talk and everlasting chatter was to tune himself out of our wavelength. It seemed a sensible system and we were all used to it, so when Dad suddenly tuned himself back in, the shock was horrible. It happened without any warning.

My sister Mandy had become terribly figure conscious since starting junior high. Her ideal was, Carolyn Jacobs. Carolyn happened to be in my class, but we weren't exactly friends—and we'd been outright opponents in the Student Council election. Carolyn had won by a small handful of votes, all of them male I had no doubt.

"It figures," she sighed when I told her the results. "Carolyn must be at least a 36-C. Are there any extra potatoes?"

"At least," I said. "The only question is how much is really Carolyn and how much is pillow stuffing?"

"Meow," somewhat muffled because Mandy had her mouth full.

I was building up to a real explosion when Dad suddenly spoke out.

"Just who is this—femme fatale—under discussion?"

Mandy and I gasped simultaneously. We'd forgotten he was sitting there perfectly capable of hearing everything we said. It was just that he never had before—bothered to listen, I mean.

"What are you doing?" he asked. "Imitating tropical fish? I was asking about 36-C."

I resented his sudden interest and clamped my mouth shut, but Mandy was perfectly willing to clue him in. "Carolyn Jacobs," she said, "one of Cindy's very special friends. A gorgeous blonde—"

"Ah yes," Dad said. "Big blue eyes, a permanent pout and a predilection for tight sweaters."

"How do you know?" I demanded. "You've never met her."

"A common type," Dad answered. "Given your not too subtle reactions to Mandy's not too subtle needling, the conclusion was obvious. But don't waste your time worrying about her. She'll go to fat or fade before she's 20."

Two minutes before I'd been thinking the same thing myself, but now I bristled to Carolyn's defense. "That's all you know," I said. "She's just about the prettiest, most popular girl in the sophomore class, that's all."

"You wouldn't talk that way if you'd ever seen her," Mandy bravely backed me up. "What a figure—wow!"

Dad gave her the knowing, almost uninterested, slightly superior bow of the head. "You and your measurements. It's the total effect that counts. The harmonious, if you will, resolution on all the parts to the whole. I don't have to see your Carolyn to know that—well let's say the foundation probably isn't equal to the superstructure. And that's bad building. Can't last."

That left Mandy and me exactly where we'd started. Imitating tropical fish.

It was funny though. I couldn't get Dad's remarks out of my head. The next day at school I sent more than one speculative glance in Carolyn's direction. I'd never noticed before that she had kind of thick ankles and knobby knees. If Dad knew what he was talking about—there might be some hope for the rest of us—but I couldn't quite see it yet.

Carolyn collected boys as if they were postage stamps or matchbook covers. It was a hobby with her. This year she was concentrating on football players. She'd already dated half of the boys on the first team, and her current target was Budge Harrison. I wouldn't have minded except that Budge was the only boy on any team who'd even shown the slightest interest in me.

Budge was so big and so mysteriously silent most of the time that I never knew quite how to act when I was with him. I'd never dated anyone in his crowd, and neither had any of my friends, so he remained something of an unknown quantity. I supposed I could have asked Carolyn, but—I'd managed without her so far, mostly because Budge and I hadn't progressed beyond walking to classes together. That didn't give me much time to make an impression, so I began resorting to extra-long grooming sessions before school everyday.

Only I had reckoned without Dad and his new total-interest-in-us program.

When I finally turned away from the mirror one Monday morning, I found Dad looking me over. The expression on his face told me he was suffering, but he was being brave about it. "What's the matter with you?" I asked.

He shrugged slightly. "The hair," he said in the light insinuating tone. "Are you going to school? Or to a Ubangi tribal ceremony?"

I checked the mirror again. "What's wrong with it? I've been wearing it this way for months."

He took a sip of his high powered low calorie breakfast concentrate. "I don't believe it," he said. "Do you have any idea what it looks like from the back? You're not leaving this house till you flatten it down—at least six inches."

"Flatten it down!" I yelped. "I just spent 15 whole minutes getting it to look this way! Anyway I'm going to be late for school if I don't get going *right now.*"

Dad swished the goo in his glass around for a while, a slow easy turn of the wrist. "The essence of any art," he said, "karate or what you will, is control. Discipline. Now the trick here is to get the contents of the glass swirling around right to the top-edge—all around—but not over. You see?"

I said I saw.

"You see, but you're not terribly interested. Well, that's understandable." He balanced the glass on the edge of my vanity. "Don't worry about that," he said. "It won't fall. (It didn't.) And don't worry about being late for school. You just may not go at all. I was thinking," he went on, just as if he were consulting me, "of making up a list of proscribed articles—that means a list of things totally forbidden to all members of this household. Things like padded bras and white lipstick, mini skirts and iridescent nail polish. I wonder if you think we should include hair spray with all of that?"

I flattened down the hair and got to school on time. He sure had a way of making his points.

At least Dad's interference didn't have any disastrous results, as I was afraid it might. Budge didn't seem to notice the difference in my appearance. And it had to be purely coincidental that I suddenly found myself with hopes for the football banquet at the end of the month. It came about in the easiest way imaginable.

I'd gone to the Shack with the girls after a Friday night game, and Budge had turned up with the boys. Luckily Carolyn had a date with the team quarterback and wasn't free to distract Budge. So I found myself saying yes to his quiet request to see me home.

As we left the Shack, I asked casually about the plays that set up the winning touchdown, and Budge turned positively garrulous. He expounded on all the beauties of the T-formation and the strategy from opening play to last (a banana pass). I had plenty of time to study his profile in the moonlight and to enjoy feeling very small and fragile walking beside him. When he finally took my hand in his just a few steps from home, I shivered all the way to my toes.

He showed a little reluctance to leave me at the front door, so I dragged him inside to show him off to Mom and Dad. He happened to catch my hand again just as I got the door open behind me, otherwise I'd never have dared. In a way I'd made a good move, but in a way I hadn't, though I didn't realize it till much later.

We caught Dad in the middle of a karate practice session. He acknowledged my introduction civilly enough, but he didn't bother to interrupt his work on the punching board. He excused himself, but I still didn't feel he was being altogether polite. And as soon as Budge left, I told Dad what I thought of him and his punching board.

He gave me his great stone face look. "You are not seriously interested in *that*," he said.

"Whether I am or not has nothing to do with it." I gave him my coldest Snow Queen glance, "And you know it."

"Granted," he said. "But your—acquaintance—didn't mind."

"How could *you* know?"

"He has the mental aptitude of a gorilla," Dad said, "and undoubtedly the instincts of one, as well as the sensibilities. I judge by what I see and hear. How else would I know?"

"That's not fair. You've barely seen him—even this once—and how could he be at his best? How would you feel if you walked into somebody's house at 11 P.M. and found their father stripped to the waist and wrestling with furniture?" I turned away abruptly, with the intention of stalking off to my room.

Dad laughed. "Not so fast, sweetheart. I trust we've seen the last of—him, but—. If you're going to be exposed to that type, you'd better learn at least a few simple things." And he grabbed my wrists, a little harder than I liked. I yelped and tried to pull away, but the more I pulled the tighter his grip became.

"Now instead of struggling to no purpose and tiring yourself all the way out, just don't move. Stand still and look demure. And count—to yourself. When you get to five, pull your hands together and break away—down—sharply. In the split second that you're free, clasp your hands together and bring them back up as hard as you can."

"All right," I muttered, "I'll play your silly game." And wow! It really worked!

"Beautiful," he said. "If I hadn't been expecting that, you'd have torn my head off."

"Honestly," I said. "What do you think this is, the Dark Ages? You've been watching too much television, Dad."

"Just keep going out with that kind," he said, "you'll—whatever happened to that kid down the block, by the way? Eric Stevens. Now there's a decent clean-cut type."

"Four-sided figure," I said, "all sides equal in length." Dad couldn't have known he'd touched a sore spot there. I'd spent the entire summer trying to make an impression on Eric, but he was a lost cause. "All he cares about is his stupid electronics. He's building a computer in his basement, but he is not—definitely not—going to program it for any dating bureau."

But Dad had already turned from his punching board to his isometric routine, and I doubt if he even heard me.

I was careful not to mention Budge around the house after that. Dad hadn't actually *said* I couldn't go out with him, and there wasn't any point in getting into a fight about it until—if and when—Budge made some positive move.

And then it happened! Budge actually asked me to the football banquet! At 9:45 in the morning, outside my English class, a full week ahead of time. I didn't come down to earth till late that afternoon at the Shack.

After I'd announced the news, as casually as I could, and the squeals had died away, Carolyn spoke up.

"How about that?" she said. "So I suppose I'll see you there, Cindy. It might be fun, watching you handle a boy like Budge."

Thud. That's how I came down to earth again. Carolyn had said just enough. But I was game.

"If I can help you learn anything at all, Carolyn," I said, "you're welcome."

"Thank you, Cindy. Now I have something really to look forward to."

That was Carolyn for you. Somehow she *always* got in the last word.

And then there was Dad. I told Mom about the banquet first thing. She agreed we might just as well keep it to ourselves, at least until we caught Dad in a good mood.

Only Dad's sunlamp burned out next day and there wasn't a replacement bulb for it anywhere in town. It had to be special ordered, week to 10 days, and honestly it was like living with a bear poked out of hibernation. Friday night arrived in its turn and Dad still didn't know about the banquet. When I turned up at the dinner table with my hair in rollers, I was sure he'd notice and begin the third degree. But he didn't—until Mandy opened her big mouth.

We'd finished dinner and I was hurriedly clearing the table when she said it. "Hey, what's the big rush. You going someplace special tonight?"

Dad had already left the table and was leaning over the TV, ready to switch it on. He frowned and half turned to glance at me, and I braced myself for the "who-where-when-how late" routine.

And then this crazy thing happened. The TV has the usual (I guess) push-pull off-on button, and since Dad already had his arm extended to pull it on he completed the action. Only the set remained dark even though the button came off in dad's hand. He looked at it in disbelief, then automatically pushed it back into its place on the control panel.

"You broke it," Mandy wailed. "And U.N.C.L.E. comes on tonight!"

Dad snarled something unintelligible then tried to turn the set on again. The button came out just as easily as the first time. In the confusion that followed, I slipped off to my room and wasn't even missed.

After 15 minutes Mandy came up with a progress report. "He's tried an instant epoxy resin and friction tape and body English and just plain slamming it a good one. Nothing works. He keeps saying that no machine is going to get the best of him, but I guess the set isn't listening. —And where *are* you going tonight, Cindy?"

I told her.

She sighed. "Lucky! But Dad wouldn't let you go if he knew about Budge."

"So let's not tell him. Okay?" I said. "He's got enough troubles as is."

By the time Budge rang the doorbell, Dad had his head buried deep in the back of the set, trying to get at the switch through the tangle of wires and tubes and things. I'm sure he didn't even hear us leave.

Maybe I should have had a guilty conscience about it all, but what it boiled down to was Dad's opinion of Budge against mine. I felt I was in a better position to judge him than Dad was. So I was determined to enjoy myself no matter what.

The dinner was boss, and after the program and awards we drove to the gym for the dance. Budge had been the perfect escort so far, and now he turned out to be wonderfully easy on his feet for someone so big. We really clicked on the dance floor—so well that we took the spotlight several times. I was so thrilled I was almost paralyzed, but Budge just took it for granted and eased me out of any tenseness that might have spoiled us as a couple.

Toward the end of the evening Budge suggested we get some fresh air, and I said sure. I was in the midst of a lovely walking dream by then, a dream that starred Budge and me—at the winter prom, holiday vacation parties and on and on. I didn't really wake up till he opened the door of his car and maneuvered me into the back seat.

"Budge," I said, "I didn't really have anything like this in mind." I said it with a kind of sweet desperation that I hoped he would find moving, but all he said was, "I did."

A firm and vigorous "no" repeated at intervals didn't work either. I managed to stay out of the corner and on the edge of the seat. Then Budge decided taking hold of my wrists might keep my hands from actually pushing him away.

"Oh, Budge," I said. "I am sorry."

He sort of grinned, rather nicely, considering. "For what, Cindy?"

I brought my hands together and snapped them downward suddenly. He didn't even have time to look surprised. I clipped him under the chin so hard he fell back against the door which (I guess) wasn't latched properly so he went right on out of the car. I scrambled out of my side and ran for the gym. I made it to the girl's lounge without actually bumping into anyone, then I sort of collapsed. I mean I was winded and scared too.

What a mess I'd made of everything! And I couldn't face Budge again, not tonight anyway—some time maybe, if he could ever come to understand that a girl likes to be asked—for anything, no matter what—and a boy has to learn how to enjoy yes, and how to accept no. And now I'd have to call home and ask Dad to pick me up—and how would I ever live that down?

It was all decidedly sobering. Then while I was trying to work up my courage for the trip to the phone booth, who should walk into the lounge but Carolyn.

"What did you do to Budge?" she asked breathlessly. "I mean he could hardly talk, his jaw was that swollen. And then he called your house and asked somebody to come pick you up, please, and he didn't mean anything out of the way, really, but he just wasn't feeling too well. I mean he was kind of pathetic."

"We had a quiet misunderstanding," I said. "And that's all."

"I'll bet," Carolyn said. "I'll bet I can figure it out anyway."

But I was only half-listening—what an unexpected thing for Budge to do—oh, I hoped I hadn't really hurt him! And that Dad hadn't been too hard on him—I was working up a good case of the black worries when half a dozen girls burst into the lounge more or less at once.

In between the shrieks they managed to tell us that *Napoleon Solo* was right out there *on the dance floor*. They made it sound as though it were going to be consecrated territory forever and after. And then their wild rush to the balcony carried Carolyn and me right along with them.

There he stood, well inside the door of the gym, handsome trim and tanned, casual and completely self-assured in a checkered sport jacket with a red, I mean scarlet, handkerchief three-pointing from his pocket. The handkerchief almost threw me, but there was something awfully familiar—that jacket, of course. It was only Dad come to pick me up.

And then Carolyn said it. "He is the most gorgeous man!"

Dad became aware of the commotion on the balcony and spotted me, signaling with an easy move of his hand. I think it was the first time in ages that I really noticed how white his teeth were and how winning his smile.

The girls were just limp. "That was meant for me," Carolyn said. "I know that was meant for me."

"Honestly!" I broke in. "You girls are—you're just exasperating. Now if you'll excuse me, I believe he's waiting for me."

And that was the only time in my life that I ever left Carolyn speechless. Now if only Dad wouldn't spoil it.

I rushed across the floor half-expecting to be ranked out on the spot, but he only bowed gallantly, ever so slightly, ever so effectively, and offered me his arm. Then we were safely outside.

"Well?" he asked gently.

"Oh—" and I had to laugh suddenly, "you were halfway right about Budge, I guess you know."

"That about says it," he admitted. "You still interested in him?"

"I've probably scared him off for good," I sighed. "But if we could ever sort of reach an understanding—I mean he isn't all that bad."

"Fair enough," Dad said and put his arm around my shoulder. "What do you say we go home and watch the late show?"

"You got it fixed!" I shrieked. "Honestly? I never thought you could."

He told me about it on the way home. "The trick," he said, "was to bypass the switch entirely and put a cut-off switch directly on the line cord. Otherwise the miserable thing would have to go off to the shop and good-bye for two weeks. The only trouble was I didn't know which wires to cut and resolder."

"So what happened?"

Dad cleared his throat. "So I called young Stevens."

I sighed, Eric. What an opportunity missed.

"You don't have to look disappointed," Dad said. "He'll still be there."

Eric was just packing up his tool kit when we arrived home. "I gave it a good going over," he said. "Everything checks out fine. Fascinating how they crammed all that equipment in there."

Dad thanked him again for stopping by, and then Eric and I were alone in the doorway.

"I think it was terribly clever—and good—of you to fix the set," I said.

"Oh I'd have still had it all in pieces yet," Eric blushed. "It was your Dad's idea that made it easy. You know he's quite a guy. I've never met anybody so—determined."

"Yes," I said, suddenly subdued and thoughtful. "He is, isn't he?"

"I'd sure like to know him a little better," Eric said. "I mean, it might help— to get to know you even a little. You're an awfully attractive girl, Cindy. It used to scare me—how nice you looked. But it won't anymore."

And he was gone before I could say a word. I heard him whistling all the way down the walk.

Eric Stevens, of all people! I hummed a few bars of the same tune. What was it? Something awfully familiar. I smiled at myself in the hall mirror, then took a second look. The theme from "That Girl," that was it. I turned my head slowly. It just could be true. In a dim light, if you didn't look too closely, it just could be . . . .

DISCUSSION

1 What is the point of view? How does the point of view help the writer with meaning?

2 How complicated is the plot?

3 How does the father usually survive in the household?

4 In the first part of the story what is Cindy's opinion of her father?

5 When does Cindy first begin to feel differently about her father?

6 What was Dad's opinion of Budge?

7 What silly game does Cindy play with her father?

8 What happens that enables Cindy to go to the football banquet with Budge with no trouble from her father? How does the father solve the problem?

9 How much humor is in the story? Does this approach clue you to the writer's purpose?

10 What is the significance of the ending?

THE WONDERFUL ICE CREAM SUIT
Ray Bradbury

It was summer twilight in the city, and out front of the quiet-clicking pool hall three young Mexican-American men breathed the warm air and looked around at the world. Sometimes they talked and sometimes they said nothing at all but watched the cars glide by like black panthers on the hot asphalt or saw trolleys loom up like thunderstorms, scatter lightning, and rumble away into silence.

"Hey," sighed Martínez at last. He was the youngest, the most sweetly sad of the three. "It's a swell night, huh? Swell."

As he observed the world it moved very close and then drifted away and then came close again. People, brushing by, were suddenly across the street. Buildings five miles away suddenly leaned over him. But most of the time everything—people, cars, and buildings—stayed way out on the edge of the world and could not be touched. On this quiet warm summer evening Martínez's face was cold.

"Nights like this you wish . . . lots of things."

"Wishing," said the second man, Villanazul, a man who shouted books out loud in his room but spoke only in whispers on the street. "Wishing is the useless pastime of the unemployed."

"Unemployed?" cried Vamenos, the unshaven. "Listen to him! We got no jobs, no money!"

"So," said Martínez, "we got no friends."

"True." Villanazul gazed off toward the green plaza where the palm trees swayed in the soft night wind. "Do you know what I wish? I wish to go into that plaza and speak among the businessmen who gather there nights to talk big

SOURCE NOTE: "The Wonderful Ice Cream Suit" originally published in *The Saturday Evening Post* as "The Magic White Suit." Copyright 1958 by Ray Bradbury. Reprinted by permission of Harold Matson Company, Inc.

talk. But dressed as I am, poor as I am, who would listen? So, Martínez, we have each other. The friendship of the poor is real friendship. We—"

But now a handsome young Mexican with a fine thin mustache strolled by. And on each of his careless arms hung a laughing woman.

"*Madre mía!*" Martínez slapped his own brow. "How does that one rate *two* friends?"

"It's his nice new white summer suit." Vamenos chewed a black thumbnail. "He looks sharp."

Martínez leaned out to watch the three people moving away, and then at the tenement across the street, in one fourth-floor window of which, far above, a beautiful girl leaned out, her dark hair faintly stirred by the wind. She had been there forever, which was to say for six weeks. He had nodded, he had raised a hand, he had smiled, he had blinked rapidly, he had even bowed to her, on the street, in the hall when visiting friends, in the park, downtown. Even now, he put his hand up from his waist and moved his fingers. But all the lovely girl did was let the summer wind stir her dark hair. He did not exist. He was nothing.

"*Madre mía!*" He looked away and down the street where the man walked his two friends around a corner. "Oh, if just I had one suit, one! I wouldn't need money if I *looked* okay."

"I hesitate to suggest," said Villanazul, "that you see Gómez. But he's been talking some crazy talk for a month now about clothes. I keep on saying I'll be in on it to make him go away. That Gómez."

"Friend," said a quiet voice.

"Gómez!" Everyone turned to stare.

Smiling strangely, Gómez pulled forth an endless thin yellow ribbon which fluttered and swirled on the summer air.

"Gómez," said Martínez, "what are you doing with that tape measure?"

Gómez beamed. "Measuring people's skeletons."

"Skeletons!"

"Hold on." Gómez squinted at Martínez. "*Caramba!* Where you *been* all my life! Let's try *you!*"

Martínez saw his arm seized and taped, his leg measured, his chest encircled.

"Hold still!" cried Gómez. "Arm—perfect. Leg—chest—*perfecto!* Now quick, the height! There! Yes! Five foot five! You're in! Shake!" Pumping Martínez's hand, he stopped suddenly. "Wait. You got . . . ten bucks?"

"I have!" Vamenos waved some grimy bills. "Gómez, measure me!"

"All I got left in the world is nine dollars and ninety-two cents." Martínez searched his pockets. "That's enough for a new suit? Why?"

"Why? Because you got the right skeleton, that's why!"

"Señor Gómez, I don't hardly know you—"

"Know me? You're going to live with me! Come on!"

Gómez vanished into the poolroom. Martínez, escorted by the polite Villan-azul, pushed by an eager Vamenos, found himself inside.

"Domínguez!" said Gómez.

Domínguez, at a wall telephone, winked at them. A woman's voice squeaked on the receiver.

"Manulo!" said Gómez.

Manulo, a wine bottle tilted bubbling to his mouth, turned.

Gómez pointed at Martínez.

"At last we found our fifth volunteer!"

Domínguez said, "I got a date, don't bother me—" and stopped. The receiver slipped from his fingers. His little black telephone book full of fine names and numbers went quickly back into his pocket. "Gómez, you—?"

"Yes, yes! Your money, now! *Ándale!*"

The woman's voice sizzled on the dangling phone.

Domínguez glanced at it uneasily.

Manulo considered the empty wine bottle in his hand and the liquor-store sign across the street.

Then very reluctantly both men laid ten dollars each on the green velvet pool table.

Villanazul, amazed, did likewise, as did Gómez, nudging Martínez. Martínez counted out his wrinkled bills and change. Gómez flourished the money like a royal flush.

"Fifty bucks! The suit costs sixty! All we need is ten bucks!"

"Wait," said Martínez. "Gómez, are we talking about *one* suit? *Uno?*"

"Uno!" Gómez raised a finger. "One wonderful white ice cream summer suit! White, white as the August moon!"

"But who will own this one suit?"

"Me!" said Manulo.

"Me!" said Domínguez.

"Me!" said Villanazul.

"Me!" cried Gómez. "*And* you, Martínez. Men, let's show him. Line up!"

Villanazul, Manulo, Domínguez, and Gómez rushed to plant their backs against the poolroom wall.

"Martínez, you too, the other end, line up! Now, Vamenos, lay that billiard cue across our heads!"

"Sure, Gómez, sure!"

Martínez, in line, felt the cue tap his head and leaned out to see what was happening. "Ah!" he gasped.

The cue lay flat on all their heads, with no rise or fall, as Vamenos slid it along, grinning.

"We're all the same height!" said Martínez.

"The same!" Everyone laughed.

Gómez ran down the line, rustling the yellow tape measure here and there on the men so they laughed even more wildly.

"Sure!" he said. "It took a month, four weeks, mind you, to find four guys the same size and shape as me, a month of running around measuring. Sometimes I found guys with five-foot-five skeletons, sure, but all the meat on their bones was too much or not enough. Sometimes their bones were too long in the legs or too short in the arms. Boy, all the bones! I tell you! But now, five of us, same shoulders, chests, waists, arms, and as for weight? Men!"

Manulo, Domíguez, Villanazul, Gómez, and at last Martínez stepped onto the scales which flipped ink-stamped cards at them as Vamenos, still smiling wildly, fed pennies. Heart pounding, Martínez read the cards.

"One hundred thirty-five pounds . . . one thirty-six . . . one thirty-three . . . one thirty-four . . . one thirty-seven . . . a miracle!"

"No," said Villanazul simply, "Gómez."

They all smiled upon that genius who now circled them with his arms.

"Are we not fine?" he wondered. "All the same size, all the same dream— the suit. So each of us will look beautiful at least one night each week, eh?"

"I haven't looked beautiful in years," said Martínez. "The girls run away."

"They will run no more, they will freeze," said Gómez, "when they see you in the cool white summer ice cream suit."

"Gómez," said Villanazul, "just let me ask one thing."

"Of course, *compadre*."

"When we get this new white ice cream summer suit, some night you're not going to put it on and walk down to the Greyhound bus in it and go live in El Paso for a year in it, are you?"

"Villanazul, Villanazul, how can you say that?"

"My eye sees and my tongue moves," said Villanazul. "How about the *Everybody Wins!* Punchboard Lotteries you ran and you kept running when nobody won? How about the United Chili Con Carne and Frijole Company you were going to organize and all that ever happened was the rent ran out on a two-by-four office?"

"The errors of a child now grown," said Gómez. "Enough! In this hot weather someone may buy the special suit that is made just for us that stands waiting in the window of SHUMWAY'S SUNSHINE SUITS! We have fifty dollars. Now we need just one more skeleton!"

Martínez saw the men peer around the pool hall. He looked where they looked. He felt his eyes hurry past Vamenos, then come reluctantly back to examine his dirty shirt, his huge nicotined fingers.

"Me!" Vamenos burst out at last. "My skeleton, measure it, it's great! Sure, my hands are big, and my arms, from digging ditches! But—"

Just then Martínez heard passing on the sidewalk outside that same terrible man with his two girls, all laughing together.

He saw anguish move like the shadow of a summer cloud on the faces of the other men in this poolroom.

Slowly Vamenos stepped onto the scales and dropped his penny. Eyes closed, he breathed a prayer.

"*Madre mía,* please . . ."

The machinery whirred; the card fell out. Vamenos opened his eyes.

"Look! One thirty-five pounds! Another miracle!"

The men stared at his right hand and the card, at his left hand and a soiled ten-dollar bill.

Gómez swayed. Sweating, he licked his lips. Then his hand shot out, seized the money.

"The clothing store! The suit! *Vamos!*"

Yelling, everyone ran from the poolroom.

The woman's voice was still squeaking on the abandoned telephone. Martínez, left behind, reached out and hung the voice up. In the silence he shook his head. "*Santos,* what a dream! Six men," he said, "one suit. What will come of this? Madness? Debauchery? Murder? But I go with God. Gómez, wait for me!"

Martínez was young. He ran fast.

Mr. Shumway, of SHUMWAY'S SUNSHINE SUITS, paused while adjusting a tie rack, aware of some subtle atmosphere change outside his establishment.

"Leo," he whispered to his assistant. "Look . . ."

Outside, one man Gómez, strolled by, looking in. Two men, Manulo and Domínguez, hurried by, staring in. Three men, Villanazul, Martínez, and Vamenos, jostling shoulders, did the same.

"Leo." Mr. Shumway swallowed. "Call the police!"

Suddenly six men filled the doorway.

Martínez, crushed among them, his stomach slightly upset, his face feeling feverish, smiled so wildly at Leo that Leo let go the telephone.

"Hey," breathed Martínez, eyes wide. "There's a great suit over there!"

"No." Manulo touched a lapel. "*This* one!"

"There is only one suit in all the world!" said Gómez coldly. "Mr. Shumway, the ice cream white, size thirty-four, was in your window just an hour ago! It's gone! You didn't—"

"Sell it?" Mr. Shumway exhaled. "No, no. In the dressing room. It's still on the dummy."

Martínez did not know if he moved and moved the crowd or if the crowd moved and moved him. Suddenly they were all in motion. Mr. Shumway, running, tried to keep ahead of them.

"This way, gents. Now which of you . . .?"

"All for one, one for all!" Martínez heard himself say, and laughed. "We'll all try it on!"

"All?" Mr. Shumway clutched at the booth curtain as if his shop were a steamship that had suddenly tilted in a great swell. He stared.

That's it, thought Martínez, look at our smiles. Now, look at the skeletons behind our smiles! Measure here, there, up, down, yes, do you *see?*

Mr. Shumway saw. He nodded. He shrugged.

"All!" He jerked the curtain. "There! Buy it, and I'll throw in the dummy free!"

Martínez peered quietly into the booth, his motion drawing the others to peer too.

The suit was there.

And it was white.

Martínez could not breathe. He did not want to. He did not need to. He was afraid his breath would melt the suit. It was enough, just looking.

But at last he took a great trembling breath and exhaled, whispering, *"Ay. Ay, caramba!"*

"It puts out my eyes," murmured Gómez.

"Mr. Shumway," Martínez heard Leo hissing. "Ain't it dangerous precedent, to sell it? I mean, what if everybody bought *one* suit for *six* people?"

"Leo," said Mr. Shumway, "you ever hear one single fifty-nine-dollar suit make so many people happy at the same time before?"

"Angels' wings," murmured Martínez. "The wings of white angels."

Martínez felt Mr. Shumway peering over his shoulder into the booth. The pale glow filled his eyes.

"You know something, Leo?" he said in awe. "That's a *suit!*"

Gómez, shouting, whistling, ran up to the third-floor landing and turned to wave to the others, who staggered, laughed, stopped, and had to sit down on the steps below.

"Tonight!" cried Gómez. "Tonight you move in with me, eh? Save rent as well as clothes, eh? Sure! Martínez you got the suit?"

"Have I?" Martínez lifted the white gift-wrapped box high. "From us to us! *Ay-hah!"*

"Vamenos, you got the dummy?"

"Here!"

Vamenos, chewing an old cigar, scattering sparks, slipped. The dummy, falling, toppled, turned over twice and banged down the stairs.

"Vamenos! Dumb! Clumsy!"

They seized the dummy from him. Stricken, Vamenos looked about as if he'd lost something.

Manulo snapped his fingers. "Hey, Vamenos, we got to celebrate! Go borrow some wine!"

Vamenos plunged downstairs in a whirl of sparks.

The others moved into the room with the suit, leaving Martínez in the hall to study Gómez's face.

"Gómez, you look sick."

"I am," said Gómez. "For what have I done?" He nodded to the shadows in the room working about the dummy. "I pick Domínguez, a devil with the women. All right. I pick Manulo, who drinks, yes, but who sings as sweet as a girl, eh? Okay. Villanazul reads books. You, you go wash behind your ears. But then what do I do? Can I wait? No! I got to buy that suit! So the last guy I pick is a clumsy slob who has the right to wear *my* suit—" He stopped, confused. "Who gets to wear *our* suit one night a week, fall down in it, or not come in out of the rain in it! Why, why, why did I do it!"

"Gómez," whispered Villanazul from the room. "The suit is ready. Come see if it looks as good using *your* light bulb."

Gómez and Martínez entered.

And there on the dummy in the center of the room was the phosphorescent, the miraculously white-fired ghost with the incredible lapels, the precise stitching, the neat buttonholes. Standing with the white illumination of the suit upon his cheeks, Martínez suddenly felt he was in church. White! White! It was white as the whitest vanilla ice cream, as the bottled milk in tenement halls at dawn. White as a winter cloud all alone in the moonlit sky late at night. Seeing it here in the warm summer-night room made their breath almost show on the air. Shutting his eyes, he could see it printed on his lids. He knew what color his dreams would be this night.

"White . . ." murmured Villanazul. "White as the snow on that mountain near our town in Mexico, which is called the Sleeping Woman."

"Say that again," said Gómez.

Villanazul, proud yet humble, was glad to repeat his tribute.

". . . white as the snow on the mountain called—"

"I'm back!"

Shocked, the men whirled to see Vamenos in the door, wine bottles in each hand.

"A party! Here! Now tell us, who wears the suit first tonight? Me?"

"It's too late!" said Gómez.

"Late! It's only nine-fifteen!"

"Late?" said everyone, bristling. "Late?"

Gómez edged away from these men who glared from him to the suit to the open window.

Outside and below it was, after all, thought Martínez, a fine Saturday night in a summer month and through the calm warm darkness the women drifted like flowers on a quiet stream. The men made a mournful sound.

"Gómez, a suggestion." Villanazul licked his pencil and drew a chart on a pad. "You wear the suit from nine-thirty to ten, Manulo till ten-thirty, Domínguez till eleven, myself till eleven-thirty, Martínez till midnight, and—"

"Why me *last*?" demanded Vamenos, scowling.

Martínez thought quickly and smiled. "After midnight is the *best* time, friend."

"Hey," said Vamenos, "that's right. I never thought of that. Okay."

Gómez sighed. "All right. A half hour each. But from now on, remember, we each wear the suit just one night a week. Sundays we draw straws for who wears the suit the extra night."

"Me!" laughed Vamenos. "I'm lucky!"

Gómez held onto Martínez, tight.

"Gómez," urged Martínez, "you first. Dress."

Gómez could not tear his eyes from that disreputable Vamenos. At last, impulsively, he yanked his shirt off over his head. "Ay-yeah!" he howled. *"Ay-yeee!"*

Whisper rustle . . . the clean shirt.

"Ah . . .!"

How clean the new clothes feel, thought Martínez, holding the coat ready. How clean they sound, how clean they smell!

Whisper . . . the pants . . . the tie, rustle . . . the suspenders. Whisper . . . now Martínez let loose the coat, which fell in place on flexing shoulders.

"Ole!"

Gómez turned like a matador in his wondrous suit-of-lights.

"Ole, Gómez, ole!"

Gómez bowed and went out the door.

Martínez fixed his eyes to his watch. At ten sharp he heard someone wandering about in the hall as if they had forgotten where to go. Martínez pulled the door open and looked out.

Gómez was there, heading for nowhere.

He looks sick, thought Martínez. No, stunned, shook up, surprised, many things.

"Gómez! This is the place!"

Gómez turned around and found his way through the door.

"Oh, friends, friends," he said. "Friends, what an experience! This suit! This suit!"

"Tell us, Gómez!" said Martínez.

"I can't, how can I say it!" He gazed at the heavens, arms spread, palms up.

"Tell us, Gómez!"

"I have no words, no words. You must see, yourself! Yes, you must see—" And here he lapsed into silence, shaking his head until at last he remembered they all stood watching him. "Who's next? Manulo?"

Manulo, stripped to his shorts, leapt forward.

"Ready!"

All laughed, shouted, whistled.

Manulo, ready, went out the door. He was gone twenty-nine minutes and thirty seconds. He came back holding to doorknobs, touching the wall, feeling his own elbows, putting the flat of his hand to his face.

"Oh, let me tell you," he said. "*Compadres,* I went to the bar, eh, to have a drink? But no, I did not go in the bar, do you hear? I did not drink. For as I walked I began to laugh and sing. Why, why? I listened to myself and asked this. Because. The suit made me feel better than wine ever did. The suit made me drunk, drunk! So I went to the *Guadalajara Refritería* instead and played the guitar and sang four songs, very high! The suit, ah, the suit!"

Domínguez, next to be dressed, moved out through the world, came back through the world.

The black telephone book! thought Martínez. He had it in his hands when he left! Now, he returns, hands empty! What? What?

"On the street," said Domínguez, seeing it all again, eyes wide, "on the street I walked, a woman cried, 'Domínguez, is that *you?*" Another said, 'Domínguez? No, Quetzalcoatl, the Great White God come from the East,' do you hear? And suddenly I didn't want to go with six women or eight, no. One, I thought. One! And to this one, who knows *what* I would say? 'Be mine!' Or 'Marry me!' *Caramba!* This suit is dangerous! But I did not care! I live, I live! Gómez, did it happen this way with you?"

Gómez, still dazed by the events of the evening, shook his head. "No, no talk. It's too much. Later. Villanazul . . .?"

Villanazul moved shyly forward.

Villanazul went shyly out.

Villanazul came shyly home.

"Picture it," he said, not looking at them, looking at the floor, talking to the floor. "The Green Plaza, a group of elderly businessmen gathered under the stars and they are talking, nodding, talking. Now one of them whispers. All turn to stare. They move aside, they make a channel through which a white-hot light burns its way as through ice. At the center of the great light is this person. I take a deep breath. My stomach is jelly. My voice is very small, but it grows louder. And what do I say? I say, 'Friends. Do you know Carlyle's *Sartor Resartus?* In that book we find *his* Philosophy of Suits. . . .'"

And at last it was time for Martínez to let the suit float him out to haunt the darkness.

Four times he walked around the block. Four times he paused beneath the tenement porches, looking up at the window where the light was lit; a shadow moved, the beautiful girl was there, not there, away and gone, and on the fifth time there she was on the porch above, driven out by the summer heat, taking the cooler air. She glanced down. She made a gesture.

At first he thought she was waving to him. He felt like a white explosion that had riveted her attention. But she was not waving. Her hand gestured and the next moment a pair of dark-framed glasses sat upon her nose. She gazed at him.

Ah, ah, he thought, so that's it. So! Even the blind may see this suit! He smiled up at her. He did not have to wave. And at last she smiled back. She did not have to wave either. Then, because he did not know what else to do and he could not get rid of this smile that had fastened itself to his cheeks, he hurried, almost ran, around the corner, feeling her stare after him. When he looked back she had taken off her glasses and gazed now with the look of the nearsighted at what, at most, must be a moving blob of light in the great darkness here. Then for good measure he went around the block again, through a city so suddenly beautiful he wanted to yell, then laugh, then yell again.

Returning, he drifted, oblivious, eyes half closed, and seeing him in the door, the others saw not Martínez but themselves come home. In that moment, they sensed that something had happened to them all.

"You're late!" cried Vamenos, but stopped. The spell could not be broken.

"Somebody tell me," said Martínez. "Who am I?"

He moved in a slow circle through the room.

Yes, he thought, yes, it's the suit, yes, it had to do with the suit and them all together in that store on this fine Saturday night and then here, laughing and feeling more drunk without drinking as Manulo said himself, as the night ran and each slipped on the pants and held, toppling, to the others and, balanced, let the feeling get bigger and warmer and finer as each man departed and the next took his place in the suit until now here stood Martínez all splendid and white as one who gives orders and the world grows quiet and moves aside.

"Martínez, we borrowed three mirrors while you were gone. Look!"

The mirrors, set up as in the store, angled to reflect three Martínezes and the echoes and memories of those who had occupied this suit with him and known the bright world inside this thread and cloth. Now, in the shimmering mirror, Martínez saw the enormity of this thing they were living together and his eyes grew wet. The others blinked. Martínez touched the mirrors. They shifted. He saw a thousand, a million white-armored Martínezes march off into eternity, reflected, re-reflected, forever, indomitable, and unending.

He held the white coat out on the air. In a trance, the others did not at first recognize the dirty hand that reached to take the coat. Then:

"Vamenos!"

"Pig!"

"You didn't wash!" cried Gómez. "Or even shave, while you waited! *Compadres,* the bath!"

"The bath!" said everyone.

"No!" Vamenos flailed. "The night air! I'm dead!"

They hustled him yelling out and down the hall.

Now here stood Vamenos, unbelievable in white suit, beard shaved, hair combed, nails scrubbed.

His friends scowled darkly at him.

For was it not true, thought Martínez, that when Vamenos passed by, avalanches itched on mountaintops? If he walked under windows, people spat, dumped garbage, or worse. Tonight now, this night, he would stroll beneath ten thousand wide-opened windows, near balconies, past alleys. Suddenly the world absolutely sizzled with flies. And here was Vamenos, a fresh-frosted cake.

"You sure look keen in that suit, Vamenos," said Manulo sadly.

"Thanks." Vamenos twitched, trying to make his skeleton comfortable where all their skeletons had so recently been. In a small voice Vamenos said, "Can I go now?"

"Villanazul!" said Gómez. "Copy down these rules."

Villanazul licked his pencil.

"First," said Gómez, "don't fall down in that suit, Vamenos!"

"I won't."

"Don't lean against buildings in that suit."

"No buildings."

"Don't walk under trees with birds in them in that suit. Don't smoke. Don't drink—"

"Please," said Vamenos, "can I *sit down* in this suit?"

"When in doubt, take the pants off, fold them over a chair."

"Wish me luck," said Vamenos.

"Go with God, Vamenos."

He went out. He shut the door.

There was a ripping sound.

"Vamenos!" cried Martínez.

He whipped the door open.

Vamenos stood with two halves of a handkerchief torn in his hands, laughing.

"Rrrip! Look at your faces! Rrrip!" He tore the cloth again. "Oh, oh, your faces, your faces! Ha!"

Roaring, Vamenos slammed the door, leaving them stunned and alone.

Gómez put both hands on top of his head and turned away. "Stone me. Kill me. I have sold our souls to a demon!"

Villanazul dug in his pockets, took out a silver coin, and studied it for a long while.

"Here is my last fifty cents. Who else will help me buy back Vamenos' share of the suit?"

"It's no use." Manulo showed them ten cents. "We got only enough to buy the lapels and the buttonholes."

Gómez, at the open window, suddenly leaned out and yelled. "Vamenos! No!"

Below on the street, Vamenos, shocked, blew out a match and threw away an old cigar butt he had found somewhere. He made a strange gesture to all the men in the window above, then waved airily and sauntered on.

Somehow, the five men could not move away from the window. They were crushed together there.

"I bet he eats a hamburger in that suit," mused Villanazul. "I'm thinking of the mustard."

"Don't!" cried Gómez. "No, no!"

Manulo was suddenly at the door.

"I need a drink, bad."

"Manulo, there's wine here, that bottle on the floor—"

Manulo went out and shut the door.

A moment later Villanazul stretched with great exaggeration and strolled about the room.

"I think I'll walk down to the plaza, friends."

He was not gone a minute when Domínguez, waving his black book at the others, winked and turned the doorknob.

"Domínguez," said Gómez.

"Yes?"

"If you see Vamenos, by accident," said Gómez, "warn him away from Mickey Murrillo's Red Rooster Café. They got fights not only *on* TV but *out front* of the TV too."

"He wouldn't go into Murrillo's," said Domínguez. "That suit means too much to Vamenos. He wouldn't do anything to hurt it."

"He'd shoot his mother first," said Martínez.

"Sure he would."

Martínez and Gómez, alone, listened to Domínguez's footsteps hurry away down the stairs. They circled the undressed window dummy.

For a long while, biting his lips, Gómez stood at the window, looking out. He touched his shirt pocket twice, pulled his hand away, and then at last pulled something from the pocket. Without looking at it, he handed it to Martínez.

"Martínez, take this."

"What is it?"

Martínez looked at the piece of folded pink paper with print on it, with names and numbers. His eyes widened.

"A ticket on the bus to El Paso three weeks from now!"

Gómez nodded. He couldn't look at Martínez. He stared out into the summer night.

"Turn it in. Get the money," he said. "Buy us a nice white panama hat and a pale blue tie to go with the white ice cream suit, Martínez. Do that."

"Gómez—"

"Shut up. Boy, is it hot in here! I need air."

"Gómez. I am touched. Gómez—"

But the door stood open. Gómez was gone.

Mickey Murrillo's Red Rooster Café and Cocktail Lounge was squashed between two big brick buildings and, being narrow, had to be deep. Outside, serpents of red and sulphur-green neon fizzed and snapped. Inside, dim shapes loomed and swam away to lose themselves in a swarming night sea.

Martínez, on tiptoe, peeked through a flaked place on the red-painted front window.

He felt a presence on his left, heard breathing on his right. He glanced in both directions.

"Manulo! Villanazul!"

"I decided I wasn't thirsty," said Manulo. "So I took a walk."

"I was just on my way to the plaza," said Villanazul, "and decided to go the long way around."

As if by agreement, the three men shut up now and turned together to peer on tiptoe through various flaked spots on the window.

A moment later, all three felt a new very warm presence behind them and heard still faster breathing.

"Is our white suit in there?" asked Gómez's voice.

"Gómez!" said everybody, surprised. "Hi!"

"Yes!" cried Domínguez, having just arrived to find his own peephole. "There's the suit! And, praise God, Vamenos is still *in* it!"

"I can't see!" Gómez squinted, shielding his eyes. "What's he *doing*?"

Martínez peered. Yes! There, way back in the shadows, was a big chunk of snow and the idiot smile of Vamenos winking above it, wreathed in smoke.

"He's smoking!" said Martínez.

"He's drinking!" said Domínguez.

"He's eating a taco!" reported Villanazul.

"A *juicy* taco," added Manulo.

"No," said Gómez. "No, no, no. . . ."

"Ruby Escuadrillo's with him!"

"Let me see that!" Gómez pushed Martínez aside.

Yes, there was Ruby! Two hundred pounds of glittering sequins and tight black satin on the hoof, her scarlet fingernails clutching Vamenos' shoulder. Her cowlike face, floured with powder, greasy with lipstick, hung over him!

"That hippo!" said Domínguez. "She's crushing the shoulder pads. Look, she's going to sit on his lap!"

"No, no, not with all that powder and lipstick!" said Gómez. "Manulo, inside! Grab that drink! Villanazul, the cigar, the taco! Domínguez, date Ruby Escuadrillo, get her away. *Ándale*, men!"

The three vanished, leaving Gómez and Martínez to stare, gasping, through the peephole.

"Manulo, he's got the drink, he's *drinking* it!"

"*Ay!* There's Villanazul, he's got the cigar, he's eating the taco!"

"Hey, Domínguez, he's got Ruby! What a *brave* one!"

A shadow bulked through Murrillo's front door, traveling fast.

"Gómez!" Martínez clutched Gómez's arm. "That was Ruby Escuadrillo's boy friend, Toro Ruíz. If he finds her with Vamenos, the ice cream suit will be covered with blood, *covered* with blood—"

"Don't make me nervous," said Gómez. "Quickly!"

Both ran. Inside they reached Vamenos just as Toro Ruíz grabbed about two feet of the lapels of that wonderful ice cream suit.

"Let go of Vamenos!" said Martínez.

"Let go that *suit*!" corrected Gómez.

Toro Ruíz, tap-dancing Vamenos, leered at these intruders.

Villanazul stepped up shyly.

Villanazul smiled. "Don't hit him. Hit me."

Toro Ruíz hit Villanazul smack on the nose.

Villanazul, holding his nose, tears stinging his eyes, wandered off.

Gómez grabbed one of Toro Ruíz's arms, Martínez the other.

"Drop him, let go, *cabrón, coyote, vaca!*"

Toro Ruíz twisted the ice cream suit material until all six men screamed in mortal agony. Grunting, sweating, Toro Ruíz dislodged as many as climbed on. He was winding up to hit Vamenos when Villanazul wandered back, eyes streaming.

"Don't hit him. Hit me!"

As Toro Ruíz hit Villanazul on the nose, a chair crashed on Toro's head.

"*Ai!*" said Gómez.

Toro Ruíz swayed, blinking, debating whether to fall. He began to drag Vamenos with him.

"Let go!" cried Gómez. "Let go!"

One by one, with great care, Toro Ruíz's banana-like fingers let loose of the suit. A moment later he was ruins at their feet.

"*Compadres,* this way!"

They ran Vamenos outside and set him down where he freed himself of their hands with injured dignity.

"Okay, okay. My time ain't up. I still got two minutes and, let's see—ten seconds."

"What!" said everybody.

"Vamenos," said Gómez, "you let a Guadalajara cow climb on you, you pick fights, you smoke, you drink, you eat tacos, and *now* you have the nerve to say your time ain't up?"

"I got two minutes and one second left!"

"Hey, Vamenos, you sure look sharp!" Distantly, a woman's voice called from across the street.

Vamenos smiled and buttoned the coat.

"It's Ramona Alvarez! Ramona, wait!" Vamenos stepped off the curb.

"Vamenos," pleaded Gómez. "What can you do in one minute and"—he checked his watch—"forty seconds!"

"Watch! Hey, Ramona!"

Vamenos loped.

"Vamenos, look out!"

Vamenos, surprised, whirled, saw a car, heard the shriek of brakes.

"No," said all five men on the sidewalk.

Martínez heard the impact and flinched. His head moved up. It looks like white laundry, he thought, flying through the air. His head came down.

Now he heard himself and each of the men make a different sound. Some swallowed too much air. Some let it out. Some choked. Some groaned. Some cried aloud for justice. Some covered their faces. Martínez felt his own fist pounding his heart in agony. He could not move his feet.

"I don't want to live," said Gómez quietly. "Kill me, someone."

Then, shuffling, Martínez looked down and told his feet to walk, stagger, follow one after the other. He collided with other men. Now they were trying to run. They ran at last and somehow crossed a street like a deep river through which they could only wade, to look down at Vamenos.

"Vamenos!" said Martínez. "You're alive!"

Strewn on his back, mouth open, eyes squeezed tight, tight, Vamenos motioned his head back and forth, back and forth, moaning.

"Tell me, tell me, oh, tell me, tell me."

"Tell you what, Vamenos?"

Vamenos clenched his fists, ground his teeth.

"The suit, what have I done to the suit, the suit, the suit!"

The men crouched lower.

"Vamenos, it's . . . why, it's *okay*!"

"You lie!" said Vamenos. "It's torn, it must be, it must be, it's torn, all around, *underneath*?"

"No." Martínez knelt and touched here and there. "Vamenos, all around, underneath even, it's okay!"

Vamenos opened his eyes to let the tears run free at last. "A miracle," he sobbed. "Praise the saints!" He quieted at last. "The car?"

"Hit and run." Gómez suddenly remembered and glared at the empty street. "It's good he didn't stop. We'd have—"

Everyone listened.

Distantly a siren wailed.

"Someone phoned for an ambulance."

"Quick!" said Vamenos, eyes rolling. "Set me up! Take off our coat!"

"Vamenos—"

"Shut up, idiots!" cried Vamenos. "The coat, that's it! Now, the pants, the pants, quick, quick, *peónes*! Those doctors! You seen movies? They rip the pants with razors to get them off! They don't *care*! They're maniacs! Ah, God, quick, quick!"

The siren screamed.

The men, panicking, all handled Vamenos at once.

"Right leg, *easy,* hurry, cows! Good! Left leg, now, left, you hear, there, easy, *easy!* Ow, God! Quick! Martínez, your pants, take them off!"

"What?" Martínez froze.

The siren shrieked.

"Fool!" wailed Vamenos. "All is lost! Your pants! Give me!"

Martínez jerked at his belt buckle.

"Close in, make a circle!"

Dark pants, light pants flourished on the air.

"Quick, here come the maniacs with the razors! Right leg on, left leg, *there!*"

"The zipper, cows, zip my zipper!" babbled Vamenos.

The siren died.

"Madre mía, yes, just in time! They arrive." Vamenos lay back down and shut his eyes. *"Gracias."*

Martínez turned, nonchalantly buckling on the white pants as the interns brushed past.

"Broken leg," said one intern as they moved Vamenos onto a stretcher.

"Compadres," said Vamenos, "don't be mad with me."

Gómez snorted. "Who's mad?"

In the ambulance, head tilted back, looking out at them upside down, Vamenos faltered.

"Compadres, when . . . when I come from the hospital . . . am I still in the bunch? You won't kick me out? Look, I'll give up smoking, keep away from Murrillo's, swear off women—"

"Vamenos," said Martínez gently, "don't promise nothing."

Vamenos, upside down, eyes brimming wet, saw Martínez there, all white now against the stars.

"Oh, Martínez, you sure look great in that suit. *Compadres,* don't he look *beautiful?*"

Villanazul climbed in beside Vamenos. The door slammed. The four remaining men watched the ambulance drive away.

Then, surrounded by his friends, inside the white suit, Martínez was carefully escorted back to the curb.

In the tenement, Martínez got out the cleaning fluid and the others stood around, telling him how to clean the suit and, later, how not to have the iron too hot and how to work the lapels and the crease and all. When the suit was cleaned and pressed so it looked like a fresh gardenia just opened, they fitted it to the dummy.

"Two o'clock," murmured Villanazul. "I hope Vamenos sleeps well. When I left him at the hospital, he looked good."

Manulo cleared his throat. "Nobody else is going out with that suit tonight, huh?"

The others glared at him.

Manulo flushed. "I mean . . . it's late. We're tired. Maybe no one will use the suit for forty-eight hours, huh? Give it a rest. Sure. Well. Where do we sleep?"

The night being still hot and the room unbearable, they carried the suit on its dummy out and down the hall. They brought with them also some pillows and blankets. They climbed the stairs toward the roof of the tenement. There, thought Martínez, is the cooler wind, and sleep.

On the way, they passed a dozen doors that stood open, people still perspiring and awake, playing cards, drinking pop, fanning themselves with movie magazines.

I wonder, thought Martínez. I wonder if—Yes!

On the fourth floor, a certain door stood open.

The beautiful girl looked up as the men passed. She wore glasses and when she saw Martínez she snatched them off and hid them under her book.

The others went on, not knowing they had lost Martínez, who seemed stuck fast in the open door.

For a long moment he could say nothing. Then he said:

"José Martínez."

And she said:

"Celia Obregón."

And then both said nothing.

He heard the men moving up on the tenement roof. He moved to follow.

She said quickly, "I saw you tonight!"

He came back.

"The suit," he said.

"The suit," she said, and paused. "But not the suit."

"Eh?" he said.

She lifted the book to show the glasses lying in her lap. She touched the glasses.

"I do not see well. You would think I would wear my glasses, but no. I walk around for years now, hiding them, seeing nothing. But tonight, even without the glasses, I see. A great whiteness passes below in the dark. So white! And I put on my glasses quickly!"

"The suit, as I said," said Martínez.

"The suit for a little moment, yes, but there is another whiteness above the suit."

"Another?"

"Your teeth! Oh, such white teeth, and so many!"

Martínez put his hand over his mouth.

"So happy, Mr. Martínez," she said. "I've not often seen such a happy face and such a smile."

"Ah," he said, not able to look at her, his face flushing now.

"So, you see," she said quietly, "the suit caught my eye, yes, the whiteness filled the night below. But the teeth were much whiter. Now, I have forgotten the suit."

Martínez flushed again. She, too, was overcome with what she had said. She put her glasses on her nose, and then took them off, nervously, and hid them again. She looked at her hands and at the door above his head.

"May I—" he said, at last.

"May you—"

"May I call for you," he asked, "When next the suit is mine to wear?"

"Why must you wait for the suit?" she said.

"I thought—"

"You do not need the suit," she said.

"But—"

"If it were just the suit," she said, "anyone would be fine in it. But no, I watched. I saw many men in that suit, all different, this night. So again I say, you do not need to wait for the suit."

"*Madre mía, madre mía!*" he cried happily. And then, quieter, "I will need the suit for a little while. A month, six months, a year. I am uncertain. I am fearful of many things. I am young."

"That is as it should be," she said.

"Good night, Miss—"

"Celia Obregón."

"Celia Obregón," he said, and was gone from the door.

The others were waiting on the roof of the tenement. Coming up through the trapdoor, Martínez saw they had placed the dummy and the suit in the center of the roof and put their blankets and pillows in a circle around it. Now they were lying down. Now a cooler night wind was blowing here, up in the sky.

Martínez stood alone by the white suit, smoothing the lapels, talking half to himself.

"Ay, *caramba,* what a night! Seems ten years since seven o'clock, when it all started and I had no friends. Two in the morning. I got all *kinds* of friends. . . ." He paused and thought, Celia Obregón, Celia Obregón. ". . . all kinds of friends," he went on. "I got a room, I got clothes. You tell *me.* You know what?" He looked around at the men lying on the rooftop, surrounding the dummy and himself. "It's funny. When I wear this suit, I know I will win at pool, like Gómez. A woman will look at me like Domínguez. I will be able to sing like Manulo, sweetly. I will talk fine politics like Villanazul. I'm strong as Vamenos. So? So, tonight, I am more than Martínez. I am Gómez, Manulo, Domínguez, Villanazul, Vamenos. I am everyone. Ay . . . ay . . ." He stood a moment longer by this suit which could save all the ways they sat or stood or walked. This suit which could move fast and nervous like Gómez or slow and thoughtfully like Villanazul or drift like Domínguez, who never touched ground, who always found a wind to take him somewhere. This suit which belonged to them but which also owned them all. This suit that was—what? A parade.

"Martínez," said Gómez. "You going to sleep?"

"Sure. I'm just thinking."

"What?"

"If we ever get rich," said Martínez softly, "it'll be kind of sad. Then we'll all have suits. And there won't be no more nights like tonight. It'll break up the old gang. It'll never be the same after that."

The men lay thinking of what had just been said.

Gómez nodded gently.

"Yeah . . . it'll never be the same . . . after that."

Martínez lay down on his blanket. In darkness, with the others, he faced the middle of the roof and the dummy, which was the center of their lives.

And their eyes were bright, shining, and good to see in the dark as the neon lights from nearby buildings flicked on, flicked off, flicked on, flicked off, revealing and then vanishing, revealing and then vanishing, their wonderful white vanilla ice cream summer suit.

DISCUSSION

1 What is the setting of the story?
2 What do we learn about the men in the first part of the story?
3 Why are the men so close to being defeated by life?
4 What plan has Gómez to help them? How long has he been working on the plan?
5 Why is Vamenos included in the plan?
6 How do the comical scenes help the story?
7 When will each man wear the suit?
8 How does wearing the suit affect each man?
9 What is the climax?
10 How does Bradbury's style help the story?
11 What does Martínez discover?
12 What do they all learn?

THE CONVERT
Lerone Bennett, Jr.

A man don't know what he'll do, a man don't know what he is till he gets his back pressed up against a wall. Now you take Aaron Lott: there ain't no other way to explain the crazy thing he did. He was going alone fine, preaching the gospel, saving souls, and getting along with the white folks; and then, all of a sudden, he felt wood pressing against his back. The funny thing was that nobody knew he was hurting till he preached that Red Sea sermon where he got mixed up and seemed to think Mississippi was Egypt. As chairman of the

SOURCE NOTE: Copyright © 1963 by *Negro Digest.* Reprinted by permission.

deacons board, I felt it was my duty to reason with him. I appreciated his position and told him so, but I didn't think it was right for him to push us all in a hole. The old fool—he just laughed.

"Brother Booker," he said, "the Lord—He'll take care of me."

I knew then that that man was heading for trouble. And the very next thing he did confirmed it. The white folks called the old fool downtown to bear witness that the colored folks were happy. And you know what he did: he got down there amongst all them big white folks and he said: "Things ain't gonna change here overnight, but they gonna change. It's inevitable. The Lord wants it."

Well sir, you could have bought them white folks for a penny. Aaron Lott, pastor of the Rock of Zion Baptist Church, a man white folks had said was wise and sound and sensible, had come close—too close—to saying that the Supreme Court was coming to Melina, Mississippi. The surprising thing was that the white folks didn't do nothing. There was a lot of mumbling and whispering but nothing bad happened till the terrible morning when Aaron came a-knocking at the door of my funeral home. Now things had been tightening up—you could feel it in the air—and I didn't want no part of no crazy scheme and I told him so right off. He walked on past me and sat down on the couch. He had on his preaching clothes, a shiny blue suit, a fresh starched white shirt, a black tie, and his Sunday black shoes. I remember thinking at the time that Aaron was too black to be wearing all them dark clothes. The thought tickled me and I started to smile but then I noticed something about him that didn't seem quite right. I ran my eyes over him closely. He was kinda middle-sized and he had a big clean-shaven head, a big nose, and thin lips. I stood there looking at him for a long time but I couldn't figure out what it was till I looked at his eyes; they were burning bright, like bulbs do just before they go out. And yet he looked contented, like his mind was resting somewheres else.

"I wanna talk with you, Booker," he said, glancing sideways at my wife. "If you don't mind, Sister Brown—"

Sarah got up and went into the living quarters. Aaron didn't say nothing for a long time; he just sat there looking out the window. Then he spoke so soft I had to strain my ears to hear.

"I'm leaving for the Baptist convention," he said. He pulled out his gold watch and looked at it. "Train leaves in 'bout two hours."

"I know *that,* Aaron."

"Yeah, but what I wanted to tell you was that I ain't going Jim Crow. I'm going first class, Booker, right through the white waiting room. That's the law."

A cold shiver ran through me.

"Aaron," I said, "don't you go talking crazy now."

The old fool laughed, a great big body-shaking laugh. He started talking 'bout God and Jesus and all that stuff. Now, I'm a God-fearing man myself, but I holds that God helps those who help themselves. I told him so.

"You can't mix God up with these white folks," I said. "When you start to messing around with segregation, they'll burn you up and the Bible, too."

He looked at me like I was Satan.

"I sweated over this thing," he said. "I prayed. I got down on my knees and I asked God not to give me this cup. But He said I was the one. I heard Him, Booker, right here—he tapped his chest—in my heart."

The old fool's been having visions, I thought. I sat down and tried to figure out a way to hold him, but he got up, without saying a word, and started for the door.

"Wait!" I shouted. "I'll get my coat."

"I don't need you," he said. "I just came by to tell you so you could tell the board in case something happened."

"You wait," I shouted, and ran out of the room to get my coat.

We got in his beat-up old Ford and went by the parsonage to get his suitcase. Rachel—that was his wife—and Jonah were sitting in the living room, wringing their hands. Aaron got his bag, shook Jonah's hand, and said, "Take care of your Mamma, boy." Jonah nodded. Aaron hugged Rachel and pecked at her cheek. Rachel broke down. She throwed her arms around his neck and carried on something awful. Aaron shoved her away.

"Don't go making no fuss over it, woman. I ain't gonna be gone forever. Can't a man go to a church meeting 'thout women screaming and crying."

He tried to make light of it, but you could see he was touched by the way his lips trembled. He held his hand out to me, but I wouldn't take it. I told him off good, told him it was a sin and a shame for a man of God to be carrying on like he was, worrying his wife and everything.

"I'm coming with you," I said. "Somebody's gotta see that you don't make a fool of yourself."

He shrugged, picked up his suitcase, and started for the door. Then he stopped and turned around and looked at his wife and his boy and from the way he looked I knew that there was still a chance. He looked at the one and then at the other. For a moment there, I thought he was going to cry, but he turned, quick-like, and walked out of the door.

I ran after him and tried to talk some sense in his head. But he shook me off, turned the corner, and went on up Adams Street. I caught up with him and we walked in silence, crossing the street in front of the First Baptist Church for whites, going on around the Confederate monument where, once, they hung a boy for fooling around with white women.

"Put it off, Aaron," I begged. "Sleep on it."

He didn't say nothing.

"What you need is a vacation. I'll get the board to approve, full pay and everything."

He smiled and shifted the suitcase over to his left hand. Big drops of sweat were running down his face and spotting up his shirt. His eyes were awful, all lit up and burning.

"Aaron, Aaron, can't you hear me?"

We passed the feed store, Bill Williams' grocery store, and the movie house.

"A man's gotta think about his family, Aaron. A man ain't free. Didn't you say that once, didn't you?"

He shaded his eyes with his hand and looked into the sun. He put the suitcase on the ground and checked his watch.

"Why don't you think about Jonah?" I asked. "Answer that. Why don't you think about your own son?"

"I am," he said. "That's exactly what I'm doing, thinking about Jonah. Matter of fact, he started *me* to thinking. I ain't never mentioned it before, but the boy's been worrying me. One day we was downtown here and he asked me something that hurt. 'Daddy,' he said, 'how come you ain't a man?' I got mad, I did, and told him: 'I am a man.' He said that wasn't what he meant. 'I mean,' he said, 'how come you ain't a man where white folks concerned.' I couldn't answer him, Booker. I'll never forget it till the day I die. I couldn't answer my own son, and I been preaching forty years."·

"He don't know nothing 'bout it," I said. "He's hot-headed, like my boy. He'll find out when he grows up."

"I hopes not," Aaron said, shaking his head. "I hopes not."

Some white folks passed and we shut up till they were out of hearing. Aaron, who was acting real strange, looked up in the sky and moved his lips. He came back to himself, after a little bit, and he said: "This thing of being a man, Booker, is a big thing. The Supreme Court can't make you a man. The NAACP can't do it. God Almighty can do a lot, but even He can't do it. Ain't nobody can do it but you."

He said that like he was preaching and when he got through he was all filled up with emotion and he seemed kind of ashamed—he was a man who didn't like emotion outside the church. He looked at his watch, picked up his bag, and said, "Well, let's git it over with."

We turned into Elm and the first thing I saw at the end of the Street was the train station. It was an old red building, flat like a slab. A group of white men were fooling around in front of the door. I couldn't make them out from that distance, but I could tell they weren't the kind of white folks to be fooling around with.

We walked on, passing the dry goods store, the barber shop, and the new building that was going up. Across the street from that was the sheriff's office. I looked in the window and saw Bull Sampson sitting at his desk, his feet propped up on a chair, a fat brown cigar sticking out of his mouth. A ball about the size of a sweet potato started burning in my stomach.

"Please Aaron," I said. "Please. You can't get away with it. I know how you feel. Sometimes I feel the same way myself, but I wouldn't risk my neck to do nothing for these niggers. They won't appreciate it; they'll laugh at you."

We were almost to the station and I could make out the faces of the men sitting on the benches. One of them must have been telling a joke. He finished and the group broke out laughing.

I whispered to Aaron: "I'm through with it. I wash my hands of the whole mess."

I don't know whether he heard me or not. He turned to the right without saying a word and went on in the front door. The string-beany man who told the joke was so shocked that his cigarette fell out of his mouth.

"Y'all see that," he said. "Why, I'll—"

"Shut up," another man said. "Go git Bull."

I kept walking fast, turned at the corner, and ran around to the colored waiting room. When I got in there, I looked through the ticket window and saw Aaron standing in front of the clerk. Aaron stood there for a minute or more, but the clerk didn't see him. And that took some not seeing. In that room, Aaron Lott stood out like a pig in a chicken coop.

There were, I'd say, about ten or fifteen people in there, but didn't none of them move. They just sat there, with their eyes glued on Aaron's back. Aaron cleared his throat. The clerk didn't look up; he got real busy with some papers. Aaron cleared his throat again and opened his mouth to speak. The screen door of the waiting room opened and clattered shut.

It got real quiet in that room, hospital quiet. It got so quiet I could hear my own heart beating. Now Aaron knew who opened that door, but he didn't bat an eyelid. He turned around real slow and faced High Sheriff Sampson, the baddest man in South Mississippi.

Mr. Sampson stood there with his legs wide open, like the men you see on television. His beefy face was blood-red and his gray eyes were rattlesnake hard. He was mad; no doubt about it. I had never seen him so mad.

"Preacher," he said, "you done gone crazy?" He was talking low-like and mean.

"Nosir," Aaron said. "Nosir, Mr. Sampson."

"What you think you doing?"

"Going to St. Louis, Mr. Sampson."

"You must done lost yo' mind, boy."

Mr. Sampson started walking towards Aaron with his hand on his gun. Twenty to thirty men pushed through the front door and fanned out over the room. Mr. Sampson stopped about two paces from Aaron and looked him up and down. That look had paralyzed hundreds of niggers; but it didn't faze Aaron none—he stood his ground.

"I'm gonna give you a chance, preacher. Git on over to the nigger side and git quick."

"I ain't bothering nobody, Mr. Sampson."

Somebody in the crowd yelled: "Don't reason wit' the nigger, Bull. Hit 'em."

Mr. Sampson walked up to Aaron and grabbed him in the collar and throwed him up against the ticket counter. He pulled out his gun.

"Did you hear me, deacon. I said, 'Git.'"

"I'm going to St. Louis, Mr. Sampson. That's cross state lines. The court done said—"

Aaron didn't have a chance. The blow came from nowhere. Laying there on the floor with blood spurting from his mouth, Aaron looked up at Mr. Sampson and he did another crazy thing: he grinned. Bull Sampson jumped up in the air and came down on Aaron with all his two hundred pounds. It made a crunchy sound. He jumped again and the mob, maddened by the blood and heat, moved in to help him. They fell on Aaron like mad dogs. They beat him with chairs; they beat him with sticks; they beat him with guns.

Till this day, I don't know what come over me. The first thing I know I was running and then I was standing in the middle of the white waiting room. Mr. Sampson was the first to see me. He backed off, cocked his pistol, and said: "Booker, boy, you come one mo' step and I'll kill you. What's a matter with you niggers today? All y'all gone crazy?"

"Please don't kill him," I begged. "You ain't got no call to treat him like that."

"So you saw it all, did you? Well, then, Booker you musta saw the nigger preacher reach for my gun?"

"He didn't do that, Mr. Sampson," I said. "He didn't—"

Mr. Sampson put a big hairy hand on my tie and pulled me to him.

"Booker," he said sweetly. "You saw the nigger preacher reach for my gun, didn't you?"

I didn't open my mouth—I couldn't I was so scared—but I guess my eyes answered for me. Whatever Mr. Sampson saw there musta convinced him 'cause he throwed me on the floor besides Aaron.

"Git this nigger out of here," he said, "and be quick about it."

Dropping to my knees, I put my hand on Aaron's chest; I didn't feel nothing. I felt his wrist; I didn't feel nothing. I got up and looked at them white folks with tears in my eyes. I looked at the women, sitting crying on the benches. I looked at the men. I looked at Mr. Sampson. I said, "He was a good man."

Mr. Sampson said, "Move the nigger."

A big sigh came out of me and I wrung my hands.

Mr. Sampson said, "Move the nigger."

He grabbed my tie and twisted it, but I didn't feel nothing. My eyes were glued to his hands; there was blood under the fingernails, and the fingers—they looked like fat little red sausages. I screamed and Mr. Sampson flung me down on the floor.

He said, *"Move the nigger."*

I picked Aaron up and fixed his body over my shoulder and carried him outside. I sent for one of my boys and we dressed him up and put him away real nice-like and Rachel and the boy came and they cried and carried on and yet, somehow, they seemed prouder of Aaron than ever before. And the colored folks—they seemed proud, too. Crazy niggers. Didn't they know? Couldn't they see? It hadn't done no good. In fact, things got worse. The Northern newspapers started kicking up a stink and Mr. Rivers, the solicitor, announced they were going to hold a hearing. All of a sudden, Booker Taliaferro Brown became the biggest man in that town. My phone rang day and night; I got threats, I got promises, and I was offered bribes. Everywhere I turned somebody was waiting to ask me: "Whatcha gonna do? Whatcha gonna say?" To tell the truth, I didn't know myself. One day I would decide one thing and the next day I would decide another.

It was Mr. Rivers and Mr. Sampson who called my attention to that. They came to my office one day and called me a shifty, no-good nigger. They said they expected me to stand by "my statement" in the train station that I saw Aaron reach for the gun. I hadn't said no such thing, but Mr. Sampson said I said it and he said he had witnesses who heard me say it. "And if you say anything else," he said, "I can't be responsible for your health. Now you know"—he put that bloody hand on my shoulder and he smiled his sweet death smile—"you *know* I wouldn't threaten you, but the boys"—he shook his head—"the boys are real worked up over this one."

It was long about then that I began to hate Aaron Lott. I'm ashamed to admit it now, but it's true: I hated him. He had lived his life; he had made his choice. Why should he live my life, too, and make me choose? It wasn't fair; it wasn't right; it wasn't Christian. What made me so mad was the fact that nothing I said would help Aaron. He was dead and it wouldn't help one whit for me to say that he didn't reach for that gun. I tried to explain that to Rachel when she came to my office, moaning and crying, the night before the hearing.

"Listen to me, woman," I said. "Listen. Aaron was a good man. He lived a good life. He did a lot of good things, but he's *dead, dead, dead!* Nothing I say will bring him back. Bull Sampson's got ten niggers who are going to swear on a stack of Bibles that they saw Aaron reach for that gun. It won't do me or you or Aaron no good for me to swear otherwise."

What did I say that for? That woman liked to had a fit. She got down on her knees and she begged me to go with Aaron.

"Go wit' him," she cried. "Booker. *Booker!* If you's a man, if you's a father, if you's a friend, go wit' Aaron."

That woman tore my heart up. I ain't never heard nobody beg like that.

"Tell the truth, Booker," she said. "That's all I'm asking. Tell the truth."

"Truth!" I said. "Hah! That's all you niggers talk about: truth. What do you know about truth? Truth is eating good and sleeping good. Truth is living, Rachel. Be loyal to the living."

Rachel backed off from me. You would have thought that I had cursed her or something. She didn't say nothing; she just stood there pressed against the door. She stood there saying nothing for so long that my nerves snapped.

"Say something," I shouted. "Say something—anything!"

She shook her head, slowly at first, and then her head started moving like it wasn't attached to her body. It went back and forth, back and forth, back and forth. I started towards her, but she jerked open the door and ran out into the night, screaming.

That did it. I ran across the room to the filing cabinet, the bottom drawer, and took out a dusty bottle of Scotch. I started drinking, but the more I drank the soberer I got. I guess I fell asleep 'cause I dreamed I buried Rachel and that everything went along fine until she jumped out of the casket and started screaming. I came awake with a start and knocked over the bottle. I reached for a rag and my hand stopped in midair.

"Of course," I said out loud and slammed my fist down on the Scotch-soaked papers.

I didn't see nothing.

Why didn't I think of it before?

I didn't see nothing.

Jumping up, I walked to and fro in the office. Would it work? I rehearsed it in my mind. All I could see was Aaron's back. I don't know whether he reached for the gun or not. All I know is that *for some reason* the men beat him to death.

Rehearsing the thing in my mind, I felt a great weight slip off my shoulders. I did a little jig in the middle of the floor and went upstairs to my bed, whistling. Sarah turned over and looked me up and down.

"What you happy about?"

"Can't a man be happy?" I asked.

She sniffed the air, said, "Oh," turned over, and mumbled something in her pillow. It came to me then for the first time that she was 'bout the only person in town who hadn't asked me what I was going to do. I thought about it for a little while, shrugged, and fell into bed with all my clothes on.

When I woke up the next morning, I had a terrible headache and my tongue was a piece of sandpaper. For a long while, I couldn't figure out what I was doing laying there with all my clothes on. Then it came to me: this was the big day. I put on my black silk suit, the one I wore for big funerals, and went downstairs to breakfast. I walked into the dining room without looking and bumped into Russell, the last person in the world I wanted to see. He was my only child, but he didn't act like it. He was always finding fault. He didn't like the way I talked to Negroes; he didn't like the way I talked to white folks. He didn't like this; he didn't like that. And to top it off, the young whippersnapper wanted to be an artist. Undertaking wasn't good enough for him. He wanted to paint pictures.

I sat down and grunted.

"Good morning, Papa." He said it like he meant it. He wants something, I thought, looking him over closely, noticing that his right eye was swollen.

"You been fighting again, boy?"

"Yes, Papa."

"You younguns. Education—that's what it is. Education! It's ruining you."

He didn't say nothing. He just sat there, looking down when I looked up and looking up when I looked down. This went on through the grits and the eggs and the second cup of coffee.

"Whatcha looking at?" I asked.

"Nothing, Papa."

"Whatcha thinking?"

"Nothing, Papa."

"You lying, boy. It's written all over your face."

He didn't say nothing.

I dismissed him with a wave of my hand, picked up the paper, and turned to the sports page.

"What are you going to do, Papa?"

The question caught me unawares. I know now that I was expecting it, that I wanted him to ask it; but he put it so bluntly that I was flabbergasted. I pretended I didn't understand.

"Do 'bout what, boy? Speak up!"

"About the trial, Papa."

I didn't say nothing for a long time. There wasn't much, in fact, I could say; so I got mad.

"Questions, questions, questions," I shouted. "That's all I get in this house—questions. You never have a civil word for your pa. I go out of here and work my tail off and you keep yourself shut up in that room of yours looking at them fool books and now soon as your old man gets his back against the wall you join the pack. I expected better than that of you, boy. A son ought to back his pa."

That hurt him. He picked up the coffee pot and poured himself another cup of coffee and his hand trembled. He took a sip and watched me over the rim.

"They say you are going to chicken out, Papa."

"Chicken out? What that mean?"

"They're betting you'll 'Tom.'"

I leaned back in the chair and took a sip of coffee.

"So they're betting, huh?" The idea appealed to me. "Crazy niggers—they'd bet on a funeral."

I saw pain on his face. He sighed and said: "I bet, too, Papa."

The cup fell out of my hand and broke, spilling black water over the table-cloth.

"You did what?"

"I bet you wouldn't 'Tom.'"

"You little fool." I fell out laughing and then I stopped suddenly and looked at him closely. "How much you bet?"

"One hundred dollars."

I stood up.

"You're lying," I said. "Where'd you get that kind of money?"

"From Mamma."

"Sarah!" I shouted. "Sarah! You get in here. What kind of house you running, sneaking behind my back, giving this boy money to gamble with?"

Sarah leaned against the door jamb. She was in her hot iron mood. There was no expression on her face. And her eyes were hard.

"I gave it to him, Booker," she said. "They called you an Uncle Tom. He got in a fight about it. He wanted to bet on you, Booker. *He* believes in you."

Suddenly I felt old and used up. I pulled a chair to me and sat down.

"Please," I said, waving my hand. "Please. Go away. Leave me alone. Please."

I sat there for maybe ten or fifteen minutes, thinking, praying. The phone rang. It was Mr. Withers, the president of the bank. I had put in for a loan and it had been turned down, but Mr. Withers said there'd been a mistake. "New fellow, you know," he said, clucking his tongue. He said he knew that it was my lifelong dream to build a modern funeral home and to buy a Cadillac hearse. He said he sympathized with that dream, supported it, thought the town needed it, and thought I deserved it. "The loan will go through," he said. "Drop by and see me this morning after the hearing."

When I put that phone down, it was wet with sweat. I couldn't turn that new funeral home down and Mr. Withers knew it. My father had raised me on that dream and before he died he made me swear on a Bible that I would make it good. And here it was on a platter, just for a word, a word that wouldn't hurt nobody.

I put on my hat and hurried to the courthouse. When they called my name, I walked in with my head held high. The courtroom was packed. The white folks had all the seats and the colored folks were standing in the rear. Whoever arranged the seating had set aside the first two rows for white men. They were sitting almost on top of each other, looking mean and uncomfortable in their best white shirts.

I walked up to the bench and swore on the Bible and took a seat. Mr. Rivers gave me a little smile and waited for me to get myself set.

"State your name," he said.

"Booker Taliaferro Brown." I took a quick look at the first two rows and recognized at least ten of the men who killed Aaron.

"And your age?"

"Fifty-seven."

"You're an undertaker?"

"Yessir."

"You been living in this town all your life?"

"Yessir."

"You like it here, don't you, Booker?"

Was this a threat? I looked Mr. Rivers in the face for the first time. He smiled. I told the truth. I said, "Yessir."

"Now, calling your attention to the day of May 17th, did anything unusual happen on that day?"

The question threw me. I shook my head. Then it dawned on me. He was talking about—

"Yessir," I said. "That's the day Aaron got—" Something in Mr. Rivers' face warned me and I pulled up—"that's the day of the trouble at the train station."

Mr. Rivers smiled. He looked like a trainer who'd just put a monkey through a new trick. You could feel the confidence and the contempt oozing out of him. I looked at his prissy little mustache and his smiling lips and I got mad. Lifting my head a little bit, I looked him full in the eyes; I held the eyes for a moment and I tried to tell the man behind the eyes that I was a man like him and that he didn't have no right to be using me and laughing about it. But he didn't get the message. The bastard—he chuckled softly, turned his back to me, and faced the audience.

"I believe you were with the preacher that day."

The water was getting deep. I scroonched down in my seat, closed the lids of my eyes, and looked dense.

"Yessir, Mr. Rivers," I drawled. "Ah was, Ah was."

"Now, Booker—" he turned around—"I believe you tried to keep the nigger preacher from getting out of line."

I hesitated. It wasn't a fair question. Finally, I said: "Yessir."

"You begged him not to go in the white side?"

"Yessir."

"And when that failed, you went over to *your* side—the *colored* side—and looked through the window?"

"Yessir."

He put his hand in his coat pocket and studied my face.

"You saw *everything,* didn't you?"

"Just about." A muscle on the inside of my thigh started tingling.

Mr. Rivers shuffled some papers he had in his hand. He seemed to be thinking real hard. I pushed myself against the back of the chair. Mr. Rivers moved close, quick, and stabbed his finger into my chest.

"Booker, did you see the nigger preacher reach for Mr. Sampson's gun?"

He backed away, smiling. I looked away from him and I felt my heart trying to tear out of my skin. I looked out over the courtroom. It was still; wasn't even a fly moving. I looked at the white folks in front and the colored folks in back and I turned the question over in my mind. While I was doing that, waiting, taking my time, I noticed, out of the corner of my eye, that the smile on Mr. Rivers' face was dying away. Suddenly, I had a terrible itch to know what that smile would turn into.

I said, "Nosir."

Mr. Rivers stumbled backwards like he had been shot. Old Judge Sloan took off his glasses and pushed his head out over the bench. The whole courtroom seemed to be leaning in to me and I saw Aaron's widow leaning back with her eyes closed and it seemed to me at that distance that her lips were moving in prayer.

Mr. Rivers was the first to recover. He put his smile back on and he acted like my answer was in the script.

"You mean," he said, "that you didn't see it. It happened so quickly that you missed it?"

I looked at the bait and I ain't gonna lie: I was tempted. He knew as well as I did what I meant, but he was gambling on my weakness. I had thrown away my funeral home, my hearse, everything I owned, and he was standing there like a magician, pulling them out of a hat, one at a time, dangling them, saying: "Looka here, looka here, don't they look pretty?" I was on top of a house and he was betting that if he gave me a ladder I would come down. He was wrong, but you can't fault him for trying. He hadn't never met no nigger who would go all the way. I looked him in the eye and went the last mile.

"Aaron didn't reach for that gun," I said. "Them people, they just fell on—"

"Hold it," he shouted. "I want to remind you that there are laws in this state against perjury. You can go to jail for five years for what you just said. Now I know you've been conferring with those NAACP fellows, but I want to remind you of the statements you made to Sheriff Sampson and me. Judge—" he dismissed me with a wave of his hand—"Judge, this *man*—" he caught himself and it was my turn to smile—"this *boy* is lying. Ten niggers have testified that they saw the preacher reach for the gun. Twenty white people saw it. You've heard their testimony. I want to withdraw this witness and I want to reserve the right to file perjury charges against him."

Judge Sloan nodded. He pushed his bottom lip over his top one.

"You can step down," he said. "I want to warn you that perjury is a very grave offense. You—"

"Judge, I didn't—"

"Nigger!" He banged his gavel. "Don't you interrupt me. Now git out of here."

Two guards pushed me outside and waved away the reporters. Billy Giles, Mr. Sampson's assistant, came out and told me Mr. Sampson wanted me out of town before sundown. "And he says you'd better get out before the Northern reporters leave. He won't be responsible for your safety after that."

I nodded and went on down the stairs and started out the door.

"Booker!"

Rachel and a whole line of Negroes were running down the stairs. I stepped outside and waited for them. Rachel ran up and throwed her arms around me. "It don't take but one, Booker," she said. "It don't take but one." Somebody else said: "They whitewashed it, they whitewashed it, but you spoiled it for 'em."

Russell came out then and stood over to the side while the others crowded around to shake my hands. Then the others sensed that he was waiting and they made a little aisle. He walked up to me kind of slow-like and he said, "Thank you, sir." That was the first time in his whole seventeen years that that boy had said "sir" to me. I cleared my throat and when I opened my eyes Sarah was standing beside me. She didn't say nothing; she just put her hand in mine and stood there. It was long about then, I guess, when I realized that I wasn't seeing so good. They say I cried, but I don't believe a word of it. It was such a hot day and the sun was shining so bright that the sweat rolling down my face blinded me. I wiped the sweat out of my eyes and some more people came up and said a lot of foolish things about me showing the white folks and following in Aaron's footsteps. I wasn't doing no such fool thing. Ol' Man Rivers just put the thing to me in a way it hadn't been put before—man to man. It was simple, really. Any man would have done it.

DISCUSSION

1 Why did the writer choose Booker as the narrator?
2 How soon in the story does the writer begin the complication?
3 How complicated is the plot?
4 What is the conflict between Aaron and Booker?
5 What does Booker mean by saying his son will "find out when he grows up"? What does Aaron mean by saying "I hopes not"?
6 What role does Booker's son play in his decision?
7 What is the relationship to the story of the scene in the white waiting room?
8 What part does Mr. Rivers play in Booker's decision?
9 When do you think Booker makes up his mind?
10 What is the meaning of the line "Booker Taliaferro Brown became the biggest man in that town"?
11 What is Mr. Rivers gambling on?
12 What is Booker's life dream?
13 How do you feel about the actions of the people at the station, especially Sheriff Sampson?
14 What is the theme of the story?
15 At the end of the story, does Booker win or lose?

THE CHRYSANTHEMUMS
John Steinbeck

The high grey-flannel fog of winter closed off the Salinas Valley from the sky and from all the rest of the world. On every side it sat like a lid on the mountains and made of the great valley a closed pot. On the broad, level land floor the gang ploughs bit deep and left the black earth shining like metal where the shares had cut. On the foothill ranches across the Salinas River, the yellow stubble fields seemed to be bathed in pale cold sunshine, but there was no sunshine in the valley now in December. The thick willow scrub along the river flamed with sharp and positive yellow leaves.

It was a time of quiet and of waiting. The air was cold and tender. A light wind blew up from the southwest so that the farmers were mildly hopeful of a good rain before long; but fog and rain do not go together.

Across the river, on Henry Allen's foothill ranch there was little work to be done, for the hay was cut and stored and the orchards were ploughed up to receive the rain deeply when it should come. The cattle on the higher slopes were becoming shaggy and rough-coated.

Elisa Allen, working in her flower garden, looked down across the yard and saw Henry, her husband, talking to two men in business suits. The three of them stood by the tractor shed, each man with one foot on the side of the little Fordson. They smoked cigarettes and studied the machine as they talked.

Elisa watched them for a moment and then went back to her work. She was thirty-five. Her face was lean and strong and her eyes were as clear as water. Her figure looked blocked and heavy in her gardening costume, a man's black hat pulled low down over her eyes, clod-hopper shoes, a figured print dress almost completely covered by a big corduroy apron with four big pockets to hold the snips, the trowel and scratcher, the seeds and the knife she worked with. She wore heavy leather gloves to protect her hands while she worked.

She was cutting down the old year's chrysanthemum stalks with a pair of short and powerful scissors. She looked down toward the men by the tractor shed now and then. Her face was eager and mature and handsome; even her work with the scissors was over-eager, over-powerful. The chrysanthemum stems seemed too small and easy for her energy.

She brushed a cloud of hair out of her eyes with the back of her glove, and left a smudge of earth on her cheek in doing it. Behind her stood the neat white farm house with red geraniums close-banked around it as high as the windows. It was a hard-swept looking little house, with hard-polished windows, and a clean mud-mat on the front steps.

SOURCE NOTE: John Steinbeck, "The Chrysanthemums." From *The Long Valley* by John Steinbeck. Copyright 1937; renewal copyright © 1965 by John Steinbeck. Reprinted by permission of The Viking Press, Inc.

Elisa cast another glance toward the tractor shed. The strangers were getting into their Ford coupe. She took off a glove and put her strong fingers down into the forest of new green chrysanthemum sprouts that were growing around the old roots. She spread the leaves and looked down among the close-growing stems. No aphids were there, no sow bugs or snails or cutworms. Her terrier fingers destroyed such pests before they could get started.

Elisa started at the sound of her husband's voice. He had come near quietly, and he leaned over the wire fence that protected her flower garden from cattle and dogs and chickens.

"At it again," he said. "You've got a strong new crop coming."

Elisa straightened her back and pulled on the gardening glove again. "Yes. They'll be strong this coming year." In her tone and on her face there was a little smugness.

"You've got a gift with things," Henry observed. "Some of those yellow chrysanthemums you had this year were ten inches across. I wish you'd work out in the orchard and raise some apples that big."

Her eyes sharpened. "Maybe I could do it, too. I've a gift with things, all right. My mother had it. She could stick anything in the ground and make it grow. She said it was having planters' hands that knew how to do it."

"Well, it sure works with flowers," he said.

"Henry, who were those men you were talking to?"

"Why, sure, that's what I came to tell you. They were from the Western Meat Company. I sold those thirty head of three-year-old steers. Got nearly my own price, too."

"Good," she said. "Good for you."

"And I thought," he continued, "I thought how it's Saturday afternoon, and we might go into Salinas for dinner at a restaurant, and then to a picture show—to celebrate, you see."

"Good," she repeated. "Oh, yes. That will be good."

Henry put on his joking tone. "There's fights tonight. How'd you like to go to the fights?"

"Oh, no," she said breathlessly. "No, I wouldn't like fights."

"Just fooling, Elisa. We'll go to a movie. Let's see. It's two now. I'm going to take Scotty and bring down those steers from the hill. It'll take us maybe two hours. We'll go in town about five and have dinner at the Cominos Hotel. Like that?"

"Of course I'll like it. It's good to eat away from home."

"All right, then, I'll go get up a couple of horses."

She said: "I'll have plenty of time to transplant some of these sets, I guess."

She heard her husband calling Scotty down by the barn. And a little later she saw the two men ride up the pale yellow hillside in search of the steers.

There was a little square sandy bed kept for rooting the chrysanthemums. With her trowel she turned the soil over and over, and smoothed it and patted it firm. Then she dug ten parallel trenches to receive the sets. Back at the chrysanthemum bed she pulled out the little crisp shoots, trimmed off the leaves of each one with her scissors and laid it on a small orderly pile.

A squeak of wheels and plod of hoofs came from the road. Elisa looked up. The country road ran along the dense bank of willows and cottonwoods that bordered the river, and up this road came a curious vehicle, curiously drawn. It was an old spring-wagon, with a round canvas top on it like the cover of a prairie schooner. It was drawn by an old bay horse and a little grey-and-white burro. A big stubble-bearded man sat between the cover flaps and drove the crawling team. Underneath the wagon, between the hind wheels, a lean and rangy mongrel dog walked sedately. Words were painted on the canvas, in clumsy, crooked letters. "Pots, pans, knives, sisors, lawn mores. Fixed." Two rows of articles, and the triumphantly definitive "Fixed" below. The black paint had run down in little sharp points beneath each letter.

Elisa, squatting on the ground, watched to see the crazy, loose-jointed wagon pass. But it didn't pass. It turned into the farm road in front of her house, crooked old wheels skirling and squeaking. The rangy dog darted from between the wheels and ran ahead. Instantly the two ranch shepherds flew out at him. Then all three stopped, and with stiff and quivering tails, with taut straight legs, with ambassadorial dignity, they slowly circled, sniffing daintily. The caravan pulled up to Elisa's wire fence and stopped. Now the newcomer dog, feeling outnumbered, lowered his tail and retired under the wagon with raised hackles and bared teeth.

The man on the wagon seat called out: "That's a bad dog in a fight when he gets started."

Elisa laughed. "I see he is. How soon does he generally get started?"

The man caught up her laughter and echoed it heartily. "Sometimes not for weeks and weeks," he said. He climbed stiffly down, over the wheel. The horse and the donkey dropped like unwatered flowers.

Elisa saw that he was a very big man. Although his hair and beard were greying, he did not look old. His worn black suit was wrinkled and spotted with grease. The laughter had disappeared from his face and eyes the moment his laughing voice ceased. His eyes were dark, and they were full of the brooding that gets in the eyes of teamsters and of sailors. The calloused hands he rested on the wire fence were cracked, and every crack was a black line. He took off his battered hat.

"I'm off my general road, ma'am," he said. "Does this dirt road cut over across the river to the Los Angeles highway?"

Elisa stood up and shoved the thick scissors in her apron pocket. "Well, yes, it does, but it winds around and then fords the river. I don't think your team could pull through the sand."

He replied with some asperity: "It might surprise you what them beasts can pull through."

"When they get started?" she asked.

He smiled for a second. "Yes. When they get started."

"Well," said Elisa, "I think you'll save time if you go back to the Salinas road and pick up the highway there."

He drew a big finger down the chicken wire and made it sing. "I ain't in any hurry, ma'am. I go from Seattle to San Diego and back every year. Takes all my time. About six months each way. I aim to follow nice weather."

Elisa took off her gloves and stuffed them in the apron pocket with the scissors. She touched the under edge of her man's hat, searching for fugitive hairs. "That sounds like a nice kind of a way to live," she said.

He leaned confidentially over the fence. "Maybe you noticed the writing on my wagon. I mend pots and sharpen knives and scissors. You got any of them things to do?"

"Oh, no," she said quickly. "Nothing like that." Her eyes hardened with resistance.

"Scissors is the worst thing," he explained. "Most people just ruin scissors trying to sharpen 'em, but I know how. I got a special tool. It's a little bobbit kind of thing, and patented. But it sure does the trick."

"No. My scissors are all sharp."

"All right, then. Take a pot," he continued earnestly, "a bent pot, or a pot with a hole. I can make it like new so you don't have to buy no new ones. That's a saving for you."

"No," she said shortly. "I tell you I have nothing like that for you to do."

His face fell to an exaggerated sadness. His voice took on a whining undertone. "I ain't had a thing to do today. Maybe I won't have no supper tonight. You see I'm off my regular road. I know folks on the highway clear from Seattle to San Diego. They save their things for me to sharpen up because they know I do it so good and save them money."

"I'm sorry," Elisa said irritably. "I haven't anything for you to do."

His eyes left her face and fell to searching the ground. They roamed about until they came to the chrysanthemum bed where she had been working. "What's them plants, ma'am?"

The irritation and resistance melted from Elisa's face. "Oh, those are chrysanthemums, giant whites and yellows. I raise them every year, bigger than anybody around here."

"Kind of a long-stemmed flower? Looks like a quick puff of colored smoke?" he asked.

"That's it. What a nice way to describe them."

"They smell kind of nasty till you get used to them," he said.

"It's a good bitter smell," she retorted, "not nasty at all."

He changed his tone quickly. "I like the smell myself."

"I had ten-inch blooms this year," she said.

The man leaned farther over the fence. "Look. I know a lady down the road a piece, has got the nicest garden you ever seen. Got nearly every kind of flower but no chrysanthemums. Last time I was mending a copper-bottom washtub for her (that's a hard job but I do it good), she said to me: 'If you ever run acrost some nice chrysanthemums I wish you'd try to get me a few seeds.' That's what she told me."

Elisa's eyes grew alert and eager. "She couldn't have known much about chrysanthemums. You *can* raise them from seed, but it's much easier to root the little sprouts you see there."

"Oh," he said. "I s'pose I can't take none to her, then."

"Why yes you can," Elisa cried. "I can put some in damp sand, and you can carry them right along with you. They'll take root in the pot if you keep them damp. And then she can transplant them."

"She'd sure like to have some, ma'am. You say they're nice ones?"

"Beautiful," she said. "Oh, beautiful." Her eyes shone. She tore off the battered hat and shook out her dark pretty hair. "I'll put them in a flower pot, and you can take them right with you. Come into the yard."

While the man came through the picket gate Elisa ran excitedly along the geranium-bordered path to the back of the house. And she returned carrying a big red flower pot. The gloves were forgotten now. She kneeled on the ground by the starting bed and dug up the sandy soil with her fingers and scooped it into the bright new flower pot. Then she picked up the little pile of shoots she had prepared. With her strong fingers she pressed them into the sand and tamped around them with her knuckles. The man stood over her. "I'll tell you what to do," she said. "You remember so you can tell the lady."

"Yes, I'll try to remember."

"Well, look. These will take root in about a month. Then she must set them out, about a foot apart in good rich earth like this, see?" She lifted a handful of dark soil for him to look at. "They'll grow fast and tall. Now remember this: In July tell her to cut them down, about eight inches from the ground."

"Before they bloom?" he asked.

"Yes, before they bloom." Her face was tight with eagerness. "They'll grow right up again. About the last of September the buds will start."

She stopped and seemed perplexed. "It's the budding that takes the most care," she said hesitantly. "I don't know how to tell you." She looked deep into his eyes, searchingly. Her mouth opened a little, and she seemed to be listening. "I'll try to tell you," she said. "Did you ever hear of planting hands?"

"Can't say I have, ma'am."

"Well, I can only tell you what it feels like. It's when you're picking off the buds you don't want. Everything goes right down into your fingertips. You watch your fingers work. They do it themselves. You can feel how it is. They pick and pick the buds. They never make a mistake. They're with the plant. Do you see? Your fingers and the plant. You can feel that, right up your arm. They know. They never make a mistake. You can feel it. When you're like that you can't do anything wrong. Do you see that? Can you understand that?"

She was kneeling on the ground looking up at him. Her breast swelled passionately.

The man's eyes narrowed. He looked away self-consciously. "Maybe I know," he said. "Sometimes in the night in the wagon there—"

Elisa's voice grew husky. She broke in on him: "I've never lived as you do, but I know what you mean. When the night is dark—why, the stars are sharp-pointed, and there's quiet. Why, you rise up and up! Every pointed star gets driven into your body. It's like that. Hot and sharp and—lovely."

Kneeling there, her hand went out toward his legs in the greasy black trousers. Her hesitant fingers almost touched the cloth. Then her hand dropped to the ground. She crouched low like a fawning dog.

He said: "It's nice, just like you say. Only when you don't have no dinner, it ain't."

She stood up then, very straight, and her face was ashamed. She held the flower pot out to him and placed it gently in his arms. "Here. Put it in your wagon, on the seat, where you can watch it. Maybe I can find something for you to do."

At the back of the house she dug in the can pile and found two old and battered aluminum saucepans. She carried them back and gave them to him. "Here, maybe you can fix these."

His manner changed. He became professional. "Good as new I can fix them." At the back of his wagon he set a little anvil, and out of an oily tool box dug a small machine hammer. Elisa came through the gate to watch him while he pounded out the dents in the kettles. His mouth grew sure and knowing. At a difficult part of the work he sucked his underlip.

"You sleep right in the wagon?" Elisa asked.

"Right in the wagon, ma'am. Rain or shine I'm dry as a cow in there."

"It must be nice," she said. "It must be very nice. I wish women could do such things."

"It ain't the right kind of a life for a woman."

Her upper lip raised a little, showing her teeth. "How do you know? How can you tell?" she said.

"I don't know, ma'am," he protested. "Of course I don't know. Now here's your kettles, done. You don't have to buy no new ones."

"How much?"

"Oh, fifty cents'll do. I keep my prices down and my work good. That's why I have all them satisfied customers up and down the highway."

Elisa brought him a fifty-cent piece from the house and dropped it in his hand. "You might be surprised to have a rival some time. I can sharpen scissors, too. And I can beat the dents out of little pots. I could show you what a woman might do."

He put his hammer back in the oily box and shoved the little anvil out of sight. "It would be a lonely life for a woman, ma'am, and a scarey life, too, with animals creeping under the wagon all night." He climbed over the single-tree, steadying himself with a hand on the burro's white rump. He settled himself in the seat, picked up the lines. "Thank you kindly, ma'am," he said. "I'll do like you told me; I'll go back and catch the Salinas road."

"Mind," she called, "if you're long in getting there, keep the sand damp."

"Sand, ma'am? . . . Sand? Oh, sure. You mean around the chrysanthemums. Sure I will." He clucked his tongue. The beasts leaned luxuriously into their collars. The mongrel dog took his place between the back wheels. The wagon turned and crawled out the entrance road and back the way it had come, along the river.

Elisa stood in front of her wire fence watching the slow progress of the caravan. Her shoulders were straight, her head thrown back, her eyes half-closed, so that the scene came vaguely into them. Her lips moved silently, forming the words "Good-bye—good-bye." Then she whispered: "That's a bright direction. There's a glowing there." The sound of her whisper startled her. She shook herself free and looked about to see whether anyone had been listening. Only the dogs had heard. They lifted their heads toward her from their sleeping in the dust, and then stretched out their chins and settled asleep again. Elisa turned and ran hurriedly into the house.

In the kitchen she reached behind the stove and felt the water tank. It was full of hot water from the noonday cooking. In the bathroom she tore off her soiled clothes and flung them into the corner. And then she scrubbed herself with a little block of pumice, legs and thighs, loins and chest and arms, until her skin was scratched and red. When she had dried herself she stood in front of a mirror in her bedroom and looked at her body. She tightened her stomach and threw out her chest. She turned and looked over her shoulder at her back.

After a while she began to dress, slowly. She put on her newest underclothing and her nicest stockings and the dress which was the symbol of her prettiness. She worked carefully on her hair, pencilled her eyebrows and rouged her lips.

Before she was finished she heard the little thunder of hoofs and the shouts of Henry and his helper as they drove the red steers into the corral. She heard the gate bang shut and set herself for Henry's arrival.

His step sounded on the porch. He entered the house calling: "Elisa, where are you?"

"In my room, dressing, I'm not ready. There's hot water for your bath. Hurry up. It's getting late."

When she heard him splashing in the tub, Elisa laid his dark suit on the bed, and shirt and socks and tie beside it. She stood his polished shoes on the floor beside the bed. Then she went to the porch and sat primly and stiffly down. She looked toward the river road where the willow-line was still yellow with frosted leaves so that under the high grey fog they seemed a thin band of sunshine. This was the only color in the grey afternoon. She sat unmoving for a long time. Her eyes blinked rarely.

Henry came banging out of the door, shoving his tie under his vest as he came. Elisa stiffened and her face grew tight. Henry stopped short and looked at her. "Why—why, Elisa. You look so nice!"

"Nice? You think I look nice? What do you mean by 'nice'?"

Henry blundered on. "I don't know. I mean you look different, strong and happy."

"I am strong? Yes, strong. What do you mean 'strong'?"

He looked bewildered. "You're playing some kind of game," he said helplessly. "It's a kind of a play. You look strong enough to break a calf over your knee, happy enough to eat it like a watermelon."

For a second she lost her rigidity. "Henry! Don't talk like that. You didn't know what you said." She grew complete again. "I'm strong," she boasted. "I never knew before how strong."

Henry looked down toward the tractor shed, and when he brought his eyes back to her, they were his own again. "I'll get out the car. You can put on your coat while I'm starting."

Elisa went into the house. She heard him drive to the gate and idle down his motor, and then she took a long time to put on her hat. She pulled it here and pressed it there. When Henry turned the motor off she slipped into her coat and went out.

The little roadster bounced along on the dirt road by the river, raising the birds and driving the rabbits into the brush. Two cranes flapped heavily over the willow-line and dropped into the river-bed.

Far ahead on the road Elisa saw a dark speck. She knew.

She tried not to look as they passed it, but her eyes would not obey. She whispered to herself sadly: "He might have thrown them off the road. That wouldn't have been much trouble, not very much. But he kept the pot," she explained. "He had to keep the pot. That's why he couldn't get them off the road."

The roadster turned a bend and she saw the caravan ahead. She swung full around toward her husband so she could not see the little covered wagon and the mismatched team as the car passed them.

In a moment it was over. The thing was done. She did not look back.

She said loudly, to be heard above the motor: "It will be good, tonight, a good dinner."

"Now you're changed again," Henry complained. He took one hand from the wheel and patted her knee. "I ought to take you in to dinner oftener. It would be good for both of us. We get so heavy out on the ranch."

"Henry," she asked, "could we have wine at dinner?"

"Sure we could. Say! That will be fine."

She was silent for a while; then she said: "Henry, at those prize fights, do the men hurt each other very much?"

"Sometimes a little, not often. Why?"

"Well, I've read how they break noses, and blood runs down their chests. I've read how the fighting gloves get heavy and soggy with blood."

He looked around at her. "What's the matter, Elisa? I didn't know you read things like that." He brought the car to a stop, then turned to the right over the Salinas River bridge.

"Do any women ever go to the fights?" she asked.

"Oh, sure, some. What's the matter, Elisa? Do you want to go? I don't think you'd like it, but I'll take you if you really want to go."

She relaxed limply in the seat. "Oh, no. No. I don't want to go. I'm sure I don't." Her face was turned away from him. "It will be enough if we can have wine. It will be plenty." She turned up her coat collar so he could not see that she was crying weakly—like an old woman.

DISCUSSION

1 What qualities in Elisa's character are especially emphasized in the initial description of her?

2 What is the point of view?

3 In the opening scene, what actions of Elisa reveal she is a woman shaped by her environment? What two images reveal much about the relationship between Elisa and her husband?

4 Mention some specific incidents that make up the whole story.

5 What conflicts, other than the main conflict, are in the story?

6 How does Steinbeck's use of animal symbols contribute to the meaning?

7 What is the significance of the incident with the tinker?

8 What is important about Elisa's preparations for her trip to town?

9 What is ironic about Elisa's words, " 'I'm strong,' she boasted. 'I never knew before how strong' "?

10 What does Elisa see on the road to town? What does this scene mean?

11 What is the climax? What conflicts along with the main conflict are resolved by the climax?

12 Why does Elisa decide to go to the fights?

13 What does the wine symbolize?

14 What is the meaning of the chrysanthemums as a symbol?

15 How does the opening image contribute to the characterization of Elisa?

CORRECTION KEY FOR WRITTEN ASSIGNMENTS

This chart includes a number of abbreviations that your writing instructor will use in correcting your written work.

SYMBOL	MEANING
ab	abbreviations
adj	adjective
adv	adverb
agr	agreement
amb	ambiguous
ant	antecedent
apos	apostrophe
approp	appropriateness
awk	awkward
ca	case
cap	capitals
coh	coherence
coor	coordination
conj	conjunction
cont	contraction
cs	comma fault; comma splice
dic	dictionary
dict	diction
emp	emphasis
fig	figure of speech
frag	fragment—part of a sentence
gr	grammar
id	idiom
ital	italics
lc	unnecessary capitals; lowercase
m	mechanics
mood	mood
ms	manuscript form
m/d	dangling modifier
m/s	squinting modifier
no punc	no punctuation
num	number, numbers
n/pl	plurals of nouns
n/poss	possessive case of nouns
par	faulty parallelism
prep	preposition
pro	pronoun
pv	point of view

red	redundancy
rep	repetition
rt	run-together sentences
sc	superfluous comma
shift	shift in construction
sl	slang
sing	singular
sp	spelling
ss	sentence sense
style	style
sub	subordination
syll	syllabication
tense	tense
t/s	topic sentence
tone	tone
trite	trite
uty	unity
var	variety
vb	verb
vo	voice
wdy	wordy
wc	wrong word (word choice)

SIGNS

^	omission of letters
¶	paragraph
no ¶	no paragraph
p/,	comma
p/.	period
p/;	semicolon
p/:	colon
p/—	dash
p/-	hyphen
p/"	quotation marks
p/!	exclamation point
p/?	question mark
p/...	ellipsis dots
p/( )	parentheses
p/[ ]	brackets

CHECKLIST FOR CORRECTNESS

1. Spelling
2. Punctuation
3. Tense of verbs
4. Voice of verbs (Use active voice whenever possible.)
5. Fragments (parts of sentences written as sentences)
6. Dangling modifier
7. Squinting modifier
8. Case of pronouns
9. Agreement of pronoun and antecedent
10. Agreement of subject and verb
11. Parallel structure (parallelism)
12. Faulty diction
13. Shifts in construction
14. Subordination
15. Coordination
16. Misuse of adjectives, adverbs, prepositions, conjunctions
17. Omissions
18. Comma splices and run-together sentences
19. Comparisons
20. Sentence structure

Index

Allusion, 111
Analogy, 165–168
    defined, 165–166
    examples of, 166–167
    function of, 166
    (*See also* Known to unknown)
Analysis (*see* Causal analysis;
    Classification; Partition; Process)
Argumentation (*see* Persuasion)

Causal analysis, 215–227
    defined, 215
    establishing causal relationships in,
        215
    organization of, 216
    post hoc fallacy in, 215
    questions to ask concerning, 215
    statement of purpose in, 215
Cause to effect order in paragraphs,
        32–33
Chronological order (*see* Time order)
Classes as an order in paragraph
        development, 34–38
    basis for, 37
    complex system of, 35
    defined, 34
    organization of, 36–37
    overlapping in, 38
    purpose of, 35
    questions to ask concerning, 34–35
    simple system of, 35
Classification, 183–190
    basis for, 184–185
    complex system of, 184
    defined, 183

Classification:
    organization of, 185
    purpose of, 184
    simple system of, 184
Climax in narration, 92
Coherence, 49–54
    defined, 49
    function of, 49
    gained by: order, 49
        pronoun reference, 52
        repeated words or groups of
            words, 52–53
        synonyms, 53
        transitional sentences, 53–54
        transitional words for, 51–52
        unity, 49
Combination of methods of development:
    in developing the essay, 245–249
    in developing the paragraph, 46–47
Comparison:
    in developing the essay, 136–149
    in developing the paragraph, 38–39
Completeness in paragraph develop-
        ment, 22–23
Conceptual partition, 199–215
    defined, 199
    organization of, 200
    thesis-support-thesis frame for, 200
Concluding paragraphs, 54–56
    examples of, 55–56
    function of, 55
    less effective conclusions, 54
Conflict in narration, 92
Contrast:
    in developing the essay, 149–165
    in developing the paragraph, 39–40

Defining in paragraph development,
    42–45
    formal definition for, 43–44
    implied topic sentence for, 42
    methods of, 43–45
Definition, 230–245
    defined, 231
    limiting use of the word, 23
    types of, 232
Description, 109–132
    defined, 109
    guide to, 116–117
    kinds of, 114–132
    organization of, 112
    point of view in, 112–113
    scale in, 113–114
    selection of words for, 109–112
Dictionary definition, 232–235
    errors in, 233–234
    methods of developing, 232–233
    purpose of, 232
Discourse, 91
Distortions in persuasion, 254–259
    by false analogy, 257–259
    by flattery, 255
    by omissions, 254
    by rhetorical questions, 257
    by superlatives and connotative
        words, 255–256
Draft, rough, for organizing papers,
    81–83

Effect to cause order in paragraphs,
    33–34
Emotional appeals in persuasion,
    253–254
    to the baser passions of man, 253
    to fears of man, 254
    to love of freedom and country, 253
Emotional description, 115–116
    defined, 115
    purpose of, 115
    selection of words for, 115–116
Examples for paragraph development, 28
Exposition:
    defined, 91–92
    purpose of, 91
Expository description, 114–115
    defined, 114
    purpose of, 114
    selection of words for, 114–115

Extended definition, 237–245
    defined, 237
    organization of, 237–243

Figures:
    in paragraphs, 31
    in partition, 194
    of speech, 111
Formal definition, 235–237
    defined, 235
    examples of, 236–237
    method of development, 235–236
Formal outline, 73–77
    construction of, 74–75
    paragraph outline, 78
    sentence outline, 75–77
    topic outline, 77–78

Gathering material, 70
General to particular to general pattern
    in paragraphs, 26
General to particular pattern in para-
    graphs, 23–25

Hyperbole, 111–112

Informal outline, 71–73
Informational process, 179–183
    causal process, 179
    organization of, 179
    purpose of, 179
Instructional process, 169–179
    cautions in, 170
    purpose of, 169
    steps in, 169
    time order for, 169
Introductory paragraph, 18–20
    defined, 18
    examples of, 18–20
    function of, 18
    kinds of, 18–20
    statement of thesis in, 18–20
Issues in persuasion, 266–270
    defined, 266
    honesty in, 269
    kinds of, 267
    organization of, 268–269

Known to unknown:
   defined, 40
   examples of, 41
   function of, 40
   (*See also* Analogy)

Main idea (*see* Topic sentence)
Manuscript:
   preparation of, 81–82
   submission of, 83
Metaphor, 111–112
Middle paragraphs, 20–47
   characteristics of, 22
   defined, 20
   development of, 23–47
   examples of, 21
   function of, 20–22
   topic sentence in, 20–21

Narration, 92–109
   defined, 92
   elements in, 92–93
   guide to, 102
   point of view in, 94
   structure of, 93–94

Order in essays [*see* Patterns (frames),
      for essays]
Order in paragraphs [*see* Patterns
      (frames), paragraphs]
Outlining, 71–81
   construction of, 74–75
   kinds of, 71–81

Paragraph outline, 78
Paragraphs:
   characteristics of, 22–23
   coherence in, 49–54
   completeness in, 22–23
   defined, 17
   organization of support in, 28–47
   patterns or frames for, 23–27
   topic sentence in, 21, 23–26
   unity in, 23–26
Particular to general pattern in para-
      graphs, 25–26

Partition, 193–215
   defined, 193
   kinds of, 194
   organization of, 193
   thesis-support frame for, 193
Patterns (frames):
   for essays, 133–136
      question to answer, 136
      support-thesis, 134–135
      thesis-support, 134–135
      thesis-support-thesis, 135
   for paragraphs, 23–27
      general to particular, 23–25
      general to particular to general, 26
      particular to general, 25–26
      question to answer, 27
Personification, 111–112
Persuasion, 251–286
   defined, 252
   distortions in, 254–259
   emotional appeals in, 253–254
   issues in, 266–270
   organization of, 268–269
   purpose of, 251–252
   strategies of dishonest persuasion,
      253–259
   strategies of honest persuasion,
      259–265
   structuring of, 265
   thesis-support-thesis frame for, 268
Physical partition, 194–199
   defined, 194
   figures in, 194
   organization of, 194
   thesis-support frame for, 193
Planning the paper, 63–83
   gathering material, 70
   limiting the subject, 68–69
   making a preliminary search, 64–68
   organizing the material, 70–81
   preparing the final draft, 82–83
   revising the first draft, 81–82
   selecting a subject, 64
Poetry, 287–312
Point of view:
   in description, 112–113
   in narration, 94
Process, 169–183
   defined, 169
   kinds of, 169, 179
Pronouns in coherence, 52

Question to answer pattern in paragraphs, 27

Reasons in paragraph development, 32
Repetition for coherence, 52–53
Research:
    gathering material, 70
    preliminary search, 64
    sources for, 64–67

Scratch outline (*see* Informal outline)
Short story, 312–384
Simile, 111–112
Space order:
    in the essay, 112–113
    in the paragraph, 29–30
Statement of purpose:
    defined, 68
    examples of, 68–69, 134–135
Strategies:
    of dishonest persuasion, 253–259
        distortions for, 254–259
        emotional appeals for, 253–254
    of honest persuasion, 259–270
        characteristics of, 259
        concession in, 269
        conciliation in, 269
        example of, 260–265
        organization of, 268–270
        refutation in, 269
Subject for a paper, 64, 68–69
    limiting of, 68–69
    list of, 64
    selection of, 64
Support in paragraphs, 27–48
    function of, 27
    kinds of, 28–48
    listing of, 47–48

Thesis:
    defined, 68
    examples of, 68–69, 134–135
    patterns for developing, 134–135
    in persuasion, 268
Time order:
    in narration, 91, 93
    in the paragraph, 28–29
Title:
    aid in limiting subject, 68
    examples of, 68–69
    questions concerning, 81
Topic outline, 77–78
Topic sentence, 21, 23–26
    defined, 21
    developed by, 22
    examples of, 20–21, 23–26
    function of, 21
    position of, 22, 24–26
    repetition of, 26
Transitional paragraphs, 48
Transitional sentence, 53–54
    for coherence, 53
    example of, 54
Transitional words, 51–52
    list of, 51
Transitions within paragraphs (*see* Coherence)

Unity in paragraphs, 22

Words:
    abstract and general, 110
    concrete and specific, 110
    selection for description, 110
Written assignments, 2–4
    assigned by instructor, 2–3
    student choice, 4